TAKING SIDES

Clashing Views on Controversial

Economic Issues

ELEVENTH EDITION

TAKING SIDES

Clashing Views on Controversial

Economic Issues

ELEVENTH EDITION

Selected, Edited, and with Introductions by

Thomas R. Swartz
University of Notre Dame

and

Frank J. Bonello
University of Notre Dame

McGraw-Hill/Dushkin
A Division of The McGraw-Hill Companies

This book is dedicated to the thousands of students who have persevered in the "Bonello/Swartz (B.S.)" introductory economics course sequence at the University of Notre Dame. It is also dedicated to our children and grandchildren. In order of their births, they are Mary Elizabeth, Karen Ann, Jennifer Lynne, John Anthony, Anne Marie, Rebecca Jourdan, David Joseph, Stephen Thomas, Chelsea Margaret, Kevin Joseph, Meghan Claire, Maureen Keeting, Michael Thomas, Thomas Jourdan, and Amanda Marie.

Cover image: © 2004 by PhotoDisc, Inc.

Cover Art Acknowledgment
Charles Vitelli

Copyright © 2004 by McGraw-Hill/Dushkin,
A Division of The McGraw-Hill Companies, Inc., Guilford, Connecticut 06437

Manufactured in the United States of America

Eleventh Edition

23456789BAHBAH7654

Library of Congress Cataloging-in-Publication Data
Main entry under title:
Taking sides: clashing views on controversial economic issues/selected, edited, and with introductions by Thomas R. Swartz and Frank J. Bonello.—11th ed.
Includes bibliographical references and index.
1. United States—Economic policy—1971–1981. 2. United States—Economic policy—1981–1993.
3. United States—Economic policy—1993–. I. Swartz, Thomas R., *comp.*
II. Bonello, Frank J., *comp.*
338.9'22
0-07-284513-9
ISSN: 1094-7612

Printed on Recycled Paper

Preface

Where there is much desire to learn, there of necessity will be much arguing.

—John Milton (1608–1674), English poet and essayist

Presented here are 17 debates on important and compelling economic issues, which are designed to stimulate critical thinking skills and initiate lively and informed discussion. These debates take economic theory and show how it is applied to current, real-world public policy decisions, the outcomes of which will have an immediate and personal impact. How these debates are resolved will affect our taxes, jobs, wages, educational system, and so on; in short, they will shape the society in which we live.

It has been our intent throughout each of the 11 editions of *Taking Sides: Clashing Views on Controversial Economic Issues* to select issues that reveal something about the nature of economics itself and something about how economics relates to current, everyday newspaper headlines and television news stories on public policy concerns. To assist the reader, we begin each issue with an *issue introduction*, which sets the stage for the debate as it is argued in the "yes" and "no" selections. Each issue concludes with a *postscript* that briefly reviews the arguments and makes some final observations. The introduction and postscript do not preempt what is the reader's own task: to achieve a critical and informed view of the economic issue at stake. Certainly, the reader should not feel confined to adopt one or the other of the positions presented. The views presented should be used as starting points, and the suggestions for further reading that appear in each issue postscript offer additional resources on the topic. Internet site addresses (URLs) have been provided at the beginning of each part, which should also prove useful as resources for further research. At the back of the book is a listing of all the *contributors to this volume,* which provides information on the economists, policymakers, political leaders, and commentators whose views are debated here.

Changes to this edition This new edition of *Taking Sides* represents a considerable revision. Of the 17 issues, 7 are completely new. Thus, as we continue our journey into the new millennium, this substantially revised book will help us to understand the implications of a changing set of economic issues that were not part of our world just a few years ago. The new issues are: *Is It Time to Reform Medical Malpractice Litigation?* (Issue 6); *Should the Double Taxation of Corporate Dividends Be Eliminated?* (Issue 9); *Should a Program of Universal Service Be Created?* (Issue 10); *Are Declining Caseloads a Sign of Successful Welfare Reform?* (Issue 12); *Are Protectionist Policies Bad for America?* (Issue 13); *Are the Costs of Global Warming Too High to Ignore?* (Issue 15); and *Has the North American Free Trade Agreement Hurt the American Economy?* (Issue 17).

As with all of the previous editions, the issues in the 11th edition can be used in any sequence. Although the general organization of the book loosely parallels the sequence of topics found in a standard introductory economics textbook, you can pick and choose which issues to read first, since they are designed to stand alone. Note that we have retained the modification to Part 3 introduced in the 7th edition. That part, "The World Around Us," allows us to more fully represent the host of problems our society faces in the ever-changing world in which we live.

A word to the instructor   *An Instructor's Manual With Test Questions* (multiple-choice and essay) is available through the publisher. A general guidebook, *Using Taking Sides in the Classroom*, which discusses methods and techniques for integrating the pro/con approach into any classroom setting, is also available. An online version of *Using Taking Sides in the Classroom* and a correspondence service for *Taking Sides* adopters can be found at http://www.dushkin.com/usingts/.

Taking Sides: Clashing Views on Controversial Economic Issues is only one title in the Taking Sides series. If you are interested in seeing the table of contents for any of the other titles, please visit the Taking Sides Web site at http://www.dushkin.com/takingsides.

Acknowledgments   We have received many helpful comments and suggestions from our friends and readers across the United States and Canada. As always, their suggestions were very welcome and have markedly enhanced the quality of this edition of *Taking Sides.* If as you read this book you are reminded of an essay that could be included in a future edition, we hope that you will drop us a note. We very much appreciate your interest and help, and we are always pleased to hear from you.

We also offer our special thanks to Ronald W. Francis, retired CEO of Impressions/CMG, who repeatedly helped us to keep sight of how the "real world" actually works. Additionally, we are most appreciative of the encouragement and the effort that two individuals at McGraw-Hill/Dushkin have expended on our behalf in expediting this edition of *Taking Sides.* They are Theodore Knight, managing editor, and David Brackley, senior developmental editor for the Taking Sides series.

To all those mentioned above, we owe a huge debt, many thanks, and none of the blame for any shortcomings that remain in this edition of *Taking Sides.*

Thomas R. Swartz
University of Notre Dame

Frank J. Bonello
University of Notre Dame

Contents in Brief

Contents

The U.S. Department of Health and Human Services (HHS) argues that
although the United States has a health care system that "is the envy of
the world," it is a system that is about to be brought to its knees by aggressive attorneys who force the medical community to practice costly
"defensive medicine." Jackson Williams, legal counsel for the watchdog
group Public Citizen, charges that the position taken by the HHS is factually "incorrect, incomplete, or misleading" and even contradicted by other
governmental agencies.

PART 2   MACROECONOMIC ISSUES   157

Issue 7.   Should Social Security Be Privatized?   158

Michael Tanner, director of health and welfare studies at the Cato Institute, argues that Social Security needs to be replaced with a retirement
system based on individually owned, privately invested accounts. He
maintains that Social Security fails as it is currently structured both as an
antipoverty program and as a retirement program, that it is unfair, and that
it makes workers dependent on politicians for their retirement incomes.
Catherine Hill, a study director at the Institute for Women's Policy Research, contends that privatization of Social Security is a bad idea because it would create significant transition and administrative costs,
create a void with respect to disability and life insurance, and lower the
retirement income of women.

Issue 8.   Does the Consumer Price Index Overstate Inflation and Changes in the Cost of Living?   180

Economist Michael J. Boskin and his colleagues argue that the Consumer
Price Index (CPI) suffers from quality and new product bias, which means
that the CPI overstates inflation and increases in the cost of living. Professor of economics James Devine counters that the Consumer Price Index
understates inflation and changes in the cost of living because it fails to
account for all pertinent changes in the quality of life.

Free-market economists Norbert J. Michel, Alfredo Goyburu, and Ralph A. Rector applaud the George W. Bush administration's initiative to eliminate the double taxation of corporate dividends. They assert that this action will improve economic efficiency and that, in the long run, this tax cut will pay for itself because it will stimulate economic growth. Economic policy analysts Joel Friedman and Robert Greenstein argue that there are no valid economic justifications to propose the elimination of the tax on dividends. All that cutting dividend taxes will really do, they say, is reduce the tax burden of high-income individuals.

Robert E. Litan, director of the Brookings Institution, contends that the government can promote and encourage the sentiment for public service unleashed by the terrorist attacks of September 11, 2001, by instituting a program of universal service. Bruce Chapman, president of the Discovery Institute, maintains that universal service is a bad idea because it cannot be justified morally, militarily, politically, or financially.

Orthodox neoclassical economist Thomas Rustici asserts that the effects of the minimum wage are clear: it creates unemployment among the least-skilled workers. Labor economist Charles Craypo argues that a high minimum wage is good for workers, employers, and consumers alike and that it is therefore good for the economy as a whole.

Cato Institute researcher Michael J. New presents statistical evidence that welfare reform, and not a growing economy, is the primary cause of the recent decline in welfare caseloads. This means that welfare reform has been a success. Evelyn Z. Brodkin, an associate professor in the School of Social Service Administration at the University of Chicago Law School, contends that in assessing welfare reform, one must look beyond the decline in welfare caseloads and ask, What has happened to those who no longer receive welfare? Her answer to this question evokes in Brodkin nostalgia for the "bad old days" of unreformed welfare.

PART 3   THE WORLD AROUND US   291

Free trade economist Murray N. Rothbard objects to the prospect of protectionism, which he sees as an attempt by the few who make up special interest groups "to repress and loot the rest of us" who make up the many. Social critic and three-time presidential hopeful Patrick J. Buchanan argues that America's "new corporate elite" is willing to sacrifice the country's best interests on "the altar of that golden calf, the global economy."

Sociologist Richard Appelbaum and political scientist Peter Dreier chronicle the rise of student activism on American campuses over the issue of sweatshops abroad. Students demand that firms be held responsible for "sweatshop conditions" and warn that if conditions do not improve, American consumers will not "leave their consciences at home when they shop for clothes." News correspondents Nicholas D. Kristof and Sheryl WuDunn agree that the working conditions in many offshore plant sites "seem brutal from the vantage point of an American sitting in his living room." But they argue that these work opportunities are far superior to the alternatives that are currently available in many parts of the world and that what is needed are more sweatshops, not fewer sweatshops.

Lester R. Brown, founder and president of the Earth Policy Institute, describes his vision of an environmentally sustainable economy, which includes food supplies, population growth issues, water availability, climatic changes, and renewable energy. Lenny Bernstein, head of L. S. Bernstein & Associates, which advises companies and trade associations on political and scientific developments on global environmental issues, acknowledges that ecosystems are sensitive to climate change, but he argues that the change that we have seen repeated again and again over the course of history can lead to benefits for our children and our children's children.

Alan S. Blinder, a former member of the Board of Governors of the Federal Reserve System, urges policymakers to use the energy of the market to solve America's environmental problems. Economist Frank Ackerman and environmental policy analyst Kevin Gallagher contend that there is an important distinction between using market forces as a "tool" and using competitive markets as a "blueprint" to solve environmental problems. They argue that environmental goals should be set through the use of "public deliberation" and that at times those goals "may have no inherent relationship to the market."

Economic Policy Institute director Robert E. Scott argues that besides the loss of a significant number of jobs, the North American Free Trade Agreement (NAFTA) has generated a number of less visible harmful effects on the American economy. These include increased income inequality and reduced fringe benefits. Daniel T. Griswold, associate director of the Cato Institute's Center for Trade Policies Studies, contends that NAFTA has helped the American economy by producing better-paying jobs and contributing to increased manufacturing output in the United States between 1993 and 2001.

Introduction

Economics and Economists: The Basis for Controversy

Thomas R. Swartz
Frank J. Bonello

I think that Capitalism, wisely managed, can probably be more efficient for attaining economic ends than any alternative system yet in sight, but that in itself it is in many ways extremely objectionable.

—Lord John Maynard Keynes, *The End of Laissez-Faire* (1926)

Although more than 70 years have passed since Lord Keynes (1883–1946) penned these lines, many economists still struggle with the basic dilemma he outlined. The paradox rests in the fact that a free-market system is extremely efficient. It is purported to produce more at a lower cost than any other economic system. But in producing this wide array of low-cost goods and services, problems arise. These problems—most notably a lack of economic equity and economic stability—concern some economists.

If the problems raised and analyzed in this book were merely the product of intellectual gymnastics undertaken by egg-headed economists, we could sit back and enjoy these confrontations as theoretical exercises. The essays contained in this book, however, touch each and every one of us in tangible ways. They are real-world issues. Some focus upon *macroeconomic* topics, such as the minimum wage and the measurement of inflation and changes in the cost of living. Another set of issues deals with *microeconomic* topics. We refer to these issues as micro problems not because they are small problems, but because they deal with small economic units, such as households, firms, and individual industries. The issue of state and local government subsidies for sports teams and sport venues is a good example. A third set of issues deals with matters that do not fall neatly into the macroeconomic or microeconomic classification. This set includes three issues relating to the international aspects of economic activity, including the effects of the North American Free Trade Agreement on the American economy and the question of whether or not we should import goods produced in sweatshops in foreign countries. We have also included two issues that focus on pollution.

The range of issues and disagreements raises a fundamental question: Why do economists disagree? One explanation is suggested by Lord Keynes's 1926 remark. How various economists will react to the strengths and weaknesses found in an economic system will depend upon how they view the relative importance of efficiency, equity, and stability. These are central terms, and we will define them in detail in the following pages. For now the important point is that some economists may view efficiency as overriding. In other cases, the same economists may be willing to sacrifice the efficiency generated by the market in order to ensure increased economic equity and/or increased economic stability.

Given the extent of conflict, controversy, and diversity, it might appear that economists rarely, if ever, agree on any economic issue. We would be most misleading if we left the reader with this impression. Economists rarely challenge the internal logic of the theoretical models that have been developed and articulated by their colleagues. Rather, they will challenge either the validity of the assumptions used in these models or the value of the ends these models seek to achieve. For example, it is most difficult to discredit the internal logic of the microeconomic models employed by the free-market economist. These models are elegant, and their logical development is most persuasive. However, these models are challenged. The challenges typically focus upon such issues as the assumption of functioning, competitive markets, and the desirability of perpetuating the existing distribution of income. In this case, those who support and those who challenge the operation of the market agree on a large number of issues. But they disagree most assuredly on a few issues that have dramatic implications.

This same phenomenon of agreeing more often than disagreeing is also true in the area of economic policy. In this area, where the public is most acutely aware of differences among economists, these differences are not generally over the kinds of changes that will be brought about by a particular policy. The differences more typically concern the timing of the change, the specific characteristics of the policy, and the size of the resulting effect or effects.

Economists: What Do They Represent?

Newspaper, magazine, and TV commentators all use handy labels to describe certain members of the economics profession. What do the headlines mean when they refer to the Chicago School, the Keynesians, the institutional economists, or the radical economists? What do these individuals stand for? Since we too use our own labels throughout this book, we feel obliged to identify the principal groups, or camps, in our profession. Let us warn you that this can be a misleading venture. Some economists—perhaps most of them—defy classification. They drift from one camp to another, selecting a gem of wisdom here and another there. These are practical men and women who believe that no one camp has all the answers to all the economic problems confronting society.

Recognizing this limitation, four major groups of economists can be identified. These groups are differentiated on the basis of two basic criteria: how they view efficiency relative to equity and stability, and what significance they attach to imperfectly competitive market structures. Before describing the four groups' views on these criteria, it is essential to understand the meaning of certain terms to be used in this description.

Efficiency, equity, and stability represent goals for an economic system. An economy is efficient when it produces those goods and services that people want without wasting scarce resources. Equity in an economic sense has several dimensions. It means that income and wealth are distributed according to accepted principles of fairness, that those who are unable to care for themselves receive adequate care, and that mainstream economic activity is open to all people. Stability is viewed as the absence of sharp ups and downs in business activity, in prices, and in employment. In other words, stability is marked by steady increases in output, little inflation, and low unemployment.

When the term *market structures* is used, it refers to the number of buyers and sellers in the market and the amount of control they exercise over price. At one extreme is a perfectly competitive market where there are so many buyers and sellers that no one has any ability to influence market price. One seller or buyer obviously could have great control over price. This extreme market structure, which we call pure monopoly, and other market structures that result in some control over price are grouped under the broad label of imperfectly competitive markets. That is, imperfect competition is a situation where the number of market participants is limited and, as a consequence, the participants have the ability to influence price. With these terms in mind, we can begin to examine the various schools of economic thought.

Free-Market Economists

One of the most visible groups of economists and perhaps the easiest group to identify and classify is the *free-market economists*. These economists believe that the market, operating freely without interference from government or labor unions, will generate the greatest amount of well-being for the greatest number of people.

Economic efficiency is one of the priorities for free-market economists. In their well-developed models, *consumer sovereignty*—consumer demand for goods and services—guides the system by directly influencing market prices. The distribution of economic resources caused by these market prices not only results in the production of an array of goods and services that are demanded by consumers, but this production is undertaken in the most cost-effective fashion. The free-market economists hold that, at any point, some individuals must earn incomes that are substantially greater than those of other individuals. They contend that these higher incomes are a reward for greater efficiency or productivity and that this reward-induced efficiency will result in rapid economic growth that will benefit all people in the society. They might also admit that a system driven by these freely operating markets will be subject to occasional bouts of instability (slow growth, inflation, and unemployment). However, they maintain that government action to eliminate or reduce this periodic instability will only make matters worse. Consequently, according to the free-market economist, government should play a minor role in the economic affairs of society.

Although the models of free-market economists are dependent upon functioning, competitive markets, the lack of these competitive markets in the real world does not seriously jeopardize their position. First, they assert that large firms are necessary to achieve low per unit costs; that is, a single large firm may be able to produce a given level of output with fewer scarce resources than a large number of small firms. Second, they suggest that the benefits associated with the free operation of markets are so great compared to government intervention that even a second-best solution of imperfectly competitive markets still yields benefits far in excess of government intervention.

These advocates of the free market have been given various labels over time. The oldest and most persistent label is *classical economists*. This is because the classical economists of the eighteenth century, particularly Adam Smith, were the first to point out the virtues of the market. In *The Wealth of Nations* (1776), Smith captured the essence of the system with the following words:

> Every individual endeavors to employ his capital so that its produce may be of greatest value. He generally neither intends to promote the public interest nor knows how much he is promoting it. He intends only his own security, only his own gain. And he is in this led by an invisible hand to promote an end that was no part of his intention. By pursuing his own interest he frequently promotes that of society more effectively than when he really intends to promote it.

Liberal Economists

Another significant group of economists in the United States can be classified as *liberal economists*. Liberal in this instance refers to the willingness to intervene in the free operation of the market. These economists share with the free-market economists a great respect for the market. The liberal economist, however, does not believe that the explicit and implicit costs of a freely operating market should or can be ignored. Rather, the liberal maintains that the costs of an uncontrolled marketplace are often borne by those in society who are least capable of bearing them: the poor, the elderly, and the infirm. Additionally, liberal economists maintain that the freely operating market sometimes results in economic instability and the resultant bouts of inflation, unemployment, and slow or negative growth.

Consider for a moment the differences between free-market economists and liberal economists at the microeconomic level. Liberal economists take exception to the free market on two grounds. First, these economists find a basic problem with fairness in the marketplace. Since the market is driven by the forces of consumer spending, there are those who through no fault of their own (they may be aged, young, infirm, or physically or mentally handicapped) may not have the wherewithal to participate in the economic system. Second, the unfettered marketplace does not and cannot handle spillover effects, or what are known as externalities. These are the third-party effects that may occur as a result of some action. Will a firm willingly compensate its neighbors for the pollutants it pours into the nearby lake? Will a truck driver willingly drive at the speed limit and in the process reduce the highway accident rate? Liberal economists think not. These economists are therefore willing to have the government intervene in these and other, similar cases.

The liberal economists' role in macroeconomics is more readily apparent. Ever since the failure of free-market economics during the Great Depression of the 1930s, Keynesianism (still another label for liberal economics) has become widely known. In his 1935 book *The General Theory of Employment, Interest, and Money,* Lord John Maynard Keynes laid the basic groundwork for this school of thought. Keynes argued that the history of freely operating market economies was marked by periods of recurring recessions, sometimes very deep recessions, which we call depressions. He maintained that government intervention through its fiscal policy—government tax and spending power—could eliminate, or at least soften, these sharp reductions in economic activity and as a result move the economy along a more stable growth path. Thus, for the Keynesians, or liberal economists, one of the "extremely objectionable" aspects of a free-market economy is its inherent instability.

Liberal economists are also far more concerned about the existence of imperfections in the marketplace than are their free-market counterparts. They reject the notion that imperfect competition is an acceptable substitute for competitive markets. These economists may agree that the imperfectly competitive firms can achieve some savings because of their large size and efficiency, but they assert that since there is little or no competition, the firms are not forced to pass these cost savings on to consumers. Thus, liberal economists, who in some circles are labeled "antitrusters," are willing to intervene in the market in two ways: They are prepared to allow some monopolies, such as public utilities, to exist, but they contend that these must be regulated by government. In other cases they maintain that there is no justification for monopolies, and they are prepared to invoke the powers of antitrust legislation to break up existing monopolies or prevent the formation of new ones.

Mainstream Critics and Radical Reform Economists

There two other groups of economists we must identify. One group can be called *mainstream critics.* Included in this group are individuals like Thorstein Veblen (1857–1929), with his critique of conspicuous consumption, and John Kenneth Galbraith (b. 1908), with his views on industrial structure. One reasonably cohesive subgroup of mainstream critics are the post-Keynesians. They are post-Keynesian because they believe that as the principal economic institutions have changed over time, they have remained closer to the spirit of Keynes than have the liberal economists. As some have suggested, the key aspect of Keynes as far as the post-Keynesians are concerned is his assertion that "expectations of the future are not necessarily certain." On a more practical level, post-Keynesians assert, among other things, that the productivity of the economic system is not significantly affected by changes in income distribution, that the system can still be efficient without competitive markets, that conventional fiscal policies cannot control inflation, and that "incomes policies" are the means to an effective and equitable answer to the inflationary dilemma. This characterization of post-

Keynesianism is drawn from Alfred S. Eichner's introduction in *A Guide to Post-Keynesian Economics* (M. E. Sharpe, 1978).

The fourth and last group can be called *radical reform economists*. Many in this group trace their ideas back to the nineteenth-century philosopher-economist Karl Marx and his most impressive work, the three volumes of *Das Kapital*. As with the other three groups of economists, there are subgroups of radical reform economists. One subgroup, which may be labeled contemporary Marxists, is best represented by those who have published their research results over the years in the *Review of Radical Political Economy*. These economists examine issues that have been largely ignored by mainstream economists, such as war, sexism, racism, imperialism, and civil rights. In their analyses of these issues, they borrow from and refine the work of Marx. In the process, they emphasize the role of class in shaping society and the role of the economy in determining class structures. Moreover, they see a need to encourage explicitly the development of some form of democratic socialism, for only then will the greatest good for the greatest number be ensured.

In concluding this section we must warn you to use these labels with extreme care. Our categories are not hard and fast. There is much grayness around the edges and little that is black and white in these classifications. This does not mean, however, that they have no value. It is important to understand the philosophical background of the individual authors. This background does indeed color or shade their work.

Summary

It is clear that there is no shortage of economic problems. These problems demand solutions. At the same time there is no shortage of proposed solutions. In fact, there is often an oversupply of solutions. The 17 issues included in this volume will acquaint you—or, more accurately, reacquaint you—with some of these problems. And, of course, there are at least two proposed solutions for each of the problems. Here we hope to provide new insights regarding the available alternatives and the differences and similarities of these alternative remedies.

If this introduction has served its purpose, you will be able to identify common elements in the proposed solutions to the different problems. For example, you will be able to identify the reliance on the forces of the market advocated by free-market economists as the remedy for several economic ills. This introduction should also help you to understand why there are at least two proposed solutions for every economic problem; each group of economists tends to interpret a problem from its own philosophical position and to advance a solution that is grounded in that philosophical framework.

Our intention, of course, is not to connect persons to one philosophic position or another. We hope instead to generate discussion and promote understanding. To do this, not only must each of us see a proposed solution, we must also be aware of the foundation that supports that solution. With greater understanding, meaningful progress in addressing economic problems can be achieved.

On the Internet . . .

The Dismal Scientist

The Dismal Scientist provides free economic data, analysis, and forecasts on a variety of topics.

http://www.dismal.com

Economist.com

The Web edition of *The Economist* is available free to subscribers of the print edition or for an annual fee to those who wish to subscribe online. A selection of articles is available free to those who want to dip into the journal.

http://www.economist.com

The Electronic Policy Network

This site offers timely information and ideas about national policy on economics and politics, welfare and families, education, civic participation, and health policy in the form of a virtual magazine.

http://epn.org

Resources for Economists on the Internet

This is the table of contents for Resources for Economists on the Internet. This resource of the WWW Virtual Library on Economics is an excellent starting point for any research in economics by academic and practicing economists and anyone interested in economics. It has many Web links.

http://rfe.wustl.edu/sc.html

Statistical Resources on the Web: Comprehensive Economics

Here is an excellent source of statistics collated from federal bureaus, economic indicators (both historical and current), the Federal Reserve Board, economic sources, federal statistical tables, and a consumer price inflator/deflator, plus many links to other sources.

http://www.lib.umich.edu/libhome/Documents.center/stecon.html

WebEc: WWW Resources in Economics

This is a complete virtual library of economics facts, figures, and thoughts.

http://netec.wustl.edu/webec.html

PART 1

Microeconomic Issues

*O*ur lives are profoundly affected by economic decisions made at the microeconomic level. Some important decisions are those regarding the profit motives of businesses, city subsidies for sport venues, discrimination in labor markets, the health care industry, deregulation of public utilities, and medical malpractice litigation reform.

- Are Profits the Only Business of Business?

- Should Cities Subsidize Sports and Sport Venues?

- Is There Discrimination in U.S. Labor Markets?

- Should California's Electric Utility Industry Be Deregulated?

- Should Markets Be Allowed to Solve the Shortage in Body Parts?

- Is It Time to Reform Medical Malpractice Litigation?

ISSUE 1

Are Profits the Only Business of Business?

YES: Milton Friedman, from "The Social Responsibility of Business Is to Increase Its Profits," *The New York Times Magazine* (September 13, 1970)

NO: Robert Almeder, from "Morality in the Marketplace," in Milton Snoeyenbos, Robert Almeder, and James Humber, eds., *Business Ethics,* rev. ed. (Prometheus Press, 1998)

ISSUE SUMMARY

YES: Free-market economist Milton Friedman contends that the sole responsibility of business is to increase its profits.

NO: Philosopher Robert Almeder maintains that if capitalism is to survive, it must act in socially responsible ways that go beyond profit making.

E very economic society—whether it is a traditional society in Central Africa, a fossilized planned economy such as Cuba's, or a wealthy capitalist society such as those found in North America, Western Europe, and the Pacific Rim—must address the basic economic problem of resource allocation. These societies must determine *what* goods and services they can and will produce, *how* these goods and services will be produced, and *for whom* these goods and services will be produced.

The *what, how,* and *for whom* questions must be answered because of the problem of scarcity. Even if a given society were indescribably rich, it would still confront the problem of scarcity—in the case of a rich society, "relative scarcity." It might have all the resources it needs to produce all the goods and services it would ever want, but it could not produce all these things simultaneously. Thus, even a very rich society must set priorities and produce first those goods and services with the highest priority and postpone the production of those goods and services with lower priorities. If time is of the essence, this society would determine *how* these goods and services should be produced. And since this wealthy society cannot produce all it wants instantly, it must also determine *for whom* the first bundle of goods and services will be produced.

Few, if any, economic societies are indescribably rich. On the other hand, there are many examples of economic societies that face grinding deprivation daily. In these societies and in all the societies that fall between poverty and great affluence, the *what, how,* and *for whom* questions are immediately apparent. Somehow these questions must be answered.

In some societies, such as the Amish communities of North America, the answers to these questions are found in tradition: Sons and daughters follow in their parents' footsteps. Younger generations produce *what* older generations produced before them. The methods of production—the horsedrawn plow, the hand-held scythe, the use of natural fertilizers—remain unchanged; thus, the *how* question is answered in the same way that the *for whom* question is answered—by following historic patterns. In other societies, such as self-sustaining religious communities, there is a different pattern of responses to these questions. In these communities, the "elder" of the community determines *what* will be produced, *how* it will be produced, and *for whom* it will be produced. If there is a well-defined hierarchical system, it is similar to one of the former stereotypical command economies of Eastern Europe.

Although elements of tradition and command are found in the industrialized societies of Western Europe, North America, and Japan, the basic answers to the three questions of resource allocation in these countries are determined by profit. In these economic societies, *what* will be produced is determined by what will yield the greatest profit. Consumers, in their search for maximum satisfaction, will bid for those goods and services that they want most. This consumer action drives the prices of these goods and services up, which, in turn, increases producers' profits. The higher profits attract new firms into the industry and encourage existing firms to increase their output. Thus, profits are the mechanism that ensures that consumers get what they want. Similarly, the profit-seeking behavior of business firms determines *how* the goods and services that consumers want will be produced. Since firms attempt to maximize their profits, they select those means of production that are economically most efficient. Lastly, the *for whom* question is also linked to profits. Wherever there is a shortage of goods and services, profits will be high. In the producers' attempts to increase their output, they must attract factors of production (land, labor, and capital) away from other economic activities. This bidding increases factor prices or factor incomes and ensures that these factors will be able to buy goods and services in the open marketplace.

Both Milton Friedman and Robert Almeder recognize the merits of a profit-driven economic system. They do not quarrel over the importance of profits. But they do quarrel over whether or not business firms have obligations beyond making profits. In the following selection, Friedman holds that the *only* responsibility of business is to make profits and that anyone who maintains otherwise is "preaching pure and unadulterated socialism." In the second selection, Almeder, who is clearly not a "socialist," contends that business must act in socially responsible ways "if capitalism is to survive."

Milton Friedman

 **YES**

The Social Responsibility of Business Is to Increase Its Profits

When I hear businessmen speak eloquently about the "social responsibilities of business in a free-enterprise system," I am reminded of the wonderful line about the Frenchman who discovered at the age of 70 that he had been speaking prose all his life. The businessmen believe that they are defending free enterprise when they declaim that business is not concerned "merely" with profit but also with promoting desirable "social ends; that business has a social conscience" and takes seriously its responsibilities for providing employment, eliminating discrimination, avoiding pollution and whatever else may be the catchwords of the contemporary crop of reformers. In fact they are—or would be if they or anyone else took them seriously—preaching pure and unadulterated socialism. Businessmen who talk this way are unwitting puppets of the intellectual forces that have been undermining the basis of a free society these past decades.

The discussions of the "social responsibilities of business" are notable for their analytical looseness and lack of rigor. What does it mean to say that "business" has responsibilities? Only people can have responsibilities. A corporation is an artificial person and in this sense may have artificial responsibilities, but "business" as a whole cannot be said to have responsibilities, even in this vague sense. The first step toward clarity in examining the doctrine of the social responsibility of business is to ask precisely what it implies for whom.

Presumably, the individuals who are to be responsible are businessmen, which means individual proprietors or corporate executives. Most of the discussion of social responsibility is directed at corporations, so in what follows I shall mostly neglect the individual proprietor and speak of corporate executives.

In a free-enterprise, private-property system, a corporate executive is an employee of the owners of the business. He has direct responsibility to his employers. That responsibility is to conduct the business in accordance with their desires, which generally will be to make as much money as possible while conforming to the basic rules of the society, both those embodied in law and those embodied in ethical custom. Of course, in some cases his employers may have a different objective. A group of persons might establish a corporation for an eleemosynary purpose—for example, a hospital or a school. The manager of such a corporation will not have money profit as his objective but the rendering of certain services.

In either case, the key point is that, in his capacity as a corporate executive, the manager is the agent of the individuals who own the corporation or establish the eleemosynary institution, and his primary responsibility is to them.

Needless to say, this does not mean that it is easy to judge how well he is performing his task. But at least the criterion of performance is straightforward, and the persons among whom a voluntary contractual arrangement exists are clearly defined.

Of course, the corporate executive is also a person in his own right. As a person, he may have many other responsibilities that he recognizes or assumes voluntarily—to his family, his conscience, his feelings of charity, his church, his clubs, his city, his country. He may feel impelled by these responsibilities to devote part of his income to causes he regards as worthy, to refuse to work for particular corporations, even to leave his job, for example, to join his country's armed forces. If we wish, we may refer to some of these responsibilities as "social responsibilities." But in these respects he is acting as a principal, not an agent; he is spending his own money or time or energy, not the money of his employers or the time or energy he has contracted to devote to their purposes. If these are "social responsibilities," they are the social responsibilities of individuals, not of business.

What does it mean to say that the corporate executive has a "social responsibility" in his capacity as businessman? If this statement is not pure rhetoric, it must mean that he is to act in some way that is not in the interest of his employers. For example, that he is to refrain from increasing the price of the product in order to contribute to the social objective of preventing inflation, even though a price increase would be in the best interests of the corporation. Or that he is to make expenditures on reducing pollution beyond the amount that is in the best interests of the corporation or that is required by law in order to contribute to the social objective of improving the environment. Or that, at the expense of corporate profits, he is to hire "hard-core" unemployed instead of better-qualified available workmen to contribute to the social objective of reducing poverty.

In each of these cases, the corporate executive would be spending someone else's money for a general social interest. Insofar as his actions in accord with his "social responsibility" reduce returns to stockholders, he is spending their money. Insofar as his actions raise the price to customers, he is spending the customers' money. Insofar as his actions lower the wages of some employees, he is spending their money.

The stockholders or the customers or the employees could separately spend their own money on the particular action if they wished to do so. The executive is exercising a distinct "social responsibility," rather than serving as an agent of the stockholders or the customers or the employees, only if he spends the money in a different way than they would have spent it.

But if he does this, he is in effect imposing taxes, on the one hand, and deciding how the tax proceeds shall be spent, on the other.

This process raises political questions on two levels: principle and consequences. On the level of political principle, the imposition of taxes and the expenditure of tax proceeds are governmental functions. We have established elaborate constitutional, parliamentary and judicial provisions to control these functions, to assure that taxes are imposed so far as possible in accordance with the preferences and desires of the public—after all, "taxation without representation" was one of the battle cries of the American Revolution. We have a system of checks and balances to separate the legislative function of imposing taxes and enacting expenditures from the executive function of collecting taxes and administering expenditure programs and from the judicial function of mediating disputes and interpreting the law.

Here the businessman—self-selected or appointed directly or indirectly by stockholders—is to be simultaneously legislator, executive and jurist. He is to decide whom to tax by how much and for what purpose, and he is to spend the proceeds—all this guided only by general exhortations from on high to restrain inflation, improve the environment, fight poverty and so on and on.

The whole justification for permitting the corporate executive to be selected by the stockholders is that the executive is an agent serving the interests of his principal. This justification disappears when the corporate executive imposes taxes and spends the proceeds for "social" purposes. He becomes in effect a public employee, a civil servant, even though he remains in name an employee of a private enterprise. On grounds of political principle, it is intolerable that such civil servants—insofar as their actions in the name of social responsibility are real and not just window-dressing—should be selected as they are now. If they are to be civil servants, then they must be selected through a political process. If they are to impose taxes and make expenditures to foster "social" objectives, then political machinery must be set up to guide the assessment of taxes and to determine through a political process the objectives to be served.

This is the basic reason why the doctrine of "social responsibility" involves the acceptance of the socialist view that political mechanisms, not market mechanisms, are the appropriate way to determine the allocation of scarce resources to alternative uses.

On the grounds of consequences, can the corporate executive in fact discharge his alleged "social responsibilities"? On the one hand, suppose he could get away with spending the stockholders' or customers' or employees' money. How is he to know how to spend it? He is told that he must contribute to fighting inflation. How is he to know what action of his will contribute to that end? He is presumably an expert in running his company—in producing a product or selling it or financing it. But nothing about his selection makes him an expert on inflation. Will his holding down the price of his product reduce inflationary pressure? Or, by leaving more spending power in the hands of his customers, simply divert it elsewhere? Or, by forcing him to produce less because of the lower price, will it simply contribute to shortages? Even if he could answer these questions, how much cost is he justified in imposing on his stockholders, customers and employees for this social purpose? What is the appropriate share and what is the appropriate share of others?

And, whether he wants to or not, can he get away with spending his stock-holders', customers' or employees' money? Will not the stockholders fire him? (Either the present ones or those who take over when his actions in the name of social responsibility have reduced the corporation's profits and the price of its stock.) His customers and his employees can desert him for other producers and employers less scrupulous in exercising their social responsibilities.

This facet of "social responsibility" doctrine is brought into sharp relief when the doctrine is used to justify wage restraint by trade unions. The conflict of interest is naked and clear when union officials are asked to subordinate the interest of their members to some more general social purpose. If the union officials try to enforce wage restraint, the consequence is likely to be wildcat strikes, rank-and-file revolts and the emergence of strong competitors for their jobs. We thus have the ironic phenomenon that union leaders—at least in the U.S.—have objected to Government interference with the market far more consistently and courageously than have business leaders.

The difficulty of exercising "social responsibility" illustrates, of course, the great virtue of private competitive enterprise—it forces people to be responsible for their own actions and makes it difficult for them to "exploit" other people for either selfish or unselfish purposes. They can do good—but only at their own expense.

Many a reader who has followed the argument this far may be tempted to remonstrate that it is all well and good to speak of government's having the responsibility to impose taxes and determine expenditures for such "social" purposes as controlling pollution or training the hard-core unemployed, but that the problems are too urgent to wait on the slow course of political processes, that the exercise of social responsibility by businessmen is a quicker and surer way to solve pressing current problems.

Aside from the question of fact—I share Adam Smith's skepticism about the benefits that can be expected from "those who affected to trade for the public good"—this argument must be rejected on grounds of principle. What it amounts to is an assertion that those who favor the taxes and expenditures in question have failed to persuade a majority of their fellow citizens to be of like mind and that they are seeking to attain by undemocratic procedures what they cannot attain by democratic procedures. In a free society, it is hard for "good" people to do "good," but that is a small price to pay for making it hard for "evil" people to do "evil," especially since one man's good is another's evil.

I have, for simplicity, concentrated on the special case of the corporate executive, except only for the brief digression on trade unions. But precisely the same argument applies to the newer phenomenon of calling upon stockholders to require corporations to exercise social responsibility (the recent G.M. crusade, for example). In most of these cases, what is in effect involved is some stockholders trying to get other stockholders (or customers or employees) to contribute against their will to "social" causes favored by the activists. Insofar as they succeed, they are again imposing taxes and spending the proceeds.

The situation of the individual proprietor is somewhat different. If he acts to reduce the returns of his enterprise in order to exercise his "social responsibility," he is spending his own money, not someone else's. If he wishes to spend his money on such purposes, that is his right, and I cannot see that there is any objection to his doing so. In the process, he, too, may impose costs on employees and customers. However, because he is far less likely than a large corporation or union to have monopolistic power, any such side effects will tend to be minor.

Of course, in practice the doctrine of social responsibility is frequently a cloak for actions that are justified on other grounds rather than a reason for those actions.

To illustrate, it may well be in the long-run interest of a corporation that is a major employer in a small community to devote resources to providing amenities to that community or to improving its government. That may make it easier to attract desirable employees, it may reduce the wage bill or lessen losses from pilferage and sabotage or have other worthwhile effects. Or it may be that, given the laws about the deductibility of corporate charitable contributions, the stockholders can contribute more to charities they favor by having the corporation make the gift than by doing it themselves, since they can in that way contribute an amount that would otherwise have been paid as corporate taxes.

In each of these—and many similar—cases, there is a strong temptation to rationalize these actions as an exercise of "social responsibility." In the present climate of opinion, with its widespread aversion to "capitalism," "profits," the "soulless corporation" and so on, this is one way for a corporation to generate goodwill as a by-product of expenditures that are entirely justified in its own self-interest.

It would be inconsistent of me to call on corporate executives to refrain from this hypocritical window-dressing because it harms the foundations of a free society. That would be to call on them to exercise a "social responsibility"! If our institutions, and the attitudes of the public make it in their self-interest to cloak their actions in this way, I cannot summon much indignation to denounce them. At the same time, I can express admiration for those individual proprietors or owners of closely held corporations or stockholders of more broadly held corporations who disdain such tactics as approaching fraud.

Whether blameworthy or not, the use of the cloak of social responsibility, and the nonsense spoken in its name by influential and prestigious businessmen, does clearly harm the foundations of a free society. I have been impressed time and again by the schizophrenic character of many businessmen. They are capable of being extremely far-sighted and clear-headed in matters that are internal to their businesses. They are incredibly short-sighted and muddle-headed in matters that are outside their businesses but affect the possible survival of business in general. This short-sightedness is strikingly exemplified in the calls from many businessmen for wage and price guidelines or controls or income policies. There is nothing that could do more in a brief period to destroy a market system and replace it by a centrally controlled system than effective governmental control of prices and wages.

The short-sightedness is also exemplified in speeches by businessmen on social responsibility. This may gain them kudos in the short run. But it helps to strengthen the already too prevalent view that the pursuit of profits is wicked and immoral and must be curbed and controlled by external forces. Once this view is adopted, the external forces that curb the market will not be the social consciences, however highly developed, of the pontificating executives; it will be the iron fist of Government bureaucrats. Here, as with price and wage controls, businessmen seem to me to reveal a suicidal impulse.

The political principle that underlies the market mechanism is unanimity. In an ideal free market resting on private property, no individual can coerce any other, all cooperation is voluntary, all parties to such cooperation benefit or they need not participate. There are no "social" values, no "social" responsibilities in any sense other than the shared values and responsibilities of individuals. Society is a collection of individuals and of the various groups they voluntarily form.

The political principle that underlies the political mechanism is conformity. The individual must serve a more general social interest—whether that be determined by a church or a dictator or a majority. The individual may have a vote and a say in what is to be done, but if he is overruled, he must conform. It is appropriate for some to require others to contribute to a general social purpose whether they wish to or not.

Unfortunately, unanimity is not always feasible. There are some respects in which conformity appears unavoidable, so I do not see how one can avoid the use of the political mechanism altogether.

But the doctrine of "social responsibility" taken seriously would extend the scope of the political mechanism to every human activity. It does not differ in philosophy from the most explicitly collectivist doctrine. It differs only by professing to believe that collectivist ends can be attained without collectivist means. That is why, in my book "Capitalism and Freedom," I have called it a "fundamentally subversive doctrine" in a free society, and have said that in such a society, "there is one and only one social responsibility of business—to use its resources and engage in activities designed to increase its profits so long as it stays within the rules of the game, which is to say, engages in open and free competition without deception or fraud."

Robert Almeder

NO

Morality in the Marketplace: Reflections on the Friedman Doctrine

Introduction

In seeking to create a climate more favorable for corporate activity, International Telephone and Telegraph allegedly contributed large sums of money to "destabilize" the duly elected government of Chile. Even though advised by the scientific community that the practice is lethal, major chemical companies reportedly continue to dump large amounts of carcinogens and mutagens into the water supply of various areas and, at the same time, lobby strongly to prevent legislation against such practices. General Motors Corporation, other automobile manufacturers, and Firestone Tire and Rubber Corporation have frequently defended themselves against the charge that they knowingly and willingly marketed a product that, owing to defective design, had been reliably predicted to kill a certain percentage of its users and, moreover, refused to recall promptly the product even when government agencies documented the large incidence of death as a result of the defective product. Finally, people often say that numerous advertising companies happily accept, and earnestly solicit, accounts to advertise cigarettes knowing full well that as a direct result of their advertising activities a certain number of people will die considerably prematurely and painfully. Most recently, of course, American Tobacco Companies have been charged with knowingly marketing a very addictive product known to kill untold numbers in slow, painful and costly deaths while the price of the stock of these companies has made fortunes for the shareholders. We need not concern ourselves with whether these and other similar charges are true because our primary concern here is with what might count as a justification for such corporate conduct were it to occur. There can be no question that such corporate behavior sometimes occurs and is frequently legal, or at least not illegal. The question is whether corporate behavior should be constrained by nonlegal or moral considerations. If so, to what extent and how could it be done? As things presently stand, it seems to be a dogma of contemporary capitalism rapidly emerging throughout the world that the sole responsibility of business is to make as much money as is *legally* possible. But the interesting question is whether this view is rationally defensible.

Sometimes, although not very frequently, corporate executives will admit to the sort of behavior depicted above and then proceed proximately to justify such behavior in the name of their responsibility to the shareholders or owners (if the shareholders are not the owners) to make as much profit as is legally possible. Thereafter, less proximately and more generally, they will proceed to urge the more general utilitarian point that the increase in profit engendered by such corporate behavior begets such an unquestionable overall good for society that the behavior in question is morally acceptable if not quite praiseworthy. More specifically, the justification in question can, and usually does, take two forms.

The first and most common form of justification consists in urging that, as long as one's corporate behavior is not illegal, the behavior will be morally acceptable because the sole purpose of being in business is to make a profit; and the rules of the marketplace are somewhat different from those in other places and must be followed if one is to make a profit. Moreover, proponents of this view hasten to add that, as Adam Smith has claimed, the greatest good for society in the long run is achieved not by corporations seeking to act morally, or with a sense of social responsibility in their pursuit of profit, but rather by each corporation seeking to maximize its own profit, unregulated in that endeavor except by the laws of supply and demand along with whatever other laws are inherent to the competition process. This, they say, is what has made capitalist societies the envy of the world while ideological socialisms sooner or later fail miserably to meet deep human needs. Smith's view, that there is an invisible hand, as it were, directing an economy governed solely by the profit motive to the greatest good for society in the long run,[1] is still the dominant motivation and justification for those who would want an economy unregulated by any moral concern that would, or could, tend to decrease profits for some *alleged* social or moral good.

Milton Friedman, for example, has frequently asserted that the sole moral responsibility of business is to make as much profit as is legally possible; and by that he means to assert that attempts to regulate or restrain the pursuit of profit in accordance with what some people believe to be socially desirable ends are in fact *subversive* of the common good because the greatest good for the greatest number is achieved by an economy maximally competitive and unregulated by moral rules in its pursuit of profit.[2] So, on Friedman's view, the greatest good for society is achieved by corporations acting legally, but with no further regard for what may be morally desirable; and this view begets the paradox that, *in business,* the greatest good for society can be achieved only by acting without regard for morality, at least in so far as moral rules are not reflected in the legal code. Moreover, adoption of this position constitutes a fairly conscious commitment to the view that while one's personal life may well need moral governance beyond the law, when pursuing profit, it is necessary that one's corporate behavior be unregulated by any moral concern other than that of making as much money as is legally possible; curiously enough, it is only in this way that society achieves the greatest good. So viewed, it is not difficult to see how a corporate executive could sincerely and consistently adopt rigorous standards of morality in his or her personal life and yet feel quite comfortable in abandoning those standards in the pursuit of profit. Albert Carr, for example, likens the conduct of business to that of playing poker.[3] As Carr would have it, moral busybodies who insist on corporations acting morally might do just as well to censure a good bluffer in poker for being deceitful. Society, of course, lacking a perspective such as Friedman's and Carr's is only too willing to view such behavior as strongly hypocritical and fostered by an unwholesome avarice.

The second way of justifying, or defending, corporate practices that may appear morally questionable consists in urging that even if corporations were to take seriously the idea of limiting profits because of a desire to be moral or more responsible to social needs, then corporations would be involved in the un-wholesome business of selecting and implementing moral values that may not be shared by a large number of people. Besides, there is the overwhelming question of whether there can be any non-questionable moral values or non-controversial list of social priorities for corporations to adopt. After all, if ethical relativism is true, or if ethical nihilism is true (and philosophers can be counted upon to argue agressively for both positions), then it would be fairly silly of cor-porations to limit profits for what may be a quite dubious reason, namely, for being moral, when there are no clear grounds for doing it, and when it is not too clear what would count for doing it. In short, business corporations could argue (as Friedman has done)[4] that corporate actions in behalf of society's inter-ests would require of corporations an ability to clearly determine and rank in noncontroversial ways the major needs of society; and it would not appear that this could be done successfully.

Perhaps another, and somewhat easier, way of formulating this second ar-gument consists in urging that because moralists and philosophers generally fail to agree on what are the proper moral rules (if any), as well as on whether we should be moral, it would be imprudent to sacrifice a clear profit for a dubious or controversial moral gain. To authorize such a sacrifice would be to abandon a clear responsibility for one that is unclear or questionable.

If there are any other basic ways of justifying the sort of corporate behav-ior noted at the outset, I cannot imagine what they might be. So, let us examine these two modes of justification. In doing this, I hope to show that neither argu-ment is sound and, moreover, that corporate behavior of the sort in question is clearly immoral if anything is immoral—and if nothing is immoral, then such corporate behavior is clearly contrary to the long-term interest of a corporation. In the end, we will reflect on ways to prevent such behavior, and on what is philosophically implied by corporate willingness to act in clearly immoral ways.

The "Invisible Hand"

Essentially, the first argument is that the greatest good for the greatest number will be, and can only be, achieved by corporations acting legally but unregu-lated by any moral concern in the pursuit of profit. As we saw earlier, the evidence for this argument rests on a fairly classical and unquestioning acceptance of Adam Smith's view that society achieves a greater good when each person is allowed to pursue her or his own self-interested ends than when each person's pursuit of self-interested ends is regulated in some way or another by moral rules or concern. But I know of no evidence Smith ever offered for this latter claim, although it seems clear that those who adopt it generally do so out of respect for the perceived good that has emerged for various modern societies as a direct result of the free enterprise system and its ability to raise the overall standard of living of all those under it.

However, there is nothing inevitable about the greatest good occurring in an unregulated economy. Indeed, we have good inductive evidence from the age of the Robber Barons that unless the profit motive is regulated in various ways (by statute or otherwise) untold social evil can, and *will,* occur because of the natural tendency of the system to place ever-increasing sums of money in ever-decreasing numbers of hands as a result of the nature of competition unregulated. If all this is so, then so much the worse for all philosophical attempts to justify what would appear to be morally questionable corporate behavior on the grounds that corporate behavior, unregulated by moral concern, is necessarily or even probably productive of the greatest good for the greatest number. Moreover, a rule utilitarian would not be very hard pressed to show the many unsavory implications to society as a whole if society were to take seriously a rule to the effect that, if one acts legally, it is morally permissible to do whatever one wants to do to achieve a profit. We shall discuss some of those implications of this rule below before drawing a conclusion.

The second argument cited above asserts that even if we were to grant, for the sake of argument, that corporations have social responsibilities beyond that of making as much money as is legally possible for the shareholders, there would be no noncontroversial way for corporations to discover just what these responsibilities are in the order of their importance. Owing to the fact that even distinguished moral philosophers predictably disagree on what one's moral responsibilities are, if any, it would seem irresponsible to limit profits to satisfy dubious moral responsibilities.

For one thing, this argument unduly exaggerates our potential for moral disagreement. Admittedly, there might well be important disagreements among corporations (just as there could be among philosophers) as to a priority ranking of major social needs; but that does not mean that most of us could not, or would not, agree that certain things ought not be done in the name of profit even when there is no law prohibiting such acts. Doubtless, there will always be a few who would do most anything for a profit; but that is hardly a good argument in favor of their having the moral right to do so rather than a good argument showing that they refuse to be moral. In sum, it is difficult to see how this second argument favoring corporate moral nihilism is any better than the general argument for ethical nihilism based on the variability of ethical judgments or practices; and apart from the fact that it tacitly presupposes that morality is a matter of what we all in fact would, or should, accept, the argument is maximally counterintuitive (as I shall show) by way of suggesting that we cannot generally agree that corporations have certain clear social responsibilities to avoid certain practices. Accordingly, I would now like to argue that if anything is immoral, a certain kind of corporate behavior is quite immoral although it may not be illegal.

Murder for Profit

Without caring to enter into the reasons for the belief, I assume we all believe that it is wrong to kill an innocent human being for no other reason than that doing so would be more financially rewarding for the killer than if he were to earn his livelihood in some other way. Nor, I assume, should our moral feeling on this matter change depending on the amount of money involved. Killing an innocent baby for fifteen million dollars would not seem to be any less objectionable than killing it for twenty cents. It is possible, however, that a self-professing utilitarian might be tempted to argue that the killing of an innocent baby for fifteen million dollars would not be objectionable if the money were to be given to the poor; under these circumstances, greater good would be achieved by the killing of the innocent baby. But, I submit, if anybody were to argue in this fashion, his argument would be quite deficient because he has not established what he needs to establish to make his argument sound. What he needs is a clear, convincing argument that raising the standard of living of an indefinite number of poor persons by the killing of an innocent person is a greater good for all those affected by the act than if the standard of living were not raised by the killing of an innocent person. This is needed because part of what we mean by having a basic right to life is that a person's life cannot be taken from him or her without a good reason. If our utilitarian cannot provide a convincing justification for his claim that a greater good is served by killing an innocent person in order to raise the standard of living for a large number of poor people, then it is hard to see how he can have the good reason that he needs to deprive an innocent person of his or her life. Now, it seems clear that there will be anything but unanimity in the moral community on the question of whether there is a greater good achieved in raising the standard of living by killing an innocent baby than in leaving the standard of living alone and not killing an innocent baby. Moreover, even if everybody were to agree that the greater good is achieved by the killing of the innocent baby, how could that be shown to be true? How does one compare the moral value of a human life with the moral value of raising the standard of living by the taking of that life? Indeed, the more one thinks about it, the more difficult it is to see just what would count as objective evidence for the claim that the greater good is achieved by the killing of the innocent baby. Accordingly, I can see nothing that would justify the utilitarian who might be tempted to argue that if the sum is large enough, and if the sum were to be used for raising the standard of living for an indefinite number of poor people, then it would be morally acceptable to kill an innocent person for money.

These reflections should not be taken to imply, however, that no utilitarian argument could justify the killing of an innocent person for money. After all, if the sum were large enough to save the lives of a large number of people who would surely die if the innocent baby were not killed, then one would as a rule be justified in killing the innocent baby for the sum in question. But this situation is obviously quite different from the situation in which one would attempt to justify the killing of an innocent person in order to raise the standard of living for an indefinite number of poor people. It makes sense to kill one innocent person in order to save, say, twenty innocent persons; but it makes no sense at all to kill one innocent person to raise the standard of living of an indefinite number of people. In the latter case, but not in the former, a comparison is made between things that are incomparable.

Given these considerations, it is remarkable and somewhat perplexing that certain corporations should seek to defend practices that are in fact instances of killing innocent persons for profit. Take, for example, the corporate practice of dumping known carcinogens into rivers. On Milton Friedman's view, we should not regulate or prevent such companies from dumping their effluents into the environment. Rather we should, if we like, tax the company after the effluents are in the water and then have the tax money used to clean up the environment.[5] For Friedman, and others, the fact that so many people will die as a result of this practice seems to be just part of the cost of doing business and making a profit. If there is any moral difference between such corporate practices and murdering innocent human beings for money, it is hard to see what it is. It is even more difficult to see how anyone could justify the practice and see it as no more than a business practice not to be regulated by moral concern. And there are a host of other corporate activities that are morally equivalent to deliberate killing of innocent persons for money. Such practices number among them contributing funds to "destabilize" a foreign government, selling cigarettes while knowing that they are highly addictive killers of innocent people, advertising cigarettes, knowingly marketing children's clothing having a known cancer-causing agent, and refusing to recall (for fear of financial loss) goods known to be sufficiently defective to directly maim or kill a certain percentage of their unsuspecting users because of the defect. On this latter item, we are all familiar, for example, with convincingly documented charges that certain prominent automobile and tire manufacturers will knowingly market equipment sufficiently defective to increase the likelihood of death as a direct result of the defect, and yet refuse to recall the product because the cost of recalling and repairing would have a greater adverse impact on profit than if the product were not recalled and the company paid the projected number of predictably successful suits. Of course, if the projected cost of the predictably successful suits were to outweigh the cost of recall and repair, then the product would be recalled and repaired, but not otherwise.

In cases of this sort, the companies involved may admit to having certain marketing problems or a design problem, and they may even admit to having made a mistake; but, interestingly enough, they do not view themselves as immoral or as murderers for keeping their product in the market place when they know people are dying from it, people who would not die if the defect were corrected.

The important point is not whether in fact these practices have occurred in the past, or occur even now; there can be no doubt that such practices have occurred and continue to occur. Rather the point is that when companies act in such ways as a matter of policy, they must either not know what they do is murder (i.e., unjustifiable killing of an innocent person), or knowing that it is murder, seek to justify it in terms of profit. And I have been arguing that it is difficult to see how any corporate manager could fail to see that these policies amount to murder for money, although there may be no civil statute against such corporate behavior. If so, then where such policies exist, we can only assume that they are designed and implemented by corporate managers who either see nothing wrong with murder for money (which is implausible) or recognize that what they do is wrong but simply refuse to act morally because it is more financially rewarding to act immorally.

Of course, it is possible that corporate executives would not recognize such acts as murder. They may, after all, view murder as a legal concept involving one non-corporate person or persons deliberately killing another non-corporate person or persons and prosecutable only under existing criminal statute. If so, it is somewhat understandable how corporate executives might fail, at least psychologically, to see such corporate policies as murder rather than as, say, calculated risks, tradeoffs, or design errors. Still, for all that, the logic of the situation seems clear enough.

Conclusion

In addition to the fact that the only two plausible arguments favoring the Friedman doctrine are unsatisfactory, a strong case can be made for the claim that corporations *do* have a clear and noncontroversial moral responsibility not to design or implement, for reasons of profit, policies that they know, or have good reason to believe, will kill or otherwise seriously injure innocent persons affected by those policies. Moreover, we have said nothing about wage discrimination, sexism, discrimination in hiring, price fixing, price gouging, questionable but not unlawful competition, or other similar practices that some will think businesses should avoid by virtue of responsibility to society. My main concern has been to show that because we all agree that murder for money is generally wrong, and since there is no discernible difference between that and certain corporate policies that are not in fact illegal, then these corporate practices are clearly immoral (that is, they ought not to be done) and incapable of being morally justified by appeal to the Friedman doctrine since that doctrine does not admit of adequate evidential support. In itself, it seems sad that this argument needs to be made and, if it were not for what appears to be a fairly strong commitment within the business community to the Friedman doctrine in the name of the unquestionable success of the free enterprise system, the argument would not need to be stated.

The fact that such practices do exist—designed and implemented by corporate managers who, for all intents and purposes appear to be upright members of the moral community—only heightens the need for effective social prevention. Presumably, of course, any company willing to put human lives into the profit and loss column is not likely to respond to moral censure. Accordingly, I submit that perhaps the most effective way to deal with the problem of preventing such corporate behavior would consist in structuring legislation such that senior corporate managers who knowingly concur in practices of the sort listed above can effectively be tried, at their own expense, for murder, rather than censured and fined a sum to be paid out of corporate profits. This may seem a somewhat extreme or unrealistic proposal. However, it seems more unrealistic to think that aggressively competitive corporations will respond to what is morally necessary if failure to do so could be very or even minimally profitable. In short, unless we take strong and appropriate steps to prevent such practices, society will be reinforcing a destructive mode of behavior that is maximally disrespectful of human life, just as society will be reinforcing a value system that so emphasizes monetary gain as a standard of human success that murder for profit could be a corporate policy if the penalty for being caught at it were not too dear.

Fortunately, a number of states in America have enacted legislation that makes corporations subject to the criminal code of that state. This practice began to emerge quite strongly after the famous Pinto case in which an Indiana superior court judge refused to dismiss a homicide indictment against the Ford Motor Company. The company was indicted on charges of reckless homicide stemming from a 1978 accident involving a 1973 Pinto in which three girls died when the car burst into flames after being slammed in the rear. This was the first case in which Ford, or any other automobile manufacturer, had been charged with a criminal offense. The indictment went forward because the state of Indiana adopted in 1977 a criminal code provision permitting corporations to be charged with criminal acts. At the time, incidentally, twenty-two other states had similar codes. At any rate, the judge, in refusing to set aside the indictment, agreed with the prosecutor's argument that the charge was based not on the Pinto design fault, but rather on the fact that Ford had permitted the car "to remain on Indiana highways knowing full well its defects." The fact that the Ford Motor company was ultimately found innocent of the charges by the jury is incidental to the point that the increasing number of states that allow corporations to fall under the criminal code is an example of social regulation that could have been avoided had corporations and corporate managers not followed so ardently the Friedman doctrine.

In the long run, of course, corporate and individual willingness to do what is clearly immoral for the sake of monetary gain is a patent commitment of a certain view about the nature of human happiness and success, a view that needs to be placed in the balance with Aristotle's reasoned argument and reflections to the effect that money and all that it brings is a means to an end, and not the sort of end in itself that will justify acting immorally to attain it. What that beautiful end is and why being moral allows us to achieve it, may well be the most rewarding and profitable subject a human being can think about. Properly understood and placed in perspective, Aristotle's view on the nature and attainment of human happiness could go a long way toward alleviating the temptation to kill for money.

In the meantime, any ardent supporter of the capitalistic system will want to see the system thrive and flourish; and this it cannot do if it invites and demands government regulation in the name of the public interest. A *strong* ideological commitment to what I have described above as the Friedman doctrine is counterproductive and not in anyone's long-range interest because it is most likely to beget an ever-increasing regulatory climate. The only way to avoid such encroaching regulation is to find ways to move the business community into the long-term view of what is in its interest, and effect ways of both determining and responding to social needs before society moves to regulate business to that end. To so move the business community is to ask business to regulate its own modes of competition in ways that may seem very difficult to achieve. Indeed, if what I have been suggesting is correct, the only kind of enduring capitalism is humane capitalism, one that is at least as socially responsible as society needs. By the same token, contrary to what is sometimes felt in the business community, the Friedman doctrine, ardently adopted for the dubious reasons generally given, will most likely undermine capitalism and motivate an economic socialism by assuring an erosive regulatory climate in a society that expects the business community to be socially responsible in ways that go beyond just making legal profits.

In sum, being socially responsible in ways that go beyond legal profit making is by no means a dubious luxury for the capitalist in today's world. It is a necessity if capitalism is to survive at all; and, presumably, we shall all profit with the survival of a vibrant capitalism. If anything, then, rigid adherence to the Friedman doctrine is not only philosophically unjustified, and unjustifiable, it is also unprofitable in the long run, and therefore, downright subversive of the long-term common good. Unfortunately, taking the long-run view is difficult for everyone. After all, for each of us, tomorrow may not come. But living for today only does not seem to make much sense either, if that deprives us of any reasonable and happy tomorrow. Living for the future may not be the healthiest thing to do; but do it we must, if we have good reason to think that we will have a future. The trick is to provide for the future without living in it, and that just requires being moral.[6]

> *This paper is a revised and expanded version of "Morality in the Marketplace,"*
> *which appears in* Business Ethics *(revised edition) eds. Milton Snoeyenbos,*
> *Robert Almeder and James Humber (Buffalo, N.Y.: Prometheus Press, 1992)*
> *82–90, and, as such, it is a revised and expanded version of an earlier piece "The*
> *Ethics of Profit: Reflections on Corporate Responsibility," which originally ap-*
> *peared in* Business and Society *(Winter 1980, 7–15).*

Notes

1. Adam Smith, *The Wealth of Nations,* ed. Edwin Canaan (New York: Modern Library, 1937), p. 423.
2. See Milton Friedman, "The Social Responsibility of Business Is to Increase Its Profits," in *The New York Times Magazine* (September 13, 1970), pp. 33, 122–126 and "Milton Friedman Responds," in *Business and Society Review* no. 1 (Spring 1972), p. 5ff.

3. Albert Z. Carr, "Is Business Bluffing Ethical?" *Harvard Business Review* (January–February 1968).

4. Milton Friedman in "Milton Friedman Responds," in *Business and Society Review* no. 1 (Spring 1972), p. 10.

5. Ibid.

6. I would like to thank J. Humber and M. Snoeyenbos for their comments and criticisms of an earlier draft.

POSTSCRIPT

Are Profits the Only Business of Business?

Friedman dismisses the pleas of those who argue for socially responsible business action on the grounds that these individuals do not understand the role of the corporate executive in modern society. Friedman points out that the executives are responsible to the corporate owners, and if the corporate executives take a "socially responsible" action that reduces the return on the owners' investment, they have spent the owners' money. This, Friedman maintains, violates the very foundation of the American political-economic system: individual freedom. If the corporate executives wish to take socially responsible actions, they should use their own money; they should not prevent the owners from spending their money on whatever social actions they might wish to support.

Almeder argues that some corporate behavior is immoral and that defense of this immoral behavior imposes great costs on society. He likens corporate acts such as advertising cigarettes, marketing automobiles that cannot sustain moderate rear-end collisions, and contributing funds to destabilize foreign governments to murdering innocent children for profit. He argues that society must not condone this behavior but, instead, through federal and state legislation, must continue to impose regulations upon businesses until businesses begin to regulate themselves.

Perhaps no single topic is more fundamental to microeconomics than the issue of profits. Many pages have been written in defense of profits; see, for example, Milton and Rose Friedman's *Free to Choose: A Personal Statement* (Harcourt Brace Jovanovich, 1980). A classic reference is Frank H. Knight's *Risk, Uncertainty, and Profits* (Kelly Press, 1921). Friedrich A. Hayek, the author of many journal articles and books, is a guru for many current free marketers. There are a number of other books and articles, however, that are highly critical of the Friedman-Knight-Hayek position, including Christopher D. Stone's *Where the Law Ends: Social Control of Corporate Behavior* (Harper & Row, 1975). Others who challenge the legitimacy of the notion that markets are morally free zones include Thomas Mulligan, "A Critique of Milton Friedman's Essay 'The Social Responsibility of Business Is to Increase Its Profits,'" *Journal of Business Ethics* (1986); Daniel M. Hausman, "Are Markets Morally Free Zones?" *Philosophy and Public Affairs* (Fall 1989); and Andrew Henley, "Economic Orthodoxy and the Free Market System: A Christian Critique," *International Journal of Social Economics* (vol. 14, no. 10, 1987).

ISSUE 2

Should Cities Subsidize Sports and Sports Venues?

YES: Thomas V. Chema, from "When Professional Sports Justify the Subsidy: A Reply to Robert Baade," *The Journal of Urban Affairs* (vol. 18, no. 1, 1996)

NO: Robert A. Baade, from "Stadium Subsidies Make Little Economic Sense for Cities: A Rejoinder," *The Journal of Urban Affairs* (vol. 18, no. 1, 1996)

ISSUE SUMMARY

YES: Attorney and economic development expert Thomas V. Chema asserts that a sports venue has both direct and indirect returns to invested dollars.

NO: Economics professor and urban sports facilities consultant Robert A. Baade argues that although one might justify a sports subsidy on the basis of "image" or "enhanced quality of life," one cannot justify spending limited development dollars on the economic returns that come from sports venues.

The cities of Vail, Colorado; Green Bay, Wisconsin; Cooperstown, New York; Indianapolis, Indiana; and Louisville, Kentucky, are all united by a common denominator. Each boasts a well-known sports venue or sporting event. South Bend, Indiana, may be known to most people as the home of the Fighting Irish football team of Notre Dame, but only our family and a few friends know, or for that matter care, that Bonello and Swartz live there too!

Is there an economic value to the city of South Bend that is totally separate and apart from the dollars spent by 90,000 college football fans who will search for the 80,000 tickets that are available six times each fall semester? In broader terms, is there an economic value for the "city fathers and mothers" associated with the ability to correctly connect ski lifts, a football team, a baseball hall of fame, an auto race, and a horse race with their respective cities? This is the essence of this issue. Robert A. Baade argues that too few individuals utilize sports facilities to make them worthy candidates for public investment. Thomas V.

Chema disagrees, particularly if the venues are strategically placed within the urban community.

We should first examine the impact of a few sports venues. Perhaps no single sports arena has had a longer, more lasting effect on its urban surroundings than the Coliseum in Rome, Italy. This marvelous, 2,000-year-old structure was home to some of the most gruesome "sports" events in Western history. In spite of its crumbling walls and hundreds of years of physical neglect, it still attracts thousands of visitors daily. In fact, this long-abandoned structure still anchors the economic development of the southeast corner of modern Rome.

Alternatively, consider the impact of the America's Cup challenge match to western Australia. The America's Cup is awarded to the winner of a worldwide sailing competition. Until 1986 the competition was always held off the New England coast because the U.S. team had never lost this international competition. Their first loss came at the hands of the Australians, who then had the right to host the challenge match in Fremantle, western Australia. This small, nineteenth-century port city had fallen into serious economic decline prior to the America's Cup challenge match. Although the Australians lost their treasured cup in 1986, they gained much in return. When the sleek racing ships sailed out of the mouth of the Swan River Bay on their return home, they left behind a transformed city awash with cappuccino shops, boutiques, restaurants, microbreweries, and pricey loft condos.

What part of Fremantle's rehabilitation is the direct result of the two or three dozen challenge teams that had to be housed and wined and dined in the two years leading up to the races? What part can be traced to the positive externalities or spillover effects associated with the presence of wealthy sailing teams and the hangers-on who could afford to go halfway around the world to see a sporting event?

In the following selections, Chema attributes large portions of economic development to the presence of sports teams, while Baade contends that it is necessary to carefully measure the dollar costs of sports enterprises to ensure that they do not result in the diversion of leisure dollars to absentee team owners and players.

Thomas V. Chema  **YES**

When Professional Sports Justify the Subsidy: A Reply to Robert Baade

Since virtually the dawn of recorded history the public has been digging into its collective pockets to subsidize the construction of sports venues. Granted, this has not always been a voluntary effort, but then the niceties of democracy were often lost on pharaohs, kings, emperors, and other potentates. The rationale for the public subsidy has varied over time and geography but, with relatively few exceptions, sports have consistently been subsidized.

Robert A. Baade has made a decade long career (or perhaps crusade) arguing against the subsidy. In his most recent paper, "Professional Sports as Catalysts for Metropolitan Economic Development," he purports to demonstrate, using two economic modeling formulae, that subsidy cannot be justified on the basis of economic development and job growth.

For a host of reasons, I disagree with the ultimate conclusion reached by Professor Baade that "cities should be wary of committing substantial portions of their capital budgets to building stadiums." Before cataloging areas of disagreement, let's accept that it is true that professional sports and sport venues are not a panacea for all urban problems. In fact, like Professor Baade, I believe that they are not necessarily even development tools. Their value as catalysts for economic development (job growth and the creation of wealth) depends upon where they are located and how they are integrated into a metropolitan area's growth strategy.

Cities of the future will be important and successful if they can create a critical mass of opportunities for people to socialize within their borders. Several millennia ago, Plato and Aristotle characterized human beings as social creatures. We want to come together, to interact.

For the past 500 years much of that interaction has taken place in cities as people did business and engaged in commerce. Today, with the information superhighway and advanced communications, we tend to be much more isolated in business transactions. Thus, we continually look for other ways to generate human contact and interaction. Cities which understand that cultural activities, recreations, sports and plain old socializing not only bring people together,

From Thomas V. Chema, "When Professional Sports Justify the Subsidy: A Reply to Robert Baade," *The Journal of Urban Affairs,* vol. 18, no. 1 (1996), pp. 19–22. Copyright © 1996 by Blackwell Publishing Ltd. Reprinted by permission.

but form a solid base for economic growth, will be the cities which prosper. Cleveland, Baltimore, Indianapolis, and Minneapolis are cities which recognize that sports venues and events can fit into an overall vision for strategic growth. They have integrated the facilities into the urban fabric and they are successful.

The key to sports venues being a catalyst for economic development is locating them in an urban setting and integrating them into the existing city infrastructure. It is the spin-off development generated by two million or more people visiting a specific area of a city during a concentrated time frame which is critical. The return on the public investment in a ballpark or arena, in dollar and cents terms as opposed to the intangible entertainment value comes not from the facility itself, but from the jobs created in new restaurants, taverns, retail, hotels, etc., that spring up on the periphery of the sports venue.

In Cleveland, for example, since the opening of Jacobs Field, 20 new restaurants employing nearly 900 people have opened within two blocks of second base. There are two new retail establishments on Prospect Avenue where there had been none since World War II. There are six projects to convert vacant upper stories of office and commercial buildings to market rate apartments and condominiums and the Gateway facility is only two years old.

This development is materializing because 5,000,000 visitors are coming to games and entertainment and they are spending their money outside the walls of the sports venues before and after the events. Moreover, they are discovering for the first time in 30 years, that downtown has much to offer. They are coming even when there are no sporting events.

Such success dramatizes the flaw in Professor Baade's past and current analyses and conclusions. Baade has researched essentially nonurban facilities which were not intended to be economic development tools. The multiuse stadiums that proliferated in the late 60s and early 70s were specifically designed to be apart from the city. The design characteristics give the impression more of a fort than a marketplace. Moreover, during the period surveyed most new venues were located in suburban or rural locations. The relatively few urban venues might as well have been in suburbs because they were separated from their host city by a moat of surface parking. These facilities became and continue to be isolated attractions. People drive to them, park on surface lots, enjoy the events in the building, and then go home. This is not bad, but it does not generate economic development spin-off. Contrary to Professor Baade's conclusion, however, it is not the sport activity, but the context which is key.

With the exception of Arlington, Texas, the post-1990 ballparks are in urban settings. They connect with the host city and give people an opportunity to spend money in that host city. Given that opportunity, people accept it and the city benefits. Drawing conclusions about the economic development impact from the last generation of sports facility is questionable at best. Certainly, there is no merit in extrapolating from the flying saucers of Pittsburgh, Cincinnati, Philadelphia, etc., and drawing conclusions as to the public return from investment in today's Camden Yards and Jacobs Field.

Moreover, the economic model proposed by Dr. Baade intuitively raises several questions. First, emphasis is placed on the assumption that most of the money generated by a stadium is "quickly disbursed beyond the stadium's environs." That may well be, but is that not equally true of a steel mill or auto plant? What is the point here, surely not that a business enterprise to be a growth generator must reinvest the income in the immediate surroundings?

Second, the fact that the current generation of public assembly facilities is a self-contained series of profit centers does not mean that spin-off development will not occur. Given the correct location and avoiding surrounding the venue with a sea of surface parking, entertainment related enterprises will spring up and flourish in the shadow of the stadiums. Witness Cleveland and Denver. Even in the dead times these businesses can survive once the public becomes familiar with them. Indeed in the modern facility there will be less true dead time because the facility will strive to maximize its usefulness, drawing people to its restaurants, team shops, etc., even when there is no event.

Third, the analysis totally ignores the fiscal impact sporting events and revenues have on the host public jurisdiction. Assuming the implausible circumstance where no sports-related revenues stay in the metropolis from a private sector perspective, there still would be the impact of tax revenues left behind. Virtually every host city has a wage or income tax, a sales tax, and/or admissions tax. This reality, multimillions of dollars, seems to be ignored by the models proposed by Professor Baade.

Fourth, it is difficult to accept the rather narrow definition of economic development posited in the study. What is the value in measuring the metropolitan growth vis-à-vis other cities? Moreover, it seems clear that the fully loaded cost of a stadium cannot be recovered from the stadium revenue alone. Indeed, that is why a subsidy is needed. The return on the subsidy investment must be judged not only on the revenue potential of the facility (and players) but on the spin-off as well. Of course, the subsidy is not made only because an economic return on investment is expected, but also because of the entertainment value of the sports activity or venue. This is not an exclusive analysis nor is the sale to the public of the subsidy ever exclusively based on the expected economic development return on investment.

Fifth, what is the rationale for measuring capital investment and sports revenue receipts on a per capita basis? I strongly suspect that any other entertainment-related industry would provide similar results to that which Professor Baade shows in his paper. In fact, if this type of analysis were applied to investments in steel mills, computer factories, supermarkets, or most other industries, the relative results would make stadium investments look pretty good. Contrary to the implication, using Professor Baade's Chicago example, the investment of $150 million in a stadium which equates to approximately $54.00 per capita is returned in less than three years based on $22.00 per capita in sports franchise revenue. A three year payback on investment is generally viewed favorably in the private sector. Such a return on a public sector investment that should last at least 40 years ought to be viewed very positively.

Sixth, the low wage, seasonal job argument which is typically made by opponents of sports facility investments is, frankly, offensive. Every community, but particularly major urban centers, need to have a diverse mixture of job types in their economy. Not everyone is a rocket scientist. Not everyone could become one even if there were such jobs available, which clearly there are not. Some members or potential members of the labor force need jobs as ushers, ticket takers, vendors, etc. These jobs are neither demeaning to their holders nor do they cause a city to gain "a comparative advantage in unskilled and seasonal labor." This type of reasoning is the product of effete snobbery.

Seventh, how does one measure the opportunity cost involved in public subsidies of sports? I have yet to see or hear of a single instance where the alternative to building a new stadium, for example, was something other than doing nothing. At least since 1989, there have been no proposals of schools v. stadiums or jails v. arenas! The real issue here is collective public investment or individual private expenditures. Economically, this is true of every public investment and sport is no exception.

Eighth, is it really appropriate to measure the economic contribution of an industry based on the growth of the host city rather than on the industry's contribution to the economy of that city? . . .

Finally, it is not clear what jobs are counted as having been created by professional sports in the Baade analysis. Clearly the team and the stadium direct employees, even including all event-related staff, constitute a small number. Most of the jobs created are not going to show up in SIC 794. This model is of very little utility.

It is appropriate for the public to review its investment in a sports venue as an investment in public infrastructure. Like a road, bridge, or water line, the return on the investment comes indirectly as well as directly. A proper analysis includes a review of the entertainment value of the facility and the spin-off value created by the facility. Similarly, a road is justified by transportation utility and the development that it opens on its periphery.

Just as not every road is equal in its economic impact, not every stadium will generate development that justifies a public subsidy. However, when a city establishes a development strategy that includes sports as part of a critical mass of attractions designed to lure people into the urban core, then a sport team or venue can and will provide significant economic value to the city.

Robert A. Baade  **NO**

Stadium Subsidies Make Little Economic Sense for Cities: A Rejoinder

The thoughtful critiques of my research authored by Messrs. Chema and Rosentraub indicate significant agreement among us about the economic impact that professional sports teams and stadiums have on local and regional economies. The areas of alleged disagreement can be broadly characterized as either technical (those monetary benefits and costs that are generally recognized and quantified) or qualitative. Some of the technical issues can be addressed, perhaps resolved, through a clarification of the methods I employed and their outcomes. Other questions can be resolved only with additional data which will enable evaluation of the urban stadiums constructed after 1990. The purpose of this rejoinder is to help advance the stadium debate by commenting on issues raised by Mr. Chema and Dr. Rosentraub.

Before elaborating on specifics relating to these issues, several matters deserve comment. First, I do not have preconceived notions on whether cities, taken individually or collectively, should subsidize the construction of sports facilities. The persistent and ubiquitous use of an economic/investment rationale for public stadium subsidies, however, compels an evaluation of the economic contribution of commercial sport to metropolitan economies. Stadium subsidies represent a classic public finance issue involving both equity and efficiency questions. My research sounds a cautionary note for governments contemplating subsidies on economic grounds. Specifically, cities should reconsider how the stadium is integrated into the urban economy and/or reconsider using the promise of economic gain as a means of selling the subsidy to a skeptical public.

On a personal note, my research about the economic impact of professional sports teams and stadiums has been inspired by my interest in public finance issues and my lifelong experience with sports. In large part my choice to teach at a liberal arts college was conditioned by my affection for both academics and sport. Lake Forest College gave me an opportunity to coach as well as teach. I raise this point in response to Mr. Chema's reference to my "decade long career (or perhaps crusade) arguing against the subsidy." While he may have mistakenly inferred from my work that I dislike sports, to the contrary, I have valued sports as a participant, coach, educator, and fan.

Given my experience, I may be in a better position than some to evaluate the intangibles so often used in discussing and defending sports. The second point I wish to make is that I have not discussed intangibles in my work except to recognize their potential importance. Because proponents of subsidies rationalize their position first and foremost on economic grounds, it is logical to evaluate first the merits of these arguments. My work focuses exclusively on the economic dimension. If we can resolve the issue as it relates to economics, then it may be necessary to move the stadium subsidy debate to the psychological arena where intangibles are properly the focus.

Third, I have chosen to do retrospective stadium analysis because I recognize that identifying and accurately measuring all the dollar inflows and outflows to an area's economy that are induced by commercial sport is a daunting task. Stadium economic impact studies are prospective in nature and are heavily dependent on the assumptions about the financial inflows and outflows to an area's economy as the consequences of professional sports activities. On a practical level, my approach has been to provide a filter through which the promises of increased economic growth for municipalities through professional sports can be evaluated. In retrospect it would appear that prospective economic impact studies in general have failed to capture all the significant inflows and outflows that are essential for even a ballpark estimate of the economic contribution of professional sports. On the other hand, retrospective analysis is limited by data availability.

In reacting to specific areas of concern, Mr. Chema notes the importance of stadium context. In referring to stadium location he observed: "Their value as catalysts for economic development . . . depends upon where they are located and how they are integrated into a metropolitan area's growth strategy." In noting the success of urban sports facilities constructed after 1990, he alleged a flaw in my research. "Such success dramatizes the flaw in Professor Baade's past and current analyses and conclusions." In response to this allegation I would refer him to Baade and Dye (1988, pp. 272–273) where we wrote:

> If an urban stadium is being planned, the plan should be expanded to incorporate ancillary development. . . . A stadium is not usually enough of a significant development to anchor an area's economy alone. Rather, in considering the revitalization of an urban neighborhood, a number of potential economic anchors should be developed simultaneously. . . . Commercial ventures require traffic. The stadium can provide infusions of people, but residential development incorporated with commercial development will ensure a balanced, nonseasonal clientele for business in the stadium neighborhood.

I have emphasized stadium context in public presentations and in my work with stadium planners and architects. Camden Yards and the Gateway Complex in Cleveland represent important experiments relating to stadium context. Research by a number of social scientists, including my own, has identified a stadium and team novelty effect. All else equal, a stadium and team will attract greater interest in the first few years of their existence. So while there is reason to be encouraged by some aspects of the economic performance of

Camden Yards and Gateway (not all the financial news from Gateway is good), I am sure that Mr. Chema recognizes that sound statistical analysis of these two projects requires more than a few observations of economic outcomes. As previously noted, retrospective analysis is limited by data availability.

Furthermore, in evaluating the stadium's economic contribution, a model must be constructed that is capable of separating the stadium from other parts of the development. An integrated development complicates the task for the scholar seeking to determine the stadium's economic contribution separate from other elements of the plan.

Mr. Chema's emphasis on context ignores at least one important contextual point. Many of the stadiums that are currently planned or under construction replace stadiums that have been deemed economically obsolete by a team. Boston, Cincinnati, Milwaukee, Minneapolis, New York, and Seattle currently are in the throes of debates about new stadiums for Major League baseball (MLB). Cincinnati, Minneapolis, and Seattle have facilities that are 25 years old or less. The dome in Minneapolis is 13 years old. This shorter stadium shelf life has important economic implications. One concern is how the new generation of facilities born out of economic imperative will affect the neighborhood's economy. Mr. Chema opines that "the fact that the current generation of public assembly facilities is a self-contained series of profit centers does not mean that spin-off development will not occur." Given the correct developmental context, that may be true, but many stadiums are being designed with the team's bottom line in mind, often to the detriment of the local economy. When a stadium is moved across the street (Chicago's Comiskey Park comes to mind) in the absence of a broader development plan to explicitly include the neighborhood, many of the economic activities and revenues appropriated by local entrepreneurs are appropriated by the stadium operatives seeking to maximize their share of stadium induced revenues.

In focusing on Cleveland and Camden Yards, Mr. Chema concentrates on the exceptions rather than the rule in stadium planning. The reality is that most stadium deals are signed at the midnight hour by legislators opting to do what is necessary to retain a team rather than formulating a plan that integrates the stadium and team into a broader development package. One could blame legislators alone for myopic stadium legislation, but these outcomes are inspired at least as much by the structure of professional sports leagues which serve their own economic interest by maintaining an excess demand for teams. St. Petersburg, Nashville, and Charlotte do not serve the economic interests of Chicago, Houston, and Milwaukee.

Mr. Chema raised other issues that are more technical in nature. He alleges that my "analysis totally ignores the fiscal impact sporting events and revenues have on the host public jurisdiction." Tax revenues are derived. If the tax base expands, tax revenues increase. Professional sports generate additional tax revenues to the extent that they expand the local economy. If sport is construed as part of the entertainment industry, as no less an authority than Bud Selig, MLB's current commissioner, contends, commercial sport from the perspective of the global economy is arguably a zero-sum game. If all the fans supporting a professional sports team within a city are residents of that city, that team will serve to realign economy activity within the city rather than expanding its tax base. Because taxes are derived, tax revenues do not change in such a situation. Does it matter much to the city whether it derives its revenues from sports entertainment or recreation provided by the local theater?

If we drew an imaginary circle from economic ground zero, the point at which the stadium activity occurs, the larger the circle the smaller the net change in economic activity. This reality should help focus the debate about stadium subsidies for various levels of government. For example, the State of Kentucky on purely economic grounds may not want to use its general funds to build a stadium for Louisville unless it can be demonstrated that either fans will pour across the Indiana, Ohio, West Virginia, and Tennessee borders or that Louisville is in need of urban renewal, a public goods argument that could justify an infusion of state funds. If the stadium replaces leisure and recreational spending in Danville with spending in Louisville, Danville may want to argue against the use of state funds for a stadium in Louisville.

Mr. Chema raised the question "what is the value in measuring the metropolitan growth vis-à-vis other cities?" As Professor Rosentraub has indicated in his critique, commercial sport contributes little in an absolute sense to a metropolitan economy. At present modeling the economies of each city that hosts professional sport is not possible and so an alternative technique must be devised to assess the actual contribution of professional sport relative to the economic promise articulated by boosters. Furthermore, an economist would be remiss if the question of opportunity cost was ignored. Public officials must evaluate the stadium not only on its own merit but relative to alternative uses of those funds. Both issues are considered at length in my paper. An argument can be made that in the municipal auction for professional sports franchises, like the auction for free agent players, the winning bid likely exceeds the team's marginal revenue product. It is likely that the greater the excess demand for professional sports teams, the greater the difference between the team's marginal revenue product and the price the host city pays.

Mr. Chema uses the figures I provided on per capita stadium investments and returns to argue that stadiums provide a good return on investment. The per capita returns were not computed for individual sports, but were calculated for commercial sports in general. For individual cities, I have calculated returns on taxpayer equity on the order of 1−2% for an individual sport and those calculations were based on figures provided from the economic impact studies of subsidy supporters. In football and baseball the trend is decidedly away from multipurpose facilities, a trend that is driven by economic imperatives (individual teams want exclusive control of stadium revenues). By the year 2000, it is not unreasonable to predict that baseball and football will no longer share a single facility in the United States.

With regard to Mr. Chema's claim that "at least since 1989, there have been no proposals of schools v. stadiums", I was puzzled by the use of the word proposals. With all due respect, I would encourage Mr. Chema to listen to the tapes of the 1995 Cincinnati City Council debates on the use of public funds for new stadiums for the NFL Bengals and the MLB Reds.

Mr. Chema understandably found offensive the use of the low wage job creation argument in conjunction with opposition to stadium subsidies. Most of us recognize the need for all types of employment. Rather than construing this argument as the product of "effete snobbery," I would ask him to recognize that some of us are trying to explain why sport might not contribute in absolute dollar terms as much as subsidy proponents suggest. My work should not be construed as a recipe for job creation, but rather as an explanation for why stadium subsidies may not have provided the projected economic boost.

As noted earlier, I argued that a retrospective approach to assessing the economic contribution of a stadium or team is necessary, given the complex manner in which dollar inflows and outflows may be affected. An after-the-fact audit of how a change in the professional sports industry influences a metropolitan economy tacitly includes both direct and indirect effects. Indirect changes include an altered city psyche or vision or a heightened spirit of cooperation. All these indirect changes may, indeed, alter the economic landscape. On page 274 of my 1988 article cited previously, I noted (Baade & Dye, 1988, p. 274):

> the most significant contribution of sports is likely to be in the area of intangibles. The image of a city is certainly affected by the presence of professional franchises. Professional sports serve as a focal point for group identification. Sports contests are a part of civic culture. There may well be a willingness of voters to pay taxes to subsidize this kind of activity just like there is for parks and museums.

Professor Rosentraub, in particular, has articulated the less visible ways in which a large public project translates into a more vibrant economy. Without repeating his words, I echo his sentiments.

An after-the-fact audit includes the economic impact of these laudable intangibles and, even then, commercial sport does not emerge as a statistically significant contributor to metropolitan economies. Dr. Rosentraub has emphasized the fact that the professional sports industry is too small to significantly influence a large metropolitan economy. I would only add that it is not only its small size which renders commercial sport relatively unimportant. It is a fact that sports spectating is but one leisure option available to the residents of a large diverse metropolis. Money spent on sports spectating is financed by reduced spending in other recreational venues and that fact contributes to the consistently statistically insignificant results for professional sports my research has yielded using a variety of models.

This fundamental principle is fortified by the fact that the primary beneficiaries of public stadium largesse are owners and players and fans for whom commercial sports produce substantial consumer surplus. For owners and players, particularly those who reside outside the city extending the subsidy, there may be adverse economic effects from diverting leisure dollars from locally owned entertainment centers to absentee owners and players.

In the final analysis I can only repeat what I have said so often. If cities subsidize commercial sports in the quest for an improved image or to enhance the quality of life for its citizens, then taxpayers should be allowed to decide the stadium subsidy issue on these bases. Using economics as a justification for the subsidy is a political expedient, perhaps necessity, but it is inconsonant with the statistical evidence.

Reference

1. Baade, R. A., & Dye, R. F. (1988). Sports stadiums and area development: a critical review. *Economic Development Quarterly, 2,* 265–275.

POSTSCRIPT

Should Cities Subsidize Sports and Sports Venues?

You probably have been directly or indirectly affected by a sports facility sometime in your life. For many of us this means being part of the crowd that shoulders its way into a baseball park or a basketball arena to watch a favorite team play. For others this means being trapped in a traffic jam as thousands of cars rush home at the end of a football game or the end of a day at the races. Are these modern-day coliseums worth the millions of dollars that taxpayers are asked to pay to support them? Would the community be better advised to spend these dollars attracting industry that supports high-paying jobs or by stabilizing neighborhoods that are in distress?

Chema advocates attracting professional sports teams to cities by offering them substantial subsidies. He argues that Baade has biased his results by focusing his analysis on suburban facilities, which he says are surrounded by "a moat of surface parking." Chema details benefits such as spin-off development, a whole range of taxes, entertainment value, and relative rates of return in other industries. Baade contends that communities should be wary of the many promises made by prospective professional sports franchises. A city should not be intimidated by a team's threat to leave for one that is willing to build a new, more costly facility. Baade argues that most of the dollars generated by sports teams are earned by absentee team owners and players and that most of the new employment opportunities associated with operating these facilities are at the minimum wage level.

A surprising amount has been written on this topic. In part this can be traced to the fact that a few conservative journals have been persuaded by Baade's position. For example, look for two essays by Raymond J. Keating: "We Wuz Robbed! The Subsidized Stadium Scam," *Policy Review* (March/April 1977) and "Pitching Socialism: Government-Financed Stadiums Invariably Enrich Owners at Public Expense," *National Review* (April 22, 1996). There is plenty written on the other side as well. See Curt Smith, "Comeback: The Triumphant Return of Old-Style Ball Parks Show That Tradition Can Be Popular," *The American Enterprise* (March/April 1997) and, on a related topic, Joanna Cagau and Neil de Mause, "Buy the Bums Out," *In These Times* (December 9, 1996). Finally, there are many articles that examine the economic impact of the Summer Olympics in Atlanta, Georgia. See, for example, Matthew Cooper, "Welcome to the Olympic Village," *The New Republic* (July 15 & 22, 1996).

ISSUE 3

Is There Discrimination in U.S. Labor Markets?

YES: William A. Darity, Jr., and Patrick L. Mason, from "Evidence on Discrimination in Employment: Codes of Color, Codes of Gender," *Journal of Economic Perspectives* (Spring 1998)

NO: James J. Heckman, from "Detecting Discrimination," *Journal of Economic Perspectives* (Spring 1998)

ISSUE SUMMARY

YES: Professor of economics William A. Darity, Jr., and associate professor of economics Patrick L. Mason assert that the lack of progress made since the mid-1970s toward establishing equality in wages between the races is evidence of persistent discrimination in U.S. labor markets.

NO: Professor of economics James J. Heckman argues that markets—driven by the profit motive of employers—will compete away any wage differentials that are not justified by differences in human capital.

O ver 45 years have passed since Rosa Parks refused to give up her seat on a segregated Montgomery, Alabama, bus. America has had these years to finally overcome discrimination, but has it? Have the domestic programs of Presidents John F. Kennedy and Lyndon Johnson that were enacted after those turbulent years following Parks's act of defiance made it possible for African Americans to succeed within the powerful economic engine that drives American society? Or does racism still stain the Declaration of Independence, with its promise of equality for all?

Before we examine the economics of discrimination, perhaps we should look backward to see where America has been, what progress has been made, and what is left—if anything—to accomplish. American history, some say, reveals a world of legalized apartheid where African Americans were denied access to the social, political, and economic institutions that are the mainstays of America. Without this access, millions of American citizens were doomed to live lives on the fringes of the mainstream. Thus, the Kennedy/Johnson programs left one legacy, which few now dispute: These programs effectively dismantled the system of legalized discrimination and, for the first time since the end of slavery, allowed blacks to dream of a better life.

The dream became a reality for many. Consider the success stories that are buried in the poverty statistics that were collected and reported in the 1960s. Poverty scarred the lives of one out of every five Americans in 1959. But poverty was part of the lives of fully one-half of all African American families. Over time fewer and fewer Americans, black and white, suffered the effects of poverty; however, even though the incidence of poverty has been cut in half for black Americans, more than 25 percent of African American families still live in poverty. Even more distressing is the reality that African American children bear the brunt of this economic deprivation. In 1997, 37.2 percent of the "next generation" of African Americans lived in families whose total family income was insufficient to lift them out of poverty. (Note that although black Americans suffer the effects of poverty disproportionately, white-not-Hispanic families are the single largest identifiable group who live in poverty: white-not-Hispanic people make up 46.4 percent of the entire poor population; white-Hispanic, 22.2 percent; and black, 25.6 percent.)

The issue for economists is why so many African Americans failed to prosper and share in the great prosperity of the 1990s. Few would deny that in part the lack of success for black Americans is directly associated with a lack of "human capital": schooling, work experiences, and occupational choices. The real question, however, is whether differences between blacks and whites in terms of human capital can explain most of the current wage differentials or whether a significant portion of these wage differentials can be traced to labor market discrimination.

In the following selections, William A. Darity, Jr., and Patrick L. Mason argue that a significant part of the reason for black Americans' lack of economic success is discrimination, while James J. Heckman maintains that the issue is all human capital differences.

37

William A. Darity, Jr., and
Patrick L. Mason

 YES

Evidence on Discrimination
in Employment

There is substantial racial and gender disparity in the American economy. As we will demonstrate, discriminatory treatment within the labor market is a major cause of this inequality. The evidence is ubiquitous: careful research studies which estimate wage and employment regressions, help-wanted advertisements, audit and correspondence studies, and discrimination suits which are often reported by the news media. Yet, there appear to have been periods of substantial reductions in economic disparity and discrimination. For example, Donohue and Heckman (1991) provide evidence that racial discrimination declined during the interval 1965–1975. Gottschalk (1997) has produced statistical estimates that indicate that discrimination against black males dropped most sharply between 1965 and 1975, and that discrimination against women declined during the interval 1973–1994. But some unanswered questions remain. Why did the movement toward racial equality stagnate after the mid-1970s? What factors are most responsible for the remaining gender inequality? What is the role of the competitive process in elimination or reproduction of discrimination in employment?

The Civil Rights Act of 1964 is the signal event associated with abrupt changes in the black-white earnings differential (Bound and Freeman, 1989; Card and Krueger, 1992; Donohue and Heckman, 1991; Freeman, 1973). Along with other important pieces of federal legislation, the Civil Rights Act also played a major role in reducing discrimination against women (Leonard, 1989). Prior to passage of the federal civil rights legislation of the 1960s, racial exclusion and gender-typing of employment was blatant. The adverse effects of discriminatory practices on the life chances of African Americans, in particular, during that period have been well-documented (Wilson, 1980; Myers and Spriggs, 1997, pp. 32–42; Lieberson, 1980). Cordero-Guzman (1990, p. 1) observes that "up until the early 1960s, and particularly in the south, most blacks were systematically denied equal access to opportunities [and] in many instances, individuals with adequate credentials or skills were not, legally, allowed to apply to certain positions in firms." Competitive market forces certainly did

From William A. Darity, Jr., and Patrick L. Mason, "Evidence on Discrimination in Employment: Codes of Color, Codes of Gender," *Journal of Economic Perspectives*, vol. 12, no. 2 (Spring 1998). Copyright © 1998 by The American Economic Association. Reprinted by permission. References and some notes omitted.

not eliminate these discriminatory practices in the decades leading up to the 1960s. They remained until the federal adoption of antidiscrimination laws.

Newspaper help-wanted advertisements provide vivid illustrations of the openness and visibility of such practices. We did an informal survey of the employment section of major daily newspapers from three northern cities, the *Chicago Tribune,* the *Los Angeles Times* and the *New York Times,* and from the nation's capital, *The Washington Post,* at five-year intervals from 1945 to 1965. (Examples from southern newspapers are even more dramatic.) . . .

With respect to gender-typing of occupations, help-wanted advertisements were structured so that whole sections of the classifieds offered job opportunities separately and explicitly for men and women. Men were requested for positions that included restaurant cooks, managers, assistant managers, auto salesmen, sales in general, accountants and junior accountants, design engineers, detailers, diemakers, drivers, and welders. Women were requested for positions that included household and domestic workers, stenographers, secretaries, typists, bookkeepers, occasionally accountants (for "girls good at figures"), and waitresses.[1] The *Washington Post* of January 3, 1960, had the most examples of racial preference, again largely for whites, in help-wanted ads of any newspaper edition we examined. Nancy Lee's employment service even ran an advertisement for a switchboard operator—presumably never actually seen by callers—requesting that all *women* applying be white! Advertisements also frequently included details about the age range desired from applicants, like men 21–30 or women 18–25. Moreover, employers also showed little compunction about specifying precise physical attributes desired in applicants.[2]

Following the passage of the Civil Rights Act of 1964, none of the newspapers carried help-wanted ads that included any explicit preference for "white" or "colored" applicants in January 1965. However, it became very common to see advertisements for "European" housekeepers (a trend that was already visible as early as 1960). While race no longer entered the help-wanted pages explicitly, national origin or ancestry seemed to function as a substitute. Especially revealing is an advertisement run by the Amity Agency in the *New York Times* on January 3, 1965, informing potential employers that "Amity Has Domestics": "Scottish Gals" at $150 a month as "mothers' helpers and housekeepers," "German Gals" at $175 a month on one-year contracts, and "Haitian Gals" at $130 a month who are "French speaking." Moreover, in the "Situations Wanted" section of the newspaper, prospective female employees still were indicating their own race in January 1965.

The case of the help-wanted pages of the *New York Times* is of special note because New York was one of the states that had a state law against discrimination and a State Commission Against Discrimination in place, long prior to the passage of the federal Civil Rights Act of 1964. However, the toothlessness of New York's State Commission Against Discrimination is well-demonstrated by the fact that employers continued to indicate their racial preferences for new hires in help-wanted ads, as well as by descriptions of personal experience like that of John A. Williams in his semi-autobiographical novel, *The Angry Ones* (1960 [1996], pp. 30–1).

Help-wanted ads were only the tip of the iceberg of the process of racial exclusion in employment. After all, there is no reason to believe that the employers who did not indicate a racial preference were entirely open-minded about their applicant pool. How successful has the passage of federal antidiscrimination legislation in the 1960s been in producing an equal opportunity environment where job applicants are now evaluated on their qualifications? To give away the answer at the outset, our response is that discrimination by race has diminished somewhat, and discrimination by gender has diminished substantially. However, neither employment discrimination by race or by gender is close to ending. The Civil Rights Act of 1964 and subsequent related legislation has purged American society of the most overt forms of discrimination. However, discriminatory practices have continued in more covert and subtle forms. Furthermore, racial discrimination is masked and rationalized by widely-held presumptions of black inferiority.

Statistical Research on Employment Discrimination

Economic research on the presence of discrimination in employment has focused largely on black-white and male-female earnings and occupational disparities. The position typically taken by economists is that some part of the racial or gender gap in earnings or occupations is due to average group differences in productivity-linked characteristics (a human capital gap) and some part is due to average group differences in treatment (a discrimination gap). The more of the gap that can be explained by human capital differences, the easier it becomes to assert that labor markets function in a nondiscriminatory manner; any remaining racial or gender inequality in employment outcomes must be due to differences between blacks and whites or between men and women that arose outside the labor market. . . .

Regression Evidence on Racial Discrimination

When we consider economic disparities by race, a difference emerges by gender. Using a Blinder-Oaxaca approach in which women are compared by their various racial and ethnic subgroups, Darity, Guilkey and Winfrey (1996) find little systematic evidence of wage discrimination based on U.S. Census data for 1980 and 1990.[3] However, when males are examined using the same Census data a standard result emerges. A significant portion of the wage gap between black and white males in the United States cannot be explained by the variables included to control for productivity differences across members of the two racial groups.

Black women are likely to have the same school quality and omitted family background characteristics as black men (the same is true for white women and men). Hence, it strains credibility to argue that the black-white earnings gap for men is due to an omitted labor quality variable unless one also argues that black women are paid more than white women conditional on the unobservables. The findings of Darity, Guilkey and Winfrey (1996), Rodgers and

Spriggs (1996) and Gottschalk (1997) indicate that in 1980 and 1990 black men in the United States were suffering a 12 to 15 percent loss in earnings due to labor market discrimination.

There is a growing body of evidence that uses color or "skin shade" as a natural experiment to detect discrimination. The approach of these studies has been to look at different skin shades within a particular ethnic group at a particular place and time, which should help to control for factors of culture and ethnicity other than pure skin color. Johnson, Bienenstock, and Stoloff (1995) looked at dark-skinned and light-skinned black males from the same neighborhoods in Los Angeles, and found that the combination of a black racial identity and a dark skin tone reduces an individual's odds of working by 52 percent, after controlling for education, age, and criminal record! Since both dark-skinned and light-skinned black males in the sample were from the same neighborhoods, the study *de facto* controlled for school quality. Further evidence that lighter-complexioned blacks tend to have superior incomes and life chances than darker-skinned blacks in the United States comes from studies by Ransford (1970), Keith and Herring (1991) and Johnson and Farrell (1995).

Similar results are found by looking at skin color among Hispanics. Research conducted by Arce, Murguia, and Frisbie (1987) utilizing the University of Michigan's 1979 National Chicano Survey involved partitioning the sample along two phenotypical dimensions: skin color, ranging from Very Light to Very Dark on a five-point scale; and physical features, ranging from Very European to Very Indian on a five-point scale. Chicanos with lighter skin color and more European features had higher socioeconomic status. Using the same data set, Telles and Murguia (1990) found that 79 percent of $1,262 of the earnings differences between the dark phenotypic group and other Mexican Americans was *not* explained by the traditional variables affecting income included in their earnings regression. Further support for this finding comes from Cotton (1993) and Darity, Guilkey, and Winfrey (1996) who find using 1980 and 1990 Census data that black Hispanics suffer close to ten times the proportionate income loss due to differential treatment of given characteristics than white Hispanics. Evidently, skin shade plays a critical role in structuring social class position and life chances in American society, even between comparable individuals within minority groups.

Cross-national evidence from Brazil also is relevant here. Despite conventional beliefs in Brazil that race is irrelevant and class is the primary index for social stratification, Silva (1985) found using the 1976 national household survey that blacks and mulattos (or "browns") shared closely in a relatively depressed economic condition relative to whites, with mulattos earning slightly more than blacks. Silva estimated that the cost of being nonwhite in Brazil in 1976 was about 566 cruzeiros per month (or $104 U.S.). But Silva found slightly greater unexplained income differences for mulattos, rather than blacks vis-à-vis whites, unexplained differences he viewed as evidence of discrimination. A new study by Telles and Lim (1997), based upon a random national survey of 5000 persons conducted by the Data Folha Institute des Pesquisas, compares economic outcomes based upon whether race is self-identified or interviewer-identified. Telles and Lim view interviewer-identification as more useful for establishing social classification and treatment. They find that self-identification underestimates white income and over-estimates brown and black incomes relative to interviewer-classification.

Despite the powerful results on skin shade, some continue to argue that the extent of discrimination is overestimated by regression techniques because of missing variables. After all, it seems likely that the general pattern of unobserved variables—for example, educational quality or labor force attachment—would tend to follow the observed variables in indicating reasons for the lower productivity of black males (Ruhm, 1989, p. 157). As a result, adjusting for these factors would reduce the remaining black-white earnings differential.[4]

As one might imagine, given the framework in which economists tackle the issue of discrimination, considerable effort has been made to find measures of all imaginable dimensions of human capital that could be used to test the presence of labor market discrimination. This effort has uncovered one variable in one data set which, if inserted in an earnings regression, produces the outcome that nearly all of the black-white male wage gap is explained by human capital and none by labor market discrimination. (However, thus far no one has suggested a reasonable missing variable for the skin shade effect.) The particular variable that eliminates evidence of discrimination in earnings against black men as a group is the Armed Forces Qualifying Test (AFQT) score in the National Longitudinal Survey of Youth (NLSY).

A number of researchers have confirmed with somewhat different sample sizes and methodologies that including AFQT scores in an earnings equation virtually will eliminate racial differences in wages. . . .

The conclusion of this body of work is that labor market discrimination against blacks is negligible or nonexistent. Using Neal and Johnson's (1996) language, the key to explaining differences in black and white labor market outcomes must instead rest with "premarket factors." These studies have led Abigail and Stephan Thernstrom (1997) in a prominent *Wall Street Journal* editorial to proclaim that "what may look like persistent employment discrimination is better described as employers rewarding workers with relatively strong cognitive skills."

But matters are not so straightforward. The essential problem is what the AFQT scores are actually measuring, and therefore what precisely is being controlled for. There is no consensus on this point. AFQT scores have been interpreted variously as providing information about school quality or academic achievement (O'Neill, 1990), about previously unmeasured skills (Ferguson, 1995; Maxwell, 1994; Neal and Johnson 1996), and even about intelligence (Herrnstein and Murray, 1994)—although the military did not design AFQT as an intelligence test (Rodgers and Spriggs, 1996).[5] The results obtained by O'Neill (1990), Maxwell (1994), Ferguson (1995), and Neal and Johnson (1996) after using the AFQT as an explanatory variable are, upon closer examination, not robust to alternative specifications and are quite difficult to interpret.

The lack of robustness can be illustrated by looking at how AFQT scores interact with other variables in the earnings equation. Neal and Johnson (1996), for example, adjust for age and AFQT score in an earnings equation, but not for years of schooling, presumably on the assumption that same-age individuals would have the same years of schooling, regardless of race. However, this assumption does not appear to be true. Rodgers, Spriggs and Waaler (1997) find that white youths had accumulated more schooling at a given age than black or Hispanic youths. When AFQT scores are both age and education-adjusted, a black-white wage gap reemerges, as the authors report (p. 3):[6]

> ... estimates from models that use our proposed age and education adjusted AFQT score [show] that sharp differences in racial and ethnic wage gaps exist. Instead of explaining three-quarters of the male black-white wage gap, the age and education adjusted score explains 40 percent of the gap. Instead of explaining the entire male Hispanic-white gap, the new score explains 50 percent of the gap . . . [B]lack women no longer earn more than white women do, and . . . Hispanic women's wage premium relative to white women is reduced by one-half.

Another specification problem arises when wage equations are estimated using both AFQT scores and the part of the NLSY sample that includes measures of psychological well-being (for "self-esteem" and "locus of control") as explanatory variables. The presence of the psychological variables restores a negative effect on wages of being African-American (Goldsmith, Veum and Darity, 1997).[7]

Yet another specification problem becomes relevant if one interprets AFQT scores as providing information about school quality. But since there is a school survey module of the NLSY which can be used to provide direct evidence on school quality, using variables like the books/pupil ratio, the percent of students classified as disadvantaged, and teacher salaries, it would surely be more helpful to use this direct data on school quality rather than the AFQT scores. In another method of controlling for school quality, Harrison (1972) compared employment and earnings outcomes for blacks and whites living in the same black ghetto communities, on grounds that school quality would not be very different between them. Harrison found sharp differences in earnings favoring whites.[8]

One severe difficulty in interpreting what differences in the AFQT actually mean is demonstrated by Rodgers and Spriggs (1996) who show that AFQT scores appear to be biased in a specific sense. . . . [They] create a hypothetical set of "unbiased" black scores by running the mean black characteristics through the equation with the white coefficients. When those scores replace the actual AFQT scores in a wage equation, then the adjusted AFQT scores no longer explain black-white wage differences. A similar result can be obtained if actual white scores are replaced by hypothetical scores produced by running white characteristics through the equation with black coefficients.[9] Apparently, the AFQT scores themselves are a consequence of bias in the underlying processes that generate AFQT scores for blacks and whites. Perhaps AFQT scores are a proxy for skills that do not capture all skills, and thus leave behind a bias of uncertain direction. Or there may be other predictors of the test that are correlated with race but which are left out of the AFQT explanatory equation.

To muddy the waters further, focusing on the math and verbal subcomponents of AFQT leads to inconsistent implications for discriminatory differentials. For example, while a higher performance on the verbal portion of the AFQT contributes to higher wages for black women versus black men, it apparently has little or no effect on the wages of white women versus white men (Currie and Thomas, 1995). However, white women gain in wages from higher scores on the math portion of the AFQT, but black women do not. Perhaps this says that white women are screened (directly or indirectly) for employment and pay on the basis of their math performance, while black women are screened based upon their verbal skills. Perhaps this is because white employers have a greater "comfort zone" with black women who have a greater verbal similarity to whites. Or perhaps something not fully understood and potentially quirky is going on with the link between these test results and wages.

Finally, since skill differentials have received such widespread discussion in recent years as an underlying cause of growing wage inequality in the U.S. economy—see, for example, the discussion in the Spring 1997 issue of *The Journal of Economic Perspectives*—it should be pointed out that growth in the rewards to skill does not mean that the effects of race have diminished. If the importance of race and skill increase simultaneously, then a rising skill premium will explain more of the changes in *intraracial* wage inequality, which may well leave a larger unexplained portion of interracial wage inequality. For example, when Murnane et al. (1995) ask whether test scores in math, reading, and vocabulary skills for respondents in the National Longitudinal Study of the High School Class of 1972 and High School and Beyond datasets have more explanatory power in wage equations for 1980 graduates than 1972 graduates, their answer is "yes"—the rate of return to cognitive skill (test scores) increased between 1978 and 1986. However, in these same regressions, the absolute value of the negative race coefficient is larger for the 1980 graduates than it is for the 1972 graduates! These results confirm that there are increasing returns to skills measured by standardized tests, but do not indicate that the rise in returns to skills can explain changes in the black-white earnings gap very well.

The upshot is the following. There is no doubt that blacks suffer reduced earnings in part due to inferior productivity-linked characteristics, like skill gaps or school quality gaps, relative to nonblack groups. However, evidence based on the AFQT should be treated with extreme caution. Given that this one variable in one particular data set is the only one that suggests racial discrimination is no longer operative in U.S. employment practices, it should be taken as far from convincing evidence. Blacks, especially black men, continue to suffer significantly reduced earnings due to discrimination and the extent of discrimination.

Direct Evidence on Discrimination: Court Cases and Audit Studies

One direct body of evidence of the persistence of employment discrimination, despite the presence of antidiscrimination laws, comes from the scope and dispensation of job discrimination lawsuits. A sampling of such cases from recent years . . . reveals [that] discriminatory practices have occurred at highly visible U.S. corporations often having multinational operations. The suits reveal racial and gender discrimination in employment, training, promotion, tenure, layoff policies, and work environment, as well as occupational segregation.

Perhaps the most notorious recent case is the $176 million settlement reached between Texaco and black employees after disclosure of taped comments of white corporate officials making demeaning remarks about blacks, remarks that revealed an outlook that translated into corresponding antiblack employment practices. Clearly, neither federal antidiscrimination laws nor the pressures of competitive markets have prevented the occurrence of discriminatory practices that have resulted in significant awards or settlements for the plaintiffs.

Another important source of direct evidence are the audit studies of the type conducted in the early 1990s by the Urban Institute (Mincy, 1993). The Urban Institute audit studies sought to examine employment outcomes for young black, Hispanic, and white males, ages 19–25, looking for entry-level jobs. Pairs of black and white males and pairs of Hispanic and non-Hispanic white males were matched as testers and sent out to apply for jobs at businesses advertising openings. Prior to application for the positions, the testers were trained for interviews to minimize dissimilarity in the quality of their self-presentation, and they were given manufactured résumés designed to put their credentials on a par. The black/white tests were conducted in Chicago and in Washington, D.C., while the Hispanic/non Hispanic tests were conducted in Chicago and in San Diego.

A finding of discrimination was confirmed if one member of the pair was offered the position and the other was not. No discrimination was confirmed if both received an offer (sequentially, since both were instructed to turn the position down) or neither received an offer. This is a fairly stringent test for discrimination, since, in the case where no offer was made to either party, there is no way to determine whether employers were open to the prospect of hiring a black or an Hispanic male, what the overall applicant pool looked like, or who was actually hired. However, the Urban Institute audits found that black males were three times as likely to be turned down for a job as white males, and Hispanic males also were three times as likely as non-Hispanic white males to experience discrimination in employment (Fix, Galster and Struyk, 1993, pp. 21–22).

Bendick, Jackson and Reinoso (1994) also report on 149 race-based (black, white) and ethnicity-based (Hispanic, non-Hispanic) job audits conducted by the Fair Employment Council of Greater Washington, Inc. in the D.C. metropolitan area in 1990 and 1991. Testers were paired by gender. The audit findings are striking. White testers were close to 10 percent more likely to receive interviews than blacks. Among those interviewed, half of the white testers received job offers versus a mere 11 percent of the black testers. When both testers received the same job offers, white testers were offered 15 cents per hour more than black testers. Black testers also were disproportionately "steered" toward lower level positions after the job offer was made, and white testers were disproportionately considered for unadvertised positions at higher levels than the originally advertised job.

Overall, the Fair Employment Council study found rates of discrimination in excess of 20 percent against blacks (in the black/white tests) and against Hispanics (in the Hispanic/non-Hispanic tests). In the Hispanic/non-Hispanic tests, Hispanic male job seekers were three times as likely to experience discrimination as Hispanic females. But, surprisingly, in the black/white tests, black females were three times as likely to encounter discrimination as black males. The racial results for women in this particular audit stand in sharp contrast with the results in the statistical studies described above.

The most severe criticisms of the audit technique have come from Heckman and Siegelman (1993). At base, their central worry is that testers cannot be paired in such a way that they will not signal a difference that legitimately can be interpreted by the prospective employer as a difference in potential to perform the job, despite interview training and doctored résumés.[10] For example, what about intangibles like a person's ability to make a first impression or the fact that certain résumés may be unintentionally superior to others?

In an audit study consciously designed to address many of the Heckman and Siegelman (1993) methodological complaints, Neumark, Bank, and Van Nort (1995) examined sex discrimination in restaurant hiring practices. Four testers (all college students, two men and two women) applied for jobs waiting tables at 65 restaurants in Philadelphia. The restaurants were separated into high, medium, and low price, according to average cost of a meal. Waiters at the high price restaurants tend to receive greater wages and tips than their counterparts in low price restaurants; specifically, the authors find that average hourly earnings for waiters were 47 and 68 percent higher in the high price restaurant than the medium and low price restaurant, respectively. One man and one woman applied for a job at each restaurant, so there were 130 attempts to obtain employment. Thirty-nine job offers were received.

One interesting twist to this methodology is that three reasonably comparable résumés were constructed, and over a three-week period each tester used a different résumé for a period of one week. This résumé-switching mitigates any differences that may have occurred because one résumé was better than another. To reduce other sources of unobserved ability—for example, the ability to make a good first impression—the testers were instructed to give their applications to the first employee they encountered when visiting a restaurant. That employee was then asked to forward the résumé to the manager. In effect, personality and appearance were eliminated as relevant variables for the interview decision, if not for the job offer decision.

Neumark et al. (1995) find that in the low-priced restaurants, the man received an offer while the woman did not 29 percent of the time. A woman never received an offer when the man did not. In the high-priced restaurants, the man received an offer while the woman did not in 43 percent of the tests, while the woman received an offer while the man did not in just 4 percent of the tests. Also, at high-priced restaurants, women had roughly a 40 percent lower probability of being interviewed and 50 percent lower probability of obtaining a job offer, and this difference is statistically significant. Hence, this audit study shows that within-occupation employment discrimination may be a contributing source to wage discrimination between men and women. . . .

The Theoretical Backdrop

Standard neoclassical competitive models are forced by their own assumptions to the conclusion that discrimination only can be temporary. Perhaps the best-known statement of this position emerges from Becker's (1957) famous "taste for discrimination" model. If two groups share similar productivity profiles under competitive conditions where at least some employers prefer profits to prejudice, eventually all workers must be paid the same wage. The eventual result may involve segregated workforces—say, with some businesses hiring only white men and others hiring only black women—but as long as both groups have the same average productivity, they will receive the same pay. Thus, in this view, discrimination only can produce temporary racial or gender earnings gaps. Moreover, alternative forms of discrimination are separable processes; wage discrimination and employment segregation are unrelated in Becker's model.

Despite the theoretical implications of standard neoclassical competitive models, we have considerable evidence that it took the Civil Rights Act of 1964 to alter the discriminatory climate in America. It did not, by any means, eliminate either form of discrimination. Indeed, the impact of the law itself may have been temporary, since there is some evidence that the trend toward racial inequality came to a halt in the mid-1970s (even though interracial differences in human capital were continuing to close) and the momentum toward gender equality may have begun to lose steam in the early 1990s. Moreover, we believe that the forms of discrimination have altered in response to the act. Therefore, it is not useful to argue that either racial or gender discrimination is inconsistent with the operation of competitive markets, especially when it has taken antidiscrimination laws to reduce the impact of discrimination in the market. Instead, it is beneficial to uncover the market mechanisms which permit or encourage discriminatory practices.

Since Becker's work, orthodox microeconomics has been massaged in various ways to produce stories of how discrimination might sustain itself against pressures of the competitive market. The tacit assumption of these approaches has been to find a way in which discrimination can increase business profits, or to identify conditions where choosing not to discriminate might reduce profits.

In the customer discrimination story, for example, businesses discriminate not because they themselves are bigoted but because their clients are bigoted. This story works especially well where the product in question must be delivered via face-to-face contact, but it obviously does not work well when the hands that made the product are not visible to the customer possessing the "taste for discrimination." Moreover, as Madden (1975, p. 150) has pointed out, sex-typing of jobs can work in both directions: "While service occupations are more contact-oriented, sexual preference can work both ways: for example, women are preferred as Playboy bunnies, airline stewardesses, and lingerie salespeople, while men seem to be preferred as tire salespeople, stockbrokers, and truck drivers."

Obviously, group-typing of employment will lead to a different occupational distributions between group A and B, but will it lead to different earnings as well? Madden (1975, p. 150, emphasis in original) suggests not necessarily:

> . . . consumer discrimination causes occupational segregation rather than wage differentials. If the female wage decreases as the amount of consumer contact required by a job increases, women seek employment in jobs where consumer contact is minimal and wages are higher. Only if there are not enough non-consumer contact jobs for working women, forcing them to seek employment in consumer-contact jobs, would consumer discrimination be responsible for wage differentials. Since most jobs do not require consumer contact, consumer discrimination would segregate women into these jobs, but not *cause* wage differentials.

Perhaps the best attempt to explain how discrimination might persist in a neoclassical framework is the statistical discrimination story, which, at base, is a story about imperfect information. The notion is that potential employers cannot observe everything they wish to know about job candidates, and in this environment, they have an incentive to seize group membership as a signal that allows them to improve their predictions of a prospective candidate's ability to perform.

However, this model of prejudicial beliefs does not ultimately wash well as a theory of why discrimination should be long-lasting. If average group differences are perceived but not real, then employers should *learn* that their beliefs are mistaken. If average group differences are real, then in a world with antidiscrimination laws, employers are likely to find methods of predicting the future performance of potential employees with sufficient accuracy that there is no need to use the additional "signal" of race or gender. It seems implausible that with all the resources that corporations put into hiring decisions, the remaining differentials are due to an inability to come up with a suitable set of questions or qualifications for potential employees.

Moreover, models of imperfect competition as explanations of discrimination do not solve the problem completely either. The reason for the immutability of the imperfection is rarely satisfactorily explained—and often not addressed at all—in models of this type (Darity and Williams, 1985). Struggle as it may, orthodox microeconomics keeps returning to the position that sustained observed differences in economic outcomes between groups must be due to an induced or inherent deficiency in the group that experiences the inferior outcomes. In the jargon, this is referred to as a deficiency in human capital. Sometimes this deficiency is associated with poor schooling opportunities, other times with culture (Sowell, 1981).[11] But the thrust of the argument is to absolve market processes, at least in a putative long run, of a role in producing the differential outcome; the induced or inherent deficiency occurs in pre-market or extra-market processes.

Certainly years of schooling, quality of education, years of work experiences and even culture can have a role in explaining racial and gender earnings differences. However, the evidence marshaled above indicates that these factors do not come close to explaining wage differentials and employment patterns observed in the economy. Instead, discrimination has been sustained both in the United States and elsewhere, for generations at a time. Such discrimination does not always even need direct legal support nor has it been eliminated by market pressures. Instead, changes in social and legal institutions have been needed to reduce it.

James Heckman (1997, p. 406) draws a similar conclusion in his examination of a specific sector of employment, the textile industry:

> . . . substantial growth in Southern manufacturing had little effect on the labor-market position of blacks in Southern textiles prior to 1965. Through tight and slack labor markets, the proportion of blacks was small and stable. After 1964, and in synchronization with the 1964 Civil Rights Act, black economic progress was rapid. Only South Carolina had a Jim Crow law prohibiting employment of blacks as textile workers, and the law was never used after the 1920s. Yet the pattern of exclusion of blacks was prevalent throughout Southern textiles, and the breakthrough in black employment in the industry came in all states at the same time. Informally enforced codes and private practices, and not formally enforced apartheid, kept segregation in place, and market forces did not break them down.

Nontraditional alternatives to orthodox microeconomic analysis can lead to a logically consistent basis for a persistent gap in wage outcomes. These alternatives typically break down the line between in-market and pre-market discrimination so often drawn in conventional economics. The first of these involves a self-fulfilling prophecy mechanism. Suppose employers believe that members of group A are more productive than members of group B on average. Suppose further that they act upon their beliefs, thereby exhibiting a stronger demand for A workers, hiring them more frequently and paying them more.

Next, suppose that members of group B become less motivated and less emotionally healthy as a consequence of the employment rebuff. Notice that the original decision not to hire may have been completely unjustified on productivity grounds; nonetheless, the decision made *in* the labor market—a decision not to hire or to hire at low pay—alters the human capital characteristics of the members of group B so that they become inferior candidates for jobs. The employers' initially held mistaken beliefs become realized over time as a consequence of the employers' initial discriminatory decisions. As Elmslie and Sedo (1996, p. 474) observe in their development of this argument, "One initial bout of unemployment that is not productivity based can lay the foundation for continued future unemployment and persistently lower job status even if no future discrimination occurs."

More broadly, depressed expectations of employment opportunities also can have an adverse effect on members of group B's inclination to acquire additional human capital—say, through additional schooling or training. The effects of the past could be passed along by the disadvantaged group from generation to generation, another possibility ignored by orthodox theory. For example, Borjas (1994) writes of the ethnic intergenerational transmission of economic advantage or disadvantage. He makes no mention of discrimination in his work but a potential interpretation is that the effects of past discrimination, both negative and positive, are passed on to subsequent generations. Other evidence along these lines includes Tyree's (1991) findings on the relationship between an ethnic group's status and performance in the past and the present, and Darity's (1989) development of "the lateral mobility" hypothesis based upon ethnic group case histories.

More narrowly, the group-typed beliefs held by employers/selectors also can have a strong effect on the performance of the candidate at the interview stage. In an experiment performed in the early 1970s, psychologists Word, Zanna and Cooper (1974, pp. 109–120) found that when interviewed by "naïve" whites, trained black applicants "received (a) less immediacy, (b) higher rates of speech error, and (c) shorter amounts of interview time" than white applicants. They then trained white interviewers to replicate the behavior received by the black applicants in the first phase of their experiment, and found that "naïve" white candidates performed poorly during interviews when they were "treated like blacks." Such self-fulfilling prophecies are familiar in the psychology literature (Sibicky and Dovidio, 1986).

A second nontraditional theory that can lead to a permanent gap in intergroup outcomes is the noncompeting groups hypothesis advanced by the late W. Arthur Lewis (1979). Related arguments emerge from Krueger's (1963) extension of the trade-based version of the Becker model, Swinton's (1978) "labor force competition" model for racial differences, and Madden's (1975) male monopoly model for gender differences, but Lewis's presentation is the most straightforward. Lewis starts with an intergroup rivalry for the preferred positions in a hierarchical occupational structure. Say that group A is able to control access to the preferred positions by influencing the required credentials, manipulating opportunities to obtain the credentials, and serving a gatekeeping function over entry and promotion along job ladders. Group B is then rendered "noncompeting."

One theoretical difficulty with this argument that its proponents rarely address is that it requires group A to maintain group solidarity even when it may have subgroups with differing interests. In Krueger's (1963) model, for example, white capitalists must value racial group solidarity sufficiently to accept a lower return on their capital as the price they pay for a generally higher level of income for all whites (and higher wages for white workers). In Madden's (1975) model, male capitalists must make a similar decision on behalf of male workers.

This noncompeting group hypothesis blurs the orthodox distinction between in-market and pre-market discrimination, by inserting matters of power and social control directly into the analysis. This approach then links discrimination to racism or sexism, rather than to simple bigotry or prejudice. It leads to the proposition that discrimination—in the sense of differential treatment of those members of each group with similar productivity-linked characteristics—is an endogenous phenomenon. "In-market" discrimination need only occur when all the earlier attempts to control access to jobs, credentials, and qualifications are quavering.

One interesting implication here is that growth in skills for what we have been calling group B, the disadvantaged group, may be accompanied by a surge of in-market discrimination, because that form of discrimination has become more necessary to preserve the position of group A. There are several instances of cross-national evidence to support this notion. Darity, Dietrich and Guilkey (1997) find that while black males were making dramatic strides in acquiring literacy between 1880 and 1910 in the United States, simultaneously they were suffering increasing proportionate losses in occupational status due to disadvantageous treatment of their measured characteristics. Geographer Peggy Lovell (1993) finds very little evidence of discrimination in earnings against blacks in northern Brazil, where blacks are more numerous, but substantial evidence of discrimination against them in southern Brazil. Northern Brazil is considerably poorer than southern Brazil and the educational levels of northern black Brazilians are more depressed than in the south.[12] It is easy to argue that the exercise of discrimination is not "needed" in the north, since blacks are not generally going to compete with whites for the same sets of jobs. Indeed, there is relatively more evidence of discrimination against mulattos than blacks, the former more likely to compete directly with whites for employment. A third example, in a study using data for males based upon a survey taken in Delhi in 1970, Desi and Singh (1989) find that the most dramatic instance of discriminatory differentials in earnings was evident for Sikh men vis-à-vis Hindu high caste men. On the other hand, most of the earnings gap for Hindu middle caste, lower caste and scheduled caste men was due to inferior observed characteristics. Since these latter groups could be excluded from preferred positions because of an inadequate educational background, it would not be necessary for the upper castes to exercise discrimination against them. Sikh males, on the other hand, possessed the types of credentials that would make them viable contestants for the positions desired by the Hindu higher castes.

A final alternative approach at construction of a consistent economic theory of persistent discrimination evolves from a reconsideration of the neoclassical theory of competition. Darity and Williams (1985) argued that replacement of neoclassical competition with either classical or Marxist approaches to competition—where competition is defined by a tendency toward equalization of rates of profit and where monopoly positions are the consequence of competition rather than the antithesis of competition—eliminates the anomalies associated with the orthodox approach (Botwinick, 1993; Mason, 1995, forthcoming-b). A labor market implication of this approach is that wage diversity, different pay across firms and industries for workers within the same occupation, is the norm for competitive labor markets. In these models, remuneration is a function of the characteristics of the individual and the job. The racial-gender composition of the job affects worker bargaining power and thereby wage differentials. In turn, race and gender exclusion are used to make some workers less competitive for the higher paying positions. This approach emphasizes that the major elements for the persistence of discrimination are racial or gender differences in the access to better paying jobs within and between occupations.

Whatever alternative approach is preferred, the strong evidence of the persistence of discrimination in labor markets calls into question any theoretical apparatus that implies that the discrimination must inevitably diminish or disappear.

Notes

1. The only significant exception to the help-wanted ads pattern of maintaining a fairly strict sexual division of labor that we could detect was evident in the *Los Angeles Times* employment section of early January 1945, where we found women being sought as aircraft riveters, assemblers, and army photographers. Of course, World War II was ongoing at that stage, and the comparative absence of men produced the "Rosie the Riveter" phenomenon. However, despite wartime conditions, even this temporary breakdown in gender-typing of occupations was not evident in the help-wanted ads for the *Chicago Tribune,* the *New York Times,* or the *Washington Post* at the same time. Moreover, racial preferences also remained strongly pronounced in wartime advertisements of each of the four newspapers.

2. The C.W. Agency, advertising in the *Los Angeles Times* on January, 1, 1950, wanted a "Girl Model 38 bust, 25 waist, 36 hips"; "Several Other Types" with physical characteristics unspecified in the advertisement apparently also were acceptable.

3. The 1980 and 1990 Censuses provide only self-reported information on interviewees' race and their ancestry, which makes it possible to partition the American population into 50 different detailed ethnic and racial groups, like Asian Indian ancestry women, Mexican ancestry women, Polish ancestry women, French Canadian ancestry women, and so on. The explanatory variables were years of school, years of college, number of children, married spouse present, years of work experience, years of work experience squared, very good or fluent English, disabled, born in the United States, assimilated (that is either married to a person with a different ethnicity or having claimed two different ethnic groups in the census), location, region, and occupation. Annual earnings was the dependent variable. There was no control for the difference between potential and actual experience; hence, to the extent that the gap between potential and actual experience and the rate of return to actual experience varies by race, the results for the female regressions may be less reliable than the results for the male regression.

4. For a view that unobservable factors might favor black male productivity, thereby meaning that the regression coefficients are underestimating the degree of discrimination, see Mason (forthcoming-a).

5. Indeed, if one uses a measure that, unlike the AFQT, was explicitly designed as a measure of intelligence, it does not explain the black-white gap in wages. Mason (forthcoming-b; 1996) demonstrates this by using in a wage equation an explanatory variable that comes from a sentence completion test given to 1972 respondents to the Panel Study of Income Dynamics (PSID)—a test which was designed to assess "g," so-called general intelligence. Mason finds that the significant, negative sign on the coefficient for the race variable is unaffected by inclusion of the PSID sentence completion test score as an explanatory variable. Indeed, Mason (1997) finds that although discrimination declined during 1968 to 1973, discrimination grew by 2.0 percent annually during 1973–1991. On the other hand, the rate of return to cognitive skill (IQ) was relatively constant during 1968–1979, but had an annual growth rate of 1.6 percent during 1979–1991.

6. Mason (1997) finds a similar result when age and education-adjusted IQ scores are used.

7. Attention to the psychological measures also provides mild evidence that blacks put forth more effort than whites, a finding consistent with Mason's (forthcoming-a) speculation that there may be unobservables that favor black productivity. Mason argues that effort or motivation is a productivity-linked variable that favors blacks, based upon his finding that blacks acquire more schooling than whites for a comparable set of resources.

8. Card and Krueger (1992) also directly control for school quality. They find that there is still a substantial wage gap left after controlling for school quality.

9. Systematic racial differences in the structural equations for the determination of standardized test scores also are evident in the General Social Survey data. Fitting equations for Wordsum scores separately for blacks and whites also yields statistically distinct structures (White, 1997).

10. Although some of their criticisms along these lines frankly strike us as ridiculous; for example, concerns about facial hair on the Hispanic male testers used by the Urban Institute.

11. To address the effects of culture, following Woodbury (1993), Darity, Guilkey, and Winfrey (1996) held color constant and varied culture by examining outcomes among blacks of differing ancestries. Unlike Sowell's expectation, black males of West Indian and non-West Indian ancestry were being confronted with the same racial penalty in U.S. labor markets by 1990.

12. The portion of the gap that can be explained by discrimination is much lower in the high black region of Brazil, the Northeast, than the rest of Brazil. We know of no evidence which suggests that this is or is not true for the U.S. south.

James J. Heckman  **NO**

Detecting Discrimination

In the current atmosphere of race relations in America, the authors of the three main papers presented in this symposium are like persons crying "fire" in a crowded theater. They apparently vindicate the point of view that American society is riddled with racism and that discrimination by employers may account for much of the well-documented economic disparity between blacks and whites. In my judgement, this conclusion is not sustained by a careful reading of the evidence.

In this article, I make three major points. First, I want to distinguish market discrimination from the discrimination encountered by a randomly selected person or pair of persons at a randomly selected firm as identified from audit studies.

Second, I consider the evidence presented by the authors in the symposium, focusing for brevity and specificity on labor markets. It is far less decisive on the issue of market discrimination than it is claimed to be. Disparity in market outcomes does not prove discrimination in the market. A careful reading of the entire body of available evidence confirms that most of the disparity in earnings between blacks and whites in the labor market of the 1990s is due to the differences in skills they bring to the market, and not to discrimination within the labor market. This interpretation of the evidence has important consequences for social policy. While undoubtedly there are still employers and employees with discriminatory intentions, labor market discrimination is no longer a first-order quantitative problem in American society. At this time, the goal of achieving black economic progress is better served by policies that promote skill formation, like improving family environments, schools and neighborhoods, not by strengthening the content and enforcement of civil rights laws—the solution to the problem of an earlier era.

Third, I want to examine the logic and limitations of the audit pair method. All of the papers in this symposium use evidence from this version of pair matching. However, the evidence acquired from it is less compelling than is often assumed. Inferences from such studies are quite fragile to alternative assumptions about unobservable variables and the way labor markets work. The audit method can find discrimination when in fact none exists; it can also disguise discrimination when it is present. These findings are especially troubling

From James J. Heckman, "Detecting Discrimination," *Journal of Economic Perspectives,* vol. 12, no. 2 (Spring 1998). Copyright © 1998 by The American Economic Association. Reprinted by permission.

because the Equal Employment Opportunity Commission has recently authorized the use of audit pair methods to detect discrimination in labor markets (Seelye, 1997).

Discrimination Definition and Measurement

The authors of these papers focus on the question of whether society is color blind, not on the specific question of whether there is market discrimination in realized transactions. But discrimination at the individual level is different from discrimination at the group level, although these concepts are often confused in the literature on the economics of discrimination.

At the level of a potential worker or credit applicant dealing with a firm, racial discrimination is said to arise if an otherwise identical person is treated differently by virtue of that person's race or gender, and race and gender by themselves have no direct effect on productivity. Discrimination is a causal effect defined by a hypothetical *ceteris paribus* conceptual experiment—varying race but keeping all else constant. Audit studies attempt to identify racial and gender discrimination so defined for the set of firms sampled by the auditors by approximating the *ceteris paribus* condition.

It was Becker's (1957) insight to observe that finding a discriminatory effect of race or gender at a randomly selected firm does not provide an accurate measure of the discrimination that takes place in the market as a whole. At the level of the market, the causal effect of race is defined by the marginal firm or set of firms with which the marginal minority member deals. The impact of market discrimination is not determined by the most discriminatory participants in the market, or even by the average level of discrimination among firms, but rather by the level of discrimination at the firms where ethnic minorities or women actually end up buying, working and borrowing. It is at the margin that economic values are set. This point is largely ignored in the papers in this symposium.

This confusion between individual firm and market discrimination arises in particular in the audit studies. A well-designed audit study could uncover many individual firms that discriminate, while at the same time the marginal effect of discrimination on the wages of employed workers could be zero. . . . Purposive sorting within markets eliminates the worst forms of discrimination. There may be evil lurking in the hearts of firms that is never manifest in consummated market transactions.

Estimating the extent and degree of distribution, whether at the individual or the market level, is a difficult matter. In the labor market, for example, a worker's productivity is rarely observed directly, so the analyst must instead use available data as a proxy in controlling for the relevant productivity characteristics. The major controversies arise over whether relevant omitted characteristics differ between races and between genders, and whether certain included characteristics systematically capture productivity differences or instead are a proxy for race or gender.

How Substantial Is Labor Market Discrimination Against Blacks?

In their paper in this symposium, [William A.] Darity [Jr.] and [Patrick L.] Mason present a bleak picture of the labor market position of African-Americans in which market discrimination is ubiquitous. They present a quantitative estimate of the magnitude of estimated discrimination: 12 to 15 percent in both 1980 and 1990 using standard regressions fit on Current Population Survey and Census data. Similar regressions show that the black/white wage gap has diminished sharply over the last half century. Comparable estimates for 1940 show a black/white wage gap ranging from 30 percentage points, for men age 25–34 to 42 percentage points, men age 55–64. In 1960, the corresponding numbers would have been 21 percent and 32 percent, for the same two age groups; in 1970, 18 and 25 percent (U.S. Commission on Civil Rights, 1986, Table 6.1, p. 191). The progress was greatest in Southern states where a blatantly discriminatory system was successfully challenged by an external legal intervention (Donohue and Heckman, 1991; Heckman, 1990).

How should the residual wage gap be interpreted? As is typical of much of the literature on measuring racial wage gaps, Darity and Mason never precisely define the concept of discrimination they use. As is also typical of this literature, the phrase "human capital variable" is thrown around without a clear operational definition. The implicit definition of these terms varies across the studies they discuss. In practice, human capital in these studies has come to mean education and various combinations of age and education, based on the available Census and Current Population Survey (CPS) data. However, there is a staggering gap between the list of productivity characteristics available to economic analysts in standard data sources and what is available to personnel departments of firms. Regressions based on the Census and/or CPS data can typically explain 20 to 30 percent of the variation in wages. However, regressions based on personnel data can explain a substantially higher share of the variation in wages; 60–80 percent in professional labor markets (for example, see Abowd and Killingsworth, 1983). It is not idle speculation to claim that the standard data sets used to estimate discrimination omit many relevant characteristics actually used by firms in their hiring and promotion decisions. Nor is it idle speculation to conjecture that disparity in family, neighborhood and schooling environments may account for systematic differences in unmeasured characteristics between race groups.

Consider just one well-documented source of discrepancy between Census variables and the productivity concepts that they proxy: the measurement of high school credentials. The standard Census and CPS data sources equate recipients of a General Equivalence Degree, or GED, with high school graduates. However, black high school certificate holders are much more likely than whites to receive GEDs (Cameron and Heckman, 1993), and a substantial portion of the widely trumpeted "convergence" in measured black educational attainment has come through GED certification. Thus, in 1987 in the NLSY data that Darity and Mason discuss, and Neal and Johnson (1996) analyze, 79 percent of black males age 25 were high school certified, and 14 percent of the credential holders were GED recipients. Among white males, 88 percent were high school certified, and only 8 percent of the white credential holders were GED certified. Given the evidence from Cameron and Heckman that GED recipients earn the same as high school dropouts, it is plausible that standard Census-based studies that use high school credentials to control for "education" will find that the wages of black high school "graduates" are lower than those of whites.

Most of the empirical literature cited by Darity and Mason takes Census variables literally and ignores these issues. The GED factor alone accounts for 1–2 percentage points of the current 12–15 percent black-white hourly wage gap. An enormous body of solid evidence on inferior inner city schools and poor neighborhoods makes the ritual of the measurement of "discrimination" using the unadjusted Census or Current Population Survey data a questionable exercise.

Darity and Mason bolster their case for rampant discrimination by appealing to audit pair evidence. They do not point out that audit pair studies have primarily been conducted for hiring in entry level jobs in certain low skill occupations using overqualified college students during summer vacations. They do not sample subsequent promotion decisions. They fail to point out that the audits undersample the main avenues through which youth get jobs, since only job openings advertised in newspapers are audited, and not jobs found through networks and friends (Heckman and Siegelman, 1993, pp. 213–215). Auditors are sometimes instructed on the "problem of discrimination in American society" prior to sampling firms, so they may have been coached to find what the audit agencies wanted to find. I have already noted that audit evidence does not translate into actual employment experiences and wages obtained by actors who purposively search markets.

Putting these objections to the side, what do the audits actually show for this unrepresentative snapshot of the American labor market? Table 1 presents evidence from three major audits in Washington, D.C., Chicago and Denver. The most remarkable feature of this evidence is the a + b column which records the percentage of audit attempts where black and white auditors were treated symmetrically (both got a job; neither got a job). In Chicago and Denver this happened about 86 percent of the time. The evidence of disparity in hiring presented in the last two columns of the table suggests only a slight preference for whites over minorities; in several pairs, minorities are favored. Only a zealot can see evidence in these data of pervasive discrimination in the U.S. labor market. And, as I will show in the next section, even this evidence on disparity has to be taken with a grain of salt, because it is based on the implicit assumption that the distribution of unobserved productivity is the same in both race groups.

Darity and Mason go on to dismiss the research of Neal and Johnson (1996) who analyze a sample of males who took an achievement or ability test in their early teens—specifically, the Armed Forces Qualifications Test (AFQT)— and ask how much of the gap in black-white wages measured a decade or so after the test was taken can be explained by the differences in the test scores.[1] It is remarkable and important that this early "premarket" measure of ability plays

Table 1

Outcomes From Major Audit Studies for Blacks
(outcome: get job or not)

Number of Audits	Pair	(a) Both Get Job	(b) Neither Gets a Job	Equal Treatment a + b	White Yes, Black No	White No, Black Yes
Chicago*						
35	1	(5) 14.3%	(23) 65.7%	80.0%	(5) 14.3%	(2) 5.7%
40	2	(5) 12.5%	(25) 62.5%	75.0%	(4) 10.0%	(2) 15.0%
44	3	(3) 6.8%	(37) 84.1%	90.9%	(3) 6.8%	(1) 2.3%
36	4	(6) 16.7%	(24) 66.7%	83.4%	(6) 16.7%	(0) 0.0%
42	5	(3) 7.1%	(38) 90.5%	97.6%	(1) 2.4%	(2) 0.0%
197	Total	(22) 11.2%	(147) 74.6%	85.8%	(19) 9.6%	(9) 4.5%
Washington*						
46	1	(5) 10.9%	(26) 56.5%	67.4%	(12) 26.1%	(3) 6.5%
54	2	(11) 20.4%	(31) 57.4%	77.8%	(9) 16.7%	(3) 5.6%
62	3	(11) 17.7%	(36) 58.1%	75.8%	(11) 17.7%	(4) 6.5%
37	4	(6) 16.2%	(22) 59.5%	75.7%	(7) 18.9%	(2) 5.4%
42	5	(7) 16.7%	(26) 61.9%	77.6%	(7) 16.7%	(2) 4.8%
241	Total	(40) 16.6%	(141) 58.5%	75.1%	(46) 19.1%	(14) 5.8%
Denver**						
18	1	(2) 11.1%	(11) 61.1%	72.1%	(5) 27.8%	(0) 0.0%
53	2	(2) 3.8%	(41) 77.4%	81.2%	(0) 0.0%	(10) 18.9%
33	3	(7) 21.2%	(25) 75.8%	97.0%	(1) 3.0%	(0) 0.0%
15	4	(9) 60.0%	(3) 20.0%	80.0%	(2) 6.7%	(2) 13.3%
265	9	(3) 11.5%	(23) 88.5%	100.0%	(0) 0.0%	(0) 0.0%
145	Total	(23) 15.8%	(103) 71.1%	86.9%	(7) 4.8%	(12) 8.3%

Note: Results are percentages; figures in parentheses are the relevant number of audits.

*This study was conducted by the Urban Institute.

**Denver pair numbers are for both black and Hispanic audits. For the sake of brevity, I only consider the black audits. The Denver study was not conducted by the Urban Institute but it was conducted to conform to Urban Institute practice.

Sources: Heckman and Siegelman (1993).

such a strong role in explaining wages measured a decade after the test is taken. This is as true for studies of white outcomes taken in isolation as it is for black-white comparisons. Their findings are important for interpreting the sources of black-white disparity in labor market outcomes. . . .

The Neal-Johnson story is not about genetic determination. They demonstrate that schooling and environment can affect their measured test score. A huge body of evidence, to which the Neal-Johnson study contributes, documents that human abilities and motivations are formed early and have a decisive effect on lifetime outcomes; the evidence is summarized in Heckman

(1995) and in Heckman, Lochner, Taber, and Smith (1997). Not only is early ability an important predictor of later success for blacks or whites, it can be manipulated. Early interventions are far more effective than late ones because early skills and motivation beget later skills and motivation. As Heckman, Lochner. Taber and Smith document, however, successful early interventions can be quite costly.

The objections raised by Darity and Mason against the Neal-Johnson study are largely specious. For example, Rodgers and Spriggs (1996) miss the point of the Neal-Johnson article by "adjusting" the test score by a later variable, such as schooling. But ability is known to be an important determinant of schooling (Cawley, Heckman and Vtylacil, 1998), so it should be no surprise that "adjusting" the score for later schooling eliminates an important component of ability and that adjusted scores play a much weaker role in explaining black-white differentials.[2]

Only one point raised by Darity and Mason concerning Neal and Johnson is potentially valid—and this is a point made by Neal and Johnson in their original article. Black achievement scores may be lower than white scores not because of the inferior environments encountered by many poor blacks, but because of expectations of discrimination in the market. If black children and their parents face a world in which they receive lower rewards for obtaining skills, they will invest less if they face the same tuition costs as whites. Poor performance in schools and low achievement test scores may thus be a proxy for discrimination to be experienced in the future.

There is solid empirical evidence that expectations about rewards in the labor market influence human capital investment decisions; for example, the reward to skills held by black workers increased following the passage of the 1964 Civil Rights Act, and a rapid rise in college enrollment of blacks followed (Donohue and Heckman, 1991). But the difficulty with the argument in this context is that it presumes that black parents and children operate under mistaken expectations about the present labor market. Although it was once true that the returns to college education were lower for blacks than for whites (Becker, 1957; U.S. Civil Rights Commission, 1986), the return to college education for blacks was higher than the return for whites by the mid-1970s, and continues to be higher today. Some parallel evidence presented by Johnson and Neal (1998) shows that the returns to (coefficient on) AFQT scores for black males in an earnings equation are now as high or higher than those for whites, although they used to be lower in the pre–Civil Rights era. Given the greater return for blacks to college education and ability, it seems implausible to argue that a rational fear of lower future returns is currently discouraging black formation of skills.

Ability as it crystallizes at an early age accounts for most of the measured gap in black and white labor market outcomes. Stricter enforcement of civil rights laws is a tenuous way to improve early childhood skills and ability.[3] The weight of the evidence suggests that this ability and early motivation is most easily influenced by enriching family and preschool learning environments and by improving the quality of the early years of schooling.

The Implicit Assumptions Behind the Audit Method

The method of audit pairs operates by controlling for systematic observed differences across pairs. It does this by attempting to create two candidates for jobs or loans who are "essentially" the same in their paper qualifications and personal characteristics, and then comparing their outcomes in their dealings with the same firm. Averaging over the outcomes at all firms for the same audit pair produces an estimate of the discrimination effect. An average is often taken over audit pairs as well to report an "overall" estimate of discrimination. More sophisticated versions of the method will allow for some heterogeneity in treatment among firms and workers or firms and applicants.

One set of difficulties arise, however, because there are sure to be many unobserved variables. As noted by Heckman and Siegelman (1993), given the current limited state of knowledge of the determinants of productivity within firms, and given the small pools of applicants from which matched pairs are constructed that are characteristic of most audit studies, it is unlikely that all characteristics that might affect productivity will be perfectly matched. Thus, the implicit assumption in the audit pair method is that controlling for some components of productivity and sending people to the same firm will reduce the bias below what it would be if random pairs of, say, whites and blacks were compared using, for example, Census data. The implicit assumption that justifies this method is that the effect of the unobserved characteristics averages out to zero across firms for the same audit pair.

However, the mean of the differences in the unobserved components need not be zero and assuming that it is begs the problem. Nowhere in the published literature on the audit pair method will you find a demonstration that matching one subset of observable variables necessarily implies that the resulting difference in audit-adjusted treatment between blacks and whites is an unbiased measure of discrimination—or indeed, that it is even necessarily a better measure of discrimination than comparing random pairs of whites and blacks applying at the same firm or even applying to different firms. . . .

Consider the following example. Suppose that the market productivity of persons is determined by the sum of two productivity components. These two productivity components are distributed independently in the population so their values are not correlated with each other. Both factors affect employer assessments of employee productivity.[4] Suppose further that average productivity of the sum is the same for both whites and blacks; however, blacks are more productive on average on one component while whites are more productive on average on the other. Now consider an audit pair study that equates only the first component of productivity and equates firm effects by sending the audit pair to the same firm. Under these conditions, the audit estimator is biased toward a finding of discrimination, since in this example, only the characteristic which makes black productivity look relatively high is being used to standardize the audit pair. The condition of zero mean of unobservable productivity differences across race groups is not especially compelling and requires a priori knowledge that is typically not available.

Now consider the case in which the observed and unobserved components of productivity are dependent. In this case, making the included components as alike as possible may accentuate the differences in the unobserved components. As a result, it can increase the bias over the case where the measured components are not aligned.

. . . [T]hink of pairing up black and white high jumpers to see if they can clear a bar set at a certain height. There is no discrimination, in the sense that they both use the same equipment and have the bar set at the same level. Suppose now that the chance of a jumper (of any race) clearing the bar depends on two additive factors: the person's height and their jumping technique. We can pair up black and white jumpers so that they have identical heights, but we can't directly observe their technique. Let us make the generous assumption, implicit in the entire audit literature, that the mean jumping technique is equal for the two groups. Then, if the variance of technique is also the same for white and black high-jumpers, we would find that the two racial groups are equally likely to clear the bar. On the other hand, if the variance differs, then whether the black or white pair is more likely to clear the bar will depend on how the bar is set, relative to their common height, and which racial group has a higher variance in jumping technique. If the bar is set at a low level so that most people of the given height are likely to clear the bar, then the group with the lower variance will be more likely to clear the bar. If the bar is set at a very high level relative to the given height, then the group with a higher variance in jumping technique will be more likely to clear the bar. A limitation of the audit method is readily apparent from this analogy: there is no discrimination, yet the two groups have different probabilities of clearing the bar.[5] And if there is discrimination—that is, the bar is being set higher for blacks—the differential dispersion in the unobserved component could still cause the minority group to clear the bar more often. The method could fail to detect discrimination when it does exist.

Thus, depending on the distribution of unobserved characteristics for each race group and the audit standardization level, the audit method can show reverse discrimination, or equal treatment, or discrimination, even though blacks and whites in this example are subject to the same cutoff and face no discrimination. The apparent bias depends on whether the level of qualifications set by the audit designer makes it more or less likely that the applicant will receive the job, and the distribution of variables that are unobservable to the audit design. The apparent disparity favoring Washington whites in Table 1 may be a consequence of differences in unobserved characteristics between blacks and whites when there is no discrimination.

Even more disturbing, suppose that there is discrimination against blacks, so the productivity cutoff used by firms is higher for blacks than whites. Depending on the audit designer's choice of what level of qualifications are given to the auditors, the audit study can find no discrimination at all. However, whether the qualifications make it relatively likely or unlikely to get the job is a fact rarely reported in audit studies. . . .

Making audit pairs as alike as possible may seem an obviously useful step, but it can greatly bias the inference about average discrimination or discrimination at the margin. Intuitively, by taking out the common components that are most easily measured, differences in hiring rates as monitored by audits arise from the idiosyncratic factors, and not the main factors, that drive actual labor markets. These examples highlight the fragility of the audit method to untested and unverifiable assumptions about the distributions of unobservables. Similar points arise in more general nonlinear models that characterize other employment decision rules.

The Becker Model

The papers in this symposium make the erroneous claim that in Becker's (1957) model, market discrimination disappears in the long run. It need not. Entrepreneurs can consume their income in any way they see fit. If a bigoted employer prefers whites, the employer can indulge that taste as long as income is received from entrepreneurial activity just as a person who favors an exotic ice cream can indulge that preference by being willing to pay the price. Only if the supply of entrepreneurship is perfectly elastic in the long run at a zero price, so entrepreneurs have no income to spend to indulge their tastes, or if there are enough nonprejudiced employers to hire all blacks, will discrimination disappear from Becker's model.

However, even if the common misinterpretation of Becker's model is accepted, it is far from clear that the prediction of no or little discrimination in the U.S. labor market in the long run is false. The substantial decline over the past 50 years in wage differentials between blacks and whites may well be a manifestation of the dynamics of the Becker model. It may take decades for the effects of past discrimination in employment and schooling as it affects current endowments of workers to fade out of the labor market. But the evidence from the current U.S. labor market is that discrimination by employers alone does *not* generate large economic disparities between blacks and whites.

Appendix

Implicit Identifying Assumptions in the Audit Method

Define the productivity of a person of race $r \in \{1, 0\}$ at firm f, with characteristics $\sim X = (X_1, X_2)$ as $P(\sim X, r, f)$. $r = 1$ corresponds to black; $r = 0$ corresponds to white. Assume that race does not affect productivity so we may write $P = P(\sim X, f)$. The treatment at the firm f for a person of race r and productivity P is $T(P(\sim X, f), r)$. Racial discrimination exists at firm f if

$$T(P(\sim X, f), r = 1) \neq T(P(\sim X, f), r = 0).$$

As noted in the text, audit methods monitor discrimination at randomly selected firms within the universe designated for sampling, not the firms where blacks are employed.

The most favorable case for auditing assumes that T (or some transformation of it) is linear in f and X. Assume for simplicity that $P = X_1 + X_2 + f$ and $T(P, r) = P + \gamma r$. When $\gamma < 0$ there is discrimination against blacks. γ may vary among firms as in Heckman and Siegelman (1993). For simplicity suppose that all firms are alike. Audit methods pair racially dissimilar workers in the following way: they match some components of $\sim X$ and they sample the same firms. Let P_1^* be the standardized productivity for the black member of the pair; P_0^* is the standardized productivity for the white member. If $P_0^* = P_1^*$,

$$T(P_1^*, 1) - T(P_0^*, 0) = \gamma.$$

When averaged over firms, the average treatment estimates the average γ.

Suppose that standardization is incomplete. We can align the first coordinate of X at $\{X_1 = X_1^*\}$ but not the second coordinate, X_2, which is unobserved by the auditor but acted on by the firm. $P_1^* = X_1^* + X_2^1$ where X_2^1 is the value of X_2 for the $r = 1$ member and $P_0^* = X_1^* + X_2^1$. In this case

$$T(P_1^*, 1) - T(P_0^*, 0) = X_2^1 - X_2^0 + \gamma.$$

For averages over pairs to estimate γ without bias, it must be assumed that $E(X_2^1) = E(X_2^0)$; i.e., that the mean of the unobserved productivity traits is the same. This is the crucial identifying assumption in the conventional audit method. Suppose that this is true so $E(X_2^1) = E(X_2^0) = \mu$. Then the pair matching as in the audit method does not increase bias and in general reduces it over comparisons of two X_1-identical persons at two randomly selected firms. Under these conditions, bias is lower than if two randomly chosen auditors are selected at the same firm if $E(X_1^1) \neq E(X_1^0)$.

However, the decision rule to offer a job or extend credit often depends on whether or not the perceived productivity P exceeds a threshold c:

$$T = 1 \text{ if } P \geq T = c$$

$$T = 0 \text{ otherwise}$$

In this case, the audit pair method will still produce bias even when it does not when T is linear in $\sim X$ and f unless the *distributions* of the omitted characteristics are identical in the two race groups. Suppose that $P = X_1 + X_2$. X_2 is uncontrolled. Then assuming no discrimination ($\gamma = 0$)

$$T(P_1^*, 1) = 1 \text{ if } X_1^* + X_2^1 + f \geq c = 0 \text{ otherwise}$$

$$T(P_0^*, 0) = 1 \text{ if } X_1^* + X_2^0 + f \geq c = 0 \text{ otherwise}.$$

Even if the distributions of f are identical across pairs, and f is independent of X, unless the *distributions* of X_2^1 and X_2^0 are identical, $\Pr(T(P_1^*, 1) = 1) \neq \Pr(T(P_0^*) = 1)$ for most values of the standardization level X_1^*. The right tail area of the distribution governs the behavior of these probabilities. This implies that even if blacks and whites face the same cutoff value, and in this sense are treated without discrimination in the labor market, even if the means of the distributions of unobservables are the same across race group, if the distributions of the unobservables are different, their probabilities of being hired will differ and will depend on the level of standardization used in the audit study—something that is rarely reported. The pattern of racial disparity in Table 1 may simply be a consequence of the choice of the level of standardization in those audits, and not discrimination.

Worse yet, suppose that the cutoff $c = c_1$ for blacks is larger than the cutoff $c = c_0$ for whites so that blacks are held to a higher standard. Then depending on the right tail area of X_2^1 and X_2^0, the values of c_1 and c_0, and the level of standardization X_1^*,

$$\Pr(T(P_1^*,) = 1) \gtrless P(T(P_0^*, 0) = 1).$$

In general, only if the *distributions* of X_2^1 and X_2^0 are the same for each race group, will the evidence reported in Table 1 be informative on the level of discrimination in the universe of sampled firms.

Figures 1 and 2 illustrate these two cases for X_2^1 and X_2^0 normally distributed (and independent of each other) where X_1^* is the level of audit standardization and firms are standardized to have $f = 0$. In Figure 1 there is no discrimination in the market. Yet the black hire rate falls short of the white rate

Figure 1

Relative Hiring Rate as a Function of the Level of Standardization. Blacks Have More Dispersion. Threshold Hiring Rule: No Discrimination Against Blacks Normally Distributed Unobservables

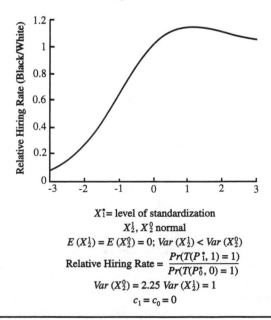

$X_1^* =$ level of standardization

X_2^1, X_2^0 normal

$E(X_2^1) = E(X_2^0) = 0$; $Var(X_2^1) < Var(X_2^0)$

Relative Hiring Rate $= \dfrac{Pr(T(P_1^*, 1) = 1)}{Pr(T(P_0^*, 0) = 1)}$

$Var(X_2^0) = 2.25\ Var(X_2^1) = 1$

$c_1 = c_0 = 0$

Figure 2

Relative Hiring Rate as a Function of the Level of Standardization. Blacks Held to Higher Standard; Blacks Have More Dispersion. Threshold Hiring Rule: No Discrimination Against Blacks Normally Distributed Unobservables

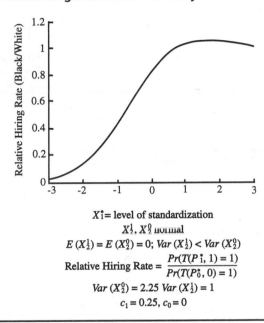

X_i^* = level of standardization

X_2^1, X_2^0 normal

$E(X_2^1) = E(X_2^0) = 0$; $Var(X_2^1) < Var(X_2^0)$

Relative Hiring Rate = $\dfrac{Pr(T(P_1^*, 1) = 1)}{Pr(T(P_0^*, 0) = 1)}$

$Var(X_2^0) = 2.25\ Var(X_2^1) = 1$

$c_1 = 0.25$, $c_0 = 0$

if the standardization rate is $X_1^* < 0$, and the lower the value of X_1^*, the greater the shortfall. In Figure 2, which is constructed for a hypothetical economy where there is discrimination against blacks, for high standardization rates, audits would appear to reveal discrimination *in favor* of blacks when in fact blacks are being held to a higher standard. The evidence in Table 1 is intrinsically ambiguous about the extent of discrimination in the market. For further discussion, see Heckman and Siegelman (1993).

Notes

1. Specifically, Darity and Mason write: "This effort has uncovered one variable in one data set which, if inserted in an earnings regression, produces the outcome that nearly all of the black male-white male wage gap is explained by human capital and none by labor market discrimination."

2. The Rodgers and Spriggs comment (1997) on Neal-Johnson raises other red herrings. Their confused discussion of endogeneity of AFQT, and their "solution" to the problem end up with an "adjusted" AFQT measure that is poorly correlated with the measured AFQT, and so is a poor proxy for black ability.

3. However, nothing I have said vindicates abolishing these laws. They have important symbolic value and they addressed and solved an important problem of blatant discrimination in the American South.

4. They need not be perfectly observed by employers but may only be proxied. However, it is easiest to think of both components as fully observed by the employer, but that the observing economist has less information.

5. I owe this analogy to Alan Krueger. This analogy also shows how artificial the audit studies are because one would expect to find athletes choosing their sports based on their chances of success, as in the purposive search in the labor market discussed earlier.

6. For simplicity, assume that γ is the same across all firms. Alternatively, assume that it is distributed independently of $\_X$ and f.

7. Allowing f to vary but assuming it is normal mean zero and variance σ_f^2 does not change the qualitive character of these calculations assuming that f is distributed independently of the characteristics.

References

Abowd, John, and Mark Killingsworth, "Sex, Discrimination, Atrophy, and the Male-Female Wage Differential," *Industrial And Labor Relations Review,* Fall 1983, *22*:3, 387–402.

Becker, Gary, *The Economics of Discrimination.* Chicago: University of Chicago Press, 1957.

Cameron, Stephen, and James Heckman, "The Nonequivalence of High School Equivalents," *Journal of Labor Economics, 1993, 11*:1, pt1, 1–47.

Cawley, John, James Heckman, and Edward Vytlacil, "Cognitive Ability and the Rising Return to Education," NBER working paper 6388, January 1998.

Donohue, John, and James Heckman, "Continuous vs. Episodic Change: The Impact of Affirmative Action and Civil Rights Policy on The Economic Status of Blacks," *Journal of Economic Literature,* December 1991. *29*:4, 1603–43.

Heckman, James, "The Central Role of the South in Accounting For The Economic Progress of Black Americans," Papers and Proceedings of The American Economic Association, May 1990.

Heckman, James, "Lessons From the Bell Curve," *Journal of Political Economy,* 1995, *103*:5, 1091–1120.

Heckman, James, and Peter Siegelman, "The Urban Institute Audit Studies: Their Methods and Findings." In M. Fix and R. Struyk, eds. *Clear and Convincing Evidence: Measurement of Discrimination in America.* Urban Institute, Fall 1993.

Heckman, James, Lance Lochner, Christopher Taber, and Jeffrey Smith, "The Effects of Government Policy on Human Capital Investment and Wage Inequality," *Chicago Policy Review,* Spring 1997, *1*:2, 1–40.

Johnson, William R., and Derek Neal, "Basic Skills and the Black-White Earnings Gaps." In Jencks, Christopher and Meredith Phillips, eds. *The Black-White Test Score Gap.* Washington, D.C. Brookings, 1998.

Neal, Derek, and William Johnson, "The Role of Premarket Factors in Black-White Wage Differences," *Journal of Political Economy, 1996, 104:5,* 869–95.

Rodgers III, William, and William Spriggs, "What Does AFQT Really Measure: Race, Wages, Schooling and the AFQT Score," *The Review of Black Political Economy,* Spring 1996, *24*:4, 13–46.

Rodgers III, William, William E. Spriggs, and Elizabeth Waaler, "The Role of Premarket Factors in Black-White Differences: Comment," Unpublished Manuscript, College of William and Mary, May 25, 1997.

Seelye, Katherine, "Employment Panel To Send People Undercover to Detect Bias in Hiring," *New York Times,* Sunday, December 7, 1997, p. 22.

U.S. Commission on Civil Rights, *The Economic Progress of Black Men in America,* Clearinghouse Publication 91, 1986.

POSTSCRIPT

Is There Discrimination in
U.S. Labor Markets?

Economists assume that markets are anonymous; that is, they assume that rational economic actors would not take race, sex, religious affiliation, or any other personal characteristic into consideration when buying or selling. Consumers are trying to maximize their consumer satisfaction, while producers are in the same marketplace trying to maximize their profits. Just as the often paraphrased axiom of Adam Smith suggests: Each acting for his or her own self-interest advances the well-being of the whole. In the world of neoclassical economics, there is simply no room for discrimination.

Yet the appearance of discrimination, if not the reality of discrimination, is all around us. Why are unemployment rates for African Americans twice those for white Americans? Why, on the average, do African American households earn 60 cents for every dollar earned by white households? Why do U.S. corporations, universities, courthouses, and even military officers' clubs have so many whites? And, more important, why do nearly 40 percent of African American children suffer the life-altering effects of poverty? Is this the product of market discrimination, or is it the consequence of deficient skill levels among African Americans?

In addition to Heckman's many contributions—he is perhaps the most prolific contributor to this debate from the neoclassical position—we suggest that you return to the source of his position, the work of Gary Becker, who in 1957 wrote *The Economics of Discrimination* (University of Chicago Press). Some of Heckman's other work is also highly recommended. See, for example, his essay "Lessons From the Bell Curve," *Journal of Political Economy* (vol. 103, 1995), pp. 1091–1120, and the book chapter he wrote with Peter Siegelman, "The Urban Institute Audit Studies: Their Methods," which appears in Michael Fix and Raymond Struyk, eds., *Clear and Convincing Evidence: Measurement of Discrimination in America* (Urban Institute Press, 1993). Finally, you might read Heckman's paper "The Value of Quantitative Evidence on the Effect of the Past on the Present," *American Economic Review* (May 1997).

Darity and Mason have also contributed extensively to this literature. See, for example, Mason's "Male Interracial Wage Differentials: Competing Explanations," *Cambridge Journal of Economics* (May 1999). You might also look for Darity and Samuel L. Myers, Jr.'s book *Persistent Disparity* (Edward Edgar, 1999). Lastly, we suggest a coauthored essay by Darity, Jason Dietrich, and David K. Guilkey, "Racial and Ethnic Inequality in the United States: A Secular Perspective," *American Economic Review* (May 1997).

ISSUE 4

Should California's Electric Utility Industry Be Deregulated?

YES: George Reisman, from "California Screaming, Under Government Blows," Ludwig von Mises Institute, http://www.mises.org/fullstory.asp?control=575 (December 22, 2000)

NO: Wenonah Hauter and Tyson Slocum, from "It's Greed Stupid! Debunking the Ten Myths of Utility Deregulation," Report of Public Citizen's Critical Mass Energy and Environment Program (January 2001)

ISSUE SUMMARY

YES: Professor of economics George Reisman asserts that the root cause of California's power problems is not the "free market" but "destructionist government policy . . . inspired by environmentalist fanaticism." He goes on to argue that this inappropriate government intrusion "has increasingly restricted the supply of electric power."

NO: Wenonah Hauter and Tyson Slocum, director and senior researcher, respectively, of Public Citizen's Critical Mass Energy and Environment Program, contend that California's attempt to deregulate its electric utilities has failed miserably. They debunk what they consider to be the 10 "myths" that proponents of deregulation used to call for the original round of deregulation in California and are currently using to call for even more deregulation of California's electric power system.

During the winter of 2000–2001, banner headline after banner headline declared, "Rolling Blackouts Hit Californians," "California is Unplugged," and "The Electricity Blame Game Is On." What happened to cause this energy crisis in California and what should be done now are the focus of this issue. It is a topic of great importance because the doubling, tripling, or even greater price increases of electricity that California has experienced may well snake across the rest of America, leaving economic chaos in the wake.

Indeed, the crisis is already impacting other western U.S. states. Many of the non-Californian utilities that generate electricity in the West are less dependent on natural gas—the most significant of several energy sources that have skyrocketed in price—than California is. Nevertheless, the fact that natural gas prices have risen sharply has increased the demand for all sources of energy that serve as substitutes, particularly hydroelectricity, coal, and nuclear energy. This problem is compounded by the fact that hydroelectricity is under its own price pressures. The drought that hit the region in the summer of 2000 coupled with the light snow pack the following winter drained the reservoirs that drive the electricity-generating turbines in that industry. Electricity prices in Idaho, Washington, and Oregon soon began to soar as the whole region competed with California for the limited amount of electricity that found its way to the marketplace.

What are the root causes of this crisis? Many people would argue that the answer to that question is rooted in AB 1890, a major deregulation bill that was passed unanimously in the California state legislature in 1996. AB 1890 had several key components. One central element was the establishment of a "Power Exchange," which was intended to serve as a centralized market for electricity. The buyers in this centralized market were the utilities, who would purchase electric power and in turn sell that electricity to their residential, commercial, and public sector customers. The sellers were those who actually generated the electric power supply. In order to ensure that no producer monopolies would have an unfair competitive advantage in this centralized market, the state's investor-owned utilities (IOUs) were required to sell their electricity-generating assets. However, the IOUs were allowed to recover their "stranded costs" by placing a monthly "competitive transition charge" on their ratepayers' bills. These stranded costs were the expenditures that IOUs had made on investments in traditional and alternative sources of energy that were formerly required by law but that would no longer be competitive in a deregulated market. Californians assumed the financial burden of compensating the IOUs for their stranded costs, and in turn the IOUs were required to reduce their rates by 10 percent and to cap them at this level until all stranded costs were recovered. Next, the deregulation mandated that the utilities participate in an electric power transmission system, which was to coordinate the distribution of electric power throughout the state. One final aspect of this deregulation was that publicly owned utilities were free to act independently. They could buy and sell in the Power Exchange, or they could sell their electricity on the open market.

In the following selections, George Reisman and Wenonah Hauter and Tyson Slocum discuss what happened in California and debate what policymakers should do to get the West Coast out of this mess and to keep it from spreading east. Reisman argues that Californians simply did not go far enough in their attempted deregulation. For him, California needs even more deregulation, not less. Hauter and Slocum maintain that this call for even more deregulation is based on the same flawed arguments that were used to get California into this situation in the first place.

George Reisman

California Screaming, Under Government Blows

The state of California is experiencing a fiasco in its electric power system. The system has repeatedly run near the overload point, necessitating brownouts and threatening rolling blackouts. Wholesale power prices in San Diego County and the southern portion of adjacent Orange County have briefly been as high as $5,000 per megawatt hour and, according to one report, as high as $11,500 per megawatt hour.

At first, the local utilities in these counties attempted to pass their greatly increased wholesale power costs on to their customers, in the form of doubled and tripled electric bills, but the state government, in response to widespread protest, soon prevented them from doing so. Now these utilities are threatened with bankruptcy, having lost approximately $6 billion dollars in the process. Out-of-state suppliers of electric power have threatened to cut off further supplies to the state, out of fear of not being paid by utilities on the verge of bankruptcy. At last report, these suppliers have been ordered by the federal government's Secretary of Energy to continue their supplies.

Incredibly, the fiasco is being blamed on deregulation and the establishment of a free market in electric power. See, for example, the disgraceful article *"California Screaming"* by Paul Krugman in *The New York Times* of December 10, 2000—on line at *The Times'* lead in to this article, which accurately conveys its tenor, is "California's blind faith in markets has led to an electricity shortage so severe that the governor has turned off the lights on the official Christmas tree."

Clearly, it is necessary to review the facts that have caused California's fiasco, in order to arrive at a rational judgment of its nature. This review will establish that the actual cause of the fiasco is not at all the free market but rather, from beginning to end, destructionist government policy, in large part inspired by environmentalist fanaticism. Assertions, such as that of *The New York Times*, which was just quoted, will be shown to constitute a literal contradiction in terms.

Destructionist government policy has increasingly restricted the supply of electric power in California and throughout the United States. It is responsible for the fact that for the last twenty years or more, there have been no new

From George Reisman, "California Screaming, Under Government Blows," Ludwig von Mises Institute, http://www.mises.org/fullstory.asp?control=575 (December 22, 2000). Copyright © 2000 by George Reisman. Reprinted by permission of The Ludwig von Mises Institute and the author.

atomic power plants constructed and few or no new coal, oil, or hydro power plants built. Indeed, it has caused existing plants of these types to be dismantled. In California, in the last decade, only power plants using natural gas as their fuel have been allowed to be constructed, and such plants now account for most of the state's generating capacity.

Because power plants using natural gas are substantially more expensive to operate in comparison with the other types of power plants, and would quickly be plunged into unprofitability if exposed to the competition of other types of power plants, investors have been unwilling to invest in additional generating capacity in California, and elsewhere, to the extent they otherwise would have. At the same time, the government-caused dependence on natural gas as the source of fuel for power plants has contributed to the recent sharp rise in the price of natural gas to record levels. The rise in the price of natural gas has been especially great in California, where lack of adequate pipeline capacity has limited natural gas supplies more than in the rest of the United States.

Over the same period that the government has restricted the supply of electric power, there has been a substantial increase in the demand for electric power. The rise in demand has been brought about both by population growth and by the increase in power consumption per capita caused by economic progress. An example of this last is the increase in power consumption caused by the use of personal computers and their peripherals by tens of millions of people.

When these facts are combined with government price controls on electric power (which have existed since the early years of the industry), *shortages* of electric power are an inevitable result. This is because the government prevents not only the increase in supply that would keep pace with the increase in demand but also the rise in the price of electric power that would keep the demand for power within the limit of the supply available, however artificially restricted that supply might be as the result of government interference.

The government's responsibility for shortages of electric power, it should be realized, inescapably implies its responsibility for power brownouts and blackouts. For their immediate cause is a demand for power too great for the power system to supply, i.e., a power shortage.

It cannot be stressed too strongly that a shortage is an excess of quantity demanded over supply available. And that it is caused by a government price control, which prevents price from rising high enough to reduce quantity demanded to the supply available, which would eliminate the shortage. Of course, the more the government holds down the supply of electric power, the higher is the price that is required to prevent a shortage of power. When the government refuses to allow a price that is high enough to keep the quantity of power demanded within the limit of the supply of power available, brownouts and blackouts are the result.

It should be understood that when taken in conjunction with price controls on electric power, the government's inflation of the money supply also contributes to power shortages. This is because inflation contributes both to the increase in the demand for power and to the restriction of its supply. The former results largely from the rise in money incomes that the spending of the additional quantity of money brings about, and which gives people the financial means to afford larger quantities of any given good at any given price. The latter results from the fact that inflation drives up the costs of constructing and operating power plants and thus correspondingly reduces their profitability in the face of controlled selling prices. The process does not have to go very far before it no longer pays to construct power plants—assuming, of course, that the environmentalists did not prevent their construction in the first place.

All this is the basic context of the fiasco now existing in California and which, on the basis of a combination of ignorance and deceit, is being blamed on, of all things, "a free market" in electric power.

The so-called free market in electric power in California consists of the fact that, last summer [2000], price controls were removed from the power supplies of San Diego County and the southern portion of adjacent Orange County, while remaining in force throughout the rest of the state.

The power supplies of this relatively small part of California were suddenly opened up to the competition of power companies throughout the rest of the state and in surrounding states who were desperate for additional power to avoid the brownouts and blackouts caused by government price controls in their operating territories. Starting last summer, by offering a higher wholesale price, these power companies could bid away power generated in this area from use by the area's local residents and businesses. Locally generated power could be retained for use in the area only at a wholesale price that matched the price generated by this competition.

It should be understood that the power companies are in a position in which any customer can turn on additional power-using devices, and they are obliged to supply the additional power needed to meet that additional demand. Price controls and the government's restrictions (described above) preventing the construction of new power-generating capacity now repeatedly compel the utilities to operate close to the limit of their existing power-generating capacity.

To avoid overloading and thereby crashing their systems and causing wide-spread blackouts, they must either find the necessary additional power or induce other customers, typically large ones, to cut back on their power consumption, by such means as the offer of substantial rate concessions. Finding additional power, wherever it is available, can serve to avoid expensive rate concessions and, worse, a system crash. This is the desperate situation for which the limited power supplies of San Diego County and the southern portion of adjacent Orange County were put in the position of having to provide a remedy.

Anyone familiar with economic theory could easily have predicted that the result would be a skyrocketing of power prices in the area. For the limited power supplies of this small area were being made to bear the burden of coping with the statewide and indeed, Western-states-regionwide power shortages caused by destructionist government policies.

Now the truth is that an immediate, partial solution to the sharp rise in power prices in this limited area is the *immediate decontrol of power prices throughout the rest of California* and, indeed, throughout the whole Western-states region, which shares a more-or-less integrated power grid. The effect of such decontrol would be an immediate substantial increase in the supply of electric power available for the decontrolled market and thus, probably within days, if not hours, a sharp drop in the price of electric power in the decontrolled market.

This increase in supply, it must be stressed, would *not* come from an increase in production, though very soon there would be such an increase and thus a further increase in supply and reduction in price in the decontrolled market. No, it would come from the more or less substantial portion of *the already existing production of electric power that is presently consumed by submarginal buyers*, i.e., by buyers unable or unwilling to pay the potential free-market price, which, of course, would be higher than the controlled price still in force over the far greater part of the state. When the price control is removed, this substantial part of the supply, presently not available for the decontrolled market, is made available for the decontrolled market, where its effect is to enlarge the supply and thus correspondingly reduce the price.

Lifting price controls in the remainder of Orange County and in Los Angeles County, for example, would add supplies from these areas to the supplies presently available only from San Diego County and the southern portion of Orange County to meet urgent needs for power throughout the state and the Western-states region in general. The rise in price in these additional areas would serve to reduce the quantity of power demanded in these areas. The supply of power previously used to meet this portion of the demand would be available for the now larger decontrolled market. The effect of this larger supply in the larger decontrolled market would be to reduce the price of power in the decontrolled market.

Decontrol throughout the state and in surrounding states would still much more substantially enlarge the supply available in the decontrolled market and drive down the price there. Indeed, at the same time that larger supplies were being made available to meet urgent needs for power, decontrol would serve greatly to diminish the urgency of those needs. This is because the rise in power prices throughout the state would serve everywhere to reduce the quantity of power demanded and thus serve to reduce the amount of power needed from outside sources to prevent brownouts or blackouts.

It should be clear that decontrol limited to the territory of just one or two counties is decontrol in a very high-pressure pressure-cooker, so to speak. It is decontrol in which all the pressure of the shortages of the whole rest of the state and surrounding states come to bear on the very limited supplies of power available just in this relatively small area. Decontrol over the whole state and region would serve to eliminate all of this pumping up of the pressure that has propelled prices so high in San Diego County and south Orange County.

A further increase in supply and reduction in price that would result from state-wide and region-wide decontrol would come from existing power capacity that is presently forced off the market by price control, coming back on to the market. That there is such capacity is confirmed by the following statement in a recent newspaper report: "Natural-gas prices traded at record levels Friday [December 8, 2000], hitting $60 per million British thermal units. *That prompted some gas-fueled generating plants to shut down* because they couldn't make a profit under the ISO's [Independent System Operator's—a state official] wholesale cap of $250 a megawatt hour." (*The Orange County Register,* December 10, 2000, News Section 1, p. 12. Italics added.)

The elimination of price control would bring such producers back into the market, increase the market supply, and reduce the market price. As matters stand, the forced withdrawal of such producers serves to further increase the pressure on the very limited supplies of the small area that is free of controls, and to further drive up their price. For buyers who might have been supplied by those producers, and now are not, must turn instead to the supplies of that small area.

The preceding makes clear that the price of a good in a fully decontrolled market is substantially less than the price of a good in an only partially decontrolled market, and is virtually certain to be very substantially less in comparison to the price in a partially decontrolled market as small as the one in California has been. Full decontrol in California would mean lower power prices both for this reason and because of the return to the market of output from existing producers that the controls had driven away by making its production unprofitable.

The following hypothetical example will serve to drive home the principle that the elimination of price control on the full supply of a good available results in a lower decontrolled price than when only a portion of the supply of a good is free of price control. Thus imagine that the full available supply of a good is 100 units and that at a fully uncontrolled, free-market price of $120, the quantity of the good demanded is also 100 units. In this case, the free-market price is $120—that is the price at which quantity demanded and supply available of the good are equal and, consequently, neither a shortage nor an unsaleable surplus of the good exists.

Now imagine that the government imposes a price control on this good of $100 per unit. At this, lower price, the quantity of the good demanded becomes greater than the 100 units of supply available. This is because now the good can be afforded by everyone who values a unit of it above the price of $100, whereas before only those who valued a unit of the good above the market price of $120 could afford it. At the free-market price, all buyers not prepared to pay at least $120 per unit would have been rendered submarginal. They would have been excluded from the market by the $120 price. Now however, as the result of the price control, a more or less substantial number of submarginal buyers become admitted to the market. They can cross the lower bar of the $100 price, while they could not have crossed the higher bar of the free-market price of $120.

Assume that as a result of the lower, controlled price, buyers are now prepared to attempt to buy 130 units of the good. Since only 100 units of the good are available, would-be buyers of 30 units must go away empty-handed. The efforts of these would-be buyers to buy 30 units that do not exist is the measure of the shortage that the price control has created.

When there is a price control and shortage, the distribution of the supply is made largely random and chaotic. That is, it becomes an essentially accidental matter *which* of the buyers seeking 130 units will be supplied and to what extent. It is entirely possible in this situation that a full 30 units of the supply could fall into the hands of buyers who at the free-market price of $120 would have been submarginal, that is, into the hands of buyers who value these units below the free-market price of $120—who value them merely above the $100 controlled price. We do not need to make such an extreme assumption, however. Assume that the effect of the price control and resulting shortage is merely to enable 10 units of the supply to fall into the hands of such submarginal buyers.

Since there are only 100 units of supply available, the diversion of 10 units into the hands of submarginal buyers, means that only 90 units of the supply remain available for buyers able and willing to pay $120 or more per unit. Thus buyers of 10 units, who value them all above $120 are excluded from the market. It is against the law—i.e., the price control—for them to outbid the submarginal buyers, as they would do in a free market. The result is that unless they are lucky, which in this case they are not, they will have to go away empty-handed.

It is entirely possible, and we will assume it to be the case, that among this group of excluded buyers are buyers who value a unit of the good far above the free-market price of $120—who would be prepared to pay as much as $1,000 for a unit of it, or even as much as $2,000. Under price controls and shortages, even buyers with the most vital and urgent need for a good, as these buyers can be assumed to be, may have to go away empty-handed, because the units they seek are obtained instead by buyers who in a free market would have been submarginal and excluded from the market by the free-market price.

Now, finally, imagine that into this situation comes the government of California, with its "blind faith in markets," as *The New York Times* has so audaciously called it. It decontrols the price of *one* unit of the hundred. What happens? The price of this unit is determined by the competition between the most desperate and second-most desperate buyer of an additional unit who have up to now been excluded from the market by the price control and resulting shortage. In the present example, it is determined at a point between the $2,000 maximum potential bid of the most desperate of these buyers and the $1,000 maximum potential bid of the second-most desperate of these buyers. Thus, the resulting price is, say, $1,500.

It should be obvious that if instead of timidly freeing just one unit of the supply from price control, the entire supply of 100 units were freed, the resulting price would be far lower—it would be the $120 free-market price.

Now although, as the above example confirms, the free-market price would be very much lower than the price prevailing in the very narrow decontrolled market of just one and a half counties, it would still be more or less substantially higher than the previously controlled price. Whatever it turned out to be, *its immediate effect would be to end the shortage of electric power and thus brownouts and blackouts*. This would be to the advantage of all consumers of power—poor consumers no less than rich ones.

The establishment of a free-market price for power means that poorer consumers are enabled to bid more for the power they need to run their one and only refrigerator, say, than many wealthier, higher-income buyers are willing to pay for the power needed to operate a second or third refrigerator. It means that they are enabled to bid more for the electric power that provides the light they need in which to read than many wealthier, higher-income buyers are able and willing to pay for power to run their pool lights or other outside lights. Retention of price control, in contrast, means that the wealthier, higher income buyer has no economic reason not to go on using power for a second or third refrigerator and for his pool lights, which serves to deprive the poorer consumer of the power for his one refrigerator or the light in which to read. A free market price guarantees the availability of electric power for the truly urgent purposes of virtually everyone who has a job.

When faced with the need to restrict consumption, a free market does so by eliminating the least important of the uses to which a good was previously devoted, i.e., its previously marginal uses. In the present case, such uses will probably turn out in large part to be power-intensive industrial uses in the production of products that are unable to bear substantially higher power costs.

To the extent that the resulting free-market price were higher than the previously controlled price, it would operate to increase the profits of power producers and thereby provide both the incentive and the means (the latter through reinvestment of the profits) to increase investment in and thus production of power. This, of course, is part of the more complete, longer-run solution to California's power fiasco. Obviously, it requires the removal of obstacles to the construction of new and additional power plants, i.e., the environmentalists must get out of the way. The freedom to construct power plants fueled by atomic energy and by coal must be restored.

The effect of stepped up investment in and production of power would be a reduction in the price of power and in the profitability of producing it. The rate of profit in power production would fall from a more or less sharply above-average rate toward the average rate. The price of electric power would gravitate toward its cost of production plus only as much profit as required to provide the average rate of profit, i.e., only enough profit to make the power industry competitive with the rest of the economic system for capital investment. While the high profits of the power industry following the removal of price controls would be temporary, what would endure is a larger-sized power industry.

Thereafter, in order for any power producer to earn a premium rate of profit, he would have become an innovator in improving power production. He would have to find ways to reduce its cost of production and/or improve what he could transmit over power lines. But these premium profits too would be temporary. They would come to an end as soon as competitors succeeded in making the improvements part of the general standard of the industry. Further high profits would have to be earned by further reductions in cost of production and/or further improvements in quality of one kind or another, and so on and on. The long-run beneficiaries would be the consumers of power, who would buy their power at progressively lower real prices.

This, indeed, is the overwhelming thrust of the free market: ever lower, not higher prices. To be sure, this result is not very obvious when prices are expressed in terms of fiat paper money, which is comparable in its cost of production to paper clips or pins, and which gets cheaper faster than businessmen can make most goods and services get cheaper, with the result that prices expressed in paper money almost always rise.

But it is very obvious when prices are expressed in terms of how many hours or minutes of labor the average worker must put in at a job in order to earn the price of something. Once prices are thought of in these terms, it is clear that the real price of almost everything has been falling for generations—precisely because of the free market and its profit motive and freedom of competition. That is the real meaning of a free market in electric power as well.

It should now be clear that the assertion of *The New York Times* that "California's blind faith in markets has led to an electricity shortage so severe that the governor has turned off the lights on the official Christmas tree" is the complete opposite of the truth, and is so by the very meaning of the terms involved.

Presenting knowledge of the actual causes of California's electric-power fiasco will prevent the enemies of the free market, such as *The New York Times* and its columnists, from getting away with blaming the free market for the consequences of the anti-free-market, destructionist policies they advocate.

In the view of writers such as Krugman, there may as well never have been any governmental restrictions on power production inspired by environmentalism. Lack of sufficient capacity is the fault of "the deregulated market." In Krugman's own words: "But in the deregulated market, where prices fluctuate constantly, companies knew that if they overinvested, prices and profits would plunge. So they were reluctant to build new plants—which is why unexpectedly strong demand has led to shortages and soaring prices."

The same gentleman knows nothing of the distorting effects of price controls on markets that are only partially decontrolled. In his eyes, the cause of the very high power prices in San Diego County and the southern portion of Orange County can only be "manipulation." To prove it, he imagines the following case:

> "Suppose that it's a hot July, with air-conditioners across the state running full blast and the power industry near the limits of its capacity. If some of that capacity suddenly went off line for whatever reason, the resulting shortage would send wholesale electricity prices sky high. So a large producer could actually increase its profits by inventing technical problems that shut down some of its generators, thereby driving up the price it gets on its remaining output."

In reality, of course, all kinds of contractual arrangements requiring delivery of specified quantities of power at specified prices would operate to prevent the kind of behavior Krugman imagines. Because of such contracts covering the greater part of their output, any rise in the price of power would go mainly to the benefit of the contract holders, rather than to the companies generating power. The amount of output on which the latter could obtain the benefit of such a short-term rise in price would be too small to make such behavior on their part worthwhile.

Putting this aside, Krugman ignores the actual, and significant, fact that in the summer of 2000, the power companies of California were operating dangerously close to the limit of their capacity, causing considerable fear of the dire consequences that would result should there be any breakdown in any of their capacity, which became all the more likely, the longer there was no down time for necessary maintenance and repairs.

Now, in the fall of 2000, when approximately twenty-five percent of California's power capacity is off line, undergoing the maintenance and repairs that could not be performed in the summer, in the face of peak demand, Krugman suggests that this too is part of a process of "manipulation." Perhaps he believes that the California utilities that have been driven to the brink of bankruptcy are growing rich in this process.

Krugman and *The New York Times* appear to suffer from the malady of substituting fantasy for knowledge of reality. The seriousness of the malady is not diminished by the fact that *The Times* is often able to pull it off with a pompousness that is exceeded only by its ignorance.

NO 　　Wenonah Hauter and Tyson Slocum

It's Greed Stupid!

Introduction

If the purpose of deregulation is really to improve the quality of people's lives by lowering the cost of a critical commodity, it is obviously failing miserably—as demonstrated in California. To understand what has happened, we must begin with the past.

Prior to "deregulation," electricity was supplied by regional monopolies that owned both the power plants and the transmission lines for the distribution of power. The California legislature set the rate of return of profit for the utilities, and the state Public Utilities Commission [CPUC] planned for future power needs and helped insure that rate increases were fair and based on the "cost of service." While this system was often abused because of the enormous political power of the electric utilities and their ability to influence policymakers, it did keep in check the profiteering that we are now witnessing in California.

By the mid-1990s, large industrial consumers sought to escape the high costs of power in some parts of the country, like California, that came as a result of building expensive nuclear power plants. At the same time, independent power producers like Enron were actively lobbying to be able to sell power to these big consumers. Political pressure for deregulation mounted because the breakup of the $300 billion dollar utility industry meant huge amounts of money could be made. Enron, an important campaign contributor to the Republican Party and to President Bush, lobbied for deregulation not only in California, but at state legislatures across the nation and in Congress.

Despite warnings from consumer groups, deregulation has been heartily embraced by both political parties, and under the Clinton administration, the U.S. Department of Energy [DOE] wrote its own federal deregulation bill that it promoted unsuccessfully.

In California, the utilities, at first, were skeptical of deregulation, because of the high cost of power from their nuclear plants. However, they began to hunger for the profits that could be made in a speculative market. They lobbied heavily for deregulation because they knew that with their enormous political clout in the state legislature, they could shape the outcome of deregulation.

From Wenonah Hauter and Tyson Slocum, "It's Greed Stupid! Debunking the Ten Myths of Utility Deregulation," Report of Public Citizen's Critical Mass Energy and Environment Program (January 2001). Notes omitted.

The legislation, written primarily by California's utilities, was extremely complex, a vast program for a vast state. It was wrangled over in a series of rapid-fire hearings, and rammed through the legislature at the last minute in a process that took only three weeks. It was unanimously passed and signed into law by Governor Pete Wilson in the fall of 1996.

The legislation, written and supported by utilities, privatized their profit and socialized their risks. The most glaring example of this was the $28 billion dollar consumer-funded bailout for their so-called "stranded costs." Stranded costs are essentially mortgage payments that the utilities make to cover their purchase of expensive boondoggle nuclear power plants. The utilities argued that the bailout was necessary because they would now be assuming market-place risk, and the uncertainty of their future profits made the paying off of debts they incurred under regulation too burdensome. To accomplish this bailout, rates were artificially frozen for 4 years, at what was then 50% above the national average cost of electricity. To date, ratepayers have bailed out the utilities for approximately $20 billion dollars through added costs to their electric bills.

In 1998, a coalition of consumer groups, Californians Against Utility Taxes, sponsored an initiative, Proposition 9, which would have invalidated portions of the 1996 deregulation bill, and prevented the utility bailout. The proposition would have required the utilities and their shareholders, not ratepayers, to bear the burden of the $28 billion bailout. According to energy analysts at the California Energy Commission, if Proposition 9 had passed, residential power customers would have seen their energy costs "fall between 18 to 32 percent." California's utilities spent more than $30 million defeating Proposition 9, compared to the $1 million spent by consumer advocates.

The legislation not only provided them with a bailout, but it enabled them to go on an international spending spree in which they purchased power plants. It also provided them with capital they used to invest in other industries that they had been prohibited from entering under the regulated monopoly system. California's utilities have invested in telecommunications and other types of high-growth services that they plan to sell in conjunction with their sale of electricity. Between the bailout and their forays into new industries, Wall Street applauded their moves because of their increased earnings potential.

Also, the legislation provided incentives for California's utilities to sell their power plants to unregulated companies. They sold most of their fossil fuel plants at above the book value, providing them with a significant profit. However, they retained their nuclear and hydro-power generation, along with a small amount of fossil-fuel plants.

Additionally, the deregulation bill transferred pricing of California's electricity generation to the Federal Energy Regulatory Commission by creating the Power Exchange, a private nonprofit organization that would operate the auction for wholesale power.

Most of the corporations that bought the California utilities' power plants are from out-of-state—such as Virginia-based AES, North Carolina-based Duke, and Houston-based Dynegy and Reliant. Eleven companies, not all of which own power plants in California, sell electricity into the Power Exchange, where electricity is bought and sold several times (in paper transactions) before it is actually delivered to consumers. Another new privately run entity, the Independent System Operator (CAISO), acts as a traffic cop, directing electricity to where it was needed.

Myth #1: Deregulation does not work because California did not deregulate enough.

Advocates for deregulation say that if the rate freeze was removed and consumers paid for the real cost of electricity through a free market, there would not be a problem. But they fail to mention that over the past few months, the cost of wholesale electricity has at times been almost 4,000 percent higher than before deregulation because of the speculative nature of the electricity market. *If all the costs were passed on to consumers, the average residential monthly consumer, who paid approximately $55 a month before deregulation, would have paid approximately $600 a month when prices spiked in California this winter.*

Second, the utilities agreed to assume a risk under deregulation, in return for the bailout and rate freeze. However, now that their plans have soured, they want to renege on the deal that they lobbied for in 1996. The retail rate "freeze" was designed by and for the state's electric utilities, as a way to subsidize them for their bad business decisions of the past, such as nuclear power plants.

Until the spring of 2000, the utilities greatly benefited from the artificially high rates that were "frozen" in 1996 at 50% above the national average for electricity. These outrageously high rates included: 1) reimbursement for their cost-of-service (all of the expenses associated with producing power); 2) approximately an 11.75% profit margin; and 3) the $20 billion dollar bailout for utilities' bad investments of the past. The outrageous utility bailout is listed as a "Competitive Transition Charge" (CTC) on every Californian's electric bill.

The Utility Reform Network (TURN), a consumer advocacy organization in California, explains the bailout and rate freeze:

> This opportunity [the rate freeze], however, included the explicit risk that some costs might not be collected by the end of the rate freeze. With the advent of higher-than-expected power prices in recent months, these utilities now argue that they never took a risk for the costs of power under the rate freeze and therefore should be compensated for money spent to buy power for its customers.

To make matters even worse, the utilities overestimate the cost of electricity that they claim to have "under collected" from consumers in their frozen rates. As a result of the price spikes that began in 2000, the utilities are asserting that consumers have to pick up the exorbitant cost of wholesale electricity. The utilities claim to be "owed," approximately $12 billion dollars.

In fact, this number is wildly exaggerated, because the utilities did not sell all of their power generation (they retained nuclear plants, hydra-electric facilities, and a small amount of fossil generation). Under deregulation, the electricity from all utility owned or contracted generation is resold into the Power

Exchange. During periods of high energy prices, the net revenues associated with this generation can be substantial. But, instead of offsetting the costs of purchasing power for customers, under the current rules, these utility owned units provide no direct benefit to rate payers in the form of lower energy procurement prices.

For example, if it costs PG&E [Pacific Gas and Electric] approximately 1.4 cents per kilowatt hour to generate hydro-electricity and they sell this power at the Power Exchange for approximately 40 cents per kilowatt hour, they make a huge profit. This profit should be subtracted from the amount that the utilities estimate they have been overcharged for wholesale power. But, the utilities have not subtracted in their estimates of how they have been overcharged, their own substantial profits in wholesale market, which is roughly estimated at $6 billion dollars. This means that the $12 billion dollar figure that they claim to have over-paid in the wholesale market is wildly inflated by at least $6 billion.

Because of the profiteering on electricity trading at the Power Exchange, the city of San Francisco initiated a lawsuit on January 18, 2001, against a number of companies for unfair business practices. The companies being sued include Dynegy Power Marketing; Enron Power Marketing, Inc.; PG&E Energy Trading Holding Corporation; Reliant Energy Services; Sempra Energy Trading Corporation (owner of San Diego Gas and Electric); Southern Company Energy Marketing; Duke Energy Trading and Marketing; NRG Energy, Inc.; and Morgan Stanley Capital Group, Inc.

The California Public Utilities Commission comments that the pricing patterns in the Power Exchange's "day ahead" and "day of" markets raise questions about the bidding behavior of market participants that cannot be coincidental.

California is suffering today because of no regulation—not because of over-regulation.

Myth #2: Deregulation will lower costs for consumers.

Deregulation has been sold to the public as a way to lower prices. Unfortunately, the inverse is often true, with deregulation resulting in higher prices over time. When deregulation legislation sailed through the California legislature with unanimous bipartisan support in 1996, proponents claimed that consumers would see *at least* a 20 percent reduction in their electric rates eventually. Now, as wholesale prices have skyrocketed since last year, proponents argue that consumer rates will have to *increase* to encourage more competition. Long-term contracts are being promoted as the antidote for the crisis. But, the price being quoted for electricity under these contracts is at least three times more expensive than under regulation. What happened to lower rates under deregulation?

The answer is that California's power producers have no restrictions on the prices they can charge for electricity, and regulators no longer set minimum energy reserve requirements to prevent power shortages. Advocates of deregulation said that prices and reserves would be set at optimum levels by the free market. But the opposite has been true. Power marketers restrict supplies by reducing the amount of electricity that is produced, creating shortages and price spikes (see Myth 4). Predictably, gaming the system has meant skyrocketing profits for power marketers in California.

An analysis of the effects on consumer prices in another deregulated energy industry—natural gas—is a good indication of what will happen to consumers' electric bills if they are left to the vagaries of a deregulated market. Since the natural gas industry was deregulated a decade ago, wellhead, or wholesale, costs have actually fallen. But the price at which natural gas is sold to residential consumers has skyrocketed. In 1984, just prior to complete deregulation, residential prices for natural gas were 44 percent above the wellhead price. By 1987, it was 110 percent above. By 1999, it was 181 percent above. At the same time, prices to larger, industrial consumers rose, but not as much as for residential consumers. In 1984, industrial prices were 28 percent above the wholesale price of electricity. In 1987, they were 39 percent of the wellhead price. By 1999, it was 42 percent of the wholesale price. This price discrimination indicates a noncompetitive market.

Even with high natural gas prices—which according to economic theory causes sellers to increase supplies—reserves are low and there are indications that some type of market manipulation may be occurring. It seems that we have our own natural gas cartel operating in the U.S., which behaves like OPEC [Organization of Petroleum Exporting Countries]. With government regulators no longer protecting consumers and defining the rules of the road, control has been ceded to a handful of energy companies that in many cases are also [in] the business of selling electricity in places like California.

At the very least, if the market is not being manipulated, years of experience show that the natural gas market is failing for consumers. After 15 years of higher prices, it is time to reexamine natural gas deregulation.

Meanwhile, we have a very different example set by publicly owned electric power systems. While energy companies defend their high prices, California's 30 communities with municipally owned and controlled power offer the same electricity at lower prices. The City of Los Angeles' Department of Water and Power charges 20 to 25 percent less than comparable privately run utilities elsewhere in the state.

Myth #3: Prices for electricity are being driven up because the demand for electricity is increasing.

Planning for new power plants is based on the need for electricity at the time of year that maximum usage of power occurs—the time of peak demand. Indeed, California's Independent System Operator (CAISO), the traffic cop for the transmission of electricity under the deregulated market, has records showing that the state's peak demand for electricity in 2000 occurred on July 12 and was approximately 45,600 megawatts. (For comparison, a large nuclear power plant is approximately 2000 megawatts.) California uses the most electricity in the summer, when air conditioners run.

CAISO uses this information about demand to find out how much energy must be produced by various plants to meet California's energy needs. The agency records the highest amounts of demand by hour within the state of California. The data shows that while demand did soar in May, in four out of the past six months—July, August, October and December—California saw a lower peak demand in 2000 than during the same months in 1999.

Overall, according to the California Energy Commission and confirmed by California Public Utilities Commission President, Loretta Lynch, the average amount of electricity used throughout the day grows at about 2% a year. This does not mean that peak demand is growing; it does mean that consumers use more power at midnight because they are using their computers.

In fact, recently, there have been blackouts when demand was less than 30,000 megawatts, approximately 15,600 megawatts less demand than the peak amount of electricity needed in California in the summer. Obviously, it is supplies of electricity being held back, not demand that is causing the problems with deregulation.

Myth #4: The problems are being caused because there is not enough power to supply California.

So, why are suppliers short? *Because under deregulation, power producers have no incentive to run plants at full capacity.* As noted above, California has 55,500 megawatts of power generating capacity and 4,500 megawatts of power on contract. Following is a breakdown of plant ownership:

- unregulated power suppliers: 21,231 megawatts (40%)
- public agencies: 11,934 megawatts (23%)
- qualifying facilities, large industrial consumers and others: 11,745 megawatts (22%)
- utilities: 8,245 megawatts (15%)

Of this power, the Independent System Operator has access to approximately 45,000 megawatts to provide electricity for the state. But large numbers of power plants are not running at full capacity or are down for unscheduled maintenance, keeping supplies short.

The tighter the supply, the more prices rise. As much as 13,000 MW of capacity was off-line in January for undisclosed reasons. According to *The Wall Street Journal,* on August 2000, 461% percent more capacity was off-line than a year earlier.

Because details about why these plants are off-line is confidential, the public is literally left in the dark. According to CAISO, many suppliers are not even complying with the requirement to turn in an annual plan for when they will have plants off-line for maintenance, and there are no penalties for this lack of cooperation. Regardless of whether one suspects that power producers are intentionally taking capacity off-line to hike prices, these statistics illustrate that under deregulation, the public has little control over pricing and reliability.

The fact is that today, the state of California has access to more capacity than the 45,000 MW of summertime peak demand—the maximum amount used during the highest usage time of year.

California has 55,000 megawatts of in-state electricity generating capacity through about 1,000 power plants. In addition, the state is able to import about 4,500 megawatts of electricity, which is under existing long-term contracts. These thousands of megawatts of capacity could easily meet demand if wholesaler suppliers were not manipulating the system. The situation would be even better if energy efficiency strategies were maximized. New plants are not needed; instead, stricter scrutiny of existing plant operations is needed. Even so, many new plants are *already* under construction, which will even further increase the amount of electricity that is available.

Myth #5: California's environmental laws are preventing new power plants from being built in the state.

It is untrue that California's environmental laws have prevented new plants from being built and are responsible for the current crisis. As noted earlier, there is enough existing capacity tied into the state's grid to meet even summertime peak demand. And while the state's sensible environmental laws get the blame for the lack of new construction, it is important to note that California's utilities did not want to make investments in new power plants. The state's utilities blocked decisions by the CPUC to build new capacity because under deregulation, the utilities realized they would have assumed the economic risk for bad decisions—rather than consumers—who paid for past mistakes as part of rates.

Southern California Edison (SCE) even went so far as stopping the development of 1,500 MW of new renewable energy and cogeneration (the heat from industrial processes is used to generate electricity) projects. This more environmentally friendly electricity would have been available to help meet the current crisis, and would have cost under 5.5 cents per kilowatt-hour. But, SCE's Chief Executive Officer, John Bryson, in the mid-1990s petitioned the Federal Energy Regulatory Commission (FERC) to stop the construction of these projects.

Before deregulation, California had a planning process for building the infrastructure for the energy sources to meet demand. In 1993, this Biennial Resource Planning Update (BRPU) process set a price that was below 5.5 cents per kilowatt (a much lower price than the cost of power from long-term contracts today), and a bidding process was initiated. The cost of environmental damage was taken into consideration in the bidding process. The Public Utilities Commission accepted bids and planned to build 1,500 MW of new wind, geothermal and cogeneration plants. Bryson then started a petitioning process at FERC, which resulted in none of the generation being built because he did not want to risk investments in new capacity. FERC voted to not allow the California Utilities Commission to require the new projects. Today, California is suffering from the FERC's bad decision and Bryson's efforts to stop new renewable energy capacity from being built.

Even so some power plants were built, according to the agency that permits new power plants:

> In the 1990s before the state's electricity generation industry was restructured, the California Energy Commission certified 12 new power plants. Of these, three were never built. Nine plants are now in operation producing 952 megawatts of generation. . . . Since April 1999, the Energy Commission has approved nine major power plant projects with a combined generation capacity of 6,278 megawatts. Six power plants, with a generation capacity of 4,308 megawatts are now under construction, with 2,368 megawatts expected to be on-line by the end of the year 2001.
>
> In addition, another 14 electricity generating projects, totaling 6,734 megawatts of generation and an estimated capital investment of more than $4.3 billion, are currently being considered for licensing by the Commission.

Although new power plants are under construction and in the planning process, the best way to address California's energy needs is through energy efficiency measures and renewable energy projects. Building more centralized plants may be a way to obtain higher profits for power producers, but it is a poor investment in light of the new technologies that are rapidly becoming available. For instance, the expanded use of distributed generation, where small amounts of generation (roof top solar power is an example) is located on a utility's distribution system to help meet energy demand.

Energy efficiency is always the cheapest and best method of lowering the demand for electricity. It cuts energy use, saves consumers money, offers predictable financial requirements, and benefits the environment by reducing energy use. Examples include: the use of compact fluorescent bulbs—which last ten times longer than conventional ones and use one quarter of the energy; double-paned windows; and more efficient appliances and industrial production lines.

According to the Center for Renewable Energy and Sustainable Technology, higher energy efficiency standards for central air conditioners (over the course of its lifetime) would save as much electricity as more than 1.2 million Californians would use. And more efficient clothes washers would save the electricity consumed by more than 700,000 Californians.

Renewable energy projects should be built to replace old, dirty generation. Renewable energy projects can now be built at the same cost as conventional facilities. Today wind turbines show great promise, tomorrow, fuel cells are likely to change the face of energy production. Renewable energy offers dependable, even fixed-cost power that is particularly important in a state that is facing blackouts and price roller coasters.

Myth #6: Deregulation is good for the environment.

While deregulation creates short-term incentives to gouge consumers by artificially ensuring low supplies of electricity, in the long run deregulation creates economic incentives for power suppliers to sell more electricity. As prices rise, suppliers push to build new plants in an attempt to maximize profit. At the same time, deregulation provides an incentive to keep cheap, dirty coal power plants running longer. The market forces driving deregulation will not shut down old plants and replace them with cleaner ones. Instead, the old plants will run, and new plants will be built as well, because deregulation encourages more energy use.

This situation means that nationally the likely environmental effects of deregulation will be sharply increasing emissions, particularly if existing coal-fueled power plants remain exempt from air pollution standards.

In addition, because a speculative electricity market is inherently volatile, and because some suppliers have an alarming amount of market power, a larger reserve margin of power is necessary. The independent power producers are using the uncertainty of the market to push for relaxing environmental regulations, to drill for natural gas in sensitive areas and to build more power plants and more transmission lines.

If utility deregulation continues on its current course, not only will air pollution increase and ecologically sensitive areas be degraded, but our global climate will be further threatened by more greenhouse gases.

Myth #7: California's energy crisis is best resolved through state, not federal, actions (as stated by President Bush).

Unfortunately, the Clinton administration promoted electricity deregulation relentlessly, and now the new Republican administration is supporting the same reckless deregulation scheme that we are seeing unfold in California today.

The Bush administration argues that blame for the current crisis lies with the state: allow the utilities to pass their costs on to consumers and ease the state's environmental standards to quickly build new power plants to increase supply.

The cause of California's deregulation crisis is the result of the removal of any government oversight on producing and selling electricity. With government regulators no longer present to protect the public interest, power producers and marketers are charging outrageous prices for electricity, and the utilities then attempt to pass on the cost to consumers (see Myth 3).

While the Bush administration seems content to blame the state for the problems with deregulation and to claim that raising rates and building new power plants would solve everything, the federal government is sitting on the one action that will directly address today's high prices. Under the authority of the Federal Energy Regulatory Commission (FERC), which is now chaired by Bush-appointee Curt L. Hebert, Jr., the federal government is the sole entity that can impose cost-based rates on these power producers. If the administration was willing to order power plant owners to sell their product at the cost-of-service (the cost of generating power) and a reasonable profit, California's utilities could buy the electricity needed and the pressure to raise consumer's electric rates would be removed. Meanwhile, the state could investigate the price-gouging and act thoughtfully in solving the problems caused by deregulation.

But, Enron, Reliant, and the other power producers and power marketers operating in California heavily financed the Bush administration. Bush and his new energy secretary, Spencer Abraham, who lost his recent run for the Senate and who once advocated the abolition of DOE, received more than $2.5 million from energy interests during the campaign and for the inauguration events. The new power suppliers for California are making so much money from their profiteering that they will maintain pressure on the Bush administration to keep the current system in place.

To date, the only federal action Bush has called for is to drill in the unique and pristine coastal area of Alaska's National Arctic Wildlife Refuge to tap into a supply of oil that would amount to only a six month supply of oil and would take 10 years to bring to market. Furthermore, oil is rarely used for electric power generation today.

Myth #8: California's three big utilities were forced, against their will, to sell their power plants.

As described in the introduction, California's three big utilities lobbied intensely to pass the 1996 deregulation bill, which provided incentives for them to sell their power plants. Some nuclear and hydropower facilities were retained by the utilities. The California utilities believed that they would thrive from electric utility deregulation and become international energy companies.

The sale of the power plants, along with the infusion of consumer-funded subsidies, gave the two utilities accelerated depreciation, enabling them to build up cash on their parent companies' balance sheets to finance the stock buyback plans and pour investments into Mission Energy, the National Energy Group and other unregulated divisions. According to a report released by TURN in October 2000, the generation owned or contracted by Pacific Gas and Electric (PG&E) and Southern California Edison (SCE) produced large profits between May and August of 2000, amounting to $2.7 billion. Because the power is credited to stranded costs, the average monthly collection of stranded costs was accelerated by 79% for PG&E and 56% for SCE. Accelerated depreciation has provided large amounts of cash for the utilities.

However, now that they have been beat at their own game by bigger and meaner companies like Enron, they are crawling back to the legislature and begging for another consumer bailout.

Myth #9: California's utilities are close to bankruptcy and need to be bailed out.

California's two major utilities, Southern California Edison and Pacific Gas & Electric, claim to have racked up such significant losses under deregulation that they are threatening to file for bankruptcy. In 1996, when the promise of huge profits loomed large they agreed to assume some risk. Now that the market has failed they are demanding that the state provide direct assistance, or else (they claim) they will no longer be able to afford to supply their customers with electricity.

But their parent companies, using the money they made from selling their power plants and from the bailout have spent more than $22 billion on power plants, stock buybacks and other purchases that far exceed their alleged $12 billion debt from California operations. Edison International and PG&E have done this both through those two companies and through affiliated companies, Mission Energy (a subsidiary of Edison International) and National Energy Group (a PG&E subsidiary).

Created in 1990, Mission Energy's revenues and profits didn't take off until 1999, when expensive investments began to pay off. A recent Public Citizen analysis showed that Mission Energy, along with a few other smaller Edison International subsidiaries, spent more than $10 billion on non-California investments since December 1998—more than double the SCE's stated debt of $5 billion. In addition, Edison International has spent $2.35 billion on stock buyback programs since deregulation began.

PG&E's high-growth subsidiary, National Energy Group, hasn't been as forthcoming, electing not to disclose the purchase price of many of its recent acquisitions. Information gleaned from several news reports reveals that since 1999, PG&E's purchases outside California and the Pacific Northwest have totaled at least $9 billion. This far eclipses PG&E's alleged $6.6 billion deficit from its California operations. PG&E spent more than $1 billion on its own stock buyback plans since the onset of deregulation.

Myth #10: Electricity deregulation is working in other states.

Electricity deregulation has passed (or been adopted by a regulatory process) in 23 states plus the District of Columbia. However, because of the situation in California, Utah has repealed its deregulation bill and New Mexico has delayed implementation of its deregulation legislation. Of the states that passed bills, only a handful of them have begun changing their energy supply systems. Some places, like Washington, D.C., negotiated long-term contracts at reasonable rates, which will put off by several years the disasters of a truly deregulated market. And in almost all states, deregulation is to be phased in over a period of years. To make the legislation politically viable, price caps, mandated rate reductions and other benefits that will be sunset were included.

Also, electric utilities across the country were given huge bailouts for their bad investments in nuclear power and other items as part of the deregulation deals in their states. These so-called "stranded costs" were passed on to consumers. According to a report by the Safe Energy Communications Council, utilities in 11 of the states that have deregulated (California, Illinois, Massachusetts, Michigan, Montana, New Hampshire, New Jersey, New York, Pennsylvania, Ohio and Texas) are demanding or have already received more than $112 billion to bail out their failed investments.

States such as Massachusetts, where utilities were bailed out, have had no electricity suppliers willing to serve residential suppliers. The idea that there is competition in the market has become a joke. Power suppliers that sprang up to serve customers in New England, Pennsylvania and New Jersey are now "dumping" their customers back to the old utilities. The new suppliers simply cannot compete in the region's electricity markets.

Pennsylvania, which has been touted as a deregulation success, does not really have a deregulated market. The state's utilities went through a regulatory process to determine how much their bailout should be. The cost of the bailout was included in the price of electricity that each utility can charge. Each investor-owned utility has a regulated price of electricity; depending on how large a settlement it received for its "stranded cost" recovery. This is basically a regulated price for electricity, which depending on the utility, will be in place for as many as nine years.

This regulated price of electricity is keeping prices in check in Pennsylvania. It means that suppliers must keep their prices lower than the regulated price to be competitive. For instance, PECO Energy has a winter price of 5.57 cents per kilowatt-hour. But many of the utilities in the region retained ownership of their plants, so suppliers must buy electricity from the utilities that are still regulated. This has meant that many suppliers have gone out of business.

No matter where deregulation has occurred, problems are already arising. For the past two summers, blackouts have plagued residents and businesses in other deregulated markets where prices on the wholesale market have spiked, most notably in Chicago, New York City and northern New Jersey.

New York City is an instance in which consumers were subject to the vagaries of the market and prices skyrocketed because of the volatile, speculative market for electricity. New York used a regulatory process to deregulate. Consolidated Edison, which serves New York City, *was* allowed to pass all of its costs on to consumers. So when price spikes occurred, bills skyrocketed, raising rates 43% for residential consumers and 49% for commercial users. Obviously, passing on the cost of a speculative market for electricity will not make deregulation a success.

Additionally, deregulation is encouraging dozens of mergers and acquisitions in the electric industry. We have seen this type of consolidation in other industries, and it has meant higher prices and poorer service in most cases for consumers.

We've seen what mergers do to consumers when we look at the airline industry. The largest airlines have engaged in numerous mergers, reducing competitors at every turn. They are masters at price discrimination, forcing business travelers to pay fares several times higher than vacation travelers, who can plan for travel weeks or months in advance. They also use their ticketing computers to send price signals to each other in a game of collusion that keeps profits up. Major airlines maintain "fortress hubs" where they have a monopoly on air service, allowing them to set prices due to lack of competing airlines. Deregulation in the airline industry has also led to terrible service, which is now legendary.

Consolidation does not lead to competition, lower prices or better service. On the contrary, it allows a handful of companies to exert market power and prevent consumers from receiving good service at reasonable prices. But, unfortunately, utility analysts predict that only a handful of companies will survive deregulation, if it continues to be embraced, and that these same companies will sell any number of services. This concept, called convergence, will mean that consumers will be forced to use a single company to provide necessary services such as power, water, telecommunications and Internet access. Prices for all of these services will be "bundled" (included in a single price), which will leave little room for price comparison.

Policymakers should think seriously, and there should be a public debate, before deregulation reaches this level. The bottom line is that if deregulation doesn't help real Americans, we shouldn't continue to pursue it.

Conclusion

Electricity is an absolute necessity that should not be a speculated product. Consumers have a right to affordable energy, produced in the most environmentally sustainable fashion possible. But, when treated as a speculative commodity, the cost and supply of electricity becomes uncertain. This situation invites price-gouging and profiteering, as we are witnessing today in California.

We must critically analyze the intentionally perpetuated myths by the proponents of deregulation, because it is clear that what many pro-deregulation politicians are saying just is not true. We need to carefully look at their assertions, or we will not only continue to bailout utilities, we will [also have] higher prices, less reliability, and a threatened environment. It is time to hold policymakers accountable for the mess they have created, and roll back dangerous electric utility deregulation schemes.

POSTSCRIPT

Should California's Electric Utility Industry Be Deregulated?

$\mathbf{M}$uch is riding on who is right and who is wrong in this debate. In large measure, this is because many states were expected to follow California's lead by passing their own utility deregulation legislation, and a number did follow that lead in the last few years of the 1990s. Then-governor Pete Wilson aggressively pursued the passage of this legislation in California, perhaps in the hope that his vocal and active support would gain him national recognition, which he could use to pursue his political ambitions in a national arena. For whatever reason, Governor Wilson went state to state "selling" his deregulation plan to his fellow governors, and by the year 2000 four states had joined California by initiating their own legislation: Massachusetts, New York, Pennsylvania, and Rhode Island.

Pennsylvania is perhaps the most successful deregulation experiment to date. Governor Tom Ridge initiated regulatory reform in the electric power industry in December 1996, not long after the California state legislature passed its deregulation package. Unlike in California, however, Pennsylvania's deregulation was put into place in phases. It took until January 1999 to put the system into place, and another full year passed before consumers could "shop around" for electric power suppliers. There are other fundamental differences between the Pennsylvania case and the California experience. One notable difference is the fact that although consumers could search the marketplace for the most economical electricity supplier, the utilities remained regulated in the transmission of this power. Perhaps the most important difference is the fact that Pennsylvania's utilities were not obligated to divest their generating capacity. They could if they cared to divest, but their only requirement was to "unbundle" their services—that is, they were to separate their role as a source of electric power from their corporate capacity to transmit that power. See Adrian T. Moore and Lynne Kiesling, "Powering Up California: Policy Alternatives for the California Energy Crisis," *Reason Public Policy Institute Policy Study No. 280* (February 2001).

State governments were not alone in experimenting with deregulating electric power. A number of national governments moved in this direction during the waning years of the twentieth century. Deregulation was put into place in England and Wales, New Zealand, Norway, Australia, and several South American countries, including Chile. See Vernon L. Smith, "Regulatory Reform in the Electric Power Industry," *Regulation* (vol. 19, no. 1, 1996).

Free-market economists are keen to deregulate all markets, including the market for electric power. Readers should take care to note this bias. There is, however, a nicely balanced essay that is very insightful. Although Severin

Borenstein's essay "The Trouble With Electricity Markets (and Some Solutions)," POWER Working Paper PWP 081 (January 2001) is more balanced, it does not in any way ignore market forces. Indeed, it provides the reader with an excellent market analysis of the root causes of the energy crisis in California and points toward some possible policy solutions. Borenstein's essay was published by the Program on Workable Energy Regulation (POWER). This program is part of the Energy Institute at the University of California, whose Web site is http://www.ucei.org.

In his essay, Borenstein asserts that there are fundamental problems with the market for electricity wherever that electricity is being provided. That is, this crisis is not unique to California. The basic problem, as Borenstein sees it, is that the demand for electricity is price inelastic, while the supply faces "strict production constraints." What he means is that this is a capital-intensive industry and that utilities are reluctant to create large amounts of expensive excess capacity to handle those rare occasions when there is an extraordinary "peak load" event—a prolonged heat spell, perhaps. This desire on the part of utilities to put in place the optimum-sized generating facility is frustrated by the fact that once electric power is produced, it is very difficult and expensive to store. The net result is that the industry is constantly faced with the potential for a mismatched supply and demand, and these sharp swings from a shortage to a surplus result in a natural volatility in prices and, therefore, in profitability. This is why the grid systems have come into being. Grids serve as a mechanism to shift the excess supplies in one area to areas that are experiencing shortages. When a whole region experiences a shortage, there is no inventory of electricity to fall back upon, and a crisis of brownouts or rolling blackouts occurs.

ISSUE 5

Should Markets Be Allowed to Solve the Shortage in Body Parts?

YES: Charles T. Carlstrom and Christy D. Rollow, from "The Rationing of Transplantable Organs: A Troubled Lineup," *The Cato Journal* (Fall 1997)

NO: Nancy Scheper-Hughes, from "The End of the Body: The Global Traffic in Organs for Transplant Surgery," Organs Watch, http://sunsite.berkeley.edu/biotech/organswatch/pages/cadraft.html (May 14, 1998)

ISSUE SUMMARY

YES: Free-market economists Charles T. Carlstrom and Christy D. Rollow argue that the simple use of market incentives can go a long way to solving the shortage of transplantable organs. They contend that although some people may have "qualms about the buying and selling of organs, the cost of our current approach is that shortages will remain endemic, and ultimately, more lives will be lost."

NO: Professor of anthropology Nancy Scheper-Hughes acknowledges that markets in and of themselves are not evil. But she asserts that "by their very nature markets are indiscriminate, promiscuous and inclined to reduce everything, including human beings, their labor and even their reproductive capacity to the status of commodities, to things that can be bought, sold, traded, and stolen."

The first human heart transplant in the United States took place a surprisingly short time ago. Dr. Michael DeBakey performed the first successful coronary artery bypass graft in 1964, and less than four years later, on May 3, 1968, Dr. Denton Cooley and his team of surgeons shocked the world by announcing that they had successfully transplanted a heart in Everett Thomas, who lived for 204 days with a heart donated by a 15-year-old girl. Until Cooley and DeBakey achieved this revolutionary medical breakthrough, those with progressive heart failure were doomed to die. There was simply no hope of reversing the process that destroys this vital organ.

Cooley and his team performed their second operation, which was quickly followed by a series of other transplants in their Houston, Texas, operating theater. At first there was no real shortage of transplantable organs; the carnage on U.S. highways alone was enough to supply the limited number of healthy hearts that these teams of surgeons could reasonably expect to transplant. But as the word spread among those who were dying of various heart conditions, the demand for this radical surgery skyrocketed.

Any time that a shortage appears, there are several ways to mediate between those who demand and those who control the supply. In a market economy, price performs the role of the "grand allocater." In brief, whoever is willing to pay the highest price moves to the top of the waiting list. Applying this model to body parts, those who are less fortunate in terms of their resource holdings become less fortunate in terms of access to the limited supply of organs. This seemingly "cold-blooded" solution is quick to bring a chorus of protests. But what are the alternatives? Can lessons be learned from parallel situations? Should a shortage of human hearts and other transplantable organs that are needed to save lives be treated like a shortage of gasoline, which fuels our cars, or a shortage of electricity, which runs air conditioners and traffic signals? In the cases of gasoline and electricity, price controls have been used to address the shortages.

How did these market interventions work? The gasoline shortages that arose in the 1970s were a result of the Organization of Petroleum Exporting Countries' (OPEC) successful attempts to artificially restrict the world's supply of crude oil. As a result, the price of gasoline skyrocketed. Both the Nixon administration in the early 1970s and the Carter administration at the end of the 1970s responded by imposing "ceiling prices." The price of regular grade gasoline was not allowed to rise above $1.75 a gallon. Since the equilibrium price of gasoline was well above this level, a shortage resulted. A serious question arose: Who would get the limited supply? In a market arrangement, those who were willing to pay the highest price would get the gasoline. In the case of the price-controlled world of the 1970s, those who were willing to wait in long lines got the limited supply. Whoever was in line first got a chance to buy the limited quantity that was available. Is that any more "just" or "fair" than a market solution?

In the following selection, Charles T. Carlstrom and Christy D. Rollow suggest that a price-controlled world is no more just or fair than a controlled system and that, worse, this world of market controls is inefficient. They advocate the use of market incentives to solve the shortage. In their view, markets are not only a more efficient solution but a solution that will actually save more lives than the current system. In the second selection, Nancy Scheper-Hughes takes serious exception to Carlstrom and Rollow's position. She asks, Which lives will be saved? Will those who are poor be condemned to death simply because they are poor? Will the organs that are needed for transplants be "harvested" from both rich and poor equally, or will only the poor be economically blackmailed into selling their organs so that they can survive in our market-dominated world?

Charles T. Carlstrom and
Christy D. Rollow

 **YES**

The Rationing of Transplantable Organs: A Troubled Lineup

On June 6, 1995, baseball legend Mickey Mantle was placed on the transplant waiting list after being diagnosed with end-stage liver disease caused by hepatitis, liver cancer, and years of alcohol abuse. Two days later, he underwent surgery, despite the fact that the average liver transplant patient waits 67 days. His doctors claimed that Mantle received no preferential treatment; rather, his gravely ill status placed him at the top of the list. Yet, because of Mantle's original liver cancer, he died two months later. Given that 804 patients died in 1995 while awaiting a liver transplant, Mantle's case and others like his raise questions about which of the 7,400 liver patients on the waiting list should have received the 3,900 livers that became available that year. Society has to confront this and similar questions because of the severe shortage of transplantable organs.

Organs are not the only goods rationed in the United States—they are just the most controversial. Hunting permits, oil drilling leases, cellular telephone licenses, and radio frequencies are other examples of rationed resources. The distinguishing feature of these goods is that prices alone are not permitted to allocate the commodity; as a result, someone must determine how they will be distributed.

There are many ways that goods can be rationed, such as lotteries, first-come, first-served, and coupons. As a consequence of price controls, gasoline was rationed in the 1970s, largely on a first-come, first-served basis.[1] The result was long lines at the pumps and an effective price of gasoline that included both the direct cost of purchasing gas plus the indirect cost of queuing. Although some view such a system as equitable, its inefficiencies are obvious once we factor in the time and even the gas wasted as people waited in line. Rationing also played a role during World War II, when the government issued coupons for purchasing staples such as meat and butter. This solution was also seen as equitable in many quarters, although, like lotteries, it did not ensure that those who most needed or valued a good received it.

This conflict between equity and efficiency arises whenever goods are rationed. Determining the most equitable way to allocate gasoline and food is

From Charles T. Carlstrom and Christy D. Rollow, "The Rationing of Transplantable Organs: A Troubled Lineup," *The Cato Journal,* vol. 17, no. 2 (Fall 1997). Copyright © 1997 by The Cato Institute. Reprinted by permission. References omitted.

difficult, but deciding how to allocate transplantable organs is infinitely more complex. The complexity stems from the fact that someone must choose who receives lifesaving transplants—a decision that impacts efficiency through the number of lives lost over time. Since both equity and efficiency are paramount when rationing goods, the market for transplantable organs is an ideal case to illustrate this conflict.

Ten Americans die each day while awaiting an organ transplant, and the problem is becoming more severe. Between 1988 and 1994, the median waiting time nearly doubled (see Figure 1). It is imperative, then, that society find ways to increase the supply of organs, even through buying and selling. For most goods, prices are allowed to adjust to provide incentives, thus ensuring their most efficient allocation. While some people would understandably have qualms about the buying and selling of organs, the cost of our current approach is that shortages will remain endemic, and ultimately, more lives will be lost. Allowing monetary payments may not completely eliminate this shortage, but it will undoubtedly increase the number of organs available.

This paper examines the inherent difficulties of rationing by analyzing the market for transplantable organs. We look at the current procurement and allocation system and discuss various proposals to increase the efficiency of the market. Although the particulars of this market are unique to organ transplantation, society faces similar choices whenever prices are regulated and shortages occur. As Dr. Arthur L. Caplan, director of the Center for Bioethics at the University of Pennsylvania, notes, "It [organ transplantation] is a case study of rationing. It is of fundamental interest to every American. All of us will have to confront the decision of what is fair in the allocation of scarce resources. This is a canary in a mine that all of us will have to enter."

Rationing Organs: The Current System

In 1984, Congress passed the National Organ Transplant Act, which outlawed the buying and selling of internal organs.[2] The National Task Force on Organ Transplantation recommended to Congress in 1986 that organ donation remain purely voluntary, governed by the altruism of the donor or the donor's family. Additionally, it suggested that the "selection of patients for transplant not be subject to favoritism, discrimination on the basis of race or sex, or ability to pay" (U.S. House of Representatives 1991: 44). This nondiscriminatory clause is crucial, because when prices are regulated and shortages occur, goods must be rationed. Since discrimination is one form of rationing, it is costless when markets are not allowed to operate freely.[3] In contrast, in an unregulated market, individuals and firms must forgo profits if they wish to discriminate—that is, engage in nonprice rationing.

Another concern was that political clout would influence the allocation process; hence, an independent nonprofit organization was selected to operate the Transplantation Network under the auspices of the Department of Health and Human Services. In October 1986, the United Network for Organ Sharing (UNOS) was awarded this federal contract. The group's task is twofold: establish criteria that match donors with waiting recipients, and develop policies that

Figure 1

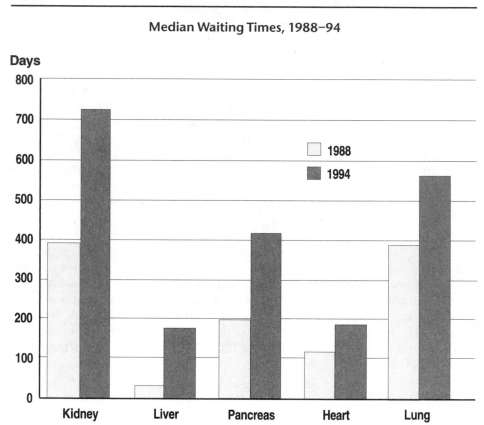

Median Waiting Times, 1988–94

Source: UNOS (1995)

facilitate the procurement of organs. Figure 2 illustrates that within the current voluntary system, UNOS has been largely unsuccessful in increasing donations; supply increases have been minimal compared to demand. The major difficulties in devising an equitable organ distribution system are summarized in Table 1.

The Sickest-First Policy

Many contend that in a fair system, organs would be given to those who "need them the most—the so-called sickest-first policy." UNOS uses this strategy in ranking liver and heart patients as part of its policy of minimizing patient deaths. The approach is myopic, however, since it ignores the impact that today's decisions have on the number of deaths over time.[4] The Mickey Mantle case is a stark example because Mantle, and hence his liver, died two months

Figure 2

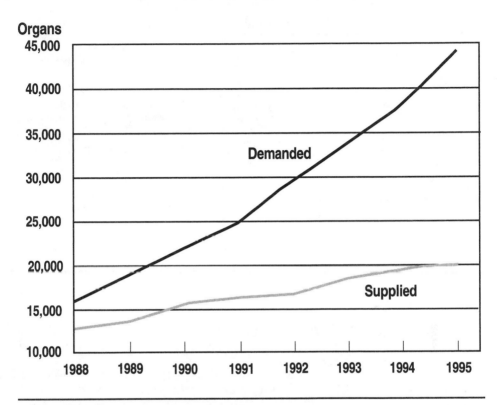

Organs Supplied and Demanded, 1988–95

Source: UNOS (1996)

after surgery. Indeed, the two-year graft (organ) survival rate for patients who are in intensive care prior to their liver transplant is approximately 50 percent, compared to 75 percent for those who are still relatively healthy. These groups' individual two-year survival rates differ by 10 to 15 percentage points.

Given the differences in two-year survival rates, the cost of transplanting 100 fewer livers into intensive-care patients today would be a loss of 85 to 90 lives versus 100 over a two-year period.[5] Since graft survival rates are higher for healthier patients, the number needing retransplantation would decline. Thus, another benefit of this one-time policy change would be to free organs for others. Another advantage is that by transplanting livers into healthier individuals, the number of critically ill patients would decrease, thereby saving additional lives. On net, this policy change would be more efficient because it would save more lives.

Table 1

Organ Rationing Schemes

Allocation Methods	Benefits	Costs
Waiting time	Equitable	Inappropriate matching; organ wastage; no consideration of urgency
Priority to sickest first	Equitable	Higher retransplantation and death rates; less benefit overall
Priority to sickest last	Higher overall survival; less retransplantation	Sickest patients die
Best biological match	Higher overall survival; less retransplantation	Fewer transplants for certain groups, including highly sensitized patients and some minorities

Source: UNOS (1977)

The Best Biological Match

Another allocation method (the one emphasized for kidneys) is biological matching, which is measured by the quality of the antigen match between donor and patient.[6] Once a kidney becomes available, UNOS searches among waiting-list patients and ranks them according to their biological match with that organ. When four of the six most critical antigens match, the one-year graft survival rate is 13 percentage points higher than for a total antigen mismatch. Four years later, that difference increases to 20 percent.

Instead of biological matching, waiting time alone could be emphasized—the first-come, first-served approach.[7] While this may seem more equitable, the cost of such a policy change would be enormous. In the first year alone, the average biological match would decrease by nearly three antigens, and graft survival rates would fall by about 6 percentage points. Even discounting subsequent declines in graft survival rates, the number of kidney transplant candidates eventually would increase by nearly 5,600, translating into approximately 202 more waiting-list deaths each year.[8] The importance of graft survival is obvious, given that nearly one-quarter of those on the kidney waiting list have received a transplant previously.

Despite their emphasis on biological matching, UNOS distributes kidneys on a regional basis, mandating that kidneys procured within a region stay local.[9] If, on the other hand, kidneys were distributed nationally, the pool of potential recipients would increase, thereby increasing the likelihood of finding a patient with a good antigen match. Thus, distributing kidneys nationally would expand the average biological match. This policy change not only would save lives, but also would eliminate inequities caused by regional variations in waiting times.[10]

Discrimination in Kidney Allocation

Certain groups of patients wait longer than others for kidney transplants and, because of equity concerns, are given special consideration. For example, highly sensitized patients are much more likely to reject an organ transplant because of antibodies acquired from multiple blood transfusions or from rejecting a previous transplant. UNOS gives them preference when a kidney is found that will not necessarily be rejected; otherwise, they may never be transplanted. Giving highly sensitized patients preference can be extremely costly, however, because it reduces the size of the waiting-recipient pool searched. In effect, UNOS limits its search to the prioritized group unless a match outside the group is considerably higher. Thus, the likelihood of finding a well-matched kidney decreases, along with patient and graft survival rates. Since highly sensitized patients make up less than 3 percent of all kidney patients awaiting transplants, discriminating for them is likely to cost more than if the group receiving preference were larger.

An even greater preference is given to patients with type-O blood. Although organs from donors with type-O blood can potentially be transplanted into patients with any blood type, transplant candidates with O blood can receive only an organ of the same type. Thus, to ensure that these patients' waits are not substantially longer, UNOS mandates that kidneys from O donors will go only to O patients, with the exception of perfectly matched kidneys. The cost of this policy is that potentially good matches are forgone.

Other groups, such as blacks, also spend a disproportionate amount of time awaiting transplants. The median waiting time for black kidney patients is twice as long as it is for whites. This has led many to conclude that UNOS's policies are inherently racist and that blacks should receive preference similar to that given to highly sensitized patients. The longer waiting time, however, is not due to discrimination but to a disproportionate number of blacks who suffer from hypertension and diabetes—the two major causes of kidney failure.

Blacks represent 29 percent of all patients with end-stage renal disease, while they make up only 12 percent of the population and donate less than 12 percent of all kidneys. These numbers are important because the quality of the biological match is usually better when both the donor and the recipient are of the same race. The fact that blacks demand more kidney transplants as a share of their population and that the supply of kidneys from blacks is, if anything, slightly less than this figure explains the wide discrepancy between black and white waiting times.[11] Thus, a policy change giving preference to blacks not only would be more inefficient, costing additional lives, but also would violate UNOS's directive not to discriminate.

Encouraged Volunteerism: The Need for Incentives

Changes in the way UNOS rations organs can potentially decrease waiting times and save lives, but major reductions in waiting-list deaths, and thus improvements in efficiency, will require a substantial increase in organ donations. Table 2 shows the gap between the number of available organs and the number of people who need a kidney, liver, pancreas, heart, or lung transplant. Although the shortages vary, most of them are critical and have shown little response to public awareness programs, professional education efforts, or legislation. "Routine inquiry laws, for example, require hospital personnel to inform the families of potential donors about their option to donate. In fact, doctors still mention this opportunity only two-thirds of the time.[12]

Table 2

U.S. Organ Waiting List and Transplant Statistics

Organ	Quantity Demand (as of 12/25/96)	Quantity Supply (January–December 1996)
Total kidney	36,013	11,949
Cadaveric		8,560
Living		3,389
Liver	7,467	4,058
Pancreas	1,786	1,022
Heart	3,935	2,381
Lung	2,546	844

Note: Multiple organ transplants are counted as more than one organ.
Source: UNOS (1997)

Trading Organs

The only way to increase the supply of organs is to increase the number of cadaveric organs, with the exception of kidneys, for which there is also the possibility of living donations.[13] More than one-quarter of the 11,700 kidneys donated each year come from living related individuals—an impressive number considering that kidney removal requires the donor to be hospitalized for five to seven days and to spend two to three months convalescing.[14]

What can be done to further increase the supply of kidneys from living donors? Currently, only 7 percent of these donations are from nonrelated individuals (primarily spouses), mainly because kidneys from nonrelated donors are usually poor matches or of the wrong blood type. To increase donations, UNOS could facilitate the trading of kidneys, allowing patients to receive a well-matched kidney in exchange for a kidney from a spouse or close friend. This policy would increase kidney donations from both related and nonrelated sources. For instance, a patient's relative or spouse may be willing to donate a kidney, but because they have the wrong blood type, they are not suitable donors for that individual.[15]

Financial Incentives

Although altruism can be a powerful factor in motivating organ donations, it works best within families and cannot be expected to function as efficiently in the market for cadaveric organs. Individuals may sign anatomical donor cards indicating their wishes, but in practice, procurement agencies will remove organs only with familial consent. Thus, to increase supply, it is necessary to provide families with additional incentives. This is especially true given the relatively few deaths (10,000 to 12,000 annually) that occur in such a way that the deceased's organs are suitable for transplantation.

To increase donations, we need to consider financial incentives mimicking those that prices provide in a market economy. Perhaps the simplest approach is to give tax incentives to families who agree to donation. Donated organs already go to UNOS, a nonprofit organization; therefore, a monetary value would need to be assigned to organs only for tax purposes. To significantly increase the donor pool, society should also reconsider its position against the buying and selling of cadaveric organs. Allowing payments to surviving family members is another way of providing market incentives.[16]

To operate efficiently, the structure of this market would still require a centralized agency like UNOS to facilitate the matching process. Donor and recipient information is critical, since an individual's willingness to pay would depend on the quality of the antigen match with the available organ. One possible market structure would be to grant authority to buy and sell organs exclusively to the federal government, an approach suggested by Nobel laureate Gary S. Becker.

Shifting Rents

A common misperception about situations in which goods are not allowed to be bought and sold is that their market value is zero. An unintended consequence of price restrictions, however, is that the quantity supplied falls and the good becomes extremely valuable. To take advantage of the difference between the regulated price and the market's valuation, black markets tend to develop. Even if the price of the good does not rise, the actual cost may increase because of queuing costs, as in the case of gasoline price controls.

Black markets for transplantable organs have not developed in the United States, but it is possible that the price of transplants is higher, because organs cannot be legally sold. The law allows for "reasonable payments to all who participate in the organ donation process." The ambiguity of this term provides an opportunity for organ procurement organizations (OPOs) to artificially inflate prices. Currently, they receive approximately $25,000 for retrieving just the kidneys from a cadaver. An interesting, but as yet unresolved, question is how much of this $25,000 includes an implicit market price for the organ.

Other medical personnel (transplant surgeons, hospitals, etc.) also benefit financially from the organ procurement process, and are probably collecting some of these profits, also known as rents. Rents accrue whenever the quantity of a good is artificially restricted, thereby giving organizations monopolistic power. In the case of organs, the price, not the quantity per se, is restricted; however, the net effect is the same. Because of this, the shadow price (value) and hence the amount collected are likely to depend on the relative scarcity of the organ. Liver transplants are among the most expensive transplant surgeries—$300,000 on average—and as Table 2 indicates, livers are in especially short supply.

Figure 3 illustrates this concept in the market for transplantable organs, where S_c represents the supply of organs under the current system, and P_H represents the price that would clear the market.[17] This is the highest price, over and above normal fees, that a hospital can potentially charge for a transplant. Area $0P_Ha0_c$ shows the maximum rents that would be collected.

It is clear, however, that all of these rents are not being collected, given current shortages. Yet, it is equally clear that some rents are being collected. For example, it is particularly telling that OPOs keep procured organs in their local area, even though UNOS's policies sometimes dictate otherwise. This is frequently true when OPOs are affiliated with hospitals' transplant centers, in which case the potential profits of keeping organs in-house can be substantial. Thus, there is an implicit market price, P, between zero and P_H that is being charged. At that price, the value of rents would be area $0PbO_c$. If P is above P^*, as shown, then selling organs would actually lower the total price of a transplant (including the equilibrium price of the organ, P^*). Similarly, if P is below the market-clearing price, the total price of a transplant would increase by less than P^*. Thus, allowing organs to be sold would increase their supply, lower their market value, and shift payments from OPOs, hospitals, and surgeons to family members.

Even if the price of transplantation did rise by the full amount of P^*, the money going to donors' families ("death benefits") would likely pale in comparison to the overall price of the operation. Consider the case where the family benefit is $5,000 and rent shifting does not occur. When allocated among two kidneys, a heart, liver, and pancreas, the extra cost per organ is probably closer to $1,000, an insignificant amount compared to the price of a transplant.

Equity Issues

Selling organs would not favor the rich at the expense of the poor, as many argue, since those receiving organ payments would likely have lower average incomes. Organ recipients, both rich and poor, would also benefit from the increased supply of organs. Currently, Medicare pays for kidney transplants, while 90 percent of liver and heart transplants are covered by Medicare, Medicaid,

Figure 3

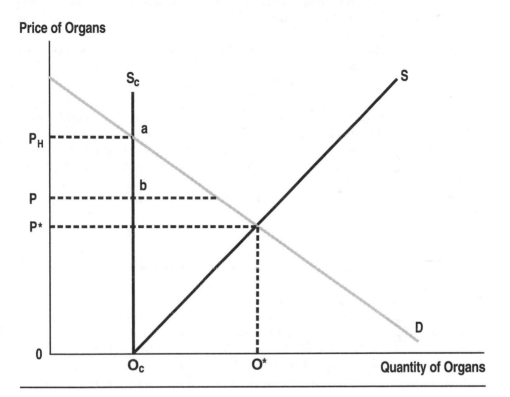

The Market for Transplantable Organs

Price of Organs

and private insurance.[18] Each additional organ supplied benefits everyone, re-gardless of wealth.

Repealing the prohibition against the buying and selling of organs could lessen the disparity between black and white waiting times for kidneys. Because the antigen match is usually higher for individuals of the same race, any policy change that increases the percentage of black donors from its present level of 12 percent will decrease their waiting time. Thus, organ payments are more likely to persuade people of lower average income, including blacks, to donate, even if the payment amount is the same across all groups.

Given the higher demand for kidneys from black donors, in the absence of nondiscriminatory laws, payments to individual black families would likely be higher than payments to whites. But even without government assistance, this would not aggravate income inequality, since the extra amount paid by blacks would largely go to blacks. Given that Medicare (and frequently Medic-aid) pays for kidney transplants, if anything, income inequality would be re-duced by allowing organs to be sold.

Budgetary Concerns

Budgetary concerns are also misplaced. As previously noted, buying and selling organs may not increase transplantation costs at all, and even if it does, this policy change would still save Medicare money. It costs Medicare more than $40,000 annually to dialyze each kidney patient, while the cost of a transplant and subsequent medication is about $100,000 the first year and $12,000 per year thereafter. Because of this, the Health Care Financing Administration estimates that transplantation is considerably more cost effective than continued dialysis.

For example, if the average life of a transplanted kidney were only three years, the budgetary impact of organ payments would be neutral. The median graft survival rate, however, is closer to six years. Therefore, as long as the family benefit is less than $180,000 ($90,000 per kidney), the government will save money. Since the vast majority (nearly 70 percent) of all waiting-list patients are waiting for kidneys, each additional dollar spent encouraging families to donate will save taxpayer money.

Conclusion

Rationing is considered anathema to most Americans, yet it is necessary when prices are regulated. Goods are frequently rationed by simplistic methods such as lotteries or first-come, first-served. These may be more "equitable" approaches, but they are also among the most inefficient and can ultimately harm everyone involved. The inefficiencies are particularly pronounced in the market for transplantable organs, where costs are measured in human lives.

Deciding what is fair and who should be first in line for organ transplants is especially troubling and difficult. Dr. Mark Siegler, who directs the University of Chicago clinical ethics program, has stated that "all alcoholics should go to the bottom of the transplant list . . . yet Dr. Siegler [also] said he would exempt Mickey Mantle from his rule because the baseball legend is 'a real American hero' . . . [W]e have got to take them with all their warts and failures and treat them differently." It is especially important that UNOS resolve these issues given the current prohibition against the buying and selling of organs.

The cost of this prohibition is that lives are being lost. Additional incentives, including monetary, are required if cadaveric organ donations are to increase substantially. Even if these incentives do not eliminate the need for rationing, each additional organ procured will reduce the difficult, and sometimes arbitrary, decisions that UNOS must make. While many feel that the distribution of organs is too important to be left to market forces, ultimately, it is too important not to be.

Notes

1. Some states developed other rationing schemes based on license plate numbers and birthdays. These were largely ineffective in reducing queuing.

2. Specifically, the law prohibits the selling of organs if the transfer affects interstate commerce. Therefore, states may allow payments for organs, as long as the organs stay within state boundaries. However, given the current distribution system, states find it problematic to allow the selling of organs. Thus, the 1984 law has effectively prohibited a market in transplantable organs.

3. There may be social costs associated with discrimination, but it is costless for the individual firm.

4. A similar tradeoff exists during wartime with the triage of combat victims. This system maximizes overall survival by allowing the most critically ill soldiers to die.

5. This assumes that all intensive-care patients would die within two years without a transplant.

6. Biological matching is not considered for livers and hearts because of time constraints. Ordinarily, when transplanting kidneys, a patient's health status is not considered given the alternative of dialysis.

7. Currently, UNOS gives only slight priority to waiting time.

8. Estimate is based on authors' calculations.

9. The exception is if an individual with a perfect match is identified in another region.

10. There are costs involved in distributing organs nationally, because of increases in ischemic (preservation) time. These costs are small for kidneys, but large for other organs such as hearts. The feasibility of distributing livers nationally is currently being debated.

11. Nevertheless, many argue that steps should be taken to end "discrimination. As a result, the number of black transplant coordinators has been increased in an effort to ensure that blacks have equal access to transplants. Not surprisingly, these efforts have failed.

12. One reason for the law's failure is lack of enforcement. There is a remarkable belief that monitoring is unnecessary. One staff member from Oregon's Health Department expresses it this way: "In a small state one does not need to coerce people to comply, especially with a requirement that is perceived as good policy."

13. Recently, however, doctors successfully transplanted a segment (lobe) of liver from a living donor.

14. A new laparoscopic procedure could reduce the recovery time from two to three months to two to three weeks. Doctors and ethicists are divided over the ethics of allowing living kidney donations.

15. UNOS's procedures do allow for the trading of cadaveric organs. For example, when one region receives a perfectly matched kidney from outside the area, UNOS requires that the receiving region eventually reimburse the sending region with a payback kidney.

16. The extent to which payments would elicit donations is unclear. The answer will likely come from pilot programs, such as the one recently introduced in Pennsylvania. Residents are offered the opportunity to contribute one dollar to a "Donor Awareness Trust Fund" when they renew their drivers' licenses or complete their state income tax forms. Up to 10 percent of this fund (a maximum of $3,000) can be redistributed to families of deceased donors for hospital, medical, and funeral costs.

17. Actually, the notion of market-clearing in this market is ambiguous. By convention, an organ shortage is defined to occur when the quantity demanded (as measured by waiting-list patients) exceeds the annual supply. At any point in

time, however, the quantity of organs demanded will exceed the available supply, even in a free market. Effectively, the relevant time frame for market-clearing should be organ-specific and should depend on the mortality rate of those awaiting transplants.

18. Medicare covers almost all kidney recipients and pays 80 percent of expenses. The remaining 20 percent is picked up by either private insurance or Medicaid.

NO

Nancy Scheper-Hughes

The End of the Body

The Global Economy and Brute Life

In a recent issue of *Atlantic Monthly* (January 1998) George Soros, best known as a world-class billionaire financier, analyzed some of the deficiencies of the global capitalist economy. It is a fairly elementary exercise, but coming from a person in his position, one tends to sit up and take notice. The benefits of world capitalism, Mr. Soros notes, are unevenly distributed. Capital is in a better position than labor. And, surely it is better to be situated at the center of the global economy than at the peripheries. Given the inherent instability of the global financial system, *busts* will inevitably follow *booms,* like night the day, and capital tends to return to its centers leaving the minor players in faraway places high and dry. Meanwhile, the rapid growth of global monopolies have compromised the authority of states and weakened their regulatory functions.

But what bothers Mr. Soros most is the erosion of social values and social cohesion in the face of the increasing dominance of anti-social market values. Not that markets are to be blamed, of course. By their very nature markets are indiscriminate, promiscuous and inclined to reduce everything, including human beings, their labor and even their reproductive capacity to the status of commodities, to things that can be bought, sold, traded, and stolen. So, while, according to Mr. Soros, a Market Economy is generally a good thing, we cannot live by markets alone. "Open" and democratic societies require strong social institutions to serve such vital goals as social justice, political freedom, bodily integrity and other human rights. The real dilemma, as Mr. Soros sees it, is one of uneven development. The evolution of the global market has outstripped the development of a mediating global society.

Indeed, amidst the neo-liberal readjustments of virtually all contemporary societies, North and South, we are experiencing today a rapid depletion, an "emptying out" even, of the traditional modernist, humanist, and pastoral ideologies and practices. But meanwhile, new mediations between capital and work, between bodies and the state, belonging and extra-territoriality, and even between, social exclusion and medical-technological inclusion are taking shape. So, rather than a conventional story of the sad decline of humanistic social values and social relations, our discussion is tethered to a frank recogni-

From Nancy Scheper-Hughes, "The End of the Body: The Global Traffic in Organs for Transplant Surgery," Organs Watch, http://sunsite.berkeley.edu/biotech/organswatch/pages/cadraft.html (May 14, 1998). Copyright © 1998 by Organs Watch. Reprinted by permission of the author. References omitted. An adapted version of this article was published as "The Global Traffic in Human Organs," *Current Anthropology,* vol. 41, no. 2 (April 2000).

tion that the conventional grounds on which those modernist values and practices were based have shifted beyond recognition.

Nowhere, perhaps, are these processes more transparent than in the rapid dissemination in the past decade of organ transplantation technologies and practices which under the ideal conditions of an "open," neo-liberal, global Market Economy has allowed for an unprecedented movement of, among other "things," mortally sick bodies moving in one direction and detached "healthy" organs (transported by commercial airlines in ordinary plastic beer coolers stored in the overhead luggage compartment of the economy section) in another direction, creating a bizarre "kula ring" of international trade. This essay critically explores—with particular reference to recent organ transplantation "developments" in Brazil, South Africa, India, the United States, and China—the new forms of bio-economics and bio-sociality (Rabinow 1996) that are now emerging in the wake of the internationalization of this immensely powerful, if crude, medical technology.

What is needed, then, is something akin to Donna Haraway's (1985) radical "manifesto" for the cyborg bodies and cyborg selves that we have, in fact, already become through the appearance of these strange markets, excess capital, advanced bio-technology, "surplus bodies" and human "spare parts." Together, these have allowed for a spectacularly lucrative world trade in organ transplantation which promises to certain, select individuals of reasonable economic "means" living almost anywhere in the world—from the Kalahari Desert in Botswana to the deserts of the Arab Emirate of Oman—a "miraculous" extension in what Giorgio Agamben (1998) refers to as "brute" or "bare" life, the elementary form of biological "species life." This, in turn, is made possible by the internal and domestic reorganization of neo-liberal, democratic states and their successful capture of the "cadaver" now redefined as the "state's body" and the concomitant politicization of death. By this we mean the increasing capacity of the post-transplantation State to define and determine the hour of death and to claim, unashamedly, the "first rights" (and first *rites*) to the disposal of the body's parts.

Until very recently, only highly deviant authoritarian and police states—Nazi Germany, Argentina in the late 1970s, Brazil in the 1960s and 1970s, and South Africa under apartheid—had assumed this capacity in the 20th century, this final word, as it were, over brute life, politicized death, and the creation and *maintenance* of a surplus population of "living dead," whether Black industrial workers kept in barbaric worker hostels in apartheid South Africa (see Ramphele 1994), the "disappeared" in Argentina, or those walking cadavers kept hostage in Nazi concentration camps. The "democratization" of practices bearing at least some family resemblances to these (i.e., the "living dead" maintained in intensive care units for the purpose of organ retrieval) in neo-liberal states has generally occurred in the absence of public outrage or resistance, with the possible exception of public unrest following democratic Brazils' passage of its authoritarian law of "presumed consent" to organ donation in 1997, which we shall discuss. . . .

In the face of this ultimate, late modern dilemma—this "end of the body" as we see it—the task of anthropology is relatively clear and straight forward: the recovery of our discipline's unrealized radical epistemological promise and a commitment to the "primacy of the ethical" (Scheper-Hughes 1994) while daring to risk practical, even political, involvement in the dangerous topic[1] under consideration. The need to define new ethical standards for the international practice of organ donation—especially in light of the abuses that undermine the bodily integrity of socially disadvantaged members of society and the public trust that is necessary for voluntary organ donation to continue, brought together a small international task force. The "Bellagio Task Force on Transplantation, Bodily Integrity, and the International Traffic in Organs," led by social historian, David Rothman, is comprised of a dozen international transplant surgeons, organ procurement specialists, human rights activists, and a medical anthropologist (myself, NS-H) meeting in 1995 and again in 1996 in the Rockefeller Conference Center in Bellagio, Italy. The task force is examining the ethical, social, and medical ramifications of these problems and is considering various strategies to impact them, including the creation of an international human rights body—a "Human Organs Watch," if you like—to monitor reports of any gross violations in the procurement and distribution of human organs in transplant surgery. An initial report of the Task Force was published in *Transplantation Proceedings* (Rothman et al., 1997). At the 1996 meeting, I was "delegated" by the Task Force to launch a very exploratory, ethnographic, comparative study of the social and economic context of organ transplantation, including the global and domestic traffic in organs.

The field research on which this discussion is based, therefore, derives from this "mission." It represents the preliminary findings from the early stages of the collaborative "Selling Life" project. . . .

The focus on the "commodification" of the body and body parts within the new global economy owes a particular debt to the writings and thought of Sidney Mintz, particularly his magisterial book, *Sweetness and Power*. This article is offered as a "transplanted" surrogate for the 1996 Sidney Mintz lecture which I was extremely honored to present at Johns Hopkins University.[2]

The Organs Ring and the Commodified Body

Indeed, as Arjun Appadurai has noted (1986) there is nothing fixed, stable, or sacrosanct about the "commodity candidacy" of things. Nowhere is this more dramatically illustrated than in the "booming" global and domestic markets in human organs and tissues from both living and deceased donors to supply the transplant industry, a medical business driven by the simple market calculus of "supply and demand." The very idea of organ "scarcity" is what Ivan Illich would call an artificially created need, invented by transplant technicians and dangled before the eyes of an ever expanding sick, aging, and dying population. This market is part of an impressive development and refinement of transplant technologies. These developments were facilitated historically through the medical definition of irreversible coma (at the end of the 1950s) and the new legal status of "brain death" (at the end of the 1960s) in which, as Giorgio Agamben (1998:163) notes, death became an epiphenomenon of transplant technologies. These transformations reveal the extent to which the sovereign power of postmodern states, both "democratic" and authoritarian, is operationalized through the life sciences and medical practices. These apparatuses, sciences, and technologies are globally integrated in markets which, in turn, increasingly reconfigure local states and local "cultures."

Lawrence Cohen, for example, who has worked in rural towns in various regions of India, from north to south, now reports that in a very brief period of time the idea of trading "a kidney for a dowry" has caught on and become one strategy for poor parents desperate to arrange a comfortable marriage for an "extra" daughter. In other words, a spare kidney for a spare daughter. Cohen notes that ten years ago when villagers and townspeople first heard through newspaper reports of kidney sales occurring in the cities of Bombay and Madras they responded with predictable alarm and revulsion. Today, some of these same villagers speak *matter of factly* about just when in the course of a family cycle it might be necessary to sell a "spare" organ. Some village parents say they can no longer complain about the fate of a dowry-less daughter. "Haven't you got a spare kidney?" one or another unsympathetic neighbor is likely to respond.

And in rural Brazil, over a similarly short period and in response to demands to "donate" a kidney to a family member, working class people have begun to view their bodies and body parts as comprised of unessential redundancies. "Nanci," I was challenged by a forty year old woman who had "given" a kidney (for a small compensation) to a distant relation, "Wouldn't you feel compelled to give an organ of which you yourself had two and the other 'fellow' had none?" I pointed out, rather lamely, that the Good Lord had given us two of quite a few organs and I hated to think of myself as selfish (*egoista*) for wanting to hang on to as many of the pairs as I could! It was not so long ago— 1986, in fact—and in this same community when I had been invited to accompany a small procession to the graveyard where we ceremoniously buried a "fellow's" amputated foot! The folk Catholic ideology of the sacredness of the body—and the integrity of its component parts— was still then the commanding ethos. And though I felt a bit silly giving that gangrenous foot the benefit of a decade of the rosary as a "send off," Rosalva's reconceptualization in the late 1990s of her body as a mere reservoir of spare parts struck me as a troublesome turn of events.

The particular and well documented case of organ selling and, more recently, of organ stealing (see *New York Times,* May 12, 1998) in Indian villages is but one small, if well documented, link in a "booming" world market in organs and human tissues (not to mention blood, semen, ova, and babies) that links east and west, north and south. Over the past 30 years, organ transplantation has been transformed from a rare and experimental procedure performed in a few advanced medical centers in the first world to a fairly common therapeutic procedure carried out in hospitals and clinics, not all of them certified and legitimate, throughout the world. Kidney transplantation, which is the most universal form of organ transplant, is now conducted in the U.S., in most European and Asian countries, in several South American and Middle Eastern countries, and in a few African countries (in North Africa and South Africa). Survival rates for kidney transplant have increased markedly over the past decade, although these still vary by country and by quality and type of organ (living or cadaveric).

Until recently the "best" medical option for kidney transplantation was using a genetically closely related living donor (Fischel 1991). Today, however, morbidity rates from infection and hepatitis are higher in countries like Brazil, India, and China, which still rely heavily on living kidney donors than in the U.S., Canada, and the countries of Western Europe which rely more on cadaveric donation. But within some poorer countries to the South, like Brazil, survival rates for kidney transplant are still better with a matched living donor than with an "anonymous" cadaveric organ which stands a good chance of not having been adequately tested or screened.

Organ transplantation now takes place in a trans-national space with both donors and recipients following the paths of capital and technology in the global economy. In general, the movement of donor organs follows modern routes of capital: *from South to North, from third world to first world, from poor to rich bodies, from black and brown to white bodies, from young to old bodies, productive to less productive, and female to male bodies.* Residents of the Gulf States (Kuwait, Saudi Arabia, Oman, United Arab Emirates) travel primarily to India to obtain kidneys, while residents of Taiwan, Hong Kong, Korea and Singapore travel to mainland China for transplant surgery, allegedly with organs removed from executed prisoners. Japanese patients travel to North America as well as to Taiwan and Singapore for organs retrieved from brain dead donors, a definition of death only very recently and reluctantly accepted in Japan.

And, a great many people—and by no means are all of them wealthy—have shown their willingness to travel great distances to secure a transplant using both legal and illegal channels. This is so even when the survival rates in some of the more commercialized contexts is quite poor. Between 1983–1988, 131 patients from just three renal units in the United Arab Emirates and Oman traveled to Bombay, India where they purchased, through local brokers, kidneys from living donors. The donors, from urban shantytowns outside Bombay, were compensated between $2,000 and $3,000 for a kidney. News of the "organs bazaars" operating in the slums of Bombay, Calcutta and Madras appeared in Indian weeklies and in special reports by ABC and the BBC. Meanwhile, prestigious medical journals, (including *The Lancet* and *Transplant Proceedings*) published dozens of articles analyzing the medical risks and poor outcomes resulting from transplantation using "poor quality" kidneys from medically compromised "donors."[3]

A medically invented, artificial scarcity in human organs for transplantation has generated a kind of panic and a desperate international search for them and for new surgical possibilities. Bearing many similarities to the international market in adoption, those looking for transplant organs are so single minded in their quest that they are sometimes willing to put aside questions about how the organ [or "the baby" in the case of adoption] was obtained. In both instances the language of "gifts," "donations," "heroic rescues" and "saving lives" masks the extent to which ethically dubious and even illegal practices are used to obtain the desired "scarce" commodity, infant or kidney, for which foreigners (or "better off" nationals) are willing to pay what to ordinary people seems a king's ransom. With desperation built in on both sides of the equation—deathly ill "buyers" and desperately needy "sellers"—once seemingly "timeless" reli-

gious beliefs in the sanctity of the body and proscriptions against body mutila-
tion have collapsed over night in some parts of the third world under the
weight of these new market's demands. These new demands are driven by the
rapid dissemination of the medical technology and expertise of transplant
surgery and a new global social imagry about the possibilities of bodily rejuve-
nation and "repair" through organ replacement.

The gap between supply and demand that drives the new global trade in
organs is exacerbated by religious sanctions and/or cultural inhibitions with respect to "brain death" and the proper handling of the dead body. Prohibitions
in one country or region can stimulate an "organs market" in more secular or
culturally pluralistic neighboring countries or regions. Meanwhile, the
"scarcity" of organs produced in the wake of centralized "waiting lists" for transplantation has provided many incentives to physicians, hospital administrators, government officials, and blatantly commercial intermediaries to engage
in ethically questionable tactics for obtaining organs. For example, heart transplantation is hardly performed at all in Japan due to deep reservations about the
social definition of brain death, while most kidney transplants are gotten with
living, related donors (see Lock 1996, 1997; Ohnuki-Tierney 1994).

For many years desperate Japanese nationals have resorted to intermediaries with connections to the underworld of organized crime (the so called
"body mafia") to locate donor hearts or (when lacking related donors), paid unrelated kidney donors in other countries, including the United States. According to Lock (personal communication, 1997) who is engaged in a comparative
study of transplant surgery in Japan and Canada (1996, 1997), a ring of Japanese
yakuza gangsters, working on behalf of desperate Japanese transplant candidates through connections at a major medical center in Boston was uncovered
by journalists and broken up by police there a decade ago. And, until recently,
Japanese kidney patients also traveled to Taiwan and Singapore to purchase organs obtained (without consent) from executed prisoners, until this practice
was roundly condemned by the World Medical Association in 1994 and was
prohibited by new regulations.

The ban on the use of organs from executed prisoners in one part of "capitalist" Asia, opened up the possibilities for a similar practice in another part of
"communist" Asia. The demand for hard currency by strapped governments
recognizes no fixed ideological or political boundaries. Recently, the *New York
Times* (February 24, 1998) reported on an FBI operation which led to the arrest
of two Chinese citizens charged with conspiring to sell human organs of executed prisoners. The undercover "sting" operation was set up by the human
rights activist, Harry Wu, who has been alerting the world since the 1980s to
this alleged, covert practice in China. This particular case is still pending investigations, but its outcome may determine once and for all the veracity of Harry
Wu's (and other human right activists') contested claims about the organs trade
in China today, which we will discuss at greater length below.

Despite the publicity and attention to the more spectacular international
traffic in human organs, an equally important though far less explored dimension of the organs trade is domestic, following the usual routes of social and
economic cleavages and obeying domestic rules of class, race, gender, and geog-

raphy. Dr. X, an elderly Brazilian surgeon and nephrologist, admitted during an interview in São Paulo in 1997 that "the commerce in organs has always been a reality in Brazil and among and between Brazilians.

"Those who suffer most," he said, are the usual "nobodies," mostly poor and uneducated, who are tricked into "donation" through illegal and unethical bodily transactions. The elderly doctor cited a transplantation scandal that occurred in Brazil in the late 1980s, one of several such cases exposed by local journalists and human rights activists. This particular one concerned a young accident victim, a mere girl of 12 years, from the interior town of Taubate, who while undergoing surgery on her broken leg, had a "spare" kidney removed by unscrupulous surgeons. Following a complaint lodged by her family who noticed a scar where none should have been, the local Public Defender began an investigation but it was interrupted by the Federal Police. Consequently, the Federal Board of Medicine was "compelled" to pass a verdict of "not guilty" due to lack of evidence.

But the poor and socially disadvantaged populations of Brazil and elsewhere in the world have not remained silent in the face of these threats and assaults to their health and to their bodily integrity, security, and dignity. For many years these marginal populations, living in urban shantytowns and hillside favelas, possessing little or no "symbolic capital" have announced their fears and their outrage through the idiom of seemingly "wild" rumors and urban legends . . . that warn of the existence and the dangerous proximity of markets in bodies and body parts (Scheper-Hughes 1996). The circulation of the rumors and "urban legends" of organ theft have produced in their wake a climate of hostile "civil" resistance toward even legitimate and altruistic organ donation and organ transplantation in some countries to the South (such as Brazil and Argentina) where voluntary donations began to drop precipitously in the 1980s. Medical associations and governments have tried, without success, to correct the "disinformation" being disseminated by the persistent organ stealing rumors.

And, in a curious reversal, these "illiterate" rumors originating in the periphery have migrated to the comfortable and affluent "core," the comfortable middle class communities of the U.S. Despite the appointment of a full-time USIA [United States Information Agency] disinformation specialist, Todd Leventhal (see USIA 1994) who has led a long and expensive U.S. government campaign to kill the "body parts" rumor, as recently as the late fall of 1997 a variant of the organ stealing rumor carrying dire warnings about the existence of seductive female (or, less often, male) medical "agents" involved in the body parts trade was circulated among thousands of Americans via an electronic mail "chain letter." One strand of the chain was passed among a network of progressive academics, and to my amusement I was one of the recipients. The warning was followed a few days later by an apology stating that the story may have been "just a rumor."

Indeed, it would seem from this that a great many people in the world, both North and South, are uneasy. Something seems amiss or profoundly wrong about the nature of the beast that medical technology has released in the name of transplant surgery. But why now, why so many years later? Has transplant surgery opened a Pandora's Box that has resulted in a long overdue, popular backlash? Or, is there something new about the current organization of transplant surgery that has turned a once proud and altruistic moment in medical history into something unseemly and grotesque?

Dr. B., a heart transplant surgeon in Cape Town, South Africa whom I interviewed in February 1998, said he has become very *"disheartened"* about his profession's recent decline in prestige, trust, and value: "Organ transplantation has moved from an era back in 1967 when the atmosphere and public attitude was very different. . . . You know, people then still spoke about organ donation as that fantastic gift. Our first organ donor, Denise Dawer, and her family, were very much hallowed here. They were given a lot of credit for what they did and their photos are displayed in our hospital's new Transplant Museum. Society at that stage was still very positive. Now that there have been hundreds of thousands of donors throughout the world, the idea of organ donation has lost some of its luster. And, donors' families throughout the world have been put under a lot more pressure. And there have been some incidents that were unfortunate. . . . So we've begun to all of a sudden to experience a sea of backlash. In Europe there has been a strong backlash because of the state's demand, the moral requirement even, to donate. Europeans have generally had a good social conscience, they tend to believe in the better good of society, and so up until now they supported organ transplantation as a social good. But, now, suddenly objections are beginning to be raised. The Lutheran Church in Germany, for example, has started to question the idea of brain death, long after it had been generally accepted there. And so we have seen a drop of about 20% in organ donations in Europe, but especially in Germany. This is entirely new. So we are experiencing a real backlash, and what happens in Germany, unfortunately, has repercussions for South Africa.". . .

The Right to Sell and Future Markets

Despite evidence of widespread moral panic about bodily integrity and organ stealing some transplant surgeons and bioethicists, like Dr. Abdullah Daar, a member of the Bellagio Task Force, [a working group set up by Columbia University to study the use of organs for transplantations] sees the commercialization and commodification of human organs, whether one likes it or not, as a fait accompli. Labor is sold, sex is sold, sperm and ova are sold, even babies are sold in international adoption. What makes kidneys so special, so exempt? Daar has asked repeatedly. What is needed, he insists, is rigorous oversight and regulation in addition to an official Donors Bill of Rights that would both inform and protect potential donors.

But other members of the Task Force argue with Daar's reliance on western notions of contract and individual "choice." They are mindful of the social and economic context that makes the "choice" to sell a kidney anything but a "free" and "autonomous" one in an urban slum of Calcutta or a shantytown of São Paulo. Similarly, the idea of "consent" is problematic in a prison with the executioner looking over one's shoulder. In response to Daar's critique of human rights "paternalism" and his defense of the autonomy of the individual and his or her right to sell an organ, Veena Das has countered that in all notions of contract there are certain exclusions—such as in family law, labor law, and anti-trust law. There are basic assumptions concerning protected areas of life—anything that would damage social or community relations—that should be taken outside of contract theory. A market price—even a fair one—on body parts exploits the desperation of the poor. In addition, many humanists and bioethicists hold it to be self-evident that certain objects (like irreplaceable, non renewable solid organs) are fundamentally "inalienable" from the person. To ask the law to negotiate, as Daar suggests, a fair and reasonable price for a live human kidney is asking the law to go against everything that contract theory (as well as society) stands for. In addition, one has to be concerned about the effects of organ sales on the coarsening of medical practice and on doctors who are forced to inflict physical harm on one person who is not viewed as a "patient" in order to save the life of another individual who is exclusively viewed as "the patient."

Nonetheless, the movement toward commercialization is gaining ground in the United States. The AMA (American Medical Association) is currently considering the possibility of financial incentives that would enable people to bequeath organs to their heirs or to charity for a price. Dr. L.R. Cohen (no relation to anthropologist Lawrence Cohen) has proposed a "futures market" in cadavcric organs that would operate through contracts offered to the general public. These contracts would provide that at the time of the seller's death, if organs are successfully transplanted from his body, a substantial sum would be paid to his designee. He suggests $5,000 per major organ utilized. Cohen's proposal is based on the idea that a market can exist side by side with and even supplement altruism. Pure gifting can always be expected among family members, but financial inducements might be necessary to provide organs for strangers.

Dr. Charles Plows, Chair of the AMA's Committee on Ethical and Judicial Affairs agrees in principle with Cohen's proposal: "The only one who doesn't get anything out of this whole transplant transaction is the person who's deceased. The hospital makes money out of furnishing the areas where this work is done. Certainly, transplant surgeons do well for themselves. The patient gets a life-saving organ. But the man or woman who's donating the organ receives nothing." At present the AMA is exploring several options. One is a fixed price per organ. Another is to let market forces—supply and demand—set the price. The idea still makes a lot of doctors in the U.S. uncomfortable, but Dr. Plows and his colleague hope to get a pilot project off the ground in 1998.

India: Kidney Bazaar

The first inklings of a commercial market in organ trafficking appeared in 1983 when an American physician, H. Barry Jacobs, established the International Kidney Exchange in an attempt to broker kidneys from living donors in the Third World, especially India. By the early 1990s upwards of 2,000 kidney *transplants with living donors* were performed each year in India, leading Prakash Chandra (1991) and other investigative journalists to refer to their country as the "great organ bazaar of the world." Proponents of paid living donors, such as Dr. K.C. Reddy, an Indian urologist with a thriving practice of kidney transplantation in Madras, argued that legalizing the trade would eliminate middle men who profit by exploiting paid donors.

Meanwhile, the free market in kidneys that catered through the 1980s to wealthy patients from the Middle East was forced underground following the passage of a law in 1994 that criminalizes organ sales. Recent reports by human rights activists, journalists, and medical anthropologists, including Lawrence Cohen, indicate that the law has produced in its wake an even larger *domestic* black market in kidneys. In some areas this new business is controlled by organized, cash-rich crime gangs expanding out from the heroin trade (in some cases with the backing of local political leaders). In other areas the business are controlled by ever more wealthy owners of profit hospitals.

An investigative report (*Frontline* December 26, 1997) found that a doctor-broker nexus in Bangalore and Madras still profits from the sale of kidneys by poor Indian donors to rich Indians, and to a smaller number of absolutely desperate foreigners with end-stage renal disease. A loophole in the law allows unrelated donors related to recipients by "ties of affection" to give a kidney following approval by local Medical Authorization Committees. These committees have been readily corrupted in areas where kidney sales have become an important source of local income. The result is that sales are now conducted with official seals of approval by the local Authorization Committee.

Today, Lawrence Cohen reports from the field, only the very rich can get an unrelated kidney. In addition to paying the donor, the middle men, and the hospital, now they must bribe the Authorization Committee members as well. As for the kidney sellers, recruited by brokers who get half the cost of the sale, almost all are trapped in terrible cycles of debt and caught in the clutches of money lenders. The kidney trade is another link, Cohen suggests, in an older and earlier system of debt peonage which has been reinforced by neo-liberal structural readjustment policies. Kidney sales are a key sign, says Cohen, of the sometimes bizarre effects of a global capitalism that seeks to turn everything into a commodity.

And there are hints and allegations of criminal practices within this climate of rampant commercialism. During the Berkeley conference on the commercialization of organs, Das told an NPR (National Public Radio, "Marketplace" program) reporter of a young woman she encountered in Delhi whose stomach pains were diagnosed as a bladder stone requiring surgery. But, in fact, the doctor, the woman charged, used the bladder stone as a pretext to operate and remove one of her kidneys which he delivered to a middleman for an undisclosed and confidential third party.

China: Collective Bodies

Today, China stands alone in continuing to use the organs of executed prisoners for transplant surgery. Although this practice has been documented by various international human rights organizations and investigated even by the FBI, Chinese public officials have impeded any form of inspection or verification of the executions. In October 1984, a Chinese government directive issued a document stating that "the use of corpses or organs of executed criminals *must be kept strictly secret,* and attention must be paid to avoid negative repercussions" (cited in *Human Rights Watch/Asia* 1994:7).

Following up on a report published by Human Rights Watch/Asia in August 1994 on "Organ Procurement and Judicial Execution in China," David Rothman visited major hospitals in Beijing and Shanghai in 1995 where he interviewed transplant surgeons and other medical officers about the technical and the social dimensions of transplant surgery as practiced at their respective units. While the surgeons and hospital administrators answered technical questions freely and accurately, they refused to respond to such questions as: Where do donated organs come from? How many foreigners come to the medical institutions seeking transplants? How much do the hospitals charge for various transplant operations?

While the "blank stares" of Chinese medical personnel that Rothman encountered in response to his questions are no proof of complicity or guilt, Dr. C.J. Lee, head of a transplant team in Taiwan, and member of the Bellagio Task Force, shared with the Task Force his personal knowledge and experience of transplant practices in Asia. The use of the organs of executed prisoners was practiced at his own unit in Taiwan until the country responded to the pressure of international human rights activists against it. China has held out, in part, Dr. Lee suggests, because of the need for foreign dollars and in part because there is less ethical soul-searching in China (as elsewhere in Asia) [or] "informed consent." And, an alternative social ethic interprets the practice as a kind of public service, an opportunity to pay the community back for wrongs committed and to gain merit for one's self.

Of course, not all Chinese embrace this collectivist ethos and some see the practice as a gross human rights abuse. Mr. Lin, a recent Chinese immigrant to California, reported a disturbing story (recorded for NPR's "Marketplace") during the Berkeley conference on the commercialization of organs, 1996. Just before arriving in California two years ago he visited a friend at a medical center in Shanghai. In the bed next to his friend was a wealthy and politically well situated professional man who told Mr. Lin that he was waiting for a kidney transplant later that day. His new kidney would arrive, he said, as soon as a prisoner was executed that morning. Minutes after the condemned prisoner was shot in the head, doctors present at the execution would quickly extract his kidneys and rush them to the hospital where two transplant surgery teams would be assembled and waiting. Reports by Human Rights Watch/Asia and by the Laogai Research Foundation (January 1995) have documented through Chinese informants and available medical and prison statistics that the state systematically takes kidneys, cornea, liver tissue and heart valves from executed prisoners. While these organs are sometimes given to reward politically well connected Chinese, often they are sold to medical "visitors" from Hong Kong, Taiwan, Singapore and other Pacific Rim nations who will pay as much as $30,000 for an organ.

Harry Wu, the human rights activist imprisoned in China until recently, was among the first to reveal the sale of prisoners' organs. At the Berkeley conference Wu said: "In 1992 I interviewed a doctor who routinely participated in removing kidneys from condemned prisoners. In one case she said, breaking down in the telling, that she had even participated in a surgery in which two kidneys were removed from a living, anesthetized prisoner late at night. The following morning the prisoner was executed by a bullet to the head." In this chilling case, brain death followed, rather than preceded, the harvesting of his vital organs.

Wu and other human rights activists claim that the Chinese Government takes organs from 2,000 executed prisoners each year. Moreover, that number is growing because the list of capital crimes in China has been expanded to accommodate the demand for organs. While the precise number of prisoners executed in China each year is unknown, Amnesty International has recently reported that a new "Strike Hard" anti-crime campaign has led to a sharp increase in the number of people executed, among them petty thieves and tax cheaters. In 1996 alone at least 6,100 death sentences were handed out and at least 4,367 confirmed executions took place. David Rothman, among others, is convinced that what lies behind the draconian anti-crime campaign is a "thriving medical business" that relies on prisoners' organs for raw materials. The state is sponsoring, he says, an "insatiable killing machine" driven by the rapacious "need" for fresh and healthy organs.

Recently, Wu's allegations have been bolstered following a sting operation he set up in New York City that led to the arrest of two Chinese citizens offering to sell cornea, kidneys, livers and other human organs to American doctors wanting them for transplant surgery. Posing in the undercover operation as a prospective customer from a dialysis center, Wu produced a video tape of the men, Mr. Wang Chenyong and Mr. Fu Xingqi in a Manhattan hotel room offering to sell him quality organs from a dependable source—fifty to two hundred prisoners executed on Hainan Island each year. Mr. Wang guaranteed this commitment by producing documents to Wu indicating that he had been deputy chief of criminal prosecutions in that prison. A pair of cornea would cost an exorbitant $5,000. In a taped telephone call, Wang boasted of making a 1000% profit (*Mail and Guardian* 2/27/1998; *San Jose Mercury News* 3/19/98; *New York Times* 2/24/98). Following their arrest by FBI agents the men were charged with conspiring to sell human organs and are being held without bond awaiting criminal proceedings. As a further fallout, a German company, Frenesius Medical Care A.G., based in a suburb of Frankfurt, announced that it was ending its half-interest in a kidney dialysis unit (next to a transplant clinic) in Guangzhou, China, citing the company's strong suspicions that foreign patients visiting the center may also be there to receive "kidneys harvested from executed Chinese criminals" (*New York Times* 3/7/98). [A] Frenesius spokesman stated that the company did not know anything about the "cover-up" role of the dialysis center and that the center was totally administered by Chinese medical personnel and controlled by military commands. . . .

The Move to Primary Care and Privatization of Organ Transplantation

. . . As organ transplantation moves into the private sector, a creeping commercialism has necessarily taken hold. In the absence of a national policy regulating transplant surgery, and no regional, let alone national, official waiting lists, the distribution of transplantable organs is appallingly informal and subject to corruption. Public and private hospitals can hire their own transplant co-ordinators who are under pressure from competing, even warring, factions to "drop" the usable heart or kidney in a bucket rather than give it to a competitor. The situation is grave. The temptation "to accommodate" patients who are able to pay is affecting both the public and private sector hospitals. At Groote-Schurr Hospital's kidney transplant unit, a steady trickle of donor "couples" arrive from Mauritius and Nimibia. Although they claim to be related, the nurses say that many are simply paid donors, but since they arrive from across the border, the doctors look the other way. While I was in Cape Town, a very ill older busi-ness man from the Cameroons arrived at the kidney transplant unit with a paid donor the man found in Johannesburg. The donor was a young university stu-dent from Burundi who agreed to part with one of his kidneys for his expenses and a bonus of 2,000 rand (about $400). The head of the kidney unit read the international medical codes against organ sales to the pair, explained the risks and dangers of living kidney donation, but as they persisted he agreed to order the blood matching tests. When they failed to match and were turned away, the symbiotic pair begged to be transplanted in any case. Such was their almost unimaginable desperation, that they were willing to face the eventuality of al-most certain organ rejection. Of course, the doctors refused their plea. Will pri-vate hospitals be as conscientious as the public ones in refusing hopeless cases among those patients willing to pay regardless of the outcome?

Meanwhile, those who live at a distance, without easy means of commu-nication and transportation, such as in the sprawling townships of Soweto out-side Johannesburg and Khayalitsha outside Cape Town have a ghost of a chance of receiving a transplant. The rule of thumb among heart and kidney transplant surgeons in Johannesburg is: "No fixed home, no phone, no organ." The ironies are striking. At the famous Chris Hani Bara Hospital on the outskirts of Soweto, I met a sprightly and playful middle aged man, flirting with nurses, during his dialysis treatment. "He's very familiar with you!" I commented to the head nurse. "And well, he might be," she replied. "He's been on the waiting list for a kidney for more than 20 years." Not a single patient at the huge Bara Hospital's kidney unit had received a transplant in the past year.

The week before I was in the splendid, suburban community of Sun Valley outside Cape Town where, in a private, gated community protected by armed guards for the comfort and security of the wealthy, white, and mostly retired residents, I met with Mr. W. Breytanbach, Ex-Deputy Minister of Defense under President P.W. Botha, still recuperating from the heart transplant he had re-ceived on his government pension and health plan in less than a month's wait. At first he was distraught on learning that he was the recipient of the heart of a young, colored nurse, and at first he blamed his difficult recovery on his "infe-rior woman's heart." He has since softened, he says, and he has even tried to contact the family of his donor through the hospital network so that he could thank them. The family has not responded. As we chatted about his time served on South Africa's notorious Security Committee, I had to control my rising sense of outrage. The sub-heading, "State Killer Gets New Heart" came several times to mind during the interview, prompting me, finally, to ask Mr. Breytan-bach if he thought he owed the new South African government something for having given him, of all people, a new lease on life. He replied:

> "To this day I still do not know why I was given a heart transplant. I know that at the time I had only 10 or 12 days at most to live and if I did not have [the operation] I would be dead. And it is great to be alive! I look at the country and I see that there may be more people more deserving than me of a heart transplant, and many who cannot get it because of a shortage of funds or of donors with so many people waiting for hearts. But by hook or by crook, I don't know how Dr. V. does it [in the private hospital] but I have been there and I can see that there are no questions asked about whether the person can really afford it or not. If need be, [heart transplant surgeon] just goes ahead and operates."

At the venerable Groote-Schuur Hospital, however, the waiting time for all major surgical procedures has increased and a virtual moratorium has brought heart transplantation to a standstill.

Concluding Remarks

Organ transplantation depends, as Cantarovitch (1990) suggests, on a social contract and social trust, the grounds for which must be explicit. This requires national and international laws protecting the rights of both organ donors and organ recipients. At a very rudimentary level, the practice of organ transplantation requires a reasonably fair and equitable health care system. For example, the Ministry of Health in Gauteng, South Africa proposed a temporary moratorium in late 1995 on heart transplants in an effort to sort out unreliable private sector doctors performing these operations under questionable medical circumstances. The present moratorium in Cape Town is more difficult to justify.

The social ethics of transplant surgery also require a reasonably democratic state in which basic human rights, especially bodily integrity, are protected and guaranteed. Organ transplantation occurring, even in elite medical centers by the most conscientious of physicians, within the milieu of a police state or authoritarian state—as the illustrations from China, and from pre-democratic transition in Brazil and South Africa exemplify—all too readily lead to gross human rights abuses of both living and dead bodies. Similarly, where vestiges of forced labor exist (especially in "debt peonage" systems which unfairly bind workers to their "owners"), and where unjust transactions keep being "legally" and "medically" covered-up (including trade in corneas, kidneys, children and facilitation of access to care) the panic and mistrust of medicine and transplant surgery in particular will persist.

Under conditions like these the most vulnerable will continue to fight back with the only resources they have—gossip, rumors, or rebuttals and resistance to "modern laws." In this way, they settle accounts, albeit obliquely, with the "situation of emergency" that continues to exist for them in this time of economic and democratic readjustments. These subaltern lives manifest their consciousness of the real and unjust processes of social exclusion/inclusion at work in the everyday, and articulate their own ethical categories and political stances in the face of the "consuming" demands which value their bodies most at the point they can be claimed by the State as "brain dead" and therefore as a reservoir of spare parts. While to transplant surgeons and to body dealers an organ is just an organ, a heart is just a pump, and a kidney is just a filter, a thing, a commodity better used than wasted, to vast numbers of ordinary people an organ is something else—a lively, animate, spiritualized part of the self that most would still like to take with them when they die.

Notes

1. I refer to this as a "dangerous" topic advisedly. The global "organs trade" is extensive, extremely lucrative, explicitly illegal in the legal codes of most countries, unethical according to every governing body of medical, professional life, and therefore, covert. The organs trade links elite surgeons and technicians from the upper reaches of bio-medical practice to "body mafia" from the lowest reaches of the criminal world. The practice involves complicity or, at least, by-stander "passivity" from within the ranks of police, mortuary workers, pathologists, civil servants, ambulance drivers, emergency room workers, eye bank and blood bank managers, and transplant coordinators. Although I have been harassed in the field before with respect to other research projects, this is the first time when in the course of my investigations into various aspects of global traffic (organs and babies) in the interior of Brazil I was warned by a close friend of being followed by a possible "hit man" representing a local (and deeply implicated) Judge, forcing me to leave the site earlier than intended.

2. The original Sidney Mintz lecture, "Small Wars: the End of Childhood", was based on my introduction to the co-edited (with Carolyn Sargent) volume, *Small Wars: the Cultural Politics of Childhood* (University of California Press) which is slated to appear in November 1998. I gratefully acknowledge the initial critical reading of that text by Richard Fox and Sidney Mintz.

3. Saalahudeen and his colleagues (1990) noted the poor medical outcomes for the large number of patients who travelled from the Gulf States to India for organ transplants in the 1980s.

POSTSCRIPT

Should Markets Be Allowed to Solve the Shortage in Body Parts?

As Carlstrom and Rollow suggest, there are some interesting parallels between the price controls and rationing that were used to contain the surge in fuel prices after OPEC flexed its muscles in the 1970s and the initial adjustments to the current shortage of body parts. As the price of fossil fuels increased and the lines outside of filling stations lengthened, alternative sources of energy began to appear in the marketplace.

If the price of kidneys, hearts, lungs, and other transplantable organs remains high, will the development of artificial organs continue? Will the practice of transplanting organs taken from other species, such as pig hearts, into humans be perfected and more generally accepted? Will the cloning of human body parts become as widespread as the raising of antibiotic cultures in laboratories?

But even if there is a universal acceptance of "human meat markets," existing law prohibits it. In 1987 Congress revised the National Organ Transplant Act to explicitly bar the sale of human organs. Should that ban be lifted, as Carlstrom and Rollow argue? They are not alone in their attempts to legalize the sale of transplantable organs; others also support the move to create a market for body parts. Indeed, the support is widespread in the Libertarian community. Perhaps the most vocal advocate is the Cato Institute (www.cato.org), but advocacy does not end there. Former Delaware governor Pete du Pont, who serves as policy chair of the National Center for Policy Analysis, has also endorsed this position. A number of Web sites support the views of Carlstrom and Rollow. See Organ Keeper (http://www.organkeeper.com); Organ Sales.com (http://www.organsales.com); and the Organ Selling Homepage (http://web. pitt.edu/~htk/).

Those who are opposed to selling organs cringe at the thought of replacing the donor system with a vendor system. In another essay by Scheper-Hughes, "Theft of Life: The Globalization of Organ Stealing Rumors," *Anthropology Today* (June 1996), the author explores the possibility of organ theft as the high price of organs and a market to sell them in become ever more present. Many people assert that the inequities that currently exist between whites and ethnic minorities would increase sharply if society moved to a market system for the allocation of human organs. H. Leon Hewitt provides an extensive bibliography on this subject at the Web site Negative Effects of Organ Transplants, sponsored by the Institute on Race, Health Care and the Law, at http://www.udayton.edu/~health/03access/98hewitt.htm.

ISSUE 6

Is It Time to Reform Medical Malpractice Litigation?

YES: U.S. Department of Health and Human Services, from "Confronting the New Health Care Crisis: Improving Health Care Quality and Lowering Costs by Fixing Our Medical Liability System" (July 24, 2002)

NO: Jackson William, from "Bush's Medical Malpractice Disinformation Campaign: A Rebuttal to the HHS Report on Medical Liability," A Report of Public Citizen's Congress Watch (January 2003)

ISSUE SUMMARY

YES: The U.S. Department of Health and Human Services (HHS) argues that although the United States has a health care system that "is the envy of the world," it is a system that is about to be brought to its knees by aggressive attorneys who force the medical community to practice costly "defensive medicine."

NO: Jackson Williams, legal counsel for the watchdog group Public Citizen, charges that the position taken by the HHS is factually "incorrect, incomplete, or misleading" and even contradicted by other governmental agencies.

The headline reads, "Princeton Senior Permanently Disabled." The newspaper story reveals that honor student John Francis slipped on the icy steps of the Harvey S. Firestone Memorial Library after the ice storm that swept through central New Jersey last February. Francis was rushed to Pokagon Hospital, where emergency surgery was required to repair his ruptured spleen. Unfortunately, Francis failed to recover his strength and vitality after the surgery. He visited the campus infirmary, where X-rays of the surgery site revealed a silhouette of a silver object in his abdominal cavity. When Francis took the X-rays to his surgeon, it was clear that a retractor had been left behind. That is not the end of this tragic story, however. During surgery to remove this foreign object, it was discovered that the retractor had caused the growth of flesh-eating bacteria: necrotizing faciitis. The damage was severe indeed; this once avid tennis player is now permanently disabled. He will be confined to a wheelchair for the rest of his life.

The question that this news article raises is the fundamental question addressed in this issue. Francis has been irreversibly damaged by a medical mistake. The liability seems clear: someone left the retractor behind, and the presence of this foreign object has caused flesh-eating bacteria to grow and invade an otherwise healthy body.

So what is owed to Francis? Few would challenge a demand to be compensated for the explicit costs he incurred: the additional medical expenditures, his wheelchair, and perhaps the costs associated with the extra semester he will spend earning his undergraduate degree. Then there is the "gray area." What of his future employment? Although Francis can be gainfully employed, are his options now limited? If his options are limited, should he be compensated for the fact that he cannot become the tennis pro he wanted to be but must now resign himself to being a stockbroker? Is he entitled to receive compensation for the pain and suffering he will endure for the rest of his life?

It is important to note that "medical misadventures" are few and far between, given the number of medical procedures that occur annually in the United States. The U.S. medical care industry is universally regarded as the best in the world. Thousands and thousands of individuals each year undergo medical procedures in the United States. Since physicians are human, however, mistakes are made. The number of people who suffer the consequences of these mistakes is a tiny fraction of those who seek medical relief, but that number is not inconsequential. Some estimate that in 2003 alone, nearly 100,000 will die of a medical misstep. A surprising number of other surgical procedures will result in some foreign object being left behind the sutures; in fact, it is estimated that in 2003, some 1,500 retractors, gauze pads, sponges, etc., will be left behind. Consequently, Francis is not alone in facing the lifelong aftereffects of a surgery gone wrong.

In light of rapidly rising medical insurance rates, it is fair to ask what underlies those rate increases. The medical community and the medical insurance industry, backed by the George W. Bush administration, allege that jury awards for "pain and suffering" are excessive and unreasonable and that they undermine the foundations of the medical industry. Attorneys for those who are impacted by alleged medical misadventures respond that the skyrocketing medical insurance rates are not the result of jury awards and court settlements; rather, they can be traced to insurance companies that have been mismanaged and the recent decline in interest rates in the U.S. economy at large.

The following selections exhibit vastly different views as to why medical malpractice insurance rates are increasing. The U.S. Department of Health and Human Services points a finger at extreme jury awards in medical malpractice cases, arguing that these awards drive the price of malpractice insurance beyond the reach of some practitioners. As a result, these doctors must either increase their fees, which reduces accessibility, or they must begin to practice "defensive medicine"—prescribing redundant medicines, making unnecessary referrals to specialists, and recommending too many invasive procedures. Jackson Williams accuses the HHS of disinformation, concluding that medical malpractice insurance rates are rising not because of jury awards but because of poor management decisions on the part of insurance companies.

U.S. Department of Health and
Human Services

 **YES**

Confronting the New Health Care Crisis

American health care is the envy of the world, but with rapidly rising health care costs, reforms are needed to make high-quality, affordable health care more widely available. These include new approaches to making employer-provided coverage more affordable, new initiatives to help states expand Medicaid and S-CHIP [State Children's Health Insurance Program] coverage for lower-income persons, and new policies including health insurance credits for persons who do not have access to employer or public health insurance. A critical element for enabling all of these reforms to provide real relief, and to help all Americans get access to better and more affordable health care, is curbing excessive litigation.

Americans spend proportionately far more per person on the costs of litigation than any other country in the world. The excesses of the litigation system are an important contributor to "defensive medicine"—the costly use of medical treatments by a doctor for the purpose of avoiding litigation. As multi-million-dollar jury awards have become more commonplace in recent years, these problems have reached crisis proportions. Insurance premiums for malpractice are increasing at a rapid rate, particularly in states that have not taken steps to make their legal systems function more predictably and effectively. Doctors are facing much higher costs of insurance, and some cannot obtain insurance despite having never lost a single malpractice judgment or even faced a claim.

This is a threat to health care quality for all Americans. Increasingly, Americans are at risk of not being able to find a doctor when they most need one because the doctor has given up practice, limited the practice to patients without health conditions that would increase the litigation risk, or moved to a state with a fairer legal system where insurance can be obtained at a lower price.

This broken system of litigation is also raising the cost of health care that all Americans pay, through out-of-pocket payments, insurance premiums, and federal taxes. Excessive litigation is impeding efforts to improve quality of care. Hospitals, doctors, and nurses are reluctant to report problems and participate in joint efforts to improve care because they fear being dragged into lawsuits, even if they did nothing wrong.

From U.S. Department of Health and Human Services, Office of the Assistant Secretary for Planning and Evaluation, "Confronting the New Health Care Crisis: Improving Health Care Quality and Lowering Costs by Fixing Our Medical Liability System" (July 24, 2002). Notes omitted.

Increasingly extreme judgments in a small proportion of cases and the settlements they influence are driving this litigation crisis. At the same time, most injured patients receive no compensation. Some states have already taken action to squeeze the excesses out of the litigation system. But federal action, in conjunction with further action by states, is essential to help Americans get high-quality care when they need it, at a more affordable cost.

Access to Care Is Threatened

There are a number of obstacles that limit access to affordable health care in this country, including lack of affordable insurance and an outdated Medicare program. We now face another—the litigation crisis that has made insurance premiums unaffordable or even unavailable for many doctors, through no fault of their own. This is making it more difficult for many Americans to find care, and threatening access for many more.

- Nevada is facing unprecedented problems in assuring quick access to urgently needed care. The University of Nevada Medical Center closed its trauma center in Las Vegas for ten days earlier this month [July 2002]. Its surgeons had quit because they could no longer afford malpractice insurance. Their premiums had increased sharply, some from $40,000 to $200,000. The trauma center was able to re-open only because some of the surgeons agreed to become county government employees for a limited time, which capped their liability for non-economic damages if they were sued. This is obviously only a temporary solution. If the Las Vegas trauma center closes again, the most severely injured patients will have to be transported to the next nearest Level 1 trauma center, five hours away. Access to trauma care is only one problem Nevada faces; access to obstetrics and many other types of care is also threatened.

- Overall, more than 10% of all doctors in Las Vegas are expected to retire, or relocate their practices by this summer. For example, Dr. Cheryl Edwards, 41, closed her decade-old obstetrics and gynecology practice in Las Vegas because her insurance premium jumped from $37,000 to $150,000 a year. She moved her practice to West Los Angeles, leaving 30 pregnant women to find new doctors.

- Dr. Frank Jordan, a vascular surgeon, in Las Vegas, left practice. "I did the math. If I were to stay in business for three years, it would cost me $1.2 million for insurance. I obviously can't afford that. I'd be bankrupt after the first year, and I'd just be working for the insurance company. What's the point?"

- Other states are facing the same problem. A doctor in a small town in North Carolina decided to take early retirement when his premiums skyrocketed from $7,500 to $37,000 per year. His partner, unable to afford the practice expenses by himself, may now close the practice, and work at a teaching hospital.

- Pennsylvania physicians are also leaving their practices. About 44 doctors at the height of their careers in Delaware County outside Philadelphia left the state in 2001 or stopped practicing medicine because of high malpractice insurance costs. . . .

Patient Safety Is Jeopardized

Because the litigation system does not accurately judge whether an error was committed in the course of medical care, physicians adjust their behavior to avoid being sued. A recent survey of physicians revealed that one-third shied away from going into a particular specialty because they feared it would subject them to greater liability exposure. When in practice, they engage in defensive medicine to protect themselves against suit. They perform tests and provide treatments that they would not otherwise perform merely to protect themselves against the risk of possible litigation. The survey revealed that over 76% are concerned that malpractice litigation has hurt their ability to provide quality care to patients.

Because of the resulting legal fear:

- 79% said that they had ordered more tests than they would, based only on professional judgment of what is medically needed, and 91% have noticed other physicians ordering more tests;
- 74% have referred patients to specialists more often than they belived was medically necessary;
- 51% have recommended invasive procedures such as biopsies to confirm diagnoses more often than they believed was medically necessary; and
- 41% said that they had prescribed more medications, such as antibiotics, than they would based only on their professional judgment, and 73% have noticed other doctors similarly prescribing excessive medications.

Every test and every treatment poses a risk to the patient, and takes away funds that could better be used to provide health care to those who need it.

Physicians' understandable fear of unwarranted litigation threatens patient safety in another way. It impedes efforts of physicians and researchers to improve the quality of care. As medical care becomes increasingly complex, there are many opportunities for improving the quality and safety of medical care, and reducing its costs, through better medical practices. According to some experts, these quality improvement opportunities hold the promise of not only significant improvements in patient health outcomes, but also reductions in medical costs of as much as 30%. . . .

However, these efforts and other efforts are impeded and discouraged by the lack of clear and comprehensive protection for collaborative quality efforts. Doctors are reluctant to collect quality-related information and work together to act on it for fear that it will be used against them or their colleagues in a lawsuit. Perhaps as many as 95% of adverse events are believed to go unreported. To make quality improvements, doctors must be able to exchange information about patient care and how it can be improved—what is the effect of care not just in one particular institution or of the care provided by one doctor—but how the patient fares in the system across all providers. These quality efforts require enhancements to information and reporting systems.

In its recent report, "To Err is Human," the Institute of Medicine (IOM) observed that, "[R]eporting systems are an important part of improving patient safety and should be encouraged. These voluntary reporting systems [should] periodically assess whether additional efforts are needed to address gaps in information to improve patient safety and to encourage health care organizations to participate in . . . reporting, and track the development of new reporting systems as they form."

However, as the IOM emphasized, fear that information from these reporting systems will be used to prepare a lawsuit against them, even if they are not negligent, deters doctors and hospitals from making reports. This fear, which is understandable in the current litigation climate, impedes quality improvement efforts. According to many experts, the "#1 barrier" to more effective quality improvement systems in health care organizations is fear of creating new avenues of liability by conducting earnest analyses of how health care can be improved. Without protection, quality discussions to improve health care provide fodder for litigants to find ways to assert that the status quo is deficient. Doctors are busy, and they face many pressures. They will be reluctant to engage in health care improvement efforts if they think that reports they make and recommendations they make will be thrown back at them or others in litigation. Quality improvement efforts must be protected if we are to obtain the full benefit of doctors' experience in improving the quality of health care.

The IOM Report emphasized the importance of shifting the inquiry from individuals to the systems in which they work: "The focus must shift from blaming individuals for past errors to a focus on preventing future errors by designing safety into the system." But the litigation system impedes this progress—not only because fear of litigation deters reporting but also because the scope of the litigation system's view is restricted. The litigation system looks at the past, not the future, and focuses on the individual in an effort to assess blame rather than considering how improvements can be made in the system. "Tort law's overly emotional and individualized approach . . . has been a tragic failure."

Health Care Costs Are Increased

The litigation and malpractice insurance problem raids the wallet of every American. Money spent on malpractice premiums (and the litigation costs that largely determine premiums) raises health care costs. Doctors alone spent $6.3 billion last year to obtain coverage. Hospitals and nursing homes spent additional billions of dollars.

The litigation system also imposes large indirect costs on the health care system. Defensive medicine that is caused by unlimited and unpredictable liability awards not only increases patients' risk but it also adds costs. The leading study estimates that limiting unreasonable awards for non-economic damages could reduce health care costs by 5–9% without adversely affecting quality of care. This would save $60–108 billion in health care costs each year. These savings would lower the cost of health insurance and permit an additional 2.4–4.3 million Americans to obtain insurance.

The costs of the runaway litigation system are paid by all Americans, through higher premiums for health insurance (which reduces workers' take home pay if the insurance is provided by an employer), higher out-of-pocket payments when they obtain care, and higher taxes.

The Federal Government—and thus every taxpayer who pays federal income and payroll taxes—also pays for health care, in a number of ways. It provides direct care, for instance, to members of the armed forces, veterans, and patients served by the Indian Health Service. It provides funding for the Medicare and Medicaid programs. It funds Community Health Centers. It also provides assistance, through the tax system, for workers who obtain insurance through their employment. The direct cost of malpractice coverage and the indirect cost of defensive medicine increases the amount the Federal Government must pay through these various channels, it is estimated, by $28.6–47.5 billion per year. If reasonable limits were placed on non-economic damages to reduce defensive medicine, it would reduce the amount of taxpayers' money the Federal Government spends by $25.3–44.3 billion per year. This is a very significant amount. It would more than fund a prescription drug benefit for Medicare beneficiaries *and* help uninsured Americans obtain coverage through a refundable health credit.

The Increasingly Unpredictable, Costly, and Slow Litigation System Is Responsible

Insurance premiums are largely determined by the expensive litigation system. The malpractice insurance system and the litigation system are inexorably linked. The litigation system is expensive, but, at the same time, it is slow and provides little benefit to patients who are injured by medical error. Its application is unpredictable, largely random, and standardless. It is traumatic for all involved.

Most victims of medical error do not file a claim—one comprehensive study found that only 1.53% of those who were injured by medical negligence even filed a claim. Most claims—57–70%—result in no payment to the patient. When a patient does decide to go into the litigation system, only a very small number recover anything. One study found that only 8–13% of cases filed went to trial; and only 1.2–1.9% resulted in a decision for the plaintiff.

Although most cases do not actually go to trial, it costs a significant amount of money to defend each claim—an average of $24,669. The most dramatic cost, however, is the cost of the few cases that result in huge jury awards. Even though few cases result in these awards, they encourage lawyers and plaintiffs in the hope that they can win this litigation lottery, and they influence every settlement that is entered into.

A large proportion of these awards is not to compensate injured patients for their economic loss—such as wage loss, health care costs, and replacing services the injured patient can longer perform (such as child care). Instead, much of the judgment (in some cases, particularly the largest judgments, perhaps 50% or more) is for non-economic damages. Awarded on top of compensation for the injured patient's actual economic loss, non-economic damages are said to be compensation for intangible losses, such as pain and suffering, loss of consortium, hedonic (loss of the enjoyment of life) damages, and various other theories that are imaginatively created by lawyers to increase the amount awarded.

Non-economic damages are an effort to compensate a plaintiff with money for what are in reality non-monetary considerations. The theories on which these awards are made however, are entirely subjective and without any standards. As one scholar has observed: "The perceived problem of pain and suffering awards is not simply the amount of money expended, but also the erratic nature of the process by which the size of the awards is determined. Juries are simply told to apply their 'enlightened conscience' in selecting a monetary figure they consider to be fair."

Unless a state has adopted limitations on non-economic damages, the system gives juries a blank check to award huge damages based on sympathy, attractiveness of the plaintiff, and the plaintiff's socio-economic status (educated, attractive patients recover more than others).

The cost of these awards for non-economic damages is paid by all other Americans through higher health care costs, higher health insurance premiums, higher taxes, reduced access to quality care, and threats to quality of care. The system permits a few plaintiffs and their lawyers to impose what is in effect a tax on the rest of the country to reward a very small number of patients who happen to win the litigation lottery. It is not a democratic process.

The number of mega-verdicts is increasing rapidly. The average award rose 76% from 1996–1999. The median award in 1999 was $800,000, a 6.7% increase over the 1998 figure of $750,000; and between 1999 and 2000, median malpractice awards increased nearly 43%. Specific physician specialties have seen disproportionate increases, especially those who deliver babies. In the small proportion of cases where damages were awarded, the median award in cases involving obstetricians and gynecologists jumped 43% in one year, from $700,000 in 1999 to $1,000,000 in 2000.

The number of million dollar plus awards has increased dramatically in recent years. In the period 1994–1996, 34% of all verdicts that specified damages assessed awards of $1 million or more. This increased by 50% in four years; in 1999-2000, 52% of all awards were in excess of $1 million. There have been 21 verdicts of $9 million or more in Mississippi since 1995—one of $100,000,000. Before 1995 there had been no awards in excess of $9,000,000.

These mega-awards for non-economic damages have occurred (as would be expected) in states that do not have limitations on the amounts that can be recovered . . . .

Mirroring the increase in jury awards, settlement payments have steadily risen over the last two decades. The average payment per paid claim increased from approximately $110,000 in 1987 to $250,000 in 1999. Defense expenses per paid claim increased by $24,000 over the same period.

The winning lottery ticket in litigation, however, is not as attractive as it may seem at first blush. A plaintiff who wins a judgment must pay the lawyer 30–40% of it, and sometimes even more. Lawyers, therefore, have an interest in finding the most attractive case. They develop a portfolio of cases and have an incentive to gamble on a big "win." If only one results in a huge verdict, they have had a good payday. Thus, they have incentives to pursue cases to the end in the hope of winning the lottery, even when their client would be satisfied by a settlement that would make them whole economically. The result of the contingency fee arrangement is that lawyers have few incentives to take on the more difficult cases or those of less attractive patients.

One prominent personal injury trial lawyer explained the secret of his success: "The appearance of the plaintiff [is] number one in attempting to evaluate a lawsuit because I think that a good healthy-appearing type, one who would be likeable and one that the jury is going to want to do something for, can make your case worth double at least for what it would be otherwise and a bad-appearing plaintiff could make the case worth perhaps half . . ."

For most injured patients, therefore, the litigation process, while offering the remote chance of a jackpot judgment, provides little real benefit, even for those who file claims and pursue them. Even successful claimants do not recover anything on average until five years after the injury, longer if the case goes to trial.

The friction generated by operating the system takes most of the money. When doctors and hospitals buy insurance (sometimes they are required to buy coverage that provides more "protection" than the total amount of their assets), it is intended to compensate victims of malpractice for their loss. However, only 28% of what they pay for insurance coverage actually goes to patients; 72% is spent on legal, administrative, and related costs. Less than half of the money that does go back to injured patients is used to compensate the patient for economic loss that is not compensated from other sources—the purpose of a compensation system. More than half of the amount the plaintiff receives duplicates other sources of compensation the patient may have (such as health insurance) and goes for subjective, non-economic damages (a large part of which, moreover, actually goes to the plaintiff's lawyer).

The malpractice system does not accurately identify negligence, deter bad conduct, or provide justice. The results it obtains are unpredictable, even random. The same study that found that only 1.53% of patients who were injured by medical error filed a claim also found, on the flip side, that most events for which claims were filed did not constitute negligence. Other studies show the same random results. "The evidence is growing that there is a poor correlation between injuries caused by negligent medical treatment and malpractice litigation."

Not surprisingly, most people involved in health care delivery on a day-to-day basis believe that the system does not accurately reflect the realities of health care or correctly identify malpractice. A recent survey indicated that 83% of physicians and 72% of hospital administrators do not believe the system achieves a reasonable result. . . .

Insurance Premiums Are Rising Rapidly

The cost of the excesses of the litigation system shows up in the cost of malpractice insurance coverage. Premiums have increased rapidly over the past several years. Experts believe we are seeing just the tip of what will happen this year and next. Rates have escalated rapidly for doctors who practice internal medicine, general surgery, and obstetrics/gynecology. The average increases ranged from 11% to 17% in 2000, were about 10% in 2001, but are accelerating rapidly. . . . A recent special report revealed that rate increases are averaging 20%.

However, these increases have varied widely across states, and some states have experienced increases of 30–75%, although there is no evidence that patient care had worsened. . . . [A] major contributing factor to the most enormous increases in liability premiums has been rapidly growing awards for non-economic damages in states that have not reformed their litigation system to put reasonable standards on these awards.

Among the states with the highest average medical malpractice insurance premiums are Florida, Illinois, Ohio, Nevada, New York, and West Virginia. These states have not reformed their litigation systems as others have. (Florida's caps apply only in limited circumstances. New York has prevented insurers from raising rates, and accordingly it is expected that substantial increases will be needed in 2003.) . . .

The effect of these premiums on what patients must pay for care can be seen from an example involving obstetrical care. The vast majority of awards against obstetricians involve poor outcomes at childbirth. As a result, payouts for poor infant outcomes account for the bulk of obstetricians' insurance costs. If an obstetrician delivers 100 babies per year (which is roughly the national average) and the malpractice premium is $200,000 annually (as it is in Florida), each mother (or the government or her employer who provides her health insurance) must pay approximately $2,000 merely to pay her share of her obstetrician's liability insurance. If a physician delivers 50 babies per year, the cost for malpractice premiums per baby is twice as high, about $4,000. It is not surprising that expectant mothers are finding their doctors have left states that support litigation systems imposing these costs.

In addition to premium increases for physicians, nursing home malpractice costs are rising rapidly because of dramatic increases in both the number of lawsuits and the size of awards. Nursing homes are a new target of the litigation system. Between 1995 and 2001, the national average of insurance costs increased from $240 per occupied skilled nursing bed per year to $2,360. From 1990 to 2001, the average size of claims tripled, and the number of claims increased from 3.6 to 11 per 1,000 beds.

These costs vary widely across states, again in relation to whether a state has implemented reforms that improve the predictability of the legal system. Florida ($11,000) had one of the highest per bed costs in 2001. Nursing homes in Mississippi have been faced with increases as great as 900% in the past two years. It has been recently reported that "nearly all companies that used to write nursing home liability [insurance] are getting out of the business." Since the costs of nursing home care are mainly paid by Medicaid and Medicare, these increased costs are borne by taxpayers, and consume resources that could otherwise be used to expand health (or other) programs.

Insurers Are Leaving the Market

The litigation crisis is affecting patients' ability to get care not only because many doctors find the increased premiums unaffordable but also because liability insurance is increasingly difficult to obtain at any price, particularly in non-reform states. Demonstrating and exacerbating the problem, several major carriers have stopped selling malpractice insurance.

- St. Paul Companies, which was the largest malpractice carrier in the United States, covering 9% of doctors, announced in December 2001 that it would no longer offer coverage to any doctor in the country.
- MIXX pulled out of every state; it will reorganize and sell only in New Jersey.
- PHICO and Frontier Insurance Group have also left the medical malpractice market.
- Doctors Insurance Reciprocal stopped writing group specialty coverage at the beginning of 2002.

States that had not enacted meaningful reforms (such as Nevada, Georgia, Oregon, Mississippi, Ohio, Pennsylvania, and Washington) were particularly affected. Fifteen insurers have left the Mississippi market in the past five years.

States With Realistic Limits on Non-Economic Damages Are Faring Better

The insurance crisis is less acute in states that have reformed their litigation systems. States with limits of $250,000 or $350,000 on non-economic damages have average combined highest premium increases of 12–15%, compared to 44% in states without caps on non-economic damages. . . .

As Table 1 shows, there is a substantial difference in the level of medical malpractice premiums in states with meaningful caps, such as California, Wisconsin, Montana, Utah and Hawaii, and states without meaningful caps.

In the early 1970s, California faced an access crisis like that facing many states now and threatening others. With bi-partisan support, including leadership from then Governor Jerry Brown and now Congressman Henry Waxman, then chairman of the Assembly's Select Committee on Medical Malpractice, California enacted comprehensive changes to make its medical liability system

Table 1

Malpractice Liability Rate Ranges by Specialty by Geography as of July 2001

	Cap in Non-Economic Damages	Low	High
INTERNISTS			
State Wide Data			
Wisconsin	$350,000	$5,000	$6,000
Montana	$250,000	5,300	7,000
Utah	$250,000	5,900	5,900
Hawaii	$350,000	6,800	6,800
Connecticut	No cap	6,200	15,800
Washington	No cap	7,100	9,000
Metropolitan Area Data			
California (Los Angeles area)	$250,000	$7,900	$13,000
Pennsylvania (Urban Philadelphia area)	No cap	10,700	11,800
Nevada (Las Vegas area)	No cap	11,600	15,800
Illinois (Chicagoland area)	No cap	16,500	28,100
Florida (Miami and Ft. Lauderdale areas)*	No cap	17,600	50,700
GENERAL SURGEONS			
State Wide Data			
Wisconsin (state wide)	$350,000	$16,000	$17,500
Montana (state wide)	$250,000	23,300	27,000
Utah (state wide)	$250,000	26,200	26,200
Hawaii (state wide)	$350,000	24,500	24,500
Connecticut (state wide)	No cap	26,200	45,800
Washington (state wide)	No cap	20,100	32,600
Metropolitan Area Data			
California (Los Angeles area)	$250,000	$23,700	$42,200
Pennsylvania (Urban Philadelphia area)	No cap	31,500	35,800
Nevada (Las Vegas area)	No cap	40,300	56,900
Illinois (Chicagoland area)	No cap	50,000	70,200
Florida (Miami and Ft. Lauderdale areas)*	No cap	63,200	126,600
OBSTETRICIANS/GYNECOLOGISTS			
State Wide Data			
Wisconsin (state wide)	$350,000	$23,800	$27,500
Montana (state wide)	$250,000	36,000	38,600
Hawaii (state wide)	$350,000	40,900	40,900
Utah (state wide)	$250,000	44,300	44,300
Connecticut (state wide)	No cap	45,400	64,800
Washington (state wide)	No cap	34,100	59,300
Metropolitan Area Data			
California (Los Angeles area)	$250,000	$46,900	$57,700
Pennsylvania (Urban Philadelphia area)	No cap	45,900	66,300
Nevada (Las Vegas area)	No cap	71,100	94,800
Illinois (Chicagoland area)	No cap	72,500	110,100
Florida (Miami and Ft. Lauderdale areas)*	No cap	108,000	208,900

Source: Medical Liability Monitor, Vol. 26, No. 10, October 2001: Shook, Hardy, Bacon, L.L.P., October 9, 2001.

*Florida imposes caps of $250,000–350,000 unless neither party demands binding arbitration or the defendant refuses to arbitrate.

more predictable and rational. The Medical Injury Compensation Reform Act of 1975 (MICRA) made a number of reforms, including:

- Placing a $250,000 limit on non-economic damages while continuing unlimited compensation for economic damages.
- Shortening the time in which lawsuits could be brought to three years (thus ensuring that memories would still be fresh and providing some assurance to doctors that they would not be sued years after an event that they may well have forgotten).
- Providing for periodic payment of damages to ensure the money is available to the patient in the future.

California has more than 25 years of experience with this reform. It has been a success. Doctors are not leaving California. Insurance premiums have risen much more slowly than in the rest of the country without any effect on the quality of care received by residents of California. Insurance premiums in California have risen by 167% over this period while those in the rest of the country have increased 505%. This has saved California residents billions of dollars in health care costs and saved federal taxpayers billions of dollars in the Medicare and Medicaid programs.

The President's Framework for Improving the Medical Liability System

Federal and state action is needed to address the impact of the medical liability crisis on health care costs and the quality of care.

Achieving a Fair, Predictable, and Timely Medical Liability Process

As years of experience in many states have proven, reasonable limits on the amount of non-economic damages that are awarded significantly restrain increases in the cost of malpractice premiums. These reforms improve the predictability of the medical liability system, reducing incentives for filing frivolous suits and for prolonged litigation. Greater predictability and more timely resolution of cases means patients who are injured can get fair compensation more quickly. They also reduce health care costs, enabling Americans to get more from their health care spending and enabling federal health programs to provide more relief. They improve access to care, by making insurance more affordable and available. They also improve the quality of health care, by avoiding unnecessary "defensive" treatments and enabling doctors to spend significantly more time focusing on patient care. Congress needs to enact legislation that would give all Americans the benefit of these reforms, eliminate the excesses of the litigation system, and protect patients' ability to get care.

The President [George W. Bush] supports federal reforms in medical liability law that would implement these proven steps for improving our health care system:

- Improve the ability of all patients who are injured by negligence to get quicker, unlimited compensation for their "economic losses," including the loss of the ability to provide valuable unpaid services like care for children or a parent.
- Ensure that recoveries for non-economic damages could not exceed a reasonable amount ($250,000).
- Reserve punitive damages for cases that justify them—where there is clear and convincing proof that the defendant acted with malicious intent or deliberately failed to avoid unnecessary injury to the patient—and avoid unreasonable awards (anything in excess of the greater of two times economic damages or $250,000).
- Provide for payment of a judgment over time rather than in one lump sum— and thus ensure that the money is there for the injured patient when needed.
- Ensure that old cases cannot be brought years after an event when medical standards may have changed or witnesses' memories have faded, by providing that a case may not be brought more than three years following the date or injury or one year after the claimant discovers or, with reasonable diligence, should have discovered the injury.
- Informing the jury if a plaintiff also has another source of payment for the injury, such as health insurance.
- Provide that defendants pay any judgment in proportion to their fault, not on the basis of how deep their pockets are.

The success of the states that have adopted reforms like these shows that malpractice premiums could be reduced by 34% by adopting these reforms. The savings to the Federal Government resulting from reduced malpractice premiums would be $1.68 billion.

Legislation such as H.R. 4600—a bill introduced by Congressman Jim Greenwood [R-Pennsylvania] with almost 100 bipartisan cosponsors—is now pending in Congress. Enactment of this legislation with improvements to ensure that its meaningful standards will apply nationally, will be a significant step toward the goals of affordable, high-quality health care for all Americans, and a fair and predictable liability system for compensating injured patients.

In addition, there are other promising approaches for compensating patients injured by negligence fairly and without requiring them to go through full-scale, time-consuming, and expensive litigation. Just as states like California have demonstrated the effectiveness of litigation reforms, they should also adopt and evaluate the impact of alternatives to litigation.

Early Offers is one innovative approach. This would provide a new set of balanced incentives to encourage doctors to make offers, quickly after an injury, to compensate the patient for economic loss, and for patients to accept. It would make it possible for injured patients to receive fair compensation quickly, and over time if any further losses are incurred, without having to enter into the litigation fray. Because doctors and hospitals would have an incentive to discover adverse events quickly in order to make a qualifying offer, it would lead to prompt identification of quality problems. The money that otherwise would be spent in conducting litigation would be recycled so that more patients get additional recovery, more quickly, with savings left over to the benefit of all Americans. It may also be possible to implement an administrative form of Early Offers as an option for care provided under federal health programs.

A second innovative approach involves strengthening medical review boards. Boards with special expertise in the technical intricacies of health care can streamline the fact-gathering and hearing process, make decisions more accurately, and provide compensation more quickly and predictably than the current litigation process. As with Early Offers, incentives are necessary for patients and health care providers to submit cases to the boards and to accept their decisions.

The Administration intends to work with states on developing and implementing these alternatives to litigation, so that injured patients can be fairly compensated quickly and without the trauma and expense that litigation entails.

NO

Jackson Williams

Bush's Medical Malpractice Disinformation Campaign

Introduction

The medical community continues to tout a report, *Confronting the New Health Care Crisis: Improving Health Care Quality and Lowering Costs by Fixing Our Medical Liability System,* issued by the Department of Health and Human Services [HHS] last summer [2002] as making an overwhelming case for medical liability "reform." In truth, a cursory examination of the report finds it to be a classic "clip job"—a collection of anecdotes, reports, and propaganda provided by lobbyists and stamped with the government's official imprimatur. The report cites such sources as Fox News Channel, Congressman Chip Pickering, and the Physician Insurers Association of America, the trade group leading the lobbying campaign. *It contains no new research nor any data generated by government health care experts or economists.*

A more intensive examination of the report shows that most of the "facts" it provides are incorrect, incomplete, or misleading; and that its conclusions are contradicted by those of other government agencies. . . .

The Bush Administration Says: "Access to Care Is Threatened"

> *"There are a number of obstacles that limit access to affordable health care in this country, including lack of affordable insurance and an outdated Medicare program. We now face another—the litigation crisis that has made insurance premiums unaffordable or even unavailable for many doctors, through no fault of their own. This is making it more difficult for many Americans to find care, and threatening access for many more. Dr. Cheryl Edwards, 41, closed her decade-old obstetrics and gynecology practice in Las Vegas because her insurance premium jumped from $37,000 to $150,000 a year. She moved her practice to West Los Angeles, leaving 30 pregnant women to find new doctors."*

The Facts: Malpractice insurance costs are a miniscule part of a doctor's expenses and don't affect decisions about where to practice medicine.

- *There is a greater likelihood of doctors withdrawing from practice due to increases in their office rents or payroll costs than due to increases in malpractice insurance costs.* While there is a temporary spike in medical malpractice insurance rates due to insurance industry economics, it is necessary to look at the larger and longer-term picture. Specifically, while physicians spend about 3.2 percent of their gross income on medical malpractice costs, they spend 17 percent on payroll costs and 5.8 percent on office rent. According to the Medicare Payment Advisory Commission (MedPAC), the average increase in medical malpractice insurance rates last year was 4.4 percent. A doctor who stops practicing because of a malpractice insurance increase would be just as likely to retire due to increased health insurance costs for office staff, or because of increased rent for office space. If increased costs to doctors justify legislative action, they could also justify repeal of wages and hours laws or enactment of rent control laws.

- *Liability laws have no effect on a doctor's decision where to practice.* Even though damage awards are higher in more affluent states, those states still have more doctors. The District of Columbia has the highest average damage award and the most doctors. Idaho, with the fewest doctors, has the third lowest median damage award. While five of the states with the lowest per capita number of doctors have enacted caps on non-economic damages, only three of the states with the highest number of doctors per capita have enacted them. According to the U.S. Chamber of Commerce, Iowa, Utah, and South Dakota rank 5th , 8th and 9th for "reasonable litigation environment," yet those states rank in the bottom ten in number of doctors. Only one state in the Chamber's legal climate top ten, Connecticut, also ranks in the top ten for doctors. California, whose damage caps supposedly drew Dr. Edwards from Las Vegas, did not add one additional doctor per 100,000 residents between 1990 and 1999, but the number of doctors per 100,000 residents increased in Nevada from 136 to 162 during that period.

- *Two factors explain almost all the variation in the number of doctors in a state: income level and urbanization.* Like anyone else, doctors want to live in places where they can earn high incomes, enjoy cultural and leisure activities, and send their children to good schools. Seven of the top ten states for doctors also rank in the top ten states in percentage of households earning $200,000 or more. Doctors want to live in areas with lots of affluent people—such areas are more likely to have the leafy suburbs, premium housing, clubs, and other amenities that doctors want. For every $1,000 increase in a state's median income for a four-person family, a state will have 2.3 more doctors per 100,000 residents. Doctors migrate to states on lists of "Best Places to Live": Forty of the top 100 cities with "strong arts, cultural programs, and higher education" were in the ten states with the highest per capita number of doctors, while there were none in the ten states with the lowest per capita number of doctors. Polled by the U.S. Chamber of Commerce, 41 percent of West Virginia doctors said that the inability of the state's poor resident to pay fees was responsible for the state's shortage of doctors, and 27 percent said that quality of life in the state was responsible.

- *There is no relationship between the level of increase in liability insurance premiums and the likelihood of discontinuing obstetric practice.* A recent study examined whether New York obstetricians facing higher premiums for obstetric liability insurance were more likely to discontinue practicing than physicians experiencing lower increases in premiums. The study found that the decrease in doctors practicing obstetrics was associated with the length of time since receiving a medical license in New York. This relationship "very likely represents the phenomenon of physicians retiring from practice or curtailing obstetrics as they age."

The Bush Administration Says: "Patient Safety Is Jeopardized"

"In its recent report, 'To Err is Human,' the Institute of Medicine (IOM) observed that, '[R]eporting systems are an important part of improving patient safety and should be encouraged. These voluntary reporting systems [should] periodically assess whether additional efforts are needed to address gaps in information to improve patient safety . . .' However, as the IOM emphasized, fear that information from these reporting systems will be used to prepare a lawsuit against them, even if they are not negligent, deters doctors and hospitals from making reports."

The Facts: Patient safety is enhanced by the tort system; it would be further enhanced by increased regulation of doctors.

- *The Administration's own Council of Economic Advisors said the opposite last year—the tort system increases patient safety.* Even the conservative appointees to the President's Council of Economic Advisors admit, "a patient purchasing a medical procedure, for example, may be unlikely to fully understand the complex risks, costs and benefits of that procedure relative to others. Such a patient must turn to a physician who serves as a 'learned intermediary,' though there remains the problem that the patient may also not be able to judge the skill of the physician from whom the procedure is 'purchased.' In such a case, the ability of the individual to pursue a liability lawsuit in the event of an improper treatment, for example, provides an additional incentive for the physician to follow good medical practice. Indeed, from a broad social perspective, this may be the least costly way to proceed—less costly than trying to educate every consumer fully. In a textbook example, recognition of the expected costs from the liability system causes the provider to undertake the extra effort or care that matches the customer's desire to avoid the risk of harm. This process is what economists refer to as 'internalizing externalities.' In other words, the liability system makes persons who injure others aware of their actions, and provides incentives for them to act appropriately."

- *Patient safety is at risk from medical providers' failure to commit to reducing medical errors.* In 1999 the Institute of Medicine released its report on patient safety in the U.S. The report estimated that between 44,000 and 98,000 Americans die annually as a result of preventable medical errors. The IOM recommended creation of a nationwide *mandatory* reporting system of serious errors—those that result in death or serious harm—for hospitals, other institutional providers and ambulatory care systems. The IOM argued that such a system is necessary to hold providers accountable for maintaining safety and to implement safety systems that reduce the likelihood of such events occurring. IOM also recommended that health professional licensing conduct periodic re-examinations and re-licensing of doctors, nurses, and other key providers, based on both competence and knowledge of safety practices. Neither of these recommendations has been implemented, due to opposition from the medical community; nor are they mentioned in the HHS report.

- *Patient safety is also at risk from incompetent doctors.* Five percent of doctors are responsible for 54 percent of malpractice in the U.S., according to records in the National Practitioner Data Bank, maintained by HHS. An inquiry to this database, which covers malpractice judgments and settlements since September 1990, found that 5.1 percent of doctors (35,009) have paid two or more malpractice awards to patients. These doctors are responsible for 54 percent of all payouts reported to the Data Bank. Of these, only 7.6 percent have ever been disciplined by state medical boards. Even physicians who have made 5 payouts have been disciplined at only a 13.3 percent rate.

The Bush Administration Says: "Health Care Costs Are Increased"

"The litigation and malpractice insurance problem raids the wallet of every American. Money spent on malpractice premiums (and the litigation costs that largely determine premiums) raises health care costs. The litigation system also imposes large indirect costs on the health care system. Defensive medicine that is caused by unlimited and unpredictable liability awards not only increases patients' risk but it also adds cost . . . The leading study estimates that limiting unreasonable awards for non-economic damages could reduce health care costs by 5–9% without adversely affecting quality of care. This would save $60–108 billion in health care costs each year."

The Facts: The Congressional Budget Office (CBO) says that limiting liability would have a negligible impact on health care costs.

- *In evaluating the impact of H.R. 4600, which would have severely limited the ability of patients to recover damages, the Congressional Budget Office projected only minimal savings.* This bill, which contained very stringent restrictions on patients' ability to recover damages, passed the U.S. House in 2002. CBO said: "The percentage effect of H.R. 4600 on overall health insurance premiums would be far smaller than the percentage impact on medical malpractice insurance premiums. Malpractice costs account for a very small fraction of total health care spending; even a very large reduction in malpractice costs would have a relatively small effect on total health plan premiums. In addition, some of the savings leading to lower medical malpractice premiums—those savings arising from changes in the treatment of collateral-source benefits—would represent a shift in costs from medical malpractice insurance to health insurance. Because providers of collateral-source benefits would be prevented from recovering their costs arising from the malpractice injury, some of the costs that would be borne by malpractice insurance under current law would instead be borne by the providers of collateral-source benefits. Most such providers are health insurers."

- *The Congressional Budget Office has rejected the "defensive medicine" theory.* CBO was asked to quantify the savings from reduced "defensive medicine" if Congress passed H.R. 4600. CBO declined, saying:

Estimating the amount of health care spending attributable to defensive medicine is difficult. Most estimates are speculative in nature, relying, for the most part, on surveys of physicians' responses to hypothetical clinical situations, and clinical studies of the effectiveness of certain intensive treatments. Compounding the uncertainty about the magnitude of spending for defensive medicine, there is little empirical evidence on the effect of medical malpractice tort controls on spending for defensive medicine and, more generally, on overall health care spending.

A small number of studies have observed reductions in health care spending correlated with changes in tort law, but that research was based largely on a narrow part of the population and considered only hospital spending for a small number of ailments that are disproportionately likely to experience malpractice claims. Using broader measures of spending, CBO's initial analysis could find no statistically significant connection between malpractice tort limits and overall health care spending. Although the provisions of H.R. 4600 could result in the initiation of fewer lawsuits, the economic incentives for individual physicians or hospitals to practice defensive medicine would appear to be little changed.

- *Overall tort expenditures are less than the cost of medical injuries.* Because so few medical injuries result in compensation to patients, the overall expenditures made for medical liability are far below the projected injury costs. The Institute of Medicine estimated the costs of preventable medical injuries in hospitals alone at between $17 billion and $29 billion a year. The Utah Colorado Medical Practice study estimated it at $20 billion. By contrast, the National Association of Insurance Commissioners reports that the total amount spent on medical malpractice insurance in 2000 was $6.4 billion. This is at least three to five times less than the cost of malpractice to society.

- *A leading actuary says the HHS report's numbers are "rubbish."* According to Robert Hunter, Director of Insurance for Consumer Federation of America, "The total cost of medical malpractice premiums is $6.4 billion (not just for doctors, as the report says, but for doctors, hospitals and other facilities). This represents about one-half of a percent of total health care expenses. In other words, if an outright ban were placed on medical malpractice lawsuits the total savings would be about $6 billion. The idea that a cap of any kind can save $60 to $108 billion is pure rubbish. How in the world could 'defensive medicine' possibly be more than equal to the total risk measured in premiums, much less 10 to 20 times the risk, as HHS assumes? This makes no economic sense at all."

The Bush Administration Says: "The Increasingly Unpredictable, Costly, and Slow Litigation System Is Responsible"

"Insurance premiums are largely determined by the expensive litigation system . . . Its application is unpredictable, largely random, and standardless . . . Although most cases do not actually go to trial, it costs a significant amount of money to defend each claim—an average of $24,669 . . . Awarded on top of compensation for the injured patient's actual economic loss, non-economic damages are said to be compensation for intangible losses, such as pain and suffering, loss of consortium, hedonic (loss of the enjoyment of life) damages, and various other theories that are imaginatively created by lawyers to increase the amount awarded . . . The average award rose 76% from 1996–1999. The median award in 1999 was $800,000, a 6.7% increase over the 1998 figure of $750,000; and between 1999 and 2000, median malpractice awards increased nearly 43%."

The Facts: The medical malpractice litigation process is logical, and awards are explained by income, cost of health care, and injury severity.

- *Government data show that medical malpractice awards have increased at a much slower pace than claimed by Jury Verdict Research.* According to the federal government's National Practitioner Data Bank (NPDB), the median medical malpractice payment by a physician to a patient rose 35 percent from 1997 to 2001, from $100,000 to $135,000. By contrast, data from Jury Verdict Research (JVR), a private research firm, which was cited in the HHS report shows that awards rose 100 percent from

1997 to 2000, from $503,000 to $1 million. The reason for the huge difference, which is explained in more detail below: JVR collects only jury *verdict* information that is reported to it by attorneys, court clerks and stringers. The NPDB is the most comprehensive source of information that exists because it includes both verdicts *and* settlements. Ninety-six percent of all medical malpractice cases are settled, as opposed to decided by a jury, and settlements result in much lower awards than jury verdicts. Jury verdicts are higher than the average settlement because cases involving severe injuries are more likely to go to trial, and the defendant has usually rejected a settlement offer for a much smaller amount. JVR reported that the median final plaintiff demand in 2000 was $562,000, and the median final settlement offer from the doctor was $80,000. Thus, in the twenty percent of trials that doctors lost, a conscious decision was made to risk a much higher jury verdict. The plaintiffs were usually willing to settle for about half of what the jury awarded. According to NPDB's database of all medical malpractice settlements and judgments, the median payment in a settlement in 2000 was $125,000, same as the median for all payments; but the median payment for a judgment was $235,000. This figure is lower than the jury verdict figure because the ultimate payment received by a successful plaintiff reflects remittiturs ordered by judges, and discounts agreed to by plaintiffs in order to avert appeals.

- *Government data show that medical malpractice awards have increased at a slower pace than health insurance premiums.* While NPDB data show that the median medical malpractice payment rose 35 percent from 1997 to 2001 (an average of 8.5 percent a year), the average premium for single health insurance coverage increased 39 percent over that time period (9.5 percent a year). Payments for health care costs, which directly affect health insurance premiums, make up the lion's share of most medical malpractice awards.

- *"Non-economic" damages are not as easy to quantify as lost wages or medical bills, but they compensate real injuries.* So-called "non-economic" damages are awarded for the pain and suffering that accompany any loss of normal functions (e.g. blindness, paralysis, sexual dysfunction, lost bowel and bladder control) and inability to engage in daily activities or to pursue hobbies, such as hunting and fishing. This category also encompasses damages for disfigurement and loss of fertility. The fact that Americans spend a great deal of money to remedy these conditions (e.g. on pain relief medication, reconstructive surgery, etc.) belies any notion that such damages are "non-economic." According to Physician Insurer Association of America (PIAA), the average payment between 1985 and 2001 for a "grave injury," which encompasses paralysis, was only $454,454.

- *No evidence supports the claim that jury verdicts are random "jackpots."* Studies conducted in California, Florida, North Carolina, New York, and Ohio have found that jury verdicts bear a reasonable relationship to the severity of the harm suffered. In total the studies examined more than 3,500 medical malpractice jury verdicts and found a consistent relationship between the severity of the injury and the size of the verdict. Uniformly the authors concluded that their findings did not support the contention that jury verdicts are frequently unpredictable and irrational.

- *The insurance industry's own numbers demonstrate that awards are proportionate to injuries.* PIAA's Data Sharing Report also demonstrates the relationship between the severity of the injury and the size of the settlement or verdict. PIAA, as do most researchers, measures severity of injury according to the National Association of Insurance Commissioners' classifications. The average indemnity paid per file was $49,947 for the least severe category of injury and increased with severity, to $454,454 for grave injuries. All researchers found that the amount of jury verdicts fell off in cases of death, for which the average indemnity was $195,723. This is not surprising, as the costs of medical treatment for a grave injury are likely to be greater and pain and suffering would be experienced over a longer time period than in the case of death.

- *The contingency fee system discourages attorneys from bringing frivolous claims.* Medical malpractice cases are brought on a contingency fee basis, meaning the attorney receives payment only in the event there is a settlement or verdict. If the claim is closed without payment, the attorney does not receive a fee. Since attorneys must earn money to stay in business, it follows that they would not intentionally take on a non-meritorious case.

- *The high cost of preparing a medical malpractice case discourages frivolous claims—and meritorious claims as well.* Medical malpractice cases are very expensive for plaintiffs' attorneys to bring, with out-of-pocket costs for cases settled at or near the time of trial (when most cases are settled) ranging from $15,000 to $25,000. If the case goes to trial, the costs can easily be doubled. These costs do not include the plaintiff's attorney's time, and an attorney pursuing a frivolous case incurs opportunity costs in not pursuing other cases. An attorney incurs expenses beginning with the determination of whether a case has merit. First, the attorney is required to obtain copies of the patient's medical records from all the providers for analysis by a competent medically trained person. If that initial consultation reveals a likelihood of medical negligence, the records must then be submitted to medical specialists, qualified to testify in court, for final review. Typically, the records must be sent to experts outside of the plaintiff's state, as physicians within the state will refuse to testify against local colleagues. As a result, the experts who agree to review records and testify can and do charge substantial fees. Fees from $1,000 per hour to several thousand dollars are not uncommon. Discovery involves taking the sworn testimony of witnesses and experts. Such depositions cost $300 and up, depending upon their length and complexity. If an expert witness is deposed, the plaintiff's attorney is charged for the witness' preparation time and time attending the deposition.

- *Plaintiffs drop 10 times more claims than they pursue.* PIAA reports that between 1985 and 2001 a total of 108,300 claims were "dropped, withdrawn or dismissed." This is 63 percent of the total number of claims (172,474) closed during the study period. It is unclear what portion constitutes involuntarily dismissed cases (dismissed after a motion was filed by the defendant) rather than cases voluntarily dismissed by plaintiffs. According to researchers at the University of Washington School of Medicine, about nine percent of claims files are closed after the defendant wins a contested motion. Based on this figure, Public Citizen estimates that about 54 percent of claims are being abandoned by patients. An attorney may send a statutorily-required notice of intent to claim or file a lawsuit in order to meet the requirements of the statute of limitations but, after collecting medical records and consulting with experts, decide not to pursue the claim. We estimate that the number of cases withdrawn voluntarily by plaintiffs was 92,621, *10 times* the number of cases that were taken to trial and lost during that period (9,293). The percentage of claims pursued by plaintiffs to final rejection by a jury is only *five percent.*

- *The small number of claims pursued to a defense verdict are not frivolous.* Researchers at the American Society of Anesthesiologists arranged for pairs of doctors to review 103 randomly selected medical negligence claims files. The doctors were asked to judge whether the anesthesiologist in question had acted reasonably and prudently. The doctors only agreed on the appropriateness of care in 62 percent of the cases; they disagreed in 38 percent of cases. The researchers concluded, "These observations indicate that neutral experts (the reviews were conducted in a situation that did not involve advocacy or financial compensation) commonly disagree in their assessments when using the accepted standard of reasonable and prudent care." The percentage of all medical malpractice claims that go to trial is only 6.6 percent, according to PIAA, meaning that the parties and their attorneys ultimately reach agreement about liability five times more often than neutral doctors do. If truly frivolous lawsuits were being pursued, the proportion of claims going to trial would exceed the 38 percent of claims on which even doctors will disagree.

- *The costs of defending claims that are ultimately dropped are not unreasonable.* Medical liability insurers have complained about the costs of defending cases that are ultimately dropped. But the professional obligation of lawyers to exercise due diligence is essentially identical to the duty of physicians. The lawyer must rule out the possibility of proving medical negligence before terminating a claim, just as doctors must rule out the possibility of illnesses suggested by their patients' symptoms. The doctor performs his duty by administering tests; the lawyer performs hers by using discovery procedures. Both processes can lead to dead ends. But plaintiffs' lawyers have no financial incentive to abuse the litigation process: they are using their own time and money to pursue discovery activities, and are only paid for work on behalf of clients whose cases are successful.

- *Award amounts correlate to plaintiff's income and the cost of living in the plaintiff's home state.* Median malpractice awards vary from state to state. Much of the variation is explained by two factors—median family income and urbanization. Public Citizen's analysis of NPDB and census data found that for every $1,000 increase in a state's median family income, the median award amount increases by about $1,100. Our analysis also found that awards increase in relation to state population density—logical, since urbanized areas have a higher cost of living than rural areas.

The Bush Administration Says: "Insurance Premiums Are Rising Rapidly"

"The cost of the excesses of the litigation system shows up in the cost of malpractice insurance coverage. Premiums have increased rapidly over the past several years."

The Facts: The spike in medical liability premiums was caused by the insurance cycle, not by an "explosion" of lawsuits or "skyrocketing" jury verdicts.

- *There is no growth in the number of new medical malpractice claims.* According to the National Association of Insurance Commissioners (NAIC), the number of new medical malpractice claims declined by about four percent between 1995 and 2000. There were 90,212 claims filed in 1995; 84,741 in 1996; 85,613 in 1997; 86,211 in 1998; 89,311 in 1999; and 86,480 in 2000.
- *For much of the 1990s, doctors benefited from artificially lower premiums.* According to the International Risk Management Institute (IRMI), one of the leading analysts of commercial insurance issues, "What is happening to the market for medical malpractice insurance in 2001 is a direct result of trends and events present since the mid to late 1990s. Throughout the 1990s, and reaching a peak around 1997 and 1998, insurers were on a quest for market share, that is, they were driven more by the amount of premium they could book rather than the adequacy of premiums to pay losses. In large part this emphasis on market share was driven by a desire to accumulate large amounts of capital with which to turn into investment income." IRMI also noted: "Clearly a business cannot continue operating in that fashion indefinitely."
- *West Virginia Insurance Commissioner blames the market.* According to the Office of the West Virginia Insurance Commission (one of the states in the throes of a medical malpractice "crisis"), "[T]he insurance industry is cyclical and necessarily competitive. We have witnessed these cycles in the Medical Malpractice line in the mid-'70's, the mid-'80's and the present situation. This particular cycle is, perhaps, worse than previous cycles as it was delayed by a booming economy in the '90's and is

now experiencing not just a shortfall in rates due to competition, but a subdued economy, lower interest rates and investment yields, the withdrawal of a major medical malpractice writer and a strong hardening of the reinsurance market. Rates will, at some point, reach an acceptable level to insurers and capital will once again flow into the Medical Malpractice market."

- *Medical liability premiums track investment results.* J. Robert Hunter, one of the country's most knowledgeable insurance actuaries and director of insurance for the Consumer Federation of America, recently analyzed the growth in medical liability premiums. He found that premiums charged do not track losses paid, but instead rise and fall in concert with the state of the economy. When the economy is booming and investment returns are high, companies maintain premiums at modest levels; however, when the economy falters and interest rates fall, companies increase premiums in response.

- *The same trends are present in other lines of insurance.* Property/casualty refers to a large group of liability lines of insurance (30 in total) including medical malpractice, homeowners, commercial, and automobile. The property/casualty insurance industry has exhibited cyclical behavior for many years, as far back as the 1920s. These cycles are characterized by periods of rising rates leading to increased profitability. Following a period of solid but not spectacular rates of return, the industry enters a down phase where prices soften, supply of the insurance product becomes plentiful, and, eventually, profitability diminishes, or vanishes completely. In the down phase of the cycle, as results deteriorate, the basic ability of insurance companies to underwrite new business or, for some companies even to renew some existing policies, can be impaired. This is because the capital needed to support the underwriting of risk has been depleted through losses. The current market began to harden in 2001, following an unusually prolonged period of soft market conditions in the property-casualty section in the 1990s. The current hard market is unusual in that many lines of insurance are affected at the same time, including medical malpractice. As a result, premiums are rising for most types of insurance. The increases have taken policyholders by surprise given that they came after several years of relatively flat to decreasing prices.

- *Insurer mismanagement compounded the problems.* Compounding the impact of the cycle has been misleading accounting practices. As the *Wall Street Journal* found in a front page investigative story on June 24, 2002, "[A] price war that began in the early 1990s led insurers to sell malpractice coverage to obstetrician-gynecologists at rates that proved inadequate to cover claims. Some of these carriers had rushed into malpractice coverage because an accounting practice widely used in the industry made the area seem more profitable in the early 1990s than it really was. A decade of short-sighted price slashing led to industry losses of nearly $3 billion last year." Moreover, "In at least one case, aggressive pricing allegedly crossed the line into fraud." According to Donald J. Zuk, chief executive of SCPIE Holdings Inc., a leading malpractice insurer in California, "Regardless of the level of . . . tort reform, the fact remains that if insurance policies are consistently under-priced, the insurer will lose money."

The Bush Administration Says: "Insurers Are Leaving the Market"

"The litigation crisis is affecting patients' ability to get care not only because many doctors find the increased premiums unaffordable but also because liability insurance is increasingly difficult to obtain at any price, particularly in non-reform states. Demonstrating and exacerbating the problem, several major carriers have stopped selling malpractice insurance."

The Facts: At least three of the four insurance companies identified by HHS as leaving the market had serious management problems during the past two years.

- *PHICO had been placed under the supervision of insurance regulators and was later sued by the state's Insurance Department.* The lawsuit alleged that PHICO directors ignored signs of financial trouble at the company and pressured the board to pay dividends at a time when the insurer's surplus "was declining drastically and significant strengthening of loss reserves was required."

- *St. Paul exited other insurance markets as well.* St. Paul Companies reported in December 2001 that it had $85 million in exposure as related to the Enron Corporation and that it held approximately $23 million in Enron Corporation senior unsecured debt. At the same time St. Paul announced it would exit its medical malpractice business, it also announced it would add reserves for claims related to the September 11 terrorist attacks, "exit certain reinsurance lines, exit countries where the company is not likely to achieve competitive scale, and reduce corporate overhead expenses, including staff reductions."

- *MIIX was found by Weiss Ratings to be the hardest hit by the property and casualty insurance industry's overall $6.6 billion decline in investment gains during the first half of 2002.* MIXX reported the largest capital losses. Weiss, a leading independent provider of ratings and analyses of financial services companies, downgraded MIIX from D- to E+, E being the lowest score possible. A former MIIX official has alleged conflicts of interest on the company's board that may have affected the situation.

The Bush Administration Says: "States With Realistic Limits on Non-Economic Damages Are Faring Better"

"The insurance crisis is less acute in states that have reformed their litigation systems. States with limits of $250,000 or $350,000 on non-economic damages have average combined highest premium increases of 12–15%, compared to 44% in states without caps on non-economic damages . . . "

The Facts: Neither the HHS report nor anyone else has presented a factual case that caps lower premiums; Public Citizen's analysis found that premiums are higher in states with caps.

- *The HHS report's "comparison" of premiums in ten states with caps to just ten states without caps is pure baloney.* HHS omitted data from other states without damage caps that did not have high premium increases. The Pennsylvania Medical Society . . . released a critique of another premium comparison, concluding that "Multivariate modeling must be used to control for outside influences . . . An issue as important as liability insurance reform deserves no less than a careful scientific approach to assessment of the impact of policy changes." While they did not prepare a multivariate model, Public Citizen did.
- *Public Citizen's analysis finds that, controlling for other factors, premiums are higher in states with caps than in states without caps.* Public Citizen entered U.S. Census, NPDB, and Medical Liability Monitor data into a multiple regression model to determine the effect that damage caps have on awards and on doctors' liability insurance premiums. Our preliminary finding is that a damage cap lowers the median payment made by doctors to plaintiffs by $29,000, in turn lowering a doctor's premium by about $11,000. Nevertheless, controlling for this and the rate of lawsuits against doctors in each state, states with caps still have premiums that are $14,000 higher than in states without caps, a $3,000 net increase. We believe that the cap encourages doctors to take more cases to trial, and the resulting higher defense attorney costs more than offset the lower indemnity payments.

POSTSCRIPT

Is It Time to Reform Medical Malpractice Litigation?

The question of medical malpractice litigation must be placed in context. No one disputes the fact that doctors make mistakes. Physicians are human and are therefore subject to human fallibilities. It should be noted that the large majority of these medical errors never result in legal action. But since the United States does not have in place a nationally mandated reporting system for medical mishaps and near mishaps, the public does not have certain knowledge of just how many medical mistakes are made annually. Doctors and their insurance carriers would have people believe that every medical mistake is litigated and that many other lawsuits are brought to the courts when there are no grounds for them. Lawyers, for their part, argue that they file lawsuits for only a small fraction of the medical mistakes that are made annually in the United States. Indeed, they contend that if it were not for the cases they did bring to light, the public would naively believe that doctors are infallible.

The truth of the matter may lie somewhere in the middle. Outside observers generally assume that about one out of every six "medical misadventures" results in a lawsuit. Of those who do seek legal redress, about half of these malpractice lawsuits are settled out of court or withdrawn before they go to trial. It is those that find their way through the court system and result in large financial settlements that are political lightning rods.

Those who litigate medical malpractice cases contend that their jury and settlement awards have little impact on medical malpractice insurance rates. They contend that the appearance of high insurance premiums can be traced to poor management decisions. When times were good and interest rates were high, these companies engaged in excessive competition, which drove the insurance rates down too far in the most competitive markets. When times were not as good and interest rates were low, insurance companies had no choice but to increase their rates. The increase, of course, was most severe in markets where the rates had been driven to the lowest levels.

This issue has been hotly debated in recent months; consequently, you might look to the press for background reading. The *New York Times* is a good source. The March 16, 2003, issue of the *New York Times Magazine* carried an article concerning four individuals who had foreign objects left in their bodies after surgeries. "The Biggest Mistake of Their Lives" discusses the case of Dan Jennings. If the miseries suffered by John Francis, as described in the introduction to this issue, seem remarkably like those of Jennings, that is because Francis is a fictional character based on Jennings.

Those who would limit malpractice awards have written widely. See, for example, "The Tort Mess," by Michael Freeman, *Forbes* (May 13, 2002). The

154

American Medical Association has many such references, including "Medical Liability Reform Background and Talking Points." This summary, which was updated on May 8, 2002, incorporates many of the points found in the HHS report. To see how the medical community interprets history in this area, see James C. Mohr, "American Medical Malpractice Litigation in Historical Perspective," *JAMA* (April 3, 2000). Finally, to read firsthand how the insurance industry feels, see Doctor's Company chairman Richard E. Anderson's July 17, 2002, testimony before the Subcommittee on Health, Committee on Energy and Commerce, in "Harming Patient Access to Care: The Impact of Excessive Litigation."

For a good summary of President George W. Bush's statement on the medical malpractice issue and a panel discussion, see the January 16, 2003, segment of *The News Hour With Jim Lehrer*, which includes Larry Smarr, president of the Physicians Insurers Association of America; Ken Suggs, secretary to the Association of American Trial Lawyers; Donald Palmisano, president-elect of the American Medical Association; and Joanne Doroshow, executive director of the Center for Justice and Democracy.

On the Internet . . .

Financial Management Service

Available at this site is a daily treasury statement, information on the federal budget from the Office of Management and Budget, a collection of statistics on social and economic conditions in the United States, and much more.

http://www.fms.treas.gov

Joint Economic Committee

Start here to explore the work and opinions of the members of the Joint Economic Committee on many topics—tax reform and government spending, international economic policy, and who is benefiting from economic growth, to name just a few.

http://www.house.gov/jec/

The Public Debt Online

Here you will find links to the public debt of the United States "to the penny," historical debt, interest expense and the public debt, and frequently asked questions about the public debt.

http://www.publicdebt.treas.gov/opd/opd.htm

U.S. Macroeconomic and Regional Data

Hosted by the State University of New York, Oswego, Department of Economics, this site contains the full text of recent economic reports to the president and links to various global and regional economic indicators.

http://www.oswego.edu/~economic/mac-data.htm

United States Department of the Treasury

In addition to information about the U.S. Treasury Department itself, this site features the latest news and speeches from the Treasury Department, a calendar of important events in the department's history, and a public engagement schedule to find out where and when Treasury Department officials will speak.

http://www.ustreas.gov

PART 2

Macroeconomic Issues

*G*overnment policy and economics are tightly intertwined. Fiscal policy and monetary policy have a dramatic impact on the national economy, and the state of the economy can often lead to changes in tax revenues, government spending, and interest rates. Decisions regarding taxes, the minimum wage, and welfare reform must be made in the context of broad macroeconomic goals, and the debates on these issues are more than theoretical. Each has a significant impact on our lives.

- Should Social Security Be Privatized?

- Does the Consumer Price Index Overstate Inflation and Changes in the Cost of Living?

- Should the Double Taxation of Corporate Dividends Be Eliminated?

- Should a Program of Universal Service Be Created?

- Is It Time to Abolish the Minimum Wage?

- Are Declining Caseloads a Sign of Successful Welfare Reform?

ISSUE 7

Should Social Security Be Privatized?

YES: Michael Tanner, from "'Saving' Social Security Is Not Enough," *Cato Institute Project on Social Security Privatization SSP No. 20* (May 25, 2000)

NO: Catherine Hill, from "Privatizing Social Security Is Bad, Particularly for Women," *Dollars and Sense* (November/December 2000)

ISSUE SUMMARY

YES: Michael Tanner, director of health and welfare studies at the Cato Institute, argues that Social Security needs to be replaced with a retirement system based on individually owned, privately invested accounts. He maintains that Social Security fails as it is currently structured both as an antipoverty program and as a retirement program, that it is unfair, and that it makes workers dependent on politicians for their retirement incomes.

NO: Catherine Hill, a study director at the Institute for Women's Policy Research, contends that privatization of Social Security is a bad idea because it would create significant transition and administrative costs, create a void with respect to disability and life insurance, and lower the retirement income of women.

Social Security, more formally the Old Age, Survivors, and Disability Insurance program (OASDI), was signed into law on August 14, 1935, by President Franklin D. Roosevelt. As originally designed, OASDI provided three types of benefits: retirement benefits to the elderly who were no longer working, survivor benefits to the spouses and children of people who have died, and disability benefits to people who experience non-work-related illness or injury. The Medicare portion of Social Security, which provides benefits for hospital, doctor, and medical expenses, was not created until 1965.

There are many terms used to describe OASDI. It is an entitlement program in the sense that everyone who satisfies the eligibility requirements receives benefits. Eligibility is established by employment and contributions to the system (in the form of payroll taxes) for a minimum period of time. It is also a defined benefits program; that is, the level of benefits is determined by legislation. The opposite of a defined benefits program is a defined contributions program, in which benefits are determined by contributions and whatever investment income is generated by those contributions. OASDI is also described as a pay-as-you-go system; this means that payments received by recipients are financed primarily by the contributions of current workers. Still another description of OASDI is that it is an income security program. In this context, the reference is to a whole set of government programs designed to provide minimum levels of income to various people. Finally, OASDI is described as a social insurance program to distinguish it from private insurance programs. The insurance feature rests on the fact that OASDI protects against certain unforeseen events, such as disability and early death. The social feature arises from the fact that contributions and the level of benefits are determined by legislation and that the contributions are mandatory (payroll taxes that must be paid). In a private insurance program the beneficiary and the insurance issuer voluntarily negotiate the level of contributions and the level of benefits.

With respect to the administration of OASDI, there are several components to consider. One component is the Social Security and Medicare Trustees. This six-member panel annually prepares estimates of the inflows and outflows of funds and the long-term actuarial soundness of the system. A second component is the Social Security Advisory Council. This panel comes together every four years and reviews the projections of the trustees. In the process the council may offer suggestions for changes in the program. The third component involves both Congress and the president. They are involved because any changes to the system in terms of contributions and benefits requires the passage of legislation.

Members of the Social Security Advisory Council agree that there is currently a Social Security "crisis," which refers to the fact that with the currently legislated structure of revenues and benefits, the system will be unable to meet its financial obligations at some future date. Presently, revenues are greater than outpayments, and the excess is accumulated in a trust fund. Around the year 2015, outpayments will exceed revenues, and the difference will be covered by drawing down the trust fund. Eventually, the trust fund will be exhausted (around the year 2036), and revenues will only be sufficient to cover about two-thirds of outpayments.

A number of strategies have been developed for dealing with the Social Security crisis. They range from an increase in Social Security payroll taxes to a reduction in benefits, to an increase in the age at which a person would become eligible for benefits, to privatization. This issue focuses on the last strategy. In the following selections, Michael Tanner states that there are a number of problems with the current Social Security system—problems that could be redressed by replacing Social Security with a system of individually owned, privately invested accounts. Catherine Hill argues against privatization generally because it involves significant transition and administrative costs, entails market risk, and creates a void for disability and life insurance protection. She also argues against privatization because it would hurt women in particular by lowering their retirement income.

159

Michael Tanner

"Saving" Social Security Is Not Enough

Introduction

The corridors of Washington are ringing with calls to "save" Social Security. And it is certainly easy to understand why the program needs "saving." Social Security is rapidly heading for financial insolvency. By 2015 the program will begin running a deficit, paying out more in benefits than it takes in through taxes. The resulting shortfall will necessitate at least a 50 percent increase in payroll taxes, a one-third reduction in benefits, or some combination of benefit cuts and tax increases. Overall, Social Security faces a long-term funding shortfall of more than $20 trillion.[1]

As a result, there have been numerous proposals designed to shore up the program's shaky finances. Those proposals generally take one of two tracks: setting aside current Social Security surpluses in some form of "lock box" or injecting general revenue financing into the system.

There are serious flaws in both of those approaches. The lock-box proposals do not, in fact, do anything to change Social Security's financing. Currently, surplus Social Security taxes are used to purchase government bonds, which are held by the Social Security trust fund. Those bonds will eventually have to be repaid. To do so, the government will have to raise revenue. Thus the bonds represent nothing more than a claim against future tax revenues, in essence a form of IOU.[2] . . .

Some proposals go beyond setting aside Social Security surpluses and would inject all or part of the current general revenue budget surpluses into the Social Security system. Aside from the fact that Social Security's liabilities far outstrip the amount of surplus available, it is impossible to prefund Social Security under the program's current structure. Any additional funds put into the system today would simply purchase more government bonds, which would have to be paid in the future from whatever tax monies were available then.

However, setting aside the important point that none of the current proposals to save Social Security actually does so, the current focus on "saving" Social Security is itself misguided. Merely finding sufficient funding to preserve Social Security fails to address the serious shortcomings of the current system. The question should be, not whether we can save Social Security, but whether we can provide the best possible retirement system for American workers. Such a system should keep seniors out of poverty as well as improve prospects for future generations. It should provide an adequate retirement income and the best possible return on an individual's money. It should be fair, treating similarly situated people equally. Certainly, it should not penalize the disadvantaged in society such as the poor and minorities. And it should allow people to own their benefits, freeing seniors from dependence on politicians and politics for retirement benefits.

On all those scores, Social Security is an abysmal failure. It fails both as an anti-poverty program and as a retirement program. It contains numerous inequities and leaves future retirement benefits to the whims of politicians. Why should the goal of public policy be to save such a program?

Instead of saving Social Security, we should begin the transition to a new and better retirement system based on individually owned, privately invested accounts. A privatized system would allow workers to accumulate real wealth that would prevent their retiring to poverty. Because a privatized system would provide a far higher rate of return, it would yield much higher retirement benefits. Because workers would own their accounts, money in them could be passed on to future generations. That would particularly benefit the poor and minorities. Finally, again because workers would own their retirement accounts, they would no longer be dependent on politicians for their retirement incomes.

Social Security as an Anti-Poverty Program

Social Security has elements of both an insurance and a welfare program. It is, in effect, both a retirement and an anti-poverty program.[3] Although people most often think of the retirement component of the program, the system's defenders often focus on its anti-poverty elements. For example, Rep. Bill Archer (R-Tex.), chairman of the House Ways and Means Committee and author of a proposal to save Social Security, calls the program "the country's greatest anti-poverty program."[4] But is it really?

There is no question that the poverty rate among the elderly has declined dramatically in the last half century. As recently as 1959, the poverty rate for seniors was 35.2 percent, more than double the 17 percent poverty rate for the general adult population.[5] Today, it has declined to approximately 11.9 percent.[6]

Clearly, Social Security has had a significant impact on that trend. A 1999 study by the Center on Budget and Policy Priorities [CBPP] found that in the absence of Social Security benefits approximately 47.6 percent of seniors would have incomes below the poverty level.[7] That suggests that receipt of Social Security benefits lifted more than 35 percent of seniors, approximately 11.4 million people, out of poverty. CBPP also points out that the percentage of elderly who would have been in poverty in the absence of Social Security has remained relatively constant over the last several decades, while the percentage of elderly in poverty after receiving Social Security benefits has been steadily declining, indicating the increased importance of Social Security as an anti-poverty remedy.[8]

The primary problem with this line of analysis is that it assumes that any loss of Social Security benefits would not be offset by income from other sources. In other words, it simply takes a retiree's current income and subtracts Social Security benefits to discover, no surprise, that total income is now lower and, indeed, frequently low enough to throw the retiree into poverty.

Social Security benefits are a substantial component of most retirees' income. Those benefits constitute more than 90 percent of retirement income for one-quarter of the elderly. Nearly half of retirees receive at least half of their income from Social Security.[9] The question, therefore, is not whether the sudden elimination of Social Security income would leave retirees worse off—clearly it would—but whether in the absence of Social Security (or an alternative mandatory savings program) retirees would have changed their behavior to provide other sources of income for their own retirement.

For example, we could ask how many seniors, in the absence of Social Security, would still be working. If they were, they would have a source of income not considered by the CBPP study. Clearly, not all seniors are able to continue working. However, many can and would. Indeed, Congress recently repealed the Social Security earnings test precisely because there are many seniors who *want* to continue working.

A more important question is whether workers, without Social Security to depend on, would have changed their behavior and saved more for their retirement. The evidence is strong that Social Security discourages individual savings. For example, Martin Feldstein of Harvard University and Anthony Pellechio of the National Bureau for Economic Research have found that households reduce their private savings by nearly one dollar for every dollar of the present value of expected future Social Security benefits.[10] Other studies have put the amount of substitution somewhat lower but still indicate a substantial offset. Even two researchers for the Social Security Administration, Dean Leimer and David Richardson, have conceded that "a dollar of Social Security wealth substitutes for about three-fifths of a dollar of fungible assets."[11]

Therefore, given that many seniors would have replaced Social Security income with income from other sources, the impact of Social Security on reducing poverty among the elderly may be overstated.

However, even taking the arguments of Social Security's defenders on their own terms, the evidence suggests that Social Security fails as an anti-poverty tool. After all, despite receiving Social Security benefits, nearly one of eight seniors still lives in poverty. In fact, the poverty rate for seniors remains slightly higher than that for the adult population as a whole.[12]

For some subgroups, the problem is far worse. For example, although the poverty rate for elderly married women is relatively low (6.4 percent), the poverty rate is far higher for elderly women who never married (21.1 percent), widowed women (21.5 percent), and divorced or separated women (29.1 percent).[13] African American seniors are also disproportionately left in poverty. Nearly 30 percent of African Americans over the age of 65 have incomes below the poverty level.[14]

Social Security's failure as an anti-poverty program is not surprising since Social Security benefits are actually quite low. A worker earning the minimum wage over his entire working life would receive only $6,301 per year in Social

Security benefits, well below the poverty level of $7,990. As mentioned above, poor seniors receive nearly 80 percent of their retirement income from Social Security. Many have no other income at all. Social Security is insufficient to raise those seniors out of poverty.

This can be contrasted with what those people would have received had they been able to invest their payroll taxes in real capital assets. For example, if the minimum wage worker described above had been able to invest his payroll taxes, he would be receiving retirement benefits of $20,728 per year, nearly three times the poverty level.[15] Clearly, by forcing workers to invest in the current pay-as-you-go system, rather than in real capital assets, Social Security is actually contributing to poverty among the elderly.

Not only does Social Security contribute to poverty among current seniors, it also helps perpetuate poverty for future generations. Social Security benefits are not inheritable. A worker can pay Social Security taxes for 30 or 40 years, but, if that worker dies without children under the age of 18 or a spouse over the age of 65, none of the money paid into the system is passed on to his heirs.[16] As Jagadeesh Gokhale, an economist at the Federal Reserve Bank of Cleveland, and others have noted, Social Security essentially forces low-income workers to annuitize their wealth, preventing them from making a bequest of that wealth to their heirs.[17]

Moreover, because this forced annuitization applies to a larger portion of the wealth of low-income workers than of high-income workers, it turns inheritance into a "disequalizing force," leading to greater inequality of wealth in America. The wealthy are able to bequeath their wealth to their heirs, while the poor cannot. Indeed, Gokhale and Boston University economist Laurence Kotlikoff estimate that Social Security doubles the share of wealth owned by the richest 1 percent of Americans.[18]

Feldstein reaches a similar conclusion. He suggests that low-income workers substitute "Social Security wealth" in the form of promised future Social Security benefits for other forms of savings. As a result, a greater proportion of a high-income worker's wealth is in fungible assets. Since fungible wealth is inheritable, whereas Social Security wealth is not, a small proportion of the population holds a stable concentration of fungible wealth.[19] Feldstein's work suggests that the concentration of wealth in the United States would be reduced by as much as half if low-income workers were able to substitute real wealth for Social Security wealth. Individual accounts would allow them to do so.

Thus, far from being "the country's greatest anti-poverty program," Social Security appears to do a poor job of lifting seniors out of poverty and may in fact perpetuate their poverty while increasing inequality in this country.

Social Security as a Retirement Program

If Social Security is an inadequate anti-poverty program, does it at least meet its second goal as a retirement program? When Franklin Roosevelt proposed Social Security, he promised a program that would provide retirement benefits "at least as good as any American could buy from a private insurance company."[20] While that may have been true at one time, it certainly is no longer the case.

Social Security's rate of return has been steadily declining since the program's inception and is now far lower than the return from private capital investment. According to the Social Security Administration, workers born after 1973 will receive rates of return ranging from 3.7 percent for a low-wage, single-income couple to just 0.4 percent for a high-wage-earning single male.[21] The overall rate of return for all workers born in a given year was estimated at slightly below 3 percent for those born in 1940, 2 percent for those born in 1960, and below 1 percent for those who will be born this century.[22] Numerous private studies predict future rates of return for an average-wage earner ranging from 2 percent to a negative 3 percent.[23]

To make matters worse, the studies generally assume that Social Security will be able to pay all its promised benefits without increasing payroll taxes. However, the Social Security system is facing a long-term financial shortfall of more than $20 trillion. According to the system's own Board of Trustees, either taxes will have to be raised by at least 50 percent or benefits reduced by 25 percent. As a result, the rate of return will be even lower than the rates cited above. In many cases the return will actually be negative.[24]

By comparison, the average rate of return to the stock market since 1926 has been 7.7 percent.[25] That return has held despite a major depression, several recessions, World War II, two smaller wars, and the turbulent inflation-recession years of the 1970s. Of course, there have been ups and downs in the market, but there has been no 20-year period since 1926 during which the market was a net loser. Indeed, there has never been a 20-year period in which the market performed worse than projected future returns from Social Security.[26]

Even corporate bonds have consistently outperformed Social Security. Discounting the period 1941–51, when government price controls artificially reduced the return, corporate bonds have paid an average real annual return of more than 4 percent.[27]

Thus, because it deprives American workers of the ability to invest in private capital markets, the current Social Security system is costing American retirees hundreds of thousands of dollars. A single-earner couple, whose wage earner is 30 years old in 2000 and earning $24,000 per year, can expect to pay more than $134,000 in Social Security taxes over their lifetimes and receive $292,320 in lifetime Social Security benefits (including spousal benefits), assuming that both husband and wife live to normally expected ages.[28] However, had they been able to invest privately, they would have received $875,280.[29] That means the current Social Security system is depriving them of more than half a million dollars.

A second way to consider Social Security's adequacy as a retirement program is to look at the replacement rate, that portion of preretirement income replaced by Social Security benefits. Most financial planners say that a person will need retirement benefits equal to between 60 and 85 percent of preretirement wages in order to maintain his or her standard of living.[30]

However, Social Security provides only 42.4 percent of preretirement income for average-income workers. Because Social Security has a progressive benefit formula, low-income workers do better with a replacement rate of 57.1

percent, still below what is needed. That is especially true since low-income workers lack other forms of retirement income. The replacement rate for high-income workers is only 25.6 percent. In the future, the situation will grow even worse. Even under current law, replacement rates are scheduled to decline significantly. By 2030 Social Security will replace only 36.7 percent of an average-wage earner's preretirement income. However, because Social Security cannot pay all promised future benefits, the Congressional Research Service estimates that the replacement rate for an average worker will decline to as low as 26 percent, a 40 percent decline from the current already inadequate levels.[31] Clearly, Social Security, both now and in the future, leaves many seniors without the income necessary to maintain their standard of living.

Again, compare this with the replacement rates provided under a system of private investment. Assuming that the worker described previously [was] able to invest the full nondisability portion of his Social Security taxes (10.6 percent of wages), his replacement rate would be an astounding 260 percent of preretirement income! If he invested just 4 percent of wages, he would still have a replacement rate equal to 100 percent of his preretirement income.

Social Security Is Unfair

As if it were not bad enough that Social Security fails in its stated mission as an anti-poverty and retirement program, the program also contains very serious inequities that make it fundamentally unfair.

The program's most obvious unfairness is *intergenerational*. Retirees currently receiving benefits paid a relatively low payroll tax over their working lifetimes and receive a fairly high rate of return. That high return is subsidized by much higher payroll taxes on today's young workers who, in turn, can expect much lower future benefits. As Daniel Shapiro, professor of philosophy at West Virginia University, has pointed out, one of the basic precepts of social justice is the minimization of *unchosen* inequalities.[32] However, the future generations forced to bear the burden of Social Security's unfunded liabilities must do so entirely because of the time of their birth and not through any fault or choice of their own.

The program's *intragenerational* inequities are less visible but just as unfair. As we have already noted, Social Security benefits are not inheritable. Therefore, lifetime Social Security benefits depend, in part, on longevity. As a result, people with identical earnings histories will receive different levels of benefits depending on how long they live. Individuals who live to be 100 receive far more in benefits than individuals who die at 66. Therefore, those groups in our society with shorter life expectancies, such as the poor and African Americans, are put at a severe disadvantage.

Of course, Social Security does have a progressive benefit formula, whereby low-income individuals receive proportionately higher benefits per dollar paid into the system than do high-income workers.[33] The question, therefore, is to what degree shorter life expectancies offset this progressivity.

The findings of studies that use income as the sole criterion are mixed. Some studies, such as those by Eugene Steuerle and Jan Bakja of the Urban

Institute and Dean Leimer of the Social Security Administration, conclude that shorter life expectancies diminish but do not completely offset Social Security's progressivity.[34] However, there is a growing body of literature—including studies by Daniel Garrett of Stanford University, the RAND Corporation, and others—that shows that the progressive benefit formula is completely offset, resulting in redistribution of wealth from poor people to the already wealthy.[35]

The question of Social Security's unfairness to ethnic minorities appears more straightforward, particularly in the case of African Americans. African Americans of all income levels have shorter life expectancies than do whites. As a result, a black man or woman, earning exactly the same lifetime wages and paying exactly the same lifetime Social Security taxes as his or her white counterpart, will likely receive far less in lifetime Social Security benefits. For example, assume that a 30-year-old black man and a 30-year-old white man both earn $30,000 per year over their working lifetimes. By the time they retire, they will each have paid $136,740 in Social Security taxes over their lifetimes[36] and will be entitled to monthly Social Security benefits of $1,162. However, the white man can expect to live until age 81.[37] If he does, he will receive $189,389 in total Social Security benefits. The black man, in contrast, can expect to live only to age 79.[38] He can expect to receive only $161,750, almost $27,000 less than his white counterpart. This may actually understate the unfairness of the current system, since it is based on life expectancies at age 65. However, if both men are age 30 today, the life expectancy for the white man is 78; for the black man it is only 69.[39] If those projections are accurate, the black man can expect to receive nearly $100,000 less in lifetime Social Security benefits than his white counterpart and, indeed, will receive less than half what he actually paid into the program.

It seems amazing that this disparate impact, which would not be tolerated in any other government program, is so easily accepted within the current Social Security system.[40]

The current program is also unfair to women who work outside the home. Under the current system, a woman is automatically entitled to 50 percent of her husband's benefits, whether or not she has worked outside the home or paid Social Security taxes.[41] However, if a woman is able to claim benefits both as a spouse and in her own right, she may receive only the larger of the two. Because many women work only part-time, take years off from work to raise children, or earn lower wages than their husbands, 50 percent of the husband's benefits is frequently larger than the benefits a woman would be entitled to as a result of her own earnings. She will, therefore, receive only the benefits based on her husband's earnings. She will receive no additional benefits even though she may have worked and paid thousands of dollars in payroll taxes. Indeed, she would receive exactly the same benefits as if she had never worked a day outside the home or paid a dime in Social Security taxes. The taxes she paid earn her exactly *nothing*.[42]

Anyone concerned with fairness and equity in government programs must acknowledge that our current Social Security system falls far short of meeting those goals.

Social Security and the Dignity of Older Americans

Finally, it should be noted that the current Social Security system makes American seniors dependent on government and the political process for their retirement income. In essence, it reduces American seniors to supplicants, robbing them of their dignity and control over their own lives.

Americans, of course, do not get back the money that they individually paid into Social Security. Under our pay-as-you-go Social Security system, the money that workers pay in Social Security taxes is not saved or invested for their own retirement; it is instead used to pay for benefits for current retirees. Any overpayment is used by the federal government to pay its general operating expenses or, under various lock-box proposals, to pay down the national debt.

In exchange, workers receive a promise that the government will tax future workers in order to provide benefits to today's workers when they retire. However, that promise is not any sort of legally enforceable contract. It has long been settled law that there is no legal right to Social Security. In two important cases, *Helvering v. Davis* and *Flemming v. Nestor,* the U.S. Supreme Court has ruled that Social Security taxes are simply taxes and convey no property or contractual rights to Social Security benefits.[43]

As a result, a worker's retirement security is entirely dependent on political decisions made by the president and Congress. Benefits may be reduced or even eliminated at any time and are not directly related to Social Security taxes paid into the system.

Therefore, retirees are left totally dependent on the whims of politicians for their retirement income. A person can work hard, play by the rules, and pay thousands of dollars in Social Security taxes but at retirement his benefits depend entirely on the decisions of the president and Congress. Despite their best intentions, seniors have been turned into little more than wards of the state.

Conclusion

If Social Security didn't exist today, would we invent it? The current Social Security system is a failure by almost every criterion. It fails to lift many seniors out of poverty or to improve prospects for future generations. Indeed, it may actually redistribute money from the poor to the wealthy. Because it forces the poor to annuitize their savings, it prevents the accumulation of real wealth and prevents the poor from passing that wealth on to future generations. Social Security also fails as a retirement program. It does not provide an adequate retirement income or yield the best possible return on an individual's money. Nor is the program fair. It includes numerous inequities that unfairly discriminate against minorities, the poor, and working women. And, finally, because people do not have any legal ownership of their benefits, it leaves seniors dependent on politicians and politics for their retirement benefits.

Surely this cannot be what we seek from Social Security, especially when there are alternatives available. Workers should be allowed to take the money they are currently paying in Social Security taxes and redirect it to individually owned, privately invested accounts, similar to individual retirement accounts or 401(k) plans. The funds that accumulated in those accounts would be invested in real assets such as stocks and bonds, with safeguards against highly risky or speculative investments. The funds would be the account holders' personal property. At retirement, workers could convert all or part of their accumulated funds into an annuity or take a series of programmed withdrawals from the principal. If they choose the latter option, any funds remaining at their death would become part of their estate, fully inheritable by their heirs.

A retirement program based on individually owned, privately invested accounts would provide higher retirement benefits and a better rate of return than does Social Security. It would lift more seniors out of poverty, and, because funds are inheritable, accumulated wealth could be passed on to future generations. It would not penalize groups with shorter life expectancies and would eliminate the penalty on working women. And workers would own their benefits and thus be free from political risk and dependence.[44]

When it comes to Social Security, policymakers should consider whether it is more important to save a system or to provide a better retirement for American seniors.

Notes

1. Board of Trustees, Federal Old-Age and Survivors Insurance and Disability Insurance Trust Funds, *2000 Annual Report* (Washington: Government Printing Office, 2000).

2. As President Clinton's own budget notes: "[Trust fund] balances are available to finance future benefit payments and other trust fund expenditures—but only in a bookkeeping sense. These funds are not set up to be pension funds like the funds of private pension plans. They do not consist of real economic assets that can be drawn down in the future to fund benefits. Instead, they are claims on the Treasury that, when redeemed, will have to be financed by raising taxes, borrowing from the public, or reducing benefits or other expenditures. The existence of large trust fund balances, therefore, does not, by itself, have any impact on the government's ability to pay benefits." Executive Office of the President of the United States, *Analytical Perspectives: Budget of the United States Government, Fiscal Year 2000* (Washington: Government Printing Office, 1999), p. 337.

3. W. Andrew Achenbaum, *Social Security: Visions and Revisions* (Cambridge: Cambridge University Press, 1986), pp. 54–55. See also Peter Ferrara, *Social Security: The Inherent Contradiction* (Washington: Cato Institute, 1980).

4. Bill Archer, Comments at Hearing on Social Security before the House Committee on Ways and Means, 106th Cong., 1st sess., June 9, 1999, transcript, p. 48, Federal News Service.

5. Daryl Jackson et al., "Understanding Social Security: The Issues and Alternatives," American Institute of Certified Public Accountants, Washington, November 1998, p. 17.

6. Bureau of the Census, Current Population Reports, Series P60, 1998.

7. Kathryn Porter, Kathy Larin, and Wendell Primus, "Social Security and Poverty among the Elderly: A National and State Perspective," Center on Budget and Policy Priorities, Washington, April 1999.

8. Ibid., p. 16.

9. Neil Gilbert and Neung-Hoo Park, "Privatization, Provision, and Targeting: Trends and Policy Implications for Social Security in the United States," *International Social Security Review* 49 (January 1996): 22.

10. Martin Feldstein and Anthony Pellechio, "Social Security and Household Wealth Accumulation: New Microeconomic Evidence," *Review of Economics and Statistics* 61 (August 1979): 361–68.

11. Dean Leimer and David Richardson, "Social Security, Uncertainty, Adjustments, and the Consumption Decision," *Economica* 59 (August 1992): 29.

12. Bureau of the Census, Current Population Reports, Series P60.

13. Steven Sandell, "Adequacy and Equity of Social Security," *Report of the 1994–1995 Advisory Council on Social Security* (Washington: Government Printing Office, 1997), vol. 2, pp. 321–27.

14. Bureau of the Census, Population Report P60-175, 1996, Table 6, p. 18.

15. Assumes investment in stocks earning actual returns and that the individual was born in 1935, earned the minimum wage his entire working life, and retires in 2000.

16. Survivors' benefits may be extended to age 21 if the child is enrolled in college.

17. Jagadeesh Gokhale et al., "Simulating the Transmission of Wealth Inequality via Bequests," *Journal of Public Economics* (forthcoming, 2000).

18. Jagadeesh Gokhale and Laurence Kotlikoff, "The Impact of Social Security and Other Factors on the Distribution of Wealth," National Bureau of Economic Research, Cambridge, Mass., October 1999.

19. Martin Feldstein, "Social Security and the Distribution of Wealth," *Journal of the American Statistical Association* 71 (December 1976): 800–807.

20. Quoted in Warren Shore, *Social Security: The Fraud in Your Future* (New York; Macmillan, 1975), p. 2.

21. Barbara Bovbjerg, "Social Security: Issues in Comparing Rates of Return with Market Investments," U.S. General Accounting Office Report HEHS-99-110, August 1999.

22. Dean Leimer, "Cohort-Specific Measures of Lifetime Net Social Security Transfers," Social Security Administration, Office of Research and Statistics, Working Paper no. 59, February 1994.

23. For example, in our 1998 book, *A New Deal for Social Security,* Peter Ferrara and I updated a study that Ferrara conducted for the National Chamber Foundation in 1986. Using economic and demographic assumptions taken from the Social Security trustees' intermediate assumptions, adjusting for survivors' and disability benefits, and assuming that, somehow, Social Security would pay all promised benefits, we found that most workers who entered the workforce after 1985 would receive rates of return of 1.0 to 1.5 percent or less. Peter J. Ferrara and Michael Tanner, *A New Deal for Social Security* (Washington: Cato Institute, 1998), p. 69. Those results closely matched the results of a study that Ferrara conducted in 1985 with Professor John Lott, then at the Wharton School and now at Yale Law School. The 1985 study, which looked at workers entering the workforce in 1983, also showed rates of return from Social Security for most workers in the range of 1.0 to 1.5 percent. Peter J. Ferrara and John Lott, "Social Security's Rates of Return for Young Workers," in *Social Security: Prospects for Real Reform,* ed. Peter Ferrara (Washington: Cato Institute, 1985), pp. 13–36. The Heritage Foundation concluded in 1998 that the rate of return to an average two-earner family (both 30 years old) was just 1.23 percent, while the return to African American men was actually negative. William Beach and Gareth Davis, "Social Security's Rate of Return," Report no. 98-01 of the Heritage Center for Data Analysis, Washington, January 15, 1998. In a 1988 study for the National

Bureau of Economic Research, John Geanakopolis, Olivia Mitchell, and Stephen Zeldes concluded that workers born after 1970 could expect a rate of return of less than 2 percent. John Geanakopolis, Olivia Mitchell, and Stephen Zeldes, "Social Security's Money Worth," National Bureau of Economic Research Working Paper no. 6722, Washington, September 1988. The U.S. General Accounting Office reports that a two-earner couple born in 1973 and making average wages would receive a rate of return from Social Security of approximately 2.1 percent. Bovbjerg, p. 13. The nonpartisan Tax Foundation suggests future rates of return as low as a negative 3 percent. Arthur Hall, "Forcing a Bad Investment on Retiring Americans," Tax Foundation Special Report no. 55, November 1995.

24. See, for example, Jagadeesh Gokhale and Laurence Kotlikoff, "Social Security's Treatment of Postwar Americans: How Bad Can It Get?" National Bureau of Economic Research Working Paper no. 7362, Cambridge, Mass., September 1999. See also Hall; Beach and Davis; and Geanakopolis, Mitchell, and Zeldes.

25. Gokhale and Kotlikoff, "Social Security's Treatment of Postwar Americans," p. 15.

26. Jeremy J. Siegel, *Stocks for the Long Run* (New York: McGraw-Hill, 1998), p. 26. Of course, critics of privatization point out, correctly, that the past is no guarantee of future performance. But the critics' contention that the future performance of private capital markets will be significantly lower than past averages is unpersuasive. See, for example, Peter Ferrara, "Social Security Is Still a Hopelessly Bad Deal for Today's Workers," Cato Institute Social Security Paper no. 18, November 29, 1999.

The critics generally argue that, using the Social Security trustees' projections for future economic growth, economic growth will be too slow to sustain continued stock market gains. Dean Baker and Mark Weisbrot, for example, suggest that future returns will be below 3.5 percent. Dean Baker and Mark Weisbrot, *Social Security: The Phony Crisis* (Chicago: University of Chicago Press, 1999), pp. 88–104. However, the critics fail to acknowledge that the issue is not simply the return to capital markets but the spread between the return to capital markets and the return to Social Security. As Gokhale and Kotlikoff point out, Social Security tax payments and benefit receipts are closely linked to overall labor productivity growth, which is highly correlated with economic performance, which, in turn, is correlated with stock market performance. It is entirely reasonable to compare the real rate of return from stocks with the return from Social Security. Gokhale and Kotlikoff, "Social Security's Treatment of Postwar Americans," p. 15. In other words, if economic growth is so slow as to reduce the returns from private capital investment, it will also reduce the taxes collected by the Social Security system, exacerbating its fiscal imbalance, leading to lower benefits or higher taxes and a reduced Social Security rate of return. Thus, both Social Security's return and the return on capital could go up or they could go down, but private capital markets will always outperform Social Security. It is even possible to envision a scenario in which capital returns increase while Social Security tax receipts do not, for example, if wage growth takes place largely above the cap, or if economic growth translates to nonwage compensation rather than increased real wages. However, it is difficult to foresee a scenario under which real wages (and therefore Social Security revenues) rise while private capital markets do not.

Critics of privatization also suggest that the return to private capital markets should be reduced to reflect administrative costs and the costs associated with the transition to a privatized system. Both arguments have been refuted extensively elsewhere. However, it is worth noting that the U.S. General Accounting Office suggests that administrative costs would range from a low of 10 basis points to a high of 300 basis points, with most estimates closer to the low end of the range. U.S. General Accounting Office, "Social Security Reform: Administrative Costs for Individual Accounts Depends on System Design," GAO/HEHS-99-131, June 1999. A study for the Cato Institute concluded that administrative costs would range between 30 and 65 basis points. Robert Genetski, "Administrative Costs and the Relative Efficiency of Public and Private Social Security Systems," Cato Institute Social Security Paper no. 15, March 9, 1999.

The question of transition costs is also highly misleading. First, it has been clearly demonstrated that it is possible to pay for the transition without additional taxes. See, for example, Ferrara and Tanner, pp. 175–204. Even more important, however, Milton Friedman and others have shown that, when Social Security's current unfunded liabilities are considered, there are no new costs associated with the transition. Milton Friedman, "Speaking the Truth about Social Security Reform," Cato Institute Briefing Paper no. 46, April 12, 1999. Indeed, as William Shipman has demonstrated, the cost of paying for the transition, regardless of the financing mechanism chosen, will always be less than the cost of preserving the current system. William Shipman, "Facts and Fantasies about Transition Costs," Cato Institute Social Security Paper no. 13, October 13, 1998.

27. Calculated from Moody's Investor Service, *Moody's Industrial Manual and Moody's Bond Survey,* 1920–96.

28. Assumes husband retires at age 67, husband collects full Social Security benefit, and wife collects spousal benefit until husband dies at age 75. Wife then collects widow's benefit until she dies at age 81.

29. Assuming historical rates of return.

30. A. Haeworth Robertson, *Social Security: What Every Taxpayer Should Know* (Washington: Retirement Policy Institute, 1992), p. 218.

31. David Koitz, "Social Security Reform: Assessing Changes to Future Retirement Benefits," Congressional Research Service Report for Congress RL-30380, December 14, 1999.

32. Daniel Shapiro, "The Moral Case for Social Security Privatization," Cato Institute Social Security Paper no. 14, October 29, 1998.

33. Social Security benefits are based on a formula that provides benefits equal to 90 percent of the first $495 of monthly income (adjusted according to a formula that takes into account the growth in wages), 32 percent of the next $2,286, and 15 percent of remaining income up to the wage cap.

34. See C. Eugene Steuerle and John Bakija, *Retooling Social Security for the 21st Century: Right and Wrong Approaches to Reform* (Washington: Urban Institute, 1994), pp. 91–132; and Dean Leimer, "Lifetime Redistribution under the Social Security Program: A Literature Synopsis," *Social Security Bulletin* 62 (1999): 43–51.

35. Daniel Garrett, "The Effects of Differential Mortality Rates on the Progressivity of Social Security," *Economic Inquiry* 33 (July 1995): 457–75; W. Constantijn, A. Panis, and Lee Lillard, "Socioeconomic Differentials in the Return to Social Security," RAND Corporation Working Paper no. 96-05. February 1996; and Beach and Davis.

36. Counting only the OASI portion of the payroll tax. This figure does not include the disability portion.

37. Bureau of the Census, *Statistical Abstract of the United States, 1995* (Washington: Government Printing Office, 1996), Table B-1.

38. Ibid.

39. Projected life expectancy at age 30. Centers for Disease Control, "United States Abridged Life Tables, 1996," *National Vital Statistics Report,* no 13 (December 24, 1998): Table 3.

40. Supporters of the current system maintain that, overall, African Americans benefit from the current Social Security system because they earn lower incomes than whites and are more likely to have periods of unemployment. Therefore, they are more likely to benefit from the program's progressive benefit formula. However, as we have seen, the lifetime progressivity of Social Security is questionable. Supporters of the status quo also suggest that African Americans benefit disproportionately from the program's disability and survivors' benefits. However, there are no empirical studies to support that contention. Indeed, the Social Security Administration rejected a request from the 1996–98 Social Security Advisory Council to conduct such a study. Sylvester Schieber and John Shoven, *The Real Deal: The History and Future of Social Security* (New Haven, Conn.: Yale University Press, 1999), p. 227.

41. The provision is gender neutral, applying to both men and women. However, because of earning patterns in the United States, it affects women almost exclusively.

42. For a full discussion of the impact of the current Social Security system on women and the benefits of privatization for women, see Darcy Ann Olsen, "Greater Financial Security for Women with Personal Retirement Accounts," Cato Institute Briefing Paper no. 38, July 20, 1998; and Ekaterina Shirley and Peter Spiegler, "The Benefits of Social Security Privatization for Women," Cato Institute Social Security Paper no. 12, July 20, 1998.

43. For a thorough discussion of this issue, see Charles Rounds, "Property Rights: The Hidden Issue of Social Security Reform," Cato Institute Social Security Paper no. 19 April 19, 2000.

44. For a full discussion of how a privatized Social Security system would work, see Ferrara and Tanner.

NO

Catherine Hill

Privatizing Social Security Is Bad, Particularly for Women

You've probably heard the rumor that Social Security won't be there for you when you retire. And you've also probably heard that [President] George Bush promised to "save" Social Security by allowing individuals to divert 2% of their wages (or earnings) into individual accounts. Stocks generally have higher returns than government bonds, so setting up individual accounts that take advantage of these higher returns should mean more money when you retire. Right? Wrong. In fact, privatizing Social Security will mean less income in retirement for almost all American workers, and it will be particularly damaging for women.

Social Security—The Basics

Since 1935, Social Security has been America's most successful social program, currently providing income to 48 million retired and disabled Americans and their families. More than three fifths of retired households depend on Social Security for more than half of their income. For 25% of older women living alone, it is their only source of income. Without Social Security, half of elderly people in the United States would be poor (meaning that an elderly couple would have an income under $10,000 annually and an elderly individual would have less than $8,000 to live on).

A payroll tax supplies the revenue for Social Security. The tax is currently 12.4% on wages up to $72,600 and is split between employers and employees (6.2% each) with self-employed people paying the full tax themselves. (Workers also pay 1.45% of wages or earnings for Medicare.) Note that, because most of the payroll revenues are immediately used to pay benefits, diverting "only" 2% of wages means a one-sixth reduction in the money available to pay benefits.

Social Security benefits are available to all workers and their families regardless of income. For this reason, Social Security has historically enjoyed a stronger base of political support than programs that provide benefits only to those who can document poverty, such as Supplemental Security Income (SSI). The average monthly check for a retired worker is $825 with a maximum benefit

From Catherine Hill, "Privatizing Social Security Is Bad, Particularly for Women," *Dollars and Sense* (November/December 2000). Copyright © 2000 by *Dollars and Sense*. Reprinted by permission.

173

of $1,373 for a worker with a consistently high salary over a full career (35 years). While no one gets rich from Social Security, it is an important source of income for almost all retired and disabled Americans.

Why There Isn't a Solvency Crisis

Every year the Social Security Trustees forecast the long-term revenues and expenditures for the program over the next 75 years, based on demographic and economic assumptions. In the early 1980s, the Trustees forecasted a financial shortfall (misreported in the press as a "crisis"). In response, Congress increased the payroll tax rate slightly and increased the retirement age (eligibility for full Social Security benefits) from 65 to 67. These changes generated billions of dollars in surpluses for Social Security, which were placed in the Social Security Trust Fund (currently valued at a little more than $896 billion). The Trust Fund earns interest, and both principal and interest can be used to supplement payroll tax revenue during the peak Baby Boom retirement years. In 1991, the Trustees decided to use more pessimistic assumptions about future economic growth, resulting in the prediction that Social Security would not be able to pay full benefits after 2034. Strong economic performance in the last few years has resulted in a lengthening of the projected solvency to 2037. If the economy does not slow down as much as predicted, and payroll tax revenues continue to grow at a healthy rate, Social Security has no long-term solvency problem. In any case, if the economy does slow down, the Social Security program is well-positioned to continue paying full benefits for at least another thirty-seven years. After 2037, Social Security can provide three-quarters of promised benefits, and with small policy changes, Social Security can continue to pay full benefits indefinitely.

Who Wants You to Believe
There Is a Crisis and Why

Privatizing Social Security would be the largest undertaking in the history of the U.S. financial-services industry. It could also be the most profitable, and Wall Street knows it. For nearly two decades, Wall Street and its conservative think tanks have been cultivating the public's fear that Social Security is "going bankrupt." As Jesse Jackson and other progressive leaders have noted, financial firms such as Morgan Stanley, Quick & Reilly, Inc., and State Street Boston Corporation have given millions of dollars to conservative groups like the Cato Institute to push privatizing Social Security. However, with the facts so squarely mounted against them, the movement appeared to lose momentum, and for a while, it looked like the campaign to privatize Social Security had run its course. Activists breathed a sigh of relief and went about tackling other issues. However, this summer [2000], privatizers got a second wind when Presidential candidate George Bush pledged to "partially privatize" Social Security by diverting 2% of the payroll tax (a little less than a sixth of the program's revenue) into individual accounts. The fight is on and the privatizers have come out swinging.

Why Privatizating Social Security Is a Bad Idea

There are four major hidden flaws of privatizing Social Security: the enormous transition from a "pay as you go" to a pre-funded system, the costs associated with purchasing equivalent life and disability coverage (or maintaining the current disability and life insurance program in the context of a 16% cut in revenue), market risk, and higher administrative costs.

Transition costs   Privatizers face a costly transition period lasting 40–70 years. If pre-funded individual accounts were to be adopted, the generations living through the transition would have to pay for two systems at once, saving for their own retirement while paying for the Social Security benefits of their parents and grandparents.

Replacing disability and life insurance   A sleight of hand used by many privatizers is to compare "returns" from Social Security—a social insurance and retirement program—to returns from private savings that provide only retirement benefits. Social Security taxes pay for disability and life insurance as well as retirement benefits. The program provides life and disability insurance to American workers and their families at an estimated value of a $230,000 disability policy and a $354,000 life insurance policy for a typical worker. Privatizers argue that individuals can purchase disability and life insurance from private insurance firms. However, evidence from other countries' experiments with privatization suggests that insurance similar to Social Security would be costly. For people with pre-existing conditions, private disability and life insurance may not be available at any price.

Overly optimistic returns on stocks   Another problem with privatization is the assumption that the stock market will perform as well in the coming decades as it has in the recent past—a risky assumption. In fact, many economists believe that the stock market may be at a peak, and many stocks may be overvalued. Privatizers can't have it both ways—either the economy will be strong and the solvency problem projected for the current system won't materialize, or the economy will slow and the rate of return on stocks will drop, lowering the balances of individual accounts. Even if the stock market does well on average, individual accounts mean that there would be winners and losers. People who have greater knowledge and more money to invest will get higher returns than others. For low earners, who have less to invest and are less able to take risks, attaining average rates of return is unlikely. People who are unlucky or unwise could end up losing most or all of their money, placing additional burdens on SSI and other government programs that provide some safety net to poor people.

Administrative costs   Another problem with the privatizers' arithmetic is the failure to account for administrative costs. It costs a lot more to administer 150 million individual accounts than a single centralized system like Social Security. Experts conservatively estimate that it would cost about $25–$50 per participant per year to administer on top of the current system, which costs about

$16 per person. Even small increases in management costs that are assessed monthly or annually can result in a large loss of value over one's lifetime. For example, if the costs of operating a system of individual accounts were 1% of account balances each year (a conservative estimate of the administrative costs of a 401(k) plan), these costs would consume approximately 20% of funds in personal accounts over a 40-year career, in addition to (not instead of) the current costs for administering Social Security. For lower income workers who have smaller accounts, administrative costs would absorb a greater percentage of their total value.

Why Privatizing Social Security Is a Particularly Bad Idea for Women

Social Security is important for women because older women enter retirement with fewer economic resources than men. For example, in 1998, older women had a higher poverty rate (12.8%) than older men (7.2%). Women of color are particularly at risk for poverty in their old age. Overall, there is a substantial gender gap in all sources of retirement income including Social Security, pensions, savings, and post-retirement employment. The greatest disparity lies in accumulated pension wealth and savings, with Social Security credits partially compensating for this gap.

Furthermore, the Social Security system is progressive. Those with lower incomes have a higher proportion of their earnings replaced, which is valuable for women since they tend to earn less than men do. Income inequality would be further exacerbated in a privatized system because women investors, who have fewer resources, would get a lower yield on their investment as they would (appropriately) avoid risk.

Another important component of Social Security for women is the spousal benefit available to wives (or husbands) or widows (or widowers) who earned significantly less than their spouses. A married person is eligible for the larger of either 100% of his or her own retired worker benefit or 50% of his or her spouse's retired worker benefit. Women (or men) divorced after ten years of marriage can claim spousal benefits, even if their former partner remarries. Women make up the vast majority of recipients using the spousal benefit provision. In 1997, 13% of women beneficiaries claimed spousal benefits compared with 2% of men. While the spousal benefit is an imperfect acknowledgement of unpaid care-giving, it is preferable to a system of individual accounts" which allocates no monetary reward for child-rearing or elder care.

Social Security's "gender neutral" benefits mean that women don't have to pay more to compensate for their longer life expectancies—another advantage that would be lost in privatization.

The fact that Social Security provides an inflation-adjusted benefit guaranteed for life is particularly important to older women (who live on average three years longer than men).

Another aspect of Social Security that is especially valuable to women is the life and disability insurance, which includes benefits to spouses caring for children under 16 if the worker retires, becomes disabled, or dies. As women provide the bulk of care-giving in our society (for the elderly and disabled as well as for children), any shortcomings in disability and life insurance caused by privatization would have a special adverse impact on women.

Social Security Can Do Better

Having looked at the serious drawbacks of privatizing Social Security, we can return to the real issues facing Social Security. Certainly, it is true that people are living longer and that prudent financial planning dictates that the government should maintain adequate reserves. To the extent there are long-term solvency concerns, there are a number of ways to increase revenue into Social Security. For example, the cap on the earnings subject to the payroll tax could be lifted, meaning that everyone—even those who make six or seven figures—would pay the same payroll tax rate. Another (no doubt unpopular) approach would be to allow all Social Security benefits to be taxed as income and use these revenues for benefits. Investing a portion of the Trust Fund in higher-yield public or private securities is another option. This recommendation differs from proposals that privatize Social Security through individual accounts because investments would be made by a central, independent organization, sharing risk across the entire system and holding down administrative costs. Moreover, only a small portion of the Social Security fund reserves would be dedicated to this alternative investment strategy; thus limiting the system's overall exposure to risk.

It is also true that Americans, especially low- and moderate-income Americans, don't save enough for retirement. Even with generous tax deferment for pensions, it is increasingly clear that private pension plans will never cover the entire workforce. More than two decades after the Employee Retirement Income Security Act (ERISA), more than half of American workers are not covered by a pension plan. The economic situation for older women is particularly bleak. Among the elderly, women are only about half as likely as men to receive income from private pensions (including income from a spouse's pension), and those who do receive pension benefits that are only about half as large as men's benefits. For example, in 1996, pension income for women averaged $3,679, compared with $6,442 for men.

Differences in access to pensions represent a significant gap in federal resources. Because pension funds' earnings are not taxed, because employer contributions to pensions are considered tax-deductible business expenses, and because employees are not taxed until they retire (and begin drawing a pension), there is a significant tax advantage for pension holders. For example, in 1999, the Office of Management and Budget estimated that the federal government lost $84 billion in tax revenue. Thus, unequal access to pensions means that these tax favors are also unequally distributed.

There are a number of ways to give low- and moderate-income families access to the tax benefits associated with pensions (now disproportionately enjoyed by their wealthier counterparts). Vice President [Al] Gore's recent proposal for Retirement Savings Plus accounts would be a step in the right direction. This program would help middle-income and even low-income families save for retirement by matching private savings with government money. Lower income families would get the most help (families making less than $30,000 would receive $3 for every dollar they save), but middle- and upper-income families would also benefit (families making $100,000 would receive one dollar for every $3 saved). The accounts would be limited to $2,000 annually and savings would grow tax-free until withdrawal, like an individual retirement account or a 401(k) plan. But remember, these "individual accounts" should come on top of, rather than as a partial substitute for, guaranteed Social Security benefits.

Last, but not least, progressives should begin fighting to improve Social Security benefits. The safety net for the poorest elderly and disabled people is dropping lower and lower as means-tested programs, such as SSI, fail to keep pace with a growing economy. Under constant pressure to protect Social Security from Wall Street's wrecking ball, advocacy groups and politicians have shied away from increasing benefits for anyone. However, there is ample evidence that such improvements are needed—particularly for disabled people and older women not living with men, who are at high risk for poverty. Again, Gore's proposals to increase benefits for widows and people who took time out of the labor force (or worked part-time) to care for children are another step in the right direction. Now is a time of great prosperity, and we can afford to begin mending the safety net so frayed over the past two decades—perhaps, even raise it!

POSTSCRIPT

Should Social Security Be Privatized?

Tanner bases his support for a private retirement system to replace Social Security on four arguments. First, he states that Social Security has been a failure as an antipoverty program. Second, he contends that Social Security has been a failure as a retirement program. Third, Tanner asserts that Social Security is fundamentally unfair. Here he is concerned with both intergenerational and intragenerational transfers. Tanner's final argument is that Social Security reduces the dignity of older Americans. This is the case because seniors must depend on government and the political process for their retirement income. The solution to all these problems, according to Tanner, is to privatize Social Security; that is, to replace the current system with individually owned, privately invested accounts.

Hill defends the current Social Security system and opposes privatization. She begins her argument by lauding the current system: it is the sole source of income for 25 percent of elderly women living alone, half of all elderly Americans would be poor without Social Security, and benefits are available to all workers and their families. Turning to privatization, Hill identifies general flaws and finds additional problems with regard to the impact of privatization on women. In rejecting privatization, Hill suggests some changes to the current system that would address the Social Security crisis. These suggestions range from the expansion of the base for Social Security payroll taxes to actions to stimulate private savings for retirement.

Additional readings on this issue include "How Not to Fix Social Security," by Mark Weisbrot, *Dollars and Sense* (March/April 1997) and "The Great Social Security Scare," by Jerry L. Mashaw and Theodore R. Marmor, *The American Prospect* (November/December 1996). Also see three articles in *Economic Commentary:* "Should Social Security Be Privatized?" by Jagadeesh Gokhale (September 1995); "Social Security: Are We Getting Our Money's Worth?" by Jagadeesh Gokhale and Kevin J. Lansing (January 1, 1996); and "A Simple Proposal for Privatizing Social Security," by David Altig and Jagadeesh Gokhale (May 1, 1996). In addition, see the Institute for Women's Policy Research report *Why Privatizing Social Security Would Hurt Women: A Response to the Cato Institute's Proposal for Individual Accounts* by Catherine Hill, Lois Shaw, and Heidi Hartman (March 2000); "Strengthening Social Security for the Twenty-First Century" by Marilyn Watkins, an Economic Opportunity Institute Policy Brief; and "Assuring Retirement Income for All Workers" by Daniel I. Halperin and Alicia H. Munnell, Working Paper No. 2000–05, Center for Retirement Research, Boston College (March 2000).

ISSUE 8

Does the Consumer Price Index Overstate Inflation and Changes in the Cost of Living?

YES: Michael J. Boskin et al., from "Consumer Prices, the Consumer Price Index, and the Cost of Living," *Journal of Economic Perspectives* (Winter 1998)

NO: James Devine, from "The Cost of Living and Hidden Inflation," *Challenge* (March–April 2001)

ISSUE SUMMARY

YES: Economist Michael J. Boskin and his colleagues argue that the Consumer Price Index (CPI) suffers from quality and new product bias, which means that the CPI overstates inflation and increases in the cost of living.

NO: Professor of economics James Devine counters that the Consumer Price Index understates inflation and changes in the cost of living because it fails to account for all pertinent changes in the quality of life.

Each month the Bureau of Labor Statistics (BLS) releases a new estimate of the Consumer Price Index (CPI). This release usually merits front-page attention in U.S. newspapers because changes in the CPI are interpreted as changes in the cost of living of Americans. If nominal income does not increase to keep pace with increases in the cost of living, as determined by increases in the CPI, then real income falls.

Because of this connection between changes in the CPI and changes in the cost of living, a number of monetary arrangements in the economy are altered when the CPI changes; that is, they are indexed. For example, some private sector collective bargaining agreements tie wages to changes in the CPI. If the CPI increases, then wages automatically rise by the same percentage. But indexing is not limited to the private sector of the economy; the federal government has resorted to indexing in a variety of areas. In counting the number of poor persons, the poverty thresholds (the income levels that separate poor from nonpoor) are adjusted upward each year by the percentage increase in the CPI. With the individual income tax, the dollar value of the personal exemption is adjusted to reflect changes in the cost of living as determined by changes in the CPI. Social Security benefits are also adjusted each year to reflect changes in the cost of living and the CPI.

It is clearly important, then, to measure changes in the CPI and in the cost of living accurately. This issue addresses the question of the extent to which this accuracy is achieved. As a first step in understanding this debate, it is important to know how the CPI is calculated. The CPI, in technical terms, is a Laspeyres fixed-weight index. Accordingly, the first step in the calculation of the CPI is to determine the fixed weights—the goods and services that consumers purchase at a particular point in time known as the base period. This is known as the market basket and is accomplished by surveys of consumer purchasing behavior. The market basket can be considered the expenditure pattern of the typical consumer. The second step is to gather information regarding the prices of the goods and services in the market basket, and this is done every month. The price information is necessary to determine the cost of the market basket. The cost of the market basket changes as prices change, but the market basket itself does not (it is fixed). If the cost of the market basket increases, then it costs the typical consumer more to buy an unchanged bundle of goods and services; that is, the cost of living has increased. The ratio of the cost of the market basket in the current period to the cost of the market basket in the base period (multiplied by 100) provides the current numerical value of the CPI. The percentage change in the CPI between any two periods represents the rate of inflation in consumer prices between those two periods and, by extension, the percentage change in the cost of living between those two periods. But a number of conditions must be satisfied if the CPI is to be an accurate measure of price and cost of living changes.

One condition is that the market basket must either remain unchanged or be properly adjusted to account for new products or changes in the quality of old products. The Bureau of Labor Statistics recognizes this and attempts to make adjustments to rectify the problem. In the following selection, Michael J. Boskin et al. assert that the adjustments are insufficient. They conclude that the CPI suffers from quality and new product bias and, as a consequence, overstates price and cost of living changes.

A second condition that needs to be satisfied if the CPI is to be accurate is that the CPI must include all of the things that truly impact individual and societal well-being. In the second selection, James Devine contends that because the CPI ignores some important factors affecting the quality of life, such as environmental quality, amount of leisure time, and the distribution of income, it understates changes in the cost of living. It should be noted that Boskin et al. were members of the Advisory Commission to Study the Consumer Price Index (the Boskin commission), constituted by the Senate Finance Committee. The selection by Boskin et al. is based on the commission's final report, *Toward a More Accurate Measure of the Cost of Living*, which was submitted early in 1996.

Michael J. Boskin et al.  **YES**

Consumer Prices, the Consumer Price Index, and the Cost of Living

Accurately measuring prices and their rate of change, inflation, is central to almost every economic issue. There is virtually no other issue that is so endemic to every field of economics. Some examples include aggregate growth and productivity; industry prices and productivity; government taxes and spending programs that are indexed to inflation; budget deficits and debt; monetary policy; real financial returns; real wages, real median incomes and poverty rates; and the comparative performance of economies.

In mid-1995, the Senate Finance Committee, pursuant to a Senate Resolution, appointed an Advisory Committee to study the Consumer Price Index (CPI) with the five authors of this article as its members. The CPI Commission concluded that the change in the Consumer Price Index overstates the change in the cost of living by about 1.1 percentage points per year, with a range of plausible values of 0.8 to 1.6 percentage points (Boskin et al., 1996). That is, if inflation as measured by the percentage change in the CPI is running 3 percent, the true change in the cost of living is about 2 percent. This bias might seem small, but when compounded over time, the implications are enormous. Over a dozen years, the cumulative additional national debt from overindexing the budget would amount to more than $1 trillion. The implications of overstating inflation for understanding economic progress are equally dramatic. Over the last quarter-century, average real earnings have risen, not fallen, and real median income has grown, not stagnated. The poverty rate would be lower. Because the CPI component price indexes are inputs into the national income accounts, an overstated CPI implies that real GDP (gross domestic product] growth has been understated (Boskin and Jorgenson, 1997). . . .

Since the publication of our report, in a series of professional meetings, Congressional hearings, and other events, there has been much support for, and criticism of, the findings and recommendations of the CPI Commission. The purpose of this paper is to provide a readily accessible and self-contained discussion of the issues involved.

At this point in the debate, we see no reason to change our original estimate of a 1.1 percentage point per annum upward bias in the change in the Consumer

From Michael J. Boskin, Ellen R. Dulberger, Robert J. Gordon, Zvi Griliches, and Dale W. Jorgenson, "Consumer Prices, the Consumer Price Index, and the Cost of Living," *Journal of Economic Perspectives* (Winter 1998). Copyright © 1998 by The American Economic Association. Reprinted by permission.

Price Index. We strongly endorse the proposed improvements the Bureau of Labor Statistics (BLS) is currently planning to make, research, or explore (Abraham et al., 1998), but believe it can and should, if given the appropriate resources, do far more to improve the CPI than it currently contemplates. . . .

The Debate Over Quality Change and New Product Bias

Most of the criticism has focused on our extensive analysis of quality change and new product bias. On the question as to whether estimates of quality change bias are inevitably too "subjective" and "judgmental" to be taken seriously, it is, of course, at least as subjective to assume that every CPI category not subject to careful research has a zero bias as to extrapolate research-based estimates from one category to another. The notion that assuming zero bias is scientific, whereas attempting to generalize cautiously from related goods or practical reasoning is not precise enough, strikes us as unreasonable. Even though we will never precisely measure the value of the invention of, say, the jet airplane, as economists we *know* the consumer surplus triangles are positive, not zero. Likewise, we have known for years that PC's with Pentium processors are objectively higher quality (faster) than the 386 and 486 machines they replaced.

Hence, the Commission examined 27 subcomponents of the CPI, and most of our estimates of quality change are based on the collection of price data from independent sources and the careful quality adjustment of those independent data. Independent sources of price data are employed in our bias estimates for shelter, appliances, radio-TV, personal computers, apparel, public transportation, prescription drugs, and medical care. Estimates derived from these categories are extrapolated, sometimes partially rather than fully, to other house furnishings, nonprescription drugs, entertainment, commodities, and personal care. This leaves only a few remaining categories where we added a bias estimate to the CPI category in which there are already quality adjustments, rather than computing the bias estimate indirectly by subtracting an independent estimate from the CPI estimate for the same category. These categories are food and beverages, other utilities, new and used cars, and motor fuel, and personal expenses. The BLS does not object to our "down in the trenches" approach to the problem. Indeed, Moulton and Moses (1997) state, "This is the first time that a systematic analysis of quality bias has been done category by category, which we consider to be a noteworthy accomplishment of the Commission. . . . [the] overall approach seems to us to be a sensible and useful way to approach the problem of coming up with an overall assessment of bias, and we expect this type of structure will prove to be useful in the future."

Some outside critics of the Commission have argued that the BLS already does a great deal of quality adjustment, and that the Commission report is flawed for ignoring the extent of the BLS adjustments. However, for most categories, the extent of current BLS quality adjustments is irrelevant to an assessment of the Commission report's treatment of quality change. We were comparing our own evidence to the corresponding CPI indexes—however they are quality-adjusted, in a major or minor way—and thus our estimates of quality change bias are a residual that remains after the BLS has completed its efforts.

However, it is still instructive to discuss what the BLS calls quality adjustment, since it illustrates the substantive and communication difficulties in this field. There is presently very little explicit adjustment for quality change (Nordhaus, 1998). Most of the reported "quality adjustment" by the BLS comes from "linking" procedures, where a missing item is replaced by another.[1] *No* judgment at all is made about the quality differential between the new and old item. The price change during the link period is imputed, by using either the inflation rate in the overall CPI or of other commodities in the particular class. Roughly one out of three items disappear sometime during the year and have to be replaced by a different item in the same general class, such as a larger versus a smaller package of yogurt, a blue raincoat versus black, a 12-cubic-foot refrigerator with its freezer at the bottom rather than at the top. But this churning is not what we had in mind by "quality change," which rather involves the appearance of new and improved goods, greater speed, durability, variety, convenience, safety, energy efficiency, and so on. Some examples include the increased variety and freshness of vegetables and fish due to improving transport facilities and the globalization of trade, the substitution of laparoscopic procedures for gallstone operations, and many more.

Yes, the BLS does lots of "price adjustments." It is forced to by its sampling framework and the product turmoil in the markets. However, the BLS is not looking for the "quality change" that we were worried about. And it does not adjust explicitly for quality *change,* as we were defining it, except in the case of automobiles, apparel, and possibly rental apartment units and the occasional truly new goods caught by their substitution procedures.[2] While some of the Commission's estimates can be questioned—in both directions—there is very little overlap between them and the recent numbers produced by the BLS.

The helpful Moulton and Moses (1997) discussion of several categories would probably lead us to reduce our overall quality change bias estimate by perhaps 0.1 of the total 0.6 percentage points, if that were the only new information since the report, but other new research information and criticism goes in the opposite direction. Eventually, even though it may turn out that some of our estimates of quality change may be too high, others are likely to be too low.[3] Remember that except for a few cases, with low overall weight in the index, we did not explicitly estimate the additional welfare gain of the numerous new commodities in the economy. In the Commission's report, we indicate this is, in our view, a major source of the improvement in living standards. We also indicate that major problems occurred with the very late introduction of VCRs, microwave ovens, personal computers, and the soon to be introduced cellular telephone service. We indicated that the appropriate way to deal with new products is to value the consumer surplus from their introduction, as first demonstrated by Hicks (1940), and recently nicely elaborated and applied by Hausman (1996). However, we were *cautious* in this regard because, while we conjecture that the rate of introduction of new products is likely to be no different in the foreseeable future than it has been in the past (and some would even argue that the pace of introduction of new products is accelerating), it is difficult to predict which new products will become important that will not be picked up with the current BLS procedures. Perhaps many Internet-related activities are candidates. In any event, we chose to deal with this by being deliberately cautious, but indicating that there was an asymmetrical bias with more potential bias on the upside than the downside because of the likely future new product introductions which were unlikely to be captured in the CPI program.

Nor did we try to quantify all of the intangible aspects of quality change, such as the improved safety of home power tools or the improved quality of stereo sound and TV pictures. But we did try to do so in some cases; for example, the increased freshness and timeliness of fruits and vegetables.

Our report considered that new goods may drive out older goods which are still valued by a subgroup of the population, or the loss of economies of scale may drive up their price. Existing goods and services may deteriorate in quality, although only a few examples can be found, as on balance, the improvement in quality is overwhelming. For example, despite the recent complaints about how health maintenance organizations have tightened up the rules of access to medical care, few would argue that unrestricted access to the technologies of yesteryear is preferable to more restricted access to the recent improvements in bypass operations, ulcer treatments, or cataract surgeries. . . .

Conclusion

While the CPI is the best measure currently available, it is not a cost-of-living index and it suffers from a variety of conceptual and practical problems. Despite important BLS updates and improvements over time, the change in the CPI has substantially overstated the actual rate of inflation, and is likely to continue to overstate the change in the cost of living for the foreseeable future. This overstatement will have important unintended consequences, including overindexing government outlays and tax brackets and increasing the federal deficit and debt. Moreover, such revisions as have occurred have not been carried out in a way that can provide an internally consistent series on the cost of living over an extended span of time.

The CPI Commission's report and findings have, in our opinion, held up to criticism and scrutiny quite well. Our overall estimate of about 1.1 percentage point of upward bias per year in the growth of the CPI still seems right to us, especially because we were so cautious in the treatment of the bias from new products. The purposes of our Commission's report included: disseminating information about the complexity of constructing a cost-of-living index; generating additional intellectual capital from academe and the private sector; and suggesting potential improvements. But these improvements must be considered, as we said in the report, with more appreciation of the efforts of our colleagues in the BLS and other government statistical agencies and an understanding of the constraints under which they are working. The BLS and other government statistical agencies have a remarkably complex task in a dynamic flexible market economy.

The analytical and econometric research done over recent decades has dramatically improved economists' understanding of the issues surrounding a cost-of-living index. We believe that improvements in geometric means, superlative indexes, more rapid introduction of new goods and new outlets, speedier updating of consumption weights, making use of hedonics and of related statistical tools, the use of scanner data, and other recommendations made here can substantially reduce the bias in the CPI going forward. Now, the time has come for governments in the United States and elsewhere to recognize these problems and to commit the resources to dealing with them. Virtually every major private firm in the world is spending heavily on information technology, and we should not expect better statistics from our government agencies without a corresponding investment.

We had hoped to provide an opportunity for the BLS (and the related statistical community) to implement an agenda for the most fundamental improvements in the nation's price statistics in many decades and to obtain financing (as necessary) for it. While we strongly support the modest improvements BLS is hoping to make (BLS, 1997; Abraham et al., 1998), we would hope that over time the size and scope of the reform agenda will expand.[4]

Ultimately, the president and Congress must decide whether they wish to continue the widespread overindexing of government programs. If the purpose of the indexing is to compensate recipients of the indexed programs or taxpayers from changes in the cost of living, no more and no less, they should move to wholly or partly adjust the indexing formulas, taking due account of the partial improvements BLS will make along the way. Such changes will have profound ramifications for our fiscal futures, but these changes should be made even if the budget was in surplus and there was no long-run entitlement cost problem. They should be made first and foremost in the interest of accuracy not only for the budget and the programs, but for the economic information upon which citizens depend.

Notes

1. In Moulton and Moses (1997), 1.65 out of the 1.76 percentage points in BLS quality adjustments come from linking procedures. If one excludes outliers, defined as commodity pairs where the implicit price-quality differential exceeds 100 percent, the quality adjustment number shrinks to 0.3 percentage points.

2. In Moulton and Moses (1997), such explicit quality adjustments account for only about 6 percent of the total "treatment of substitutions" effect, and amount to only 0.08 percent per year in the "outlier-cleaned" recomputations.

3. Recent evidence that we may have underestimated the biases in some of the areas we did examine comes from an alternative measure of consumer prices, the PCE (personal consumption expenditures) deflator, which has been rising by about one-third percent less per year (since 1992) than the CPI. An unpublished examination of this difference by the BLS indicates that most of it arises from the use by the BEA of alternative price indexes for hospital expenditures and airfares. These indexes do not adjust for any of the quality changes mentioned by us.

4. We have been told by leaders in government statistics agencies around the world that they were surprised that the BLS initially reacted defensively to the Commission Report, and failed to capitalize fully on the opportunity it presented.

References

Abraham, Katherine G., John S. Greenlees, and Brent R. Moulton, "Working to Improve the Consumer Price Index," *Journal of Economic Perspectives,* Winter 1998, *12*:1.

Boskin, Michael J., and Dale W. Jorgenson, "Implications of Overstating Inflation for Indexing Government Programs and Understanding Economic Progress," 1997 Papers and Proceedings, *American Economic Review,* May 1997, *87*: 2, 89–93.

Boskin, Michael J., E. Dulberger, R. Gordon, Z. Griliches, and D. Jorgenson, "Toward a More Accurate Measure of the Cost of Living," Final Report to the Senate Finance Committee, December 4, 1996.

Hausman, Jerry, "Valuation of New Goods Under Perfect and Imperfect Competition." In Bresnahan, T. and Robert J. Gordon, eds. *The Economics of New Goods.* Chicago: University of Chicago Press, 1996.

Hicks, John R., "The Valuation of the Social Income," *Economica,* May 1940, 7:26, 105–24.

Moulton, Brent R., and Karin E. Moses, "Addressing the Quality Change Issue in the Consumer Price Index," forthcoming in *Brookings Papers on Economic Activity,* 1997.

Nordhaus, William D., "Quality Changes in Price Indexes," *Journal of Economic Perspectives,* Winter 1998, *12*:1.

U.S. Bureau of Labor Statistics, "Measurement Issues in the Consumer Price Index." Response to the U.S. Congress, Joint Economic Committee, June 1997.

James Devine

 **NO**

The Cost of Living and Hidden Inflation

Economists generally argue that inflation is overstated by the federal govern-ment because it does not sufficiently account for the improved quality of prod-ucts. This economist believes that if we account for all pertinent changes in the quality of life, inflation is understated.

Despite low reported inflation rates in recent years and official recalculations of the inflation rate that reduce it even further, these measures underestimate the true increases in the cost of living. Official measures of inflation, such as the Consumer Price Index (CPI) and the Personal Consumption Expenditure (PCE) deflator, are market-oriented, measuring only the decrease in our money's power to purchase products currently available for sale. This article presents a preliminary alternative measure of inflation, the cost-of-living (COL) inflation rate, which brings in nonmarket elements of people's existence, such as the costs arising from pollution. Compared to the government's official measures of consumer prices, these elements raise the amount of money income needed to keep real standards of living from falling.

The COL measure suggests that in terms of the issues that working people care about, inflation continues above the officially measured rate, even using the most conservative measure of the COL: For the period 1951–1998, the an-nual COL inflation rate averaged 4.1 percent, about 0.4 of a percentage point higher than the inflation rate implied by the PCE deflator and about 0.1 percent higher than the inflation rate implied by the CPI. (Since the PCE deflator's method of calculation is similar to that of the COL, the former comparison is more meaningful.) Worse, the gaps between the COL and official inflation have widened: Between 1980 and 1998, on average the COL rose about 0.7 of a per-centage point per year more than the PCE price and 0.3 more than the CPI.

These numbers imply that the gap between officially measured real wages and the real benefit received from wages has widened (at an increasing rate). To understand this assertion, however, we must reexamine the basics.

From James Devine, "The Cost of Living and Hidden Inflation," *Challenge,* vol. 44, no. 2 (March–April 2001), pp. 73–84. Copyright © 2001 by M. E. Sharpe, Inc. Reprinted by permission. References omitted.

Measuring Inflation and "Real" Wages

In addition to measuring the inflation rate (the percentage rise in prices), indices such as the CPI are commonly used to find the "real value" of nominal magnitudes. Real wages, for example, are measured as follows:

Constant-price wage = (money wage)/CPI

Thus, for example, because the CPI rose so quickly between 1970 and 1979, real average private-sector weekly earnings fell by 2 percent—even though money (nominal) wages rose by almost 90 percent.

During the late 1990s, controversy raged over technical issues concerning the method of calculation of the CPI.[1] Appointed by Congress to suggest recalculation of the CPI, Stanford professor Michael Boskin and his colleagues argued that the CPI should be reformulated to make it a more accurate measure of the "cost of living." For example, the CPI should be adjusted for the quality improvements that they assumed occurred for many products in the consumption basket used to measure the index, the availability of new products, and the rise of low-cost retail outlets like Wal-Mart.

The Bureau of Labor Statistics (BLS) has accepted many or most of the Boskin recommendations, adjusting their estimates of CPI inflation downward. According to *Business Week,* "a significant chunk of the reported downturn in inflation since 1995—perhaps three-quarters of a percentage point—reflects changes in the behavior of statisticians rather than changes in the underlying pace of price hikes" (Koretz 1999). This estimation trend has gone further, with the Federal Reserve recently shifting its emphasis to the PCE deflator for calculating the inflation rate (Cooper and Madigan 2000). This measure generally rises more slowly than even the revamped CPI, because it reflects the rise in prices of the products that consumers actually buy, while ignoring the costs of the way that inflation pushes people to substitute one product for another (chicken for steak, for example).[2]

Other economists argued that the traditional formulation of the CPI was relatively accurate and did not need Boskin-type revisions.[3] They hoped to protect social security beneficiaries and government workers with escalator clauses in their contracts from getting automatic raises below that of the actual inflation rate, which they saw as being better measured by the old version of the CPI. These revisions may not be all bad, however, since they delayed or moderated the Federal Reserve's use of economic slowdown or recession as a preemptive strike against inflation.

Often forgotten is that the official CPI is not truly a measure of the "cost of living" that people face, with or without Boskin revisions. As one BLS official notes, "A more complete cost-of-living index would go beyond [the CPI] to take into account the changes in other governmental or environmental factors that affect consumers' well-being" (Gibson 1998, p. 3). Robert Kuttner (1996) argues this point more strenuously: Official price indices leave out even more aspects of the true cost that people face in order to live, such as the cost of crime, lawsuits, pollution, and family breakdown. For example, the cutback in hours at the public library raises the cost of living by pushing people to buy books instead or lowers their quality of life by preventing them from reading. However, this cutback does not raise the measured CPI or PCE.[4] This is why I use the term "hidden inflation."

A calculation in light of Kuttner's criticism implies a gigantic and expensive research project, one that only the government could afford—and seems unlikely to engage in. Rather, I follow another hint from Kuttner: He points to the "Genuine Progress Indictor" (the GPI) calculated by the Redefining Progress think tank as an example of efforts to measure our economic welfare or "true living standards"—an alternative to real gross domestic product (GDP) as an indicator of society's progress. The GPI adjusts the official national income and product account measures for real benefits missed, such as contributions from housework, and costs that should be subtracted, such as that of using up nonreproducible natural resources. This article applies this research to calculate estimates of the "cost of living" and the "COL inflation rates" that are implied.

It is beyond this short article's scope to criticize official measures of inflation. However, even if Boskin-type adjustments are needed, if my estimates are anywhere close to being accurate, the costs of increases in pollution, commuting time, labor time, and the like more than cancel out Boskin-type adjustments.[5] As a first guess for calculating inflation rates, we might split the difference, clinging to the official price level as calculated before Boskin-type adjustments. Better, we should use different inflation rates for different purposes (Mitchell 1998). The CPI and the PCE attempt to measure purchasing power of a dollar in the market, while the COL gauges the actual cost of the benefits of everyday life.

The COL is measured by the amount of money spending needed to buy a constant quality of consumption as measured by the GPI calculations. Thus, a new version of the "real wage" can be calculated:

> Constant-COL wage = (money wage)/COL

. . .

Calculating the COL

The basic idea for calculating the COL index is similar to that behind the PCE deflator. The latter is the average price level implied by calculations of real consumption spending. As a first approximation,

> PCE deflator = (money spent on consumer goods)/(inflation-corrected sum of those goods)

The denominator is often interpreted as the "real" benefit to consumers of consumer spending.

Based on the Redefining Progress critique of real gross domestic product as a measure of social welfare, my most conservative COL estimate replaces real consumption with a measure of benefit received:

COL = (money spent on consumer goods)/(benefit received from current consumption)

where the denominator is a measure of those parts of the GPI that contribute to an individual's current enjoyment. Like those of the denominator of the PCE deflator, the components of this number are corrected for inflation. But it changes the official estimates of real consumer purchases by including the impact of extra current benefits and costs usually missed by the National Income and Product Accounts.[6]

Two types of examples explain the idea of COL inflation. Assume that consumption spending in both money and inflation-corrected terms is constant, so that the PCE price is constant and the official inflation rate using this measure equals zero. Suppose that the current benefits to consumers missed by the official accounts (extra current benefits) decrease. If the amount of unpaid housework, volunteer labor done, leisure time, or the services provided by publicly supplied streets and highways decreases, this means that fewer real benefits are received. Since money spending is constant, there has been a rise in dollars paid on the market per real benefit actually received. As with the public library example, there has been a decline in the benefit received from money spent.

Second, if the current costs missed by the official accounts (extra current costs) rise, that is, if people are suffering from increased pollution while spending the same amount of money buying consumer goods, it represents a decline in their living standard and a decrease in the value of the money spent. Similarly, if individuals suffer from increased costs of commuting (which are necessary to earn income), increased costs of auto accidents and crime, or decreased leisure time or family stability, the money that they spend is providing them with fewer benefits than it used to. Third, spending more money on necessary defensive goods (such as car locks or insurance) does not raise the real benefits received. Rather, it implies that the real benefits one does receive are more expensive to preserve.

Alternative COL Estimates

My "most conservative" COL estimates are consistent with common-sense notions of inflation and thus do not go as far away from the GDP calculations as the GPI does. First, the COL discussed above ignores distributional issues. As with the CPI, the PCE price, and most conceptions of "inflation," the concept of the cost of living used above is individualistic, referring to an average individual. While widening gaps in the distribution of income encourage the fraying of the social fabric and go against official societal goals, it is hard to assert that changes in distribution directly imply a higher cost of living for any individual. Those results of rising inequality that raise the cost of living, such as increases in street crime, are already measured as part of extra current costs and thus as part of the COL.

Next, forward-looking costs and benefits, which play a major role in the GPI, play no role in the calculation of the COL discussed above. When calculating the CPI or PCE price, aspects of living that refer to future impacts are omitted, since the concern is with current consumption, not with all benefits and costs received by future generations. In other words, the ecologically crucial cost of the destruction of wetlands or the ozone layer has little or no impact on our current cost of living or on the inflation rate as most conceive it. This attitude is very shortsighted, but exactly the same attitude is implicit in official calculations.

Less conservative estimates of COL inflation not only are higher but show an upward trend relative to official measures of the inflation rate. Though these more radical estimates of COL inflation do not fit with the common-sense meaning of the word "inflation" discussed above, these trends are important.

Table 1

Average Annual Additions to Inflation Rates (Percentage Points)

Dates	Conservative COL	With distributional adjustment	With forward-looking adjustment	With both adjustments
Additions to "conservative" COL				
1951–98	n.a.	0.2	0.8	1.4
1980–98	n.a.	0.6	1.0	2.6
Additions to PCE deflator inflation				
1951–98	0.4	0.6	1.2	1.8
1980–98	0.7	1.3	1.7	3.4
Additions to CPI inflation				
1951–98	0.1	0.2	0.9	1.8
1980–98	0.3	0.9	1.0	2.6

n.a.: not applicable.

If we drop the individualistic perspective of both the conservative COL and official numbers to include the effects of distributional shifts, my measures of COL inflation rise more in relation to official inflation rates. On average between 1951 and 1998, bringing in distributional issues added 0.2 of a percentage point to the conservative COL inflation rate and 0.6 of a percentage point to the PCE price inflation rate each year (see Table 1). For the period 1980–1998, these additions are 0.6 of a percentage point and 1.3 percentage point, respectively.

This results from the well-known widening of the gap between the rich and poor, as indicated by the falling share of total income accruing to the poorest fifth of the population. Alternatively, this says that COL inflation has hit the poorest fifth the hardest.

Another interpretation is that our ability to maintain low COL and CPI inflation rates simply means that the costs of societal problems are being shoved onto the backs of the poor. In terms of the distributional-conflict theory (cf. Rowthorn 1977), inflation can be reduced if one participant in the conflict—here, the poor—is pushed out. In other words, if the widening distributional gap could have been avoided, there would have been higher official inflation rates (or higher unemployment to restrain such inflation). Improving programs such as the minimum wage, unemployment insurance benefits, or "welfare" that help the poorest earn higher wages in order to allow constancy of the income distribution encourages businesses hiring such labor to raise prices. Recent slowing of official inflation rates despite falling unemployment rates is thus linked not only to measurement changes but to the widening distributional gap.

Both the conservative COL and the PCE-based inflation rates are also falling behind COL rates that include future-oriented costs and benefits, such as the cost of global warming and the loss of old-growth forests and the benefits of net investment. For 1951–1998, including such issues added 0.8 of a percentage point to the conservative COL estimate and 1.2 percentage points to the official inflation rate. These additions rise to 1.3 percentage points and 0.9 of a point for the 1980–1998 period. This result indicates that the paying of more and more of the costs of living on earth is being postponed to the future. We are currently enjoying relatively low inflation, as measured by both the conservative COL estimate and the CPI. However, the long-term costs in terms of the environment or slow growth of potential output (due to inadequate investment) will likely have to be paid in the future, in the form of environmental disaster, slow productivity growth, and the like. My measures suggest that if the nation were paying more of the environmental costs now or investing more in the future, both the official and COL inflation rates would be higher (or unemployment would be higher to restrain such inflation).

Policy Issues

Should the Federal Reserve make COL inflation its central concern? Under a literal interpretation of the current Fed goal of attaining zero inflation, it would spark slowdowns more than it has done already. But this is a wrong interpretation, since monetary policy cannot raise the extra current benefits or lower extra current costs as defined here. Since the Fed's main constituency (bond-holders and bankers) does not care about negative future effects, distributional changes, current external costs, or uncompensated labor, its policy experts understand this point. The job of fixing the extra costs and promoting the extra benefits belongs to other branches of the government. The problems, of course, arise because these other branches are doing inadequate jobs at dealing with these problems.

Where the COL measure is relevant is in indexing. That is, retirees, workers, and taxpayers should have their income protected (via indexing) from rises in the cost of living, not just those reflected by the official measures. Imposing Boskin-type adjustments on the CPI and thus on indexed incomes implies real cutbacks in benefits received not only because these modifications may be technically wrong, but also because they ignore the real meaning of the cost of living and thus overlook hidden inflation. Even though the idea of indexing incomes to prevent loss of real purchasing power seems politically utopian at this point, the Boskin "reforms" are nonetheless attacks on people's standards of living.

Notes

1. See the discussions in *Challenge* 40, no. 2 (March/April 1997), *Journal of Economic Perspectives* 12, no. 1 (winter 1998), and Baker (1998a, 1998b).
2. These costs are relevant only when inflation occurs relative to nominal incomes, but it is the race between prices and money incomes that evokes interest in measuring inflation in the first place.
3. See Madrick (1997a, 1997b) and the response by Gordon and Griliches (1997).
4. This example assumes that we do not benefit from tax cuts that match the decrease in public services. Throughout this paper, I assume that decreases in the tax burden do not cancel out increases in the COL. Given the relative constancy of tax obligations as a percentage of GDP, this is reasonable. But given the increasing regressivity of the tax system over recent decades, it suggests that the COL has risen faster for the bottom half of the income distribution than is indicated by the most conservative COL numbers.
5. This is in comparison to the similarly calculated CPE deflator, which, like the CPI, reflects Boskin-type revisions.
6. This makes the main assumption of the GPI calculation to calculate the benefits received from consumption, i.e., that pleasures received by people can be quantified and added up.

POSTSCRIPT

Does the Consumer Price Index Overstate Inflation and Changes in the Cost of Living?

Boskin et al. defend their estimate of the magnitude of quality change and new product bias with two fundamental arguments. First, they dismiss as unreasonable the criticism that estimates of such bias are too subjective. Second, they contend that the procedures used by the BLS are irrelevant because the Boskin et al. estimates are "a residual that remains after the BLS has completed its efforts." Boskin et al. note that most of the quality adjustments made by the BLS involve linking procedures when a new item replaces an old item. They contend that in these linking procedures there is no effort to judge the quality difference between the new and old items. This procedure thereby misses real quality differences associated with the "greater speed, durability, variety, convenience, safety, [and] energy efficiency" accompanying the introduction of new and improved goods.

Devine argues that price indexes that are used to calculate inflation and measure changes in the cost of living, such as the CPI and the Personal Consumption Expenditure (PCE) deflator, only reflect changes in money's ability to purchase products that are currently available for sale. A true measure of inflation and the cost of living, he maintains, should also include nonmarket elements that affect individual and societal well-being. Devine therefore proposes a more comprehensive measure of inflation and cost of living changes: the cost of living (COL) inflation rate. Devine finds that the conservative COL adds 0.3 percent to the average annual CPI inflation rate over the 1980–1998 period, while the COL with distribution and forward-looking adjustments adds 2.6 percent. Devine concludes that imposing the types of adjustments recommended by Boskin et al. on the CPI and on indexed incomes "implies real cutbacks in benefits received not only because these modifications may be technically wrong, but also because they ignore the real meaning of the cost of living and thus overlook hidden inflation."

Additional readings on this issue include "The Downside of Bad Data," by Everett Ehrlich, *Challenge* (March/April 1997); "How Right Is the Boskin Commission? Interview With Janet Norwood," *Challenge* (March/April 1997); "Quality Changes in the CPI: Some Missing Links," by Charles Hulten, *Challenge* (March/April 1997); "The Boskin Commission's Trillion-Dollar Fantasy," by Wynne Godley and George McCarthy, *Challenge* (May/June 1997); and "Bias in the Consumer Price Index: What Is the Evidence?" by Brent R. Moulton, *Journal of Economic Perspectives* (Fall 1996).

ISSUE 9

Should the Double Taxation of Corporate Dividends Be Eliminated?

YES: Norbert J. Michel, Alfredo Goyburu, and Ralph A. Rector, from "The Economic and Fiscal Effects of Ending the Federal Double Taxation of Dividends," A Working Paper of the Heritage Center for Data Analysis (January 27, 2003)

NO: Joel Friedman and Robert Greenstein, from "Exempting Corporate Dividends From Individual Income Taxes," A Report of the Center on Budget and Policy Priorities (January 11, 2003)

ISSUE SUMMARY

YES: Free-market economists Norbert J. Michel, Alfredo Goyburu, and Ralph A. Rector applaud the George W. Bush administration's initiative to eliminate the double taxation of corporate dividends. They assert that this action will improve economic efficiency and that, in the long run, this tax cut will pay for itself because it will stimulate economic growth.

NO: Economic policy analysts Joel Friedman and Robert Greenstein argue that there are no valid economic justifications to propose the elimination of the tax on dividends. All that cutting dividend taxes will really do, they say, is reduce the tax burden of high-income individuals.

The U.S. federal government engages in a wide variety of economic and non-economic activities. In the United States these activities range from the provision of national and domestic security to the construction and maintenance of public and private transportation systems. Additionally, the government provides economic security in the form of income transfers to the elderly, the unemployed, and the poor. Finally, it creates institutions that allow markets to flourish, since markets are the engines that drive the economic system. All of these efforts are taken for granted, are costly, and must be paid for. To finance these activities, governments have three options: they can create money, they can tax, or they can borrow. The United States does not create money, but the government certainly does tax and borrow.

Consider, for example, federal government total outlays and receipts for fiscal year 2002. That year alone the federal government spent $2.01 trillion. This was financed by $1.85 trillion in receipts or taxes, and since taxes were less than expenditures, America incurred $160 billion in new federal debt. The bulk of this tax revenue came from income-related taxes: the individual income tax raised $858 billion; payroll taxes—largely social security contributions—generated $701 billion; and last, as well as a distant third, corporate income taxes accounted for another $148 billion. All the other federal taxes combined—federal excise taxes, customs duties, estate/gift taxes, and a dozen or so miscellaneous taxes—summed to a total of $146 billion in tax revenue.

The unvarnished truth is that no one likes to pay taxes. However, making deep cuts in the tax system is not always practical, given that there is a widespread belief that all or most of the expenditures and transfers that are generally taken for granted are demanded by a majority of taxpayers. Although "taxes, like death" are inevitable, the displeasure with taxes can be minimized if the tax system meets two basic criteria: equity and efficiency.

The first criterion of equity, or fairness, from the economist's perspective, requires looking horizontally and vertically. That is, for a tax to be horizontally equitable, that tax must treat individuals in identical circumstances identically. In this case, those with the same economic characteristics should pay the same amount in taxes. Vertical equity is a bit more complicated. It assumes that unlike individuals will be treated unequally; that is, a person with greater tax-paying capacity should not pay the same amount of taxes as someone with a lower income. At a minimum, those with higher incomes should pay proportionally the same as those with lower incomes and, in some cases, share a larger percentage of the tax burden than those of more moderate means.

Besides being equitable, a tax system needs to satisfy a second general criterion. Taxes should not interfere significantly with the efficient operation of a market economy. Consider the case of an extreme tax that took all of an individual's income. Economists would argue that this tax is inefficient because it would undermine work incentives. In technical terms, since work and leisure are substitutes for one another, a 100 percent tax would make the price of an additional hour of leisure equal to zero. Why work if you are not going to be better off from working? In this case one would expect folks to work far less and therefore increase their consumption of leisure. If no one works, the size of the economic pie has to decline because resources are wasted.

Most would conclude that taxes are necessary and that policymakers should do all they can to impose taxes that take into account equitable and efficient consequences of these taxes. Unfortunately, sometimes in order to get equity, one must sacrifice efficiency. In other cases, in order to get efficiency, one has to sacrifice equity. The importance that is placed on one or the other of these two considerations helps shape which taxes we support and which we take issue with. In the following selections, Norbert J. Michel, Alfredo Goyburu, and Ralph A. Rector argue that, above all, policymakers should maximize efficiency. Joel Friedman and Robert Greenstein, on the other hand, plead the case for equity.

Norbert J. Michel, Alfredo Goyburu,
and Ralph A. Rector

The Economic and Fiscal Effects of Ending the Federal Double Taxation of Dividends

On January 7, 2003, President George W. Bush unveiled a multi-faceted proposal to improve the nation's economic growth. One of the most important features of his plan calls for abolition of the current federal double taxation of corporate dividends paid to individual shareholders. Economic analysts at the Center for Data Analysis (CDA) at The Heritage Foundation found, in a study of a dividend reform proposal similar to President Bush's, that ending the double taxation of dividends would improve the nation's economic growth, employment level, and other economic indicators over the next 10 years.

For example, CDA estimates indicate that the employment level would average 285,000 additional jobs from 2003 to 2012. In addition, CDA analysis has found that ending this double taxation would reduce federal revenue by $64 billion over ten years, or 79 percent less than an estimate that does not account for the effects of greater economic activity following the proposal's implementation. The CDA's $64 billion estimate is slightly more than one-fifth of the $364 billion cost estimated by the United States Department of the Treasury for President Bush's proposal.[1] The CDA and Treasury analyses consider slightly different proposals, but this cost difference is largely due to the more realistic estimation method used by the CDA.

The Treasury Department employs an erroneous "static" approach to estimate the revenue effect of tax law changes, while the CDA uses dynamic simulation, a method that accounts for the impact that federal tax policy may exert on economic growth.[2] Figure 1 shows that the estimation method chosen can make a large difference in the projected revenue loss. The figure compares the CDA's own static and dynamic projections of the federal revenue change resulting from a particular plan to end the double taxation of dividends.

This double taxation[3] has two stages. The first stage occurs when the federal government taxes shareholders on corporate income through corporate taxes. The second occurs after the corporation has distributed part of the post-tax profits to the shareholders in the form of dividends. In this second stage, the federal government taxes shareholders on their dividend income through the personal income tax.

From Norbert J. Michel, Alfredo Goyburu, and Ralph A. Rector, "The Economic and Fiscal Effects of Ending the Federal Double Taxation of Dividends," A Working Paper of the Heritage Center for Data Analysis (January 27, 2003). Copyright © 2003 by The Heritage Foundation. Reprinted by permission. Some notes omitted.

Figure 1

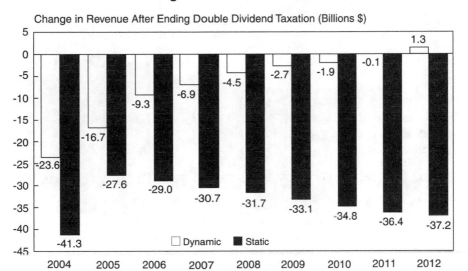

Dynamic vs. Erroneous Static Revenue Cost Estimates of Ending Double Dividend Taxation

Change in Revenue After Ending Double Dividend Taxation (Billions $)

Note: Assumes legislative enactment on September 30, 2003.

Source: Estimates by the Center for Data Analysis at The Heritage Foundation, using August 2002 Congressional Budget Office projections and the DRI–WEFA U.S. Macroeconomic Model.

Economists have long argued that the double taxation of dividends re-duces the after-tax return on capital in the nation's economy and thus discour-ages investment—in other words, purchases of new business equipment and machinery.[4] This reduced investment in turn weakens economic growth. Con-sequently, eliminating the double taxation would spur investment and im-prove the economy's long-term growth. Recognizing these economic benefits, several nations, including Australia, France, Italy, Canada, Germany, Japan, and the United Kingdom, have abolished or reduced their double taxation of corpo-rate dividends.[5]

One recent legislative proposal to abolish this double taxation in the United States was sponsored by Representative Christopher Cox (R–CA).[6] The Heritage Foundation's CDA used this proposal to illustrate the economic and federal fiscal effects of ending the double taxation of dividends.[7] To estimate these effects, Heritage analysts employed the DRI–WEFA U.S. Macroeconomic Model and the Center's own Individual Income Tax Model. Assuming the re-form becomes law in September 2003, the investigation found that:[8]

- *GDP increases.* During the period from 2003 through 2012, the Cox pro-posal would increase the nation's gross domestic product (GDP) by an inflation-adjusted[9] $32 billion per year on average, compared to what it would otherwise have been. GDP would be at least $22 billion higher in

Figure 2

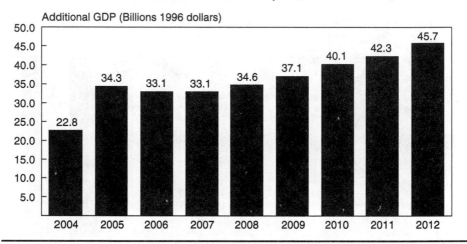

Ending Double Taxation of Dividends Bolsters Economic Growth, Gross Domestic Product Compared to Baseline

Additional GDP (Billions 1996 dollars)

Year	Additional GDP
2004	22.8
2005	34.3
2006	33.1
2007	33.1
2008	34.6
2009	37.1
2010	40.1
2011	42.3
2012	45.7

Note: Assumes legislative enactment on September 30, 2003.

Source: Estimates by the Center for Data Analysis at The Heritage Foundation, using August 2002 Congressional Budget Office projections and the DRI–WEFA U.S. Macroeconomic Model.

2004 and no less than $45 billion higher in 2012 if the proposal were to be implemented. (See Figure 2.)

- *Employment grows.* The provisions in the Cox bill would enable the economy to support 325,000 more jobs by 2012. (See Figure 3.) With these additional jobs in the economy, the unemployment rate would be 0.2 percent lower throughout the period 2005–2012 than current projections indicate.

- *Investment strengthens.* Over the 10-year period from 2003 through 2012, the proposal would result in an aggregate increase of at least $253 billion (adjusted for inflation) in non-residential investment. Because of this higher level of investment, the nation's non-residential capital stock would be $175 billion higher in 2012. (See Figure 4.)

- *Disposable income picks up.* Under the Cox legislation, disposable personal income would average an inflation-adjusted $56 billion higher from 2003 through 2012. (See Figure 5.) This higher level would raise annual disposable personal income by $192 per person on average during the period. For a family of four, this increase would correspond to $768 more in disposable income on average each year.

- *Personal savings increases.* The proposal would increase personal savings by an inflation-adjusted average of $18 billion per year from 2003 through 2012.

- *Higher economic growth reduces the "cost" to the Treasury by over 70 percent.* The CDA's own static estimates suggest the proposal would reduce federal revenue by about $300 billion from 2003 through 2012. However,

Figure 3

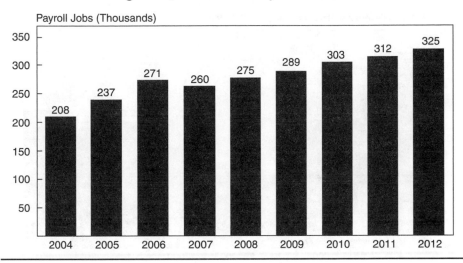

**Ending Double Taxation of Dividends
Strengthens Job Growth Compared to Baseline**

Note: Assumes legislative enactment on September 30, 2003.

Source: Estimates by the Center for Data Analysis at The Heritage Foundation, using August 2002 Congressional Budget Office projections and the DRI–WEFA U.S. Macroeconomic Model.

Figure 4

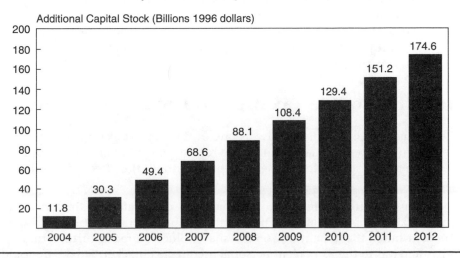

**Ending Double Taxation of Dividends Raises Net
Capital Stock Compared to Baseline**

Note: Assumes legislative enactment on September 30, 2003.

Source: Estimates by the Center for Data Analysis at The Heritage Foundation, using August 2002 Congressional Budget Office projections and the DRI–WEFA U.S. Macroeconomic Model.

Figure 5

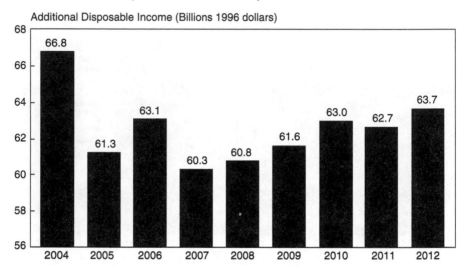

**Ending Double Taxation of Dividends Boosts
Disposable Income Compared to Baseline**

Additional Disposable Income (Billions 1996 dollars)

Note: Assumes legislative enactment on September 30, 2003.

Source: Estimates by the Center for Data Analysis at The Heritage Foundation, using August 2002 Congressional Budget Office projections and the DRI–WEFA U.S. Macroeconomic Model.

the CDA's more realistic *dynamic* estimates show that the proposal would reduce federal revenue during the period by a total of $64 billion. (See Figure 1.) During the last five years, the proposal would be nearly revenue neutral, since the improved economic growth caused by the legislation would, in turn, increase tax collections. For reasons discussed below, these estimates do not take into account the way in which the proposal's effect on capital gains tax collections would change federal tax revenue.

How the Double Taxation of Dividends Works

The double taxation of dividends[10] is one of the clearest examples of the way the nation's current tax law reduces the return on capital and, therefore, the incentive to invest. The following example illustrates the effect of this double taxation.

Consider $100 in pre-tax profit earned by a corporation in the flat 35 percent bracket. Suppose that, after paying the $35 in federal corporate taxes, the firm distributed the remaining $65 to a shareholder. Suppose, further, that this individual was in the 27 percent personal income tax bracket. This shareholder would pay $17.55 in personal income taxes on these dividends. This second round of taxation would leave only $47.45 of the original $100 in corporate profits. In other words, for every $100 in pre-tax profits, the federal government would absorb approximately $52.55 in taxes.

In contrast, consider the taxes the shareholder might have paid if that person could have received the dividend before the firm paid corporate taxes. In this case, the corporation would have paid the shareholder all $100 in the form of a dividend. The shareholder would then have paid $27 in personal income taxes on the dividends, leaving that investor with $73 out of the $100 in pre-tax corporate profit. As this example shows, the double taxation of corporate dividends reduced the shareholder's return on capital from $73 to $47.45—a reduction of 35 percent (or $25.55). In the aggregate, this lower return on capital means that there is less investment than there would otherwise have been.

Dynamic Simulation of Macroeconomic and Fiscal Effects

Heritage economists use dynamic simulation to project the economic and fiscal effects of proposals for tax changes. This method contrasts with the static approach used by the U.S. Department of the Treasury and the Congressional Joint Committee on Taxation (JCT), which assumes that federal tax policy does not affect economic growth.

In determining the fiscal effects of tax change proposals, the static approach does take into account some of the ways taxpayers alter their tax reporting and filing in response to changes in tax law. For example, the static approach takes into account that taxpayers could increase their itemized deductions or shift compensation from taxable to tax-exempt (or tax-deferred) forms in response to certain changes in the tax laws. However, the static approach does not take into account the way investors and workers alter their consumption, investment, saving, and work effort in response to changes in tax policy. This is a major shortcoming of the static approach because economic theory suggests that tax policy changes bring about such alterations.[11]

Such changes in taxpayers' behavior could affect important macroeconomic variables, including employment, personal income, and GDP. Thus, changes in tax law often exert an impact on the nation's economy. The static approach necessarily ignores these impacts, leading to systematic inaccuracies in the estimates of the fiscal effects of tax policy changes.

In contrast, The Heritage Foundation uses dynamic simulation in evaluating the fiscal and economic effects of tax policy proposals. Dynamic simulation takes into account the impact that tax policy legislation can exert on taxpayers' economic decisions, such as consumption, investment, saving, and work effort. Dynamic simulation, therefore, can reflect changes in macroeconomic variables that new tax policies can cause.

For example, if a tax rate reduction were to strengthen national economic growth and therefore increase the tax base, a resultant increase in tax collections could partially offset the federal revenue losses caused by the rate reduction. Static analysis would not take such an offset into account and therefore would overestimate the net decline in federal tax collections resulting from the tax rate reduction. Dynamic analysis would include this offset because it would take full account of the economic benefits that the tax rate reduction could cause. It would also capture the ways in which these benefits could strengthen the economy, bolster the tax base, and ameliorate the reduction in tax collections.

In analyzing the economic and fiscal impact of the Cox proposal, CDA analysts made a number of assumptions regarding the alternative minimum tax, capital gains taxation, federal spending, and the date the bill would be enacted. These assumptions were as follows.

- *Alternative minimum tax.* The form of the bill submitted for consideration in the 107th Congress does not clearly state how the dividend tax credit should be handled under those parts of the tax code that establish the alternative minimum tax (AMT). Heritage Foundation analysts assumed that taxpayers required to file under the AMT rules would be able to take advantage of the dividend tax credit. If this were not the case, the dividend tax relief for those taxpayers would be negated.

- *Capital gains tax.* The Cox proposal would be expected to cause an increase in equity prices. This increase would likely cause investors to adjust their portfolios, perhaps triggering increased capital gains tax liability. Estimating the total increase in capital gains tax collections would require both distributional and basis data that are not readily available to Heritage economists. Therefore, CDA analysts assumed that such collections would remain unchanged relative to the baseline forecast.

- *Federal spending.* Heritage Foundation analysts assumed that Congress would make no government program spending reductions to offset federal revenue cuts expected with the Cox proposal. As a result, any changes in federal spending observed in the simulation are attributable solely to the Cox proposal's effect on the national economy and, in turn, the economy's effect on federal spending.

- *Dividend increase.* Heritage analysts assumed that ending the double taxation of dividends would increase dividend payouts by 10 percent. A portion of this increase would be caused by higher shareholder demand for dividends. In response to this higher demand, corporations would increase their payouts of dividends out of after-tax profits. The remainder of this 10 percent increase would be explained by a reduction in the user cost of capital and a corresponding increase in profits. Some of these higher profits would then be returned to shareholders as higher dividends. The combined result of these two effects was assumed to be a 10 percent increase in dividends.[12]

- *Date of enactment.* Heritage economists assumed that the tax reform would become law on September 30, 2003, and apply retroactively to dividends received after January 1, 2003. Assuming an earlier date of enactment would have resulted in the proposal's benefits being realized sooner.

Macroeconomic and Fiscal Effects of the Cox Proposal

Heritage economists used a modified version of the DRI–WEFA U.S. Macroeconomic Model to conduct a dynamic simulation of the effects of Representative Cox's bill.[13] Specifically, Heritage economists developed a baseline by adapting the DRI–WEFA macroeconomic forecast from September 2002 to yield the same economic and budget projections as those of the Congressional Budget Office (CBO) in August 2002.[14] Thus, the economic baseline employed in this analysis should be comparable to baselines used by the CBO and JCT in analyzing this legislation. . . .

Specifically, the dynamic analysis projects that the Cox proposal would:

- *Increase economic growth.* GDP would increase by an average of at least $32 billion per year (adjusted for inflation) within the period from 2003 through 2012. GDP would be an inflation-adjusted $22 billion higher in 2004 and $45 billion higher in 2012. (See Figure 2.)
- *Create more job opportunities.* The proposal would increase the number of jobs by at least 325,000 in 2012. (See Figure 3.) This increase in jobs would correspond to a decline in the unemployment rate of no less than 0.2 percent per year over the next 10 years. (See Figure 3.)
- *Increase investment.* Non-residential investment would average nearly $25 billion per year (adjusted for inflation) higher between 2003 and 2012. By the end of fiscal year 2012, the net capital stock would be at least an inflation-adjusted $174 billion higher. (See Figure 4.) The user cost of capital would be about 5.4 percent lower in 2012.
- *Increase disposable personal income.* Disposable personal income would increase by an inflation-adjusted average of $56 billion or more per year from 2003 through 2012. For a family of four, this increase in disposable income would correspond to an average of at least $768 per year. (See Figure 5.)
- *Increase personal savings and personal consumption.* Personal savings would average an inflation-adjusted $18 billion higher during the 10-year period. Personal consumption expenditures would average an inflation-adjusted $36 billion higher than current projections.
- *Slightly increase consumer prices.* Under the Cox proposal, growth in the consumer price index would average 0.1 percent higher from 2004 through 2008. Over the final four years of the forecast period, increases in the price level would be virtually unchanged in comparison with those of the baseline.
- *Decrease federal tax revenue.* The Cox dividend proposal would reduce total federal tax revenues by a total of $64 billion during its first 10 years. Close to $56 billion of this reduction would take place during the first five years, for an average of $11 billion per year. During the final five years of the simulation period, the tax cut would be virtually revenue neutral, reducing federal revenue by an average of less then $2 billion per year. During this latter five-year period, increases mostly in corporate and Social Security tax collections would offset expected declines in

personal income taxes. Corporate tax collections would rise because of higher pre-tax corporate profits. Payroll taxes would increase because of higher employment levels.

- *Increase federal spending.* If Congress were not to reduce federal program spending to offset the tax revenue reductions caused by this proposal, overall federal spending would rise. Spending would average about $13 billion higher after ending the double taxation of dividends. About two-thirds of this increase would result from additional federal interest payments. The rest would be caused by increases in federal expenditures on income-maintenance programs for federal and Social Security retirees. These increases in federal income maintenance spending would be caused mainly by higher consumer prices observed during the years from 2004 through 2008.

Conclusion

President Bush has proposed reforming the U.S. tax code to abolish the federal double taxation on corporate dividends. Economists have long argued that this double taxation exerts a harmful effect on the nation's economy because it increases the user cost of capital and therefore reduces investment in the United States. Last fall [2002], Representative Christopher Cox introduced legislation that would end this double taxation.

This Heritage Foundation working paper investigates the 10-year economic and fiscal impact of Representative Cox's proposal to abolish this double taxation. It finds that the proposal would, by the year 2012, improve growth in the nation's GDP, add hundreds of thousands of jobs to the economy, increase investment, strengthen growth in disposable income, and add to the nation's capital stock.

Notes

1. United States Department of the Treasury, Office of Public Affairs, "Tax Provisions of the President's Growth Package," at *http://www.treas.gov/press/releases/kd3739.htm.*

2. Forthcoming sections of this paper further discuss the differences between static and dynamic analysis.

3. The term "double taxation" refers only to the federal taxation of dividends. When state and local taxes and estate taxes are considered, there are more than two layers of taxation on dividend income. However, this working paper limits its discussion to federal tax policy, so its language refers only to federal double taxation. Consequently, the examples discussed herein set aside the effect of state and local taxation on corporate shareholder return and the user cost of capital.

4. For more on the economic effects of federal double taxation of dividends, see James M. Poterba, "Tax Policy and Corporate Saving," *Brookings Papers on Economic Activity* No. 2, 1987, pp. 455–515; Peter Birch Sorensen, "Changing Views of the Corporate Income Tax," *National Tax Journal,* Vol. 48, Issue 2 (June 1995), pp. 279–294; James M. Poterba and Lawrence H. Summers, "The Economic Effects of Dividend Taxation," National Bureau of Economic Research *Working*

Paper No. 1353, 1984; and James M. Poterba and Lawrence H. Summers, "New Evidence that Taxes Affect the Valuation of Dividends," *The Journal of Finance,* Vol. 39, Issue 5 (December 1984), pp. 1397–1415.

5. Deborah Thomas and Keith Sellers, "Eliminate the Double Tax on Dividends," *Journal of Accountancy,* November 1994, and Ervin L. Black, Joseph Legoria, and Keith F. Sellers, "Capital Investment Effects of Dividend Imputation," *The Journal of the American Taxation Association,* Vol. 22, Issue 2 (2000), pp. 40–59.

6. H.R. 5323, 107th Congress.

7. The Center for Data Analysis was asked to evaluate this proposal in September 2002 and plans to evaluate the "exclusion method" in President Bush's proposal in a forthcoming study.

8. CDA analysts assumed that the reform would be enacted on September 30, 2003, and applicable retroactively to dividends paid after January 1, 2003.

9. All dollar values listed as "inflation-adjusted" are indexed to the general 1996 price level.

10. The Bureau of Economic Analysis (BEA) and the Internal Revenue Service (IRS) define the word "dividend" differently. This paper uses the BEA definition. There are at least two major differences between the BEA and IRS definitions. For example, the IRS defines as "dividend income" interest earned by mutual funds on the funds' non-equity holdings, while the BEA does not count this as dividend income. In contrast, the BEA counts as dividend income flows from S-Corporations, while the IRS does not. The numerical differences between the two definitions can be quite large. For example, during calendar year 2000, IRS dividends were $142.2 billion, while BEA dividends were $375.7 billion. See Thae S. Park, "Comparison of BEA Estimates of Personal Income and IRS Estimates of Adjusted Gross Income," Bureau of Economic Analysis, *Survey of Current Business,* November 2002, Table 2, at *http://www.bea.gov/bea/ARTICLES/2002/11November/1102irs&agi.pdf.*

11. For a discussion of the shortcomings of static analysis of the effects of tax policy changes, see Daniel J. Mitchell, "The Correct Way to Measure the Revenue Impact of Changes in Tax Rates," Heritage Foundation *Backgrounder* No. 1544, May 3, 2002, at *http://www.heritage.org/Research/Taxes/BG1544.cfm.* See also "The Argument for Reality-Based Scoring," Heritage Foundation *Web Memo* No. 92, March 29, 2002, at *http://www.heritage.org/Research/Taxes/WM92.cfm,* and Daniel R. Burton, "Reforming the Federal Tax Policy Process," Cato Institute, *Cato Policy Analysis* No. 463, December 17, 2002, at *http://www.cato.org/pubs/pas/pa-463es.html.*

12. Based on empirical evidence, this 10 percent increase in dividends appears to be a low-end estimate. See Martin Feldstein, "Corporate Taxation and Dividend Behavior," *The Review of Economic Studies,* Vol. 37, Issue 1 (January 1970), pp. 57–72, and Poterba, "Tax Policy and Corporate Saving." Assuming a larger increase in dividends would have resulted in a higher estimated growth in GDP.

13. The Center for Data Analysis used the Mark 11 U.S. Macroeconomic Model of DRI–WEFA, Inc., to conduct this analysis. The model was developed in the late 1960s by Nobel Prize–winning economist Lawrence Klein and several colleagues at the University of Pennsylvania. It is widely used by *Fortune* 500 companies, prominent federal agencies, and economic forecasting departments. The methodologies, assumptions, conclusions, and opinions herein are entirely the work of Heritage Foundation analysts. They have not been endorsed by, and do not necessarily reflect the views of, the owners of the model.

14. Congressional Budget Office, "The Budget and Economic Outlook: An Update," August 2002, at *http://www.cbo.gov/showdoc.cfm?index=3735&sequence=0.*

15. To maintain comparability with published CBO long-term projections, projections of changes in federal spending and revenue are not adjusted for inflation in this paper.

NO  Joel Friedman and Robert Greenstein

Exempting Corporate Dividends From Individual Income Taxes

As the centerpiece of its "growth package," the [George W.] Bush Administration proposes a large reduction in the taxes that individuals pay on dividend payments they receive from corporations. According to Administration estimates, this tax cut reduces revenues by $364 billion, representing more than half of the package's $674 billion cost through 2013. This proposal to eliminate the taxes on dividends raises a number of questions. It would do little to stimulate the economy in the near term. In addition, its high cost over the next decade and beyond would result in further damage to the federal budget, increasing deficits and thereby reducing national savings and imposing long-term costs on the economy. . . .

Proposal Likely to Have Little Effect as Economic Stimulus

Even though the current weakness in the economy is used as justification for the proposal, reducing or eliminating the taxation of dividends would be ineffective at stimulating the economy now while it is weak. Indeed, most investors would not receive a tax cut from this proposal until *well over one year from now*, when they file their 2003 taxes in early 2004.

According to the Administration's estimates, exempting certain dividends from individual income taxes would cost $364 billion over the next decade. About 95 percent of this hefty cost would not occur until after 2003, by which time the economy is expected to have recovered from the current downturn.

Adding to the proposal's inefficiency as a stimulus mechanism is the fact that it would put cash primarily into the hands of high-income individuals, a group that is likely to save rather than spend a larger portion of any additional funds it receives than middle- and lower-income families. Yet only if funds are spent will they have the desired effect of stimulating the economy now. The Congressional Research Service found that "dividends are concentrated among higher income individuals who tend to save more" and that overall "using dividend tax reductions to stimulate the economy is unlikely to be very effective."[1]

Benefits Would Be Heavily Concentrated at the Top

It should also be noted that any claims that the benefits of this tax cut would be spread broadly across a growing "investor class" would be misleading. Many middle-income families are more likely to do their investing in the context of tax-deferred retirement accounts, such as 401(k)s and Individual Retirement Accounts. Yet only dividends paid from stocks held in taxable accounts would be affected by this proposal.

According to estimates by the Urban Institute-Brookings Institution Tax Policy Center:

- Nearly two-thirds of the benefits of exempting corporate dividends from the individual income tax would flow to the top five percent of the population, because these taxpayers own the lion's share of stocks. (The top five percent includes tax filers with incomes over $140,000; these filers have average income of $350,000.)

- The top one percent of tax filers—a group whose incomes start at $330,000 and that has average income of about $1 million—would receive 42 percent of the benefits.

- Those with incomes over $1 million—the top 0.2 percent of tax filers, with an average income that exceeds $3 million—would receive nearly one-quarter of the tax-cut benefits.

- In fact, the group with incomes over $1 million—which consists of about 226,000 tax filers in 2003—would receive roughly as much in benefits as the 120 million tax filers with incomes below $100,000. Stated another way, the top 0.2 percent of tax filers would receive nearly as much from this tax cut as the bottom 90 percent of filers combined.

The dollar value of the benefits of this tax cut for different income groups is also illustrative. Exempting corporate dividends from the individual income tax would yield an average annual tax savings of $27,100 for tax filers with incomes over $1 million, according to preliminary Tax Policy Center estimates. In contrast, those with incomes between $30,000 and $40,000 would see an average annual benefit of $42. Those with incomes between $40,000 and $50,000 would see an average annual benefit of $84.

The high-income taxpayers who would reap the vast majority of these tax-cut benefits have experienced far more substantial income gains over the past two decades than families lower down on the economic spectrum. Moreover, this high-income group is also the primary beneficiary of the tax-cut package enacted in 2001. Those with incomes over $1 million can expect an annual tax cut of *over $130,000* when all of the income-tax changes enacted in 2001 are fully in effect, and this figure does not even include the benefits this group would receive from repeal of the estate tax. The benefits of a dividend tax cut would come on top of this amount.

State Budget Deficits Would Be Enlarged

Exempting dividends from the individual income tax also would undercut other federal efforts to bolster the economy by worsening the dire fiscal situation in the states, which are facing a $60 billion to $85 billion budget gap in the next fiscal year, the largest shortfall in the last half-century. As states cut spending and raise taxes to meet their balanced budget requirements, they are placing a drag on the economy. Cutting the individual tax on dividends would reduce state revenues, because of the linkages between state and federal tax codes. Eliminating the tax could reduce state revenues by approximately $4 billion a year.[2] In general, states will have to raise taxes or cut expenditures by one dollar for each dollar of revenue loss, further undermining the proposal's effectiveness as economic stimulus.

IMPACT OF A DIVIDEND EXEMPTION ON THE ELDERLY

Supporters of exempting dividends from individual taxation are stressing the impact of this tax cut on the elderly. And indeed, preliminary Tax Policy Center estimates indicate that about 41 percent of the benefits of a dividend exemption would go to those over age 65. But while the elderly as a group would receive a large relative share of the tax cut, these benefits would flow predominately to those elderly individuals who have high incomes.

- Nearly 40 percent of the benefits of the dividend exemption that would accrue to elderly individuals would flow to the 2.5 percent of elderly people with incomes exceeding $200,000.
- Nearly three-quarters of the benefits that would go to the elderly from this tax cut would flow to the 19 percent of elderly with incomes above $75,000.
- Elderly people with incomes below $50,000—a group that represents two-thirds of all of the elderly in the nation—would receive only 13 percent of the tax cut going to the elderly and *less than 6 percent* of the total tax cut.

By citing a statistic showing that a large share of the benefits from the dividend exemption would go to the elderly, some proponents of this tax cut appear to be trying to foster the impression that it would benefit the average or typical elderly person. This is not the case. Most elderly have fairly low incomes and would receive little or nothing from this tax cut.

The benefits of the proposal would flow predominately to a small group of individuals with high incomes, and a disproportionate share of these high-income taxpayers happen to be elderly. That this is so does not alter the fact that most elderly people would not benefit significantly from it. In fact, many elderly could be adversely affected if the tax cut resulted in fewer resources being available for programs upon which ordinary elderly people rely.

States would also be hard hit by the anticipated increase in interest rates expected to result from this proposal. The proposal will draw funds away from the bond market, as corporate stocks become more attractive investments following the tax cut. To compete for investor dollars with stocks paying dividends that are fully or partially exempt from taxation, entities that issue bonds—including state and local governments—would have to offer higher interest rates. In addition, the cost of reducing or eliminating taxes on dividends for individuals would enlarge the deficit and increase government borrowing. As government borrowing needs crowd out other borrowers, interest rates can rise. Overall, higher interest rates increase the cost of borrowing for states, putting further strain on their budgets.

Positive Effects on the Stock Market Appear to Be Exaggerated

Claims that this tax cut, by making stocks more valuable, would significantly buoy the stock market and thereby bolster consumer confidence and help the economy are likely to be exaggerated. A more muted response seems more likely than a strong reaction when one considers that over half of dividends would not be directly affected by the proposal (because they are paid to tax-exempt accounts, such as pension funds). Moreover, corporate investments would be negatively affected by the higher interest rates that would likely result from this tax cut.

Furthermore, trying to induce an increase in the stock market is an indirect and rather inefficient way to encourage consumers to spend more and thus stimulate the economy. The Congressional Research Service concluded that the link between a stock market increase and consumer spending "is weaker, more uncertain, and perhaps more delayed, than a direct stimulus to the economy via spending increases or cuts in taxes aimed at lower income individuals."[3] In addition, cutting dividends taxes to manipulate the market in an effort to aid investors hurt by the recent downturn is questionable public policy. As Brookings Institution economists Gale and Orszag have noted, "having the government bail out investors who voluntarily accepted risks by investing in the stock market would set a dangerous precedent."[4]

Potential Negative Impact on Certain Sectors of the Economy, Including Small Businesses

As the economy adjusted to lower taxes for corporate dividends, some sectors of the economy would likely be disadvantaged, at least in the short run. This tax cut would make stocks a more attractive investment in terms of their after-tax returns, prompting investors to pull funds out of some other investments and shift these dollars to corporate stocks.

As noted above, the tax cut would draw funds away from the bond market, which would result in higher interest rates. These higher rates not only raise costs for state and local governments and business investment but also for home mortgages and car loans. Similarly, one would also expect the non-corporate sector, which is comprised primarily of small businesses, to be affected adversely, as investment dollars shift into corporate stocks.

Effect on Economy Over the Long Run

The high cost of ending the taxation of dividends would likely mitigate any beneficial long-term impact the proposal might have on the economy. Supporters tout the positive effects of cutting dividend taxes on encouraging more investment in corporations. They often ignore the negative effects associated with the tax cut's long-term cost, however, and the resulting increase in the federal deficit. Although a one-time increase in the current deficit to pay for stimulus can be good economic medicine, permanently increasing future deficits as this proposal would do would have a corrosive effect on the economy. The preponderance of economic research indicates that sustained budget deficits reduce national savings, which results in less investment and ultimately lowers the nation's income in the future. So while the proposal may improve the efficiency of the allocation of investment dollars, it would also shrink the pool of investment dollars available by increasing the deficit. In the end, it is the combination of these positive and negative effects that will determine the overall impact on the economy.

Other Proposals Would Be More Effective Stimulus and Do Less Fiscal Damage Over the Long Run

Other proposals would be far more effective at providing immediate economic stimulus by directing funds to individuals and businesses that would spend the money—and thereby bolster the economy now when it is weak. A generous extension of unemployment benefits, for instance, would put money into the hands of families who are out of work and likely facing cash-flow constraints. Similarly, fiscal assistance to the states would pump money directly into the economy by helping states avoid making deep program cuts or increasing taxes, which would otherwise place a drag on the economy. A tax cut aimed at lower- and moderate-income working families would also offer considerably more stimulus for each dollar of cost in the ten-year budget window—than a cut in taxes on dividends.

Although a temporary increase in the deficit can be justified as providing economic stimulus in the short run, a permanent increase in the deficit is much harder to defend given the deterioration in the fiscal outlook and the knowledge that, just over the horizon, the retirement of the baby boomers will place a huge burden on the federal budget. Despite the need to begin to take steps now to reduce, or certainly not to worsen, future deficits—as well as the need to pay for the ongoing fight against terrorism at home and abroad and the generally agreed-upon need for a prescription drug benefit for seniors—this proposal would produce a substantial drain on the Treasury. These revenue losses would come on top of the massive revenue losses the 2001 tax cut will cause when it is fully in effect. Overall, a costly proposal to eliminate or reduce sharply individual taxes on corporate dividends seems particularly inappropriate.

Supporters of this tax cut are pushing for it to be part of an economic stimulus package, despite its being ineffective and inefficient as stimulus. By doing so, they may seek to create a belief that its high, permanent cost does not have to be offset. Including this proposal in a stimulus package that is said to warrant rapid congressional action avoids linking the proposal to broader consideration of corporate tax reforms that would address the "zero taxation" of much corporate income resulting from the proliferation of corporate tax avoidance and tax sheltering schemes. Any proposal to lighten the tax burden on corporate dividends should be considered, however, only in the context of a deficit-neutral package of corporate reforms, where the range of issues related to corporate taxation can be addressed together.

This analysis is divided into three sections. The first section looks at the cost and distribution of proposals to reduce or eliminate the tax on corporate dividends. The second assesses the impact on the economy of such a tax change. The final section examines the concept of the "double taxation" of corporate dividends and its relevance to the current debate.

Reducing or Eliminating the Tax on Corporate Dividends

A corporation can use dividends as a way to distribute earnings to its shareholders, with dividends being paid out of its after-tax income.[5] In other words, a corporation makes dividend payments to its shareholders out of the earnings that remain after corporate income taxes have been paid. Shareholders include these dividend payments in their income for tax purposes. To the extent that shareholders are subject to the individual income tax, they pay tax on their dividend income.

The Urban Institute-Brookings Institution Tax Policy Center estimates that in 2000, corporations paid $201 billion in dividends out of their after-tax incomes. More than half of these dividends were paid to tax-exempt entities—such as pension funds, individual retirement accounts, and non-profit foundations—or to individuals that owed no income tax. As a result, only about 46 percent of the dividends paid by corporations to individuals (or $93 billion in dividends) were subject to the individual income tax in 2000.[6]

Over the years, various options to eliminate the taxation of corporate dividends have been proposed. Some proposals would exempt from the *corporate* income tax all earnings paid out in dividends. Such proposals would be more costly than making dividends tax free for individuals, because of the large share of dividends flowing to tax-exempt accounts not currently subject to individual income taxes. . . .

Economic Impact of Eliminating the Individual Taxation of Dividends

The Treasury Department released a comprehensive report on various options to reduce the taxation of dividends in 1992.[7] Although the different options had varying effects, the Treasury Department concluded that all of the options—including ending taxes on dividends at the individual level—would have a positive impact on the economy. It concluded such a tax change "will encourage capital to shift into the corporate sector" and "stimulate improvements in overall economic well-being." But the Treasury report was able to reach these positive conclusions in large part because *it assumed that the cost of the tax cuts would be fully offset.* That is, the Treasury options were assessed assuming they had no net impact on the deficit. This assumption is in sharp contrast to the Bush Administration's tax-cut proposal, which is not expected to be offset and would result in higher deficits. These different assumptions are crucial to understanding the long-term effects of the proposals on the economy, because of the negative impact of budget deficits on future economic growth.

The Long-Term Effect—More Efficient Investments but Less Invested

Brookings Institution economists William Gale and Peter Orszag recently undertook an exhaustive review of the available economics literature on the impact of budget deficits on the economy.[8] They found a broad consensus among economists that "declines in budget surpluses (or increases in budget deficits) reduce national savings and thus reduce future national income." They also found that a wide variety of perspectives, from empirical research and leading macroeconomic models to the views of numerous leading academics and policy institutions, "all indicate that increases in expected future deficits raise long-term interest rates." Although the link between future deficits and long-term interest rates has received the most attention in the media, their paper makes the important point that because sustained budget deficits reduce national savings, they have a negative impact on the economy regardless of their effect on interest rates.[9]

As Gale and Orszag point out in their paper, an increase in the budget deficit and the resulting reduction in national savings mean the nation has less to invest. Lower investment leads to a smaller stock of capital assets and lower economic growth in the future. Exempting dividends from individual taxation may encourage a more efficient allocation of resources—that is, it may encourage more investments in those areas that will yield the highest returns for economic growth. But if the revenue losses generated by the tax cut are not offset and result in larger deficits, there will be lower national savings and thus less to invest. So even though the proposal may promote more efficient investment of the capital that is available, there will be a lower level of investment overall. It is the combined effect of these factors—more efficient investments, but less invested—that ultimately will determine the long-term impact of the proposal on the economy.

In Short Run, Tax Cut Offers Little to Boost Economy

Although the long-term impact of the proposal would be modest at best, its effects in the short term are clearer. The proposal is particularly ineffective economic stimulus, offering little "bang for the buck."

- The benefits of eliminating individual taxes on corporate dividends would flow primarily to those with higher incomes. This higher-income group, however, is likely to save more and spend less of any additional funds it receives than low- and moderate-income families would. Funds must be spent if they are to stimulate the economy in the near term.
- Despite the hefty ten-year cost of the proposal, only a small portion of the revenue losses would result in an immediate increase in spending. This undermines the proposal's effectiveness as a mechanism to deliver immediate stimulus to the economy. More than 90 percent of the revenue losses over the next ten years would occur after 2003, in years when the economy is expected to have recovered.
- The tax cut also is poorly designed to put money into the hands of consumers quickly, because most tax-cut recipients would not begin receiving the bulk of their annual tax-cut benefits until they filed their 2003 tax returns in early 2004. To receive the benefits earlier, taxpayers would have to adjust their withholding or estimated payments for the remainder of this year, a step that few—particularly those with only modest levels of dividends—would be likely to take, given the difficulty individuals would have estimating the impact of the tax cut and their fear of penalties in the event of underpayment.
- A tax cut for dividends would reduce state revenues because of the linkages between state and federal tax codes, worsening the state fiscal crisis that is imposing a drag on the economy. Preliminary estimates by the Center on Budget and Policy Priorities indicate that exempting dividends from individual income tax could cost states about $4 billion a year. Given the large budget deficits that states face and the requirements that they balance their budgets, states would be forced to make up for these revenue losses with dollar-for-dollar expenditure reductions or tax increases. Such actions by the states counteract federal efforts to stimulate the economy.[10]
- The proposal also could have a negative impact on the economy in the near-term because of its effects on long-term interest rates. As Gale and Orszag explain in their analysis, financial markets are forward looking and take into account today changes that are expected to occur in the future. Thus, a costly proposal to eliminate or substantially reduce the taxation of dividends would create the expectation of higher future deficits, which in turn could exert upward pressure on long-term interest rates today. These higher long-term rates could dampen prospects for current economic growth, because individuals and businesses make fewer large purchases when the long-term interest rates they pay on the funds they borrow to make the purchases rise to higher levels.

It also is worth noting that in the short run, a proposal to eliminate or reduce substantially the individual taxation of corporate dividends would create winners and losers—that is, it would benefit some sectors of the economy and some firms at the expense of others.

- With a tax cut for corporate stocks that pay dividends, the after-tax returns of this type of investment would rise. While more money would flow to these stocks, these funds would be drawn away from other sectors.
- Funds would likely flow out of the non-corporate sector and into corporate stocks. In the analysis it conducted in 1992, the Treasury Department concluded that the proposal would result in "the reallocation of physical capital (and other real resources) from the rest of the economy into the corporate sector." Thus, the non-corporate sector—typically comprised of small businesses, including sole proprietors—would likely experience a loss of investment funds.
- Similarly, by making equities a more attractive investment, the proposal would make bonds relatively less attractive. Interest rates on bonds would rise under these circumstances, as the bond market would have to offer higher interest rates to attract investors. This result, plus the effect on interest rates stemming from the increase in the deficit the tax cut would engender, could place significant upward pressure on rates. Higher interest rates would not only affect business investment and borrowing by state and local governments, but would also impact consumers by increasing rates on home mortgages and car loans, for instance.

Positive Impact on the Stock Market Likely Exaggerated

Eliminating individual taxes on dividends would make dividend-paying stocks more valuable in terms of their after-tax return. Supporters of this tax cut maintain that investors would seek out these higher returns, thereby bidding up the price of these stocks and boosting the stock market as a whole. This improvement in the stock market would, in turn, have a salutary effect on the economy, they argue, as consumers, heartened by the increase in their portfolios, would react by increasing their spending. This analysis is flawed in a number of respects.

It is far from clear that the proposal would lead to a significant rise in the stock market. As noted previously, about half of all dividends are not subject to individual income tax, primarily because they flow to tax-exempt pension funds, retirement accounts, and non-profit foundations. None of the investment decisions made by these groups would be directly affected by the elimination of the individual tax on corporate dividends, because they are not subject to the tax. Further, corporate investments would be negatively affected by the higher interest rates that likely would follow from this deficit-increasing tax cut.

While one might expect to see stock prices rise modestly in reaction to the proposed tax cut, it would likely be a one-time increase that primarily yielded a windfall for current holders of dividend-paying stocks, who purchased their stocks at prices that reflected the current tax treatment of dividends. University of Michigan tax expert Reuven Avi-Yonah recently wrote that "it is doubtful that cutting the tax on dividends will have a significant impact on the stock market. And even if it did, current holders of the stock, wealthy individuals who bought the stock at a discounted price anticipating that they would be taxed on future dividends, would get an unjustified windfall."[11] Similarly, the *Daily Tax Report* issued by the Bureau of National Affairs cites economists from the investment firm Credit Suisse First Boston as predicting that cutting dividend taxes would have only a "mildly positive" effect on stock prices.[12]

The key question in assessing the stimulative effect of such changes in stock prices is whether a modest increase in the market would be sufficient to increase consumer spending enough to have a meaningful impact on the economy; most estimates—including those of the Federal Reserve—indicate that consumers boost their spending by only a few cents for each dollar increase in their wealth. If the goal is to get consumers to spend more, encouraging such spending through a rise in the stock market consequently is an indirect and inefficient method of achieving that goal. Other proposals, such as extending and strengthening unemployment benefits and providing fiscal assistance for states, would have far more "bang for the buck" in terms of stimulating the economy. As the Congressional Research Service recently concluded, the link between higher stock prices and increased consumer spending "is weaker, more uncertain, and perhaps more delayed, than a direct stimulus to the economy via increases in spending or cuts in taxes aimed at lower income individuals."[13]

"Double Taxation" of Corporate Dividends

Supporters of eliminating the taxation of corporate dividends typically argue that such a change is necessary to end the "double taxation" of these dividends. Double taxation arises because, in theory, corporations pay dividends out of their after-tax earnings, and these payments are subsequently taxed as part of the shareholders' income. Thus, these corporate earnings are taxed twice—once at the corporate level and again at the individual level.

In reality, not all corporate dividends are taxed twice; some are only taxed once and some not at all. As noted above, on the individual side, more than half of all corporate dividends flow to entities, such as tax-exempt retirement funds, that are not subject to individual income tax. Further, some corporate earnings distributed to shareholders are not subject to the corporate income tax, as corporations make use of available tax preferences and other less scrupulous tax avoidance techniques to lower or eliminate their tax bills.

Significant Corporate Profits Escape Corporate Income Tax

To be taxed twice, corporate profits first have to be subjected to the corporate income tax. Yet there is significant evidence that corporations are aggressively employing tax avoidance strategies that have resulted in a growing share of corporate profits escaping corporate taxation altogether. In recent years, the Treasury Department, the congressional tax-writing committees, academics and journalists have raised concerns over the rise in corporate tax sheltering activities.

As evidence of this trend, recent studies have shown a growing divergence in the amount of profits that corporations report to their shareholders (known as book income) and the amounts that these companies report to the Internal Revenue Service for purposes of paying corporate income taxes.[14] Harvard economist Mihir Desai concludes that the traditional link between these two measures of corporate profits has "broken down" and that "the patterns of the deteriorating link between tax and book income are consistent with increased levels of sheltering over the decade." For instance, Desai found that $154 billion, or more than half of the gap between corporate book and tax income in 1998, the latest year covered in his study, could not be explained by the traditional accounting differences between these two measures.

On a related front, the Institute on Taxation and Economic Policy examined the books of 250 large companies between 1996 and 1998.[15] Together these companies pay about 30 percent of all federal corporate income taxes.

- Over that three-year period, ITEP found that 41 companies—or about one in six of the total sample—paid "less than zero" in federal corporate taxes in at least one year. Despite reporting nearly $26 billion in profits to their shareholders over the period, these companies not only paid no corporate income tax but actually received rebate checks from the federal government totaling $3 billion. This list includes companies such as General Motors, ChevronTexaco, Goodyear and CSX.
- Building on these findings, Citizens for Tax Justice currently estimates that in 2002, *less than half* of corporate profits were subject to the corporate income tax. As [a] result, CTJ concludes that only a little more than half of corporate profits were subject to tax at *any* level, corporate or individual.[16]

In a *New York Times* article on January 5, 2003, *Times* business columnist Gretchen Morgenson concluded that "companies are paying less and less in taxes each year, making the 35 percent corporate tax rate a fiction."[17] Morgenson reported, for example, that Bristol-Myers Squibb's effective tax rate fell to 15.4 percent in 2001 from 25.2 percent in the previous year. (A firm's effective tax rate is the percentage of the firm's profits paid in taxes.) Similarly, in a recent article, Robert McIntyre, executive director of Citizens for Tax Justice and an expert in corporate tax avoidance, points out that CSX, despite having U.S. profits of more than $930 million over the past four years, paid no federal corporate income taxes over the period and instead received refunds totaling $164 million.[18]

Taxing Dividends Twice Not Relevant Equity Issue

The moniker "double taxation" tends to raise the specter of some group—in this case, individuals who receive dividends—being treated unfairly by the tax system, because part of their income is being taxed twice. On its editorial page, for example, the *Wall Street Journal* has argued that the policy of taxing dividend income twice should be ended as a matter of equity.[19]

But for economists, whether this income is taxed once or twice is not the relevant equity issue. As McIntyre aptly noted, "Who wouldn't feel better, for instance, about paying two taxes of 10 percent each rather than a single tax of

40 percent?"[20] Moreover, many forms of income are taxed more than once. An obvious example is wages. While corporate dividends are theoretically double taxed first at the corporate level and then at the individual level, an individual's wages are immediately subject to both payroll and income taxes.

Equity, in the context of taxes, is about whether taxpayers in similar circumstance pay similar amounts of tax and about how the burden of taxes is borne by different income groups, not about the number of times a particular type of income is taxed. The current federal tax system as a whole (including the taxation of dividends, and also including payroll and excise taxes) is modestly progressive.[21] The most significant equity issue related to the taxation of dividends is whether eliminating the tax on dividends and thereby reducing the level of progressivity in the tax system is a desirable step.

Concerns That Dividend Taxation Distorts Investment Decisions

The more significant concern raised by many economists is that the current tax treatment of corporate dividends may interfere with the efficient allocation of the nation's resources by directing investments into less productive, but more lightly taxed, areas. In a dynamic market economy, such as in the United States, investment funds flow to those areas that yield the highest *after-tax* return—other factors, such as risk, being equal. Consequently, investors may be deterred from investing in the corporate sector because the after-tax return of a corporate investment would be lower than the after-tax return of a non-corporate investment that is taxed only as part of an individual's income tax return.[22] Although it might offer a higher after-tax return, the non-corporate investment could be a less productive use of investment dollars (as measured by its *pre-tax* return) and thus be less beneficial for overall economic growth.

Furthermore, within the corporate sector, some economists believe the current tax treatment of dividends can distort corporate financing decisions. Corporations raise funds to finance capital investment through essentially three methods: debt (i.e., issuing bonds); equity (i.e., issuing new shares of stock); and retained earnings (i.e., reinvesting after-tax earnings rather than distributing them to shareholders in the form of dividends). The concern is that current tax law biases corporate investment decisions against issuing new equity and toward debt financing and retaining earnings, which are both more lightly taxed than dividends.[23] As a result, corporations may not be using an optimal mix of these three financing mechanisms, which would ultimately be less efficient for the economy.

There is a large body of academic work examining the impact on the economy of having separate corporate and individual income taxes. Many of these studies conclude that, for the efficiency reasons discussed above, the economy would benefit if the corporate and individual taxes were integrated. The 1992 Treasury study reached this conclusion and, to that end, proposed a *deficit-neutral* dividend exclusion at the individual level. There is not unanimous agreement on this issue among economists, however, particularly when international economic issues are taken into account. As University of Michigan international tax expert Reuven Avi-Yonah recently wrote, the case for corporate tax integration in a globalizing world "is much shakier than is commonly thought," with many of our trading partners now moving away from the full exclusion of dividends from taxation.[24]

Conclusion

As short-term stimulus, exempting all or a portion of corporate dividends from individual income taxes is ill-conceived. It fails to meet the basic requirements of any stimulus proposal, which are that such a proposal be temporary and be targeted in a way that encourages as much new spending as possible in the short term. The proposal to reduce or eliminate the taxation of dividends is clearly intended to be permanent, and its benefits would flow primarily to those with the highest incomes, a group likely to save more of a tax cut than moderate- and lower-income families would.

Despite its shortcomings as stimulus, reducing or eliminating individual taxes on corporate dividends is expected to be the centerpiece of the Bush Administration's economic growth package. The Administration likely will use the continued uncertainty surrounding the state of the economy both to push for rapid consideration of its package and to argue that the package's large long-term costs need not be offset. This, however, is the wrong context for debating the dividend proposal, since it precludes consideration of other relevant corporate tax issues and thus virtually ensures this costly tax cut will impose a permanent drain on the Treasury.

Consideration of measures to reduce or eliminate the so-called "double taxation" of corporate dividends should be accompanied by consideration of measures to curb the "zero taxation" of a rising share of corporate profits as a result of the increasingly aggressive use of corporate tax shelters and other tax-avoidance techniques. A tax cut for dividends should be considered only as part of a more comprehensive, deficit-neutral package of corporate tax reforms.

Notes

1. Gregg A. Esenwein and Jane G. Gravelle, "The Taxation of Dividend Income: An Overview and Economic Analysis of the Issues," Congressional Research Service, October 7, 2002.

2. Iris J. Lav, "Bush 'Growth Plan' Would Worsen State Budget Crises," Center on Budget and Policy Priorities, January 9, 2002.

3. Esenwein and Gravelle.

4. William Gale and Peter Orszag, "A New Round of Tax Cuts," Center on Budget and Policy Priorities, August 23, 2002.

5. Dividend-paying firms tend to be large, well-established companies. For example, many of the highest-yielding stocks (i.e., pay the highest dividends relative to their share prices) tend to be familiar companies, such as Philip Morris, J.P. Morgan Chase, General Motors, Eastman-Kodak, Dow Chemical, Bristol-Myers Squibb, ConAgra Foods, Ford Motor, and ChevronTexaco. See Greg Bartalos, "New Tax Plan May Yield Sweet Dividends," *Barron's Online*, December 12, 2002.

6. William G. Gale, "About Half of Dividend Payments Do Not Face Double Taxation," *Tax Notes*, November 11, 2002.

7.   "Integration of the Individual and Corporate Tax Systems: Taxing Business Income Once," U.S. Department of the Treasury, January 1992.

8.   William G. Gale and Peter R. Orszag, "The Economic Effects of Long-Term Fiscal Discipline," Urban-Brookings Tax Policy Center Discussion Paper, December 17, 2002.

9.   Gale and Orszag point out that if lower national savings leads to increased foreign borrowing, interest rates may not rise. But if foreign borrowing increases, then America's indebtedness to rest of the world increases. The returns to these investments flow overseas, rather than raising the future incomes of Americans. As a result, higher deficits lower the nation's income in the future, regardless of whether interest rates increase.

10.   States would also be negatively affected by the proposal because it would likely result in higher interest rates and thus increase their cost of borrowing.

11.   Reuven S. Avi-Yonah, "Back to the 1930s? The Shaky Case for Exempting Dividends," *Tax Notes*, December 23, 2002

12.   Brett Ferguson, "Treasury Renews Push for Higher Debt Limit, Warns Ceiling Could be Hit in late February," *BNA Daily Tax Report*, December 27, 2002.

13.   Esenwein and Gravelle.

14.   See Mihir Desai, "The Corporate Profit Base, Tax Sheltering Activity, and the Changing Nature of Employee Compensation," NBER Working Paper 8866, April 2002, and George A. Plesko, "Reconciling Corporation Book and Tax Net Income, Tax Years 1996-1998," *Statistics of Income Bulletin*, Spring 2002.

15.   Robert S. McIntyre and T.D. Coo Nguyen, "Corporate Income Taxes in the 1990s," Institute on Taxation and Economic Policy, October 2000.

16.   Robert McIntyre, "New Gang, Old Myths," *The American Prospect*, January 13, 2003.

17.   Gretchen Morgenson, "Waiting for the President to Pass the Tax-Cut Gravy," *The New York Times*, January 5, 2003.

18.   McIntyre, "New Gang, Old Myths."

19.   "Ending Double Tax Trouble," *The Wall Street Journal*, December 26, 2002.

20.   McIntyre, "New Gang, Old Myths."

21.   Joel Friedman and Isaac Shapiro, "Are Taxes Too Concentrated at the Top? Rapidly Rising Income at the Top Lie Behind Increase in Share of Taxes Paid by High-Income Taxpayers," Center on Budget and Policy Priorities, December 18, 2002.

22.   Earnings in a non-corporate business are taxed only at the individual income tax rates. The majority of non-corporate businesses are sole proprietorships, earnings from which are taxed at the owner's individual income tax rates. Other non-corporate enterprises such as partnerships are often referred to as "pass-through" companies because the earnings pass through to the partners and shareholders and are taxed at their individual rates. See Jack H. Taylor, "Passthrough Organizations Not Taxed As Corporations," Congressional Research Service, August 20, 2002.

23.   Of these three methods, debt receives the most favorable tax treatment. Although interest payments to bondholders are treated as income to the bondholder, just as dividend payments are treated as income to shareholders, interest payments are a deductible expense for a corporation. As a deductible expense, interest payments reduce the amount of corporate profits subject to tax; in contrast, dividends are paid out of after-tax funds. Thus, interest payments are taxed at most only once, at the individual level, and are more lightly taxed than dividends, which can face both corporate and individual taxes.

Retained earnings can also be subject to double taxation, but to a much lesser degree than dividends. When a corporation retains its earnings for investment purposes, it tends to push the firm's share prices higher. Thus, shareholders become subject to higher capital gains taxes when (or if) they decide to sell their shares. But capital gains are taxed at a lower rate than regular income taxes, and shareholders can control when they will sell shares, potentially deferring capital gains taxes indefinitely. As a result, retained earnings generate lower taxes at the individual level than dividend payments, which are subject to tax in the year in which the payment is made at individual income tax rates.

24. Avi-Yohan.

POSTSCRIPT

Should the Double Taxation of Corporate Dividends Be Eliminated?

Ignore for the moment whether or not eliminating the tax on dividend income will stimulate the economy, and focus on the issue of "double taxation." If one concludes that the efficiency concerns raised by Michel, Goyburu, and Rector outweigh the equity issues raised by Friedman and Greenstein, one should ask whether or not there really is double taxation in the first place.

Before considering that discussion, it is important to understand how double taxation allegedly comes into being. Those who favor the repeal of the dividend tax argue that every time a corporation has an excess profit of one dollar that they plan to distribute as a dividend, 35 cents of that potential dividend goes to the U.S. Treasury, assuming that the corporation is in the highest corporate income tax bracket of 35 percent. As the corporation "distributes" its excess profits to its shareholders, those 65 pennies are now subject to personal income taxes. Again, assuming the highest tax bracket, this time of the personal income tax, the 65 cents that is distributed would be taxed at 38.6 percent. That represents another 24 cents in taxes for a total of 59 cents for every dollar earned and distributed to shareholders.

There are some very big assumptions here that should be underscored. One could ask, for example, just how much of a corporation's net income is subject to the corporate income tax? The taxation of corporate income is too complex to detail, but it is important to note that over the past 40 years, the amount of corporate taxes paid as a percentage of all federal taxes from all sources has steadily decreased. On the other hand, in the 1960s corporate taxes were a close second to personal income taxes as a percentage of federal tax revenue; now corporate taxes are a distant third to social security taxes. This is the result of accelerated depreciation allowances and other tax preferences that have been granted to the corporate sector. Thus, a significant amount of corporate net income never passes through the corporate tax mill. That portion of corporate net income that is distributed in the form of dividends is only taxed once—as personal income.

One could also note the consequences of corporations' having two options for their net income: they can distribute their net earnings as dividends, or they can "retain" these corporate earnings and invest them in the corporate enterprise. Over time this should increase the value of the corporation, but that increased valuation is not fully taxed as personal income. This is because any asset that is held for more than one year and that appreciates in value is subject to special rates. The maximum tax that an individual must pay on these capital gains is 20 percent, and that is not paid until the gain is realized—that is, there is no capital gain income to tax until the appreciated asset is sold. In this extreme case, the total tax is 48 percent (35 cents of corporate taxes and another 13 cents of capital gains taxes). This is not an insignificant amount, even though it is not the 60 percent that is often cited.

Much has been written in support of eliminating the tax on corporate dividends. Alan Greenspan offered an interesting view on this topic in his February 12, 2003, testimony before the House Financial Services Committee. Greenspan concluded that, in the long run, "virtually everyone" benefits from the elimination of this tax. Greenspan is not alone in this view, particularly in the conservative "think tanks." See, for example, the March 6, 2003, testimony before the House Ways and Means Committee by John H. Makin, a resident scholar of the American Enterprise Institute, which can be found on the Internet at http://www.aei.org/news/newsID.16393/news_detail.asp, and "How the Tax Code Contributed to the Corporate Scandals and Bankruptcies," by Lawrence H. Whitman, *Heritage Backgrounder No. 1578* (August 27, 2002).

Many others take exception to the tax code. Their concerns take several forms. William G. Gale and Peter R. Orszag, for example, question the growth consequences of eliminating the dividend tax in "The Economic Effects of Long Term Fiscal Discipline," Urban-Brookings Tax Policy Center Discussion Paper (December 17, 2002), which can be found at http://www.som.yale.edu/faculty/pks4/files/macro_readings/inv_gale_orszag_brookings_021217.pdf. Avrum D. Lank agrees in "Forget the Plan to Stop Taxing Dividends," *JSOnline/Milwaukee Journal Sentinel*, http://www.jsonline.com/bym/your/jan03/ 113334.asp. In this essay, Lank raises the issue of the complexities that this will introduce into the tax code. Many agree, including Gregg A. Esenwein and Jane G. Gravelle in "The Taxation of Dividends: An Overview and Economic Analysis of the Issues," Congressional Research Service (October 7, 2002) and Dean Baker in "The Dividend Tax Break: Taxing Logic," Center for Economic and Policy Research Issue Brief (January 6, 2003).

ISSUE 10

Should a Program of Universal Service Be Created?

YES: Robert E. Litan, from "September 11, 2001: The Case for Universal Service," *Brookings Review* (Fall 2002)

NO: Bruce Chapman, from "A Bad Idea Whose Time Is Past: The Case Against Universal Service," *Brookings Review* (Fall 2002)

ISSUE SUMMARY

YES: Robert E. Litan, director of the Brookings Institution, contends that the government can promote and encourage the sentiment for public service unleashed by the terrorist attacks of September 11, 2001, by instituting a program of universal service.

NO: Bruce Chapman, president of the Discovery Institute, maintains that universal service is a bad idea because it cannot be justified morally, militarily, politically, or financially.

For most Americans the images of September 11, 2001, are still vivid: the flames, the smoke, the rubble, and the human suffering as the World Trade Center towers were destroyed by terrorists. The shock of September 11 brought a surge in the public's sense of community and, correspondingly, in the willingness of Americans to participate in community service activities. In the period since then, the United States has deployed military forces in Afghanistan in pursuit of terrorists and has used military forces to overthrow the regime of Saddam Hussein in Iraq. The combination of the increased willingness to participate in community service and increased military activity has generated a number of proposals.

One set of proposals called for increased governmental support for volunteer community service. President George W. Bush was among those who offered recommendations that followed this path. Another set of proposals called for a return to compulsory military service—a return to a military draft. Among those who proceeded in this fashion was Congressman Charles Rangel (D-New York). A third group of proposals basically encompassed both of the first two, calling for a governmental program of universal service. Robert E. Litan's plan, which is elaborated on in the first of the following selections, falls into this category.

Some definitions might help to introduce the issue. First, a military draft is a requirement that young people, usually just young men, serve in the armed services. Such a draft may be universal, where all young people (or all young men) are required to enter the military. Or the draft may be selective, with certain individuals exempted from service depending on such things as luck (as with a draft lottery), marital status, or educational plans. Currently, the United States requires all young males to register for the draft but has a completely voluntary military structure—no one has to serve in the military unless he or she chooses to do so. The voluntary army has been criticized for putting too heavy a burden on minorities, so when the military action began in Iraq in March 2003, the young people put in harm's way did not reflect a representative cross-section of America. Rangel was among several congressmen who sponsored the Universal National Service Act of 2003 (H.R. 163, with the companion bill in the Senate designated as S.B. 89). The purpose of the proposed legislation is "to provide for the common defense by requiring that all young people in the United States, including women, perform a period of military service or a period of civilian service in furtherance of national defense and homeland security and for other purposes."

In the following selection, Litan describes his proposal for universal service: a one-year requirement of service imposed on all young people, which would preferably be served after high school. Young people would have the choice of spending that one year in military or community service. They would be compensated regardless of which alternative they chose, but the pay would be greater for those who selected the military option. This would provide a monetary incentive for taking the more dangerous alternative. Presumably, this structure would have several benefits. First, it would not require military service of any young person who, for whatever reason, objects to military service. Such a person could refuse military service but would still be obligated to perform a year of service to the nation. Second, everyone would be equally burdened with the one-year obligation, but society would not be asking anyone to do something that they might object to on moral or other grounds. Litan sees a number of benefits that would be created by his proposal for universal service. In the second selection, Bruce Chapman argues that service, whether of the military or community variety, should be strictly voluntary.

Robert E. Litan

 **YES**

September 11, 2001:
The Case for Universal Service

Americans are a generous people. The attacks of September 11 [2001] produced an outpouring of donations to help families of the victims. Americans took pride in the heroism of public servants—firefighters, the police, FBI agents, and men and women in the military—who responded to the call of duty. It was also widely felt that September 11 would change the lives of many young Americans, who not only would have the images of the attacks seared into their memories, but also would pursue careers in public service or the "helping" professions.

Time will tell whether those initial impulses toward helping others will last. But time alone won't determine the outcome. Public policy can and will have an impact. If Americans want more of their children to pursue service careers or at least devote time to activities that help and support others, whether in the public or private sector, it will certainly help if government encourages or provides opportunities for such service. The same is true for adults wishing to serve in some capacity, as many apparently were willing to do in the weeks following September 11.

President [George W.] Bush, for one, has recognized the role of public policy by supporting a much-expanded voluntary national service program. In his fiscal year 2003 budget, he called for the creation of the USA Freedom Corps, which would combine and expand the Peace Corps and AmeriCorps programs and add a new Senior Corps as well as a volunteer program for college students. Bush proposed increasing the funding of all national service programs by nearly $300 million and eventually placing more than 2 million Americans a year in some kind of formal national service (75,000 in full-time AmeriCorps programs). He also called on Americans to give two years over the course of their lives to service.

The Bush proposals tap into two strong American traditions—a commitment to volunteerism and a resistance to compulsory service except in wars requiring a massive call-up. With the exception of some community service programs in some high schools in certain states, this nation has never required its young citizens to perform civilian service.

From Robert E. Litan, "September 11, 2001: The Case for Universal Service," *Brookings Review*, vol. 20, no. 4 (Fall 2002). Copyright © 2002 by The Brookings Institution. Reprinted by permission.

The president's call to service may be working. Applications by college graduates to AmeriCorps are up 75 percent and applications to the Peace Corps are up 18 percent, according to a June [2002] survey in *Time*. But the surge in interest may also be linked to the poor job market this past year for college graduates.

In short, there are limits to volunteerism. Can we do more? Here I lay out the case for moving beyond even the president's new initiative toward some kind of universal service requirement, one that would offer all young Americans a choice, preferably after finishing high school, to enter military or civilian service for at least a year. Those opting and qualifying for the military would be given additional monetary incentives to do so.

Having a reasoned debate about universal service before September 11 would have been unthinkable. It isn't (or at least shouldn't be) so anymore.

The Case for Universal Service, Now

As the Bush administration has reminded us, we are at war—this time, against an enemy whose main targets of attack are American civilians. Unlike past wars, this new war on terrorism, we are told, could last a generation or more. If . . . the nation [is] at war with Iraq again, the question arises: why should the burden of the war—and the risks of getting injured or killed—rest only on the shoulders of those who volunteer to fight it?

There are answers to this question, of course. One is that the military should be able to handle even a stepped-up military campaign against terrorism. After all, the armed forces fought Iraq in 1991 with roughly 500,000 troops; this time around, the highest projections seem to fall in the 250,000 range. A second answer is that the men and women in uniform are paid to put themselves in harm's way, and they volunteered to assume any risk of war that may come about.

But unlike America's past foreign wars, the war on terrorism requires a vigilant homeland security effort in addition to an offensive military (and intelligence) campaign abroad. This time around, it is not just those in the military who are in harm's way. We are all potential targets or victims—and thus all have some obligation to help secure America. As a practical matter, neither the economy nor society could function if everyone stood guard duty or devoted their time to protecting the homeland. Paid professionals have and will continue to carry out these duties. But if this new war is, as it is said to be, a generational event, then why not also ask the next generation—all of whom may be at risk—to help shoulder the security effort?

The need is there. Young people in service, provided they were properly trained, could substantially augment the guards now in place at a wide range of public and private facilities. The nation could also use many more inspectors at its ports—perhaps our greatest vulnerability today—where only a tiny fraction of incoming containers is examined. Some highly motivated young people may even decide to train for security-related careers—as police officers, customs or immigration officials, or FBI agents—and serving in all of these jobs should qualify for universal service.

Though one good reason for adopting universal service now is to respond to the military and homeland threat, universal service makes sense in other ways in this time of national peril.

First, universal service could provide some much-needed "social glue" in an embattled American society that is growing increasingly diverse—by race, national origin, and religious preference—and where many young Americans from well-to-do families grow up and go to school in hermetically sealed social environments. Twenty years ago, when America was much less diverse than it is now and is going to be, the editorial page of the *Wall Street Journal* (of all places) opined that mandatory service would constitute a "means for acculturation, acquainting young people with their fellow Americans of all different races, creeds, and economic backgrounds."

Those words are as compelling today as when they were written. A service program in which young people from different backgrounds work and live together would do far more than college ever could to immerse young Americans in the diversity of our country. It would also help sensitize more fortunate young men and women, at an impressionable point in their lives, to the concerns and experiences of others from different backgrounds and give them an enduring appreciation of what life is like "on the other side of the tracks."

Second, universal service could promote civic engagement, which, as Harvard social scientist Robert Putnam has persuasively argued in *Bowling Alone*, has been declining—or at least was before September 11. Some who perform service for the required period may believe their civic responsibilities will thereby be discharged, but many others are likely to develop an appreciation for helping others that could change the way they lead the rest of their lives.

Third, young people serving in a civilian capacity in particular would help satisfy unmet social needs beyond those associated with homeland security: improving the reading skills of tens of millions of Americans who cannot now read English at a high school level, cleaning up blighted neighborhoods, and helping provide social, medical, and other services to the elderly and to low-income individuals and families. Allowing individuals to delay their service until after college would enable them to bring skills to their service that could prove even more useful to society and may be a desirable option. But doing so would also reduce the benefits of added social cohesion from universal service, because it would tend to create two tiers of service, one for those who don't go to college and another for those who do.

Finally, universal service would establish firmly the notion that with rights for ourselves come responsibilities to others. Of course, the Constitution guarantees all citizens certain rights—of free speech, of due process of law, to be free from discrimination, to vote—without asking anything of them in return. But why shouldn't citizens be required to give something to their country in exchange for the full range of rights to which citizenship entitles them?

Countering the Objections

. . . [I]mposing a universal service requirement would raise serious objections aside from the philosophical one—opposition to any form of government compulsion and the temporary loss of liberty it entails.

Probably the most serious argument against universal service is its cost. Roughly 4 million students graduate from high school each year. A good benchmark for costs is the AmeriCorps program. According to official figures, the federal government spent roughly $10,000 for each AmeriCorps volunteer in fiscal year 2001. A plausible assumption is that the states and the private sector added perhaps another $7,000 (according to a 1995 study by the General Accounting Office, these costs amounted then to about $5,500 per person, so they might be close to $7,000 now). Given the relatively small numbers enrolled in AmeriCorps—about 50,000 annually—its per person costs may be higher than those for a much larger universal program, which would be able to amortize overhead costs over a much larger population. On the other hand, not all AmeriCorps volunteers live in a dormitory setting. Providing dormitories for all participants in a universal civilian program would raise the cost relative to AmeriCorps.

Balancing these factors, I assume here for illustrative purposes a per person cost of $20,000, which, if funded entirely by the federal government, would bring the total annual gross cost of the entire program to about $80 billion. From this figure, it would be necessary to subtract the costs of those who already serve in AmeriCorps and the Peace Corps, as well as high school students who now volunteer for the military. In addition, some participants in a universal service program might be performing functions now carried out by paid workers. Taking all these offsets into account could bring the annual net incremental cost of the program down to, say, the $70 billion range—still a very large number.

Given the recent dramatic deterioration of the federal budget, a program of that magnitude would seem now to be a political nonstarter, and it may well be. Nonetheless, one potentially fair way to reduce costs and thereby make the idea of universal service more palatable from a budgetary perspective would be to implement the requirement initially as a lottery, much like the system that existed toward the end of the Vietnam War. Depending on the cutoff point, the program could be sized at any level that the political traffic could bear.

However large the program could turn out to be, those who may be tempted to dismiss as too costly a universal service requirement of any size must consider its benefits. A 1995 GAO cost-benefit analysis, for example, positively evaluated the findings of a 1995 study by George R. Neumann, Roger C. Kormendi, Robert F. Tamura, and Cyrus J. Gardner that had cited quantifiable monetary benefits of $1.68 to $2.58 for every dollar invested in three AmeriCorps programs. These estimates did not count the nonquantifiable, but very real, benefits of strengthening local communities and fostering civic responsibility. Nor did they include the broader benefits of added social cohesion that a universal program would entail. On the other side of the ledger, it is quite possible that there would be diminishing returns to a much broader program than

AmeriCorps, and thus at some enrollment level the costs of a universal require-ment could exceed the benefits. But even this result—which is hardly ensured—would not credit the nonquantifiable social benefits of a broader program.

The bottom line: even a universal service program as large as $70 billion a year could well produce social benefits in excess of that figure and thus repre-sent a very real net economic and social gain for American society as a whole.

Of course, the gains from universal service would be realized only if the participants were doing valuable work. And some fear that under a universal re-quirement, many participants in the civilian program in particular could be do-ing make-work (raking leaves is the image) without contributing much in the way of social value. Indeed, to the extent this happened—and some assert that it happens in the AmeriCorps program—the affected participants would come away from their service with a negative view of government and civic responsi-bility.

The concern is real. AmeriCorps tries to address it by decentralizing its ac-tivities, relying on both state governments and the private sector to develop programs that are essentially certified at the federal level. A civilian universal service program could work largely the same way, but on a much-expanded scale. At the same time, certain programs, especially those associated with homeland security, would have to be run out of Washington.

Still, it would be a challenge to develop meaningful work for all of the high school graduates who would enter the civilian program each year. Meeting this challenge provides another reason, besides cost, to begin the program on a less than universal scale, run it first as a lottery, and eventually expand it to a true universal system.

An Idea Whose Time Is Coming

Universal service is an idea whose time may not be quite here, but it is coming. For reasons of need, social cohesion, and social responsibility, universal service is a compelling idea. If adopted, it could be one of the truly transformative fed-eral initiatives of recent times, perhaps having an even greater impact on Amer-ican society than the GI bill, which helped educate much of the post–World War II generation. At the very least, universal service should be on the public agenda and actively debated. The discussion alone would be a fitting postscript to the horrible events of September 11 and the continuing search for ways to engage all Americans to serve their country.

NO

Bruce Chapman

A Bad Idea Whose Time Is Past:
The Case Against Universal Service

If each woman in China could only be persuaded to lower the hem of her skirt one inch, some 19th-century English merchants reasoned, the looms of Manchester could spin forever. Like that romantic calculation, the idea of universal service assumes a mythical economic and cultural system where people behave as you would like them to, with motivations of which you approve. Unlike it, universal service adds coercion to ensure compliance.

Universal service never was a good idea, and it grows worse with time. It fails militarily, morally, financially, and politically.

For almost a century, universal service has brought forth new advocates, each desiring to enlist all youth in something. Only the justifications keep changing. Today's justification is "homeland security." But is it realistic to suggest that youth who help guard a "public or private facility" (let alone those who stuff envelopes at some charity's office) are "shouldering the burden of war" in the same way as a soldier in Afghanistan?

I don't want to attach to Robert Litan all the customary arguments that universal service advocates have been promoting for years, especially because he states that "advocating universal service before September 11 would have been unthinkable" (at least to him). Except in times of mass conflict, such as the Civil War and the two World Wars, there has never been much of a reason for universal service. Still, the varied arguments for it need to be addressed.

No Military Case

Universal service is not needed on military grounds. We eliminated the draft three decades ago in part because the armed services found that they needed relatively fewer recruits to serve longer than conscription provided. As the numbers that were needed shrank, the unfairness of the draft became ever more apparent—and offensive. Youth, ever ingenious, found ways to get deferments, decamp to Canada, make themselves a nuisance to everyone in authority—and make those who did serve feel like chumps. Many of the young people who

From Bruce Chapman, "A Bad Idea Whose Time Is Past: The Case Against Universal Service," *Brookings Review*, vol. 20, no. 4 (Fall 2002). Copyright © 2002 by The Brookings Institution. Reprinted by permission.

objected to military service availed themselves of alternative service, but no one seriously believed that most "conscientious objectors" were "shouldering the burden of war" in a way comparable to those fighting in the field.

The government took advantage of its free supply of almost unlimited manpower by underpaying its servicemen, thereby losing many recruits who might have chosen a military career. Raising the pay when the volunteer force was introduced changed the incentives and—surprise—eliminated the need for the draft. The all-volunteer force has been a big success.

Leaders in today's increasingly sophisticated, highly trained military now are talking of further manpower cuts. They have no interest in short-term soldiers of any kind and give no support to a return to conscription. The idea of using universal service to round up young men and women who, instead of direct military service, could be counted on to guard a "public or private facility," as Litan proposes, is naive. In Litan's plan, youth would be obligated for only a year—slightly less, if AmeriCorps were the model. Philip Gold, a colleague at Discovery Institute and author of the post–September 11 book *Against All Terrors: This Nation's Next Defense,* points out that "if the object is fighting, a person trained only for a few months is useless. In a noncombat defense position, he would be worse than useless. He would be dangerous."

Litan's interest in compulsory service grew partly out of recent work on Israel. According to Gold, armed guards in Israel do protect day care centers, for example. But all have had serious military training and two to three years of active duty, followed by service in the active reserves. A population with widespread military training and service can accomplish things that a civilian volunteer program cannot.

Litan anticipates nothing comparable from short-term universal servicemen and -women. A one-year obligation, under the AmeriCorps example, works out to only 1,700 hours—roughly 10 months of 40-hour weeks. By the time the compulsory volunteers were trained, it would be time for them to muster out. The system would be roiled by constant turnover. It is surely unrealistic to expect to fill security jobs with youths who will be around for only a few months. Ask yourself, would you rather have a paid and trained person or a conscripted teenager inspecting the seaport for possible terrorists?

No Moral Justification

Trying to justify universal service on moral grounds is also a mistake, and a serious one. Morally, service isn't service to the extent it is compelled. Involuntary voluntarism is like hot snow. And allowing the pay to approach (let alone surpass) that available to ordinary workers of the same age performing the same tasks as the stipended and officially applauded "volunteers" stigmatizes the private sector. (The military recruit of today is sometimes called a volunteer only because he is not conscripted. His service is more commendable morally than that of some other paid employee because he is prepared to risk his life.)

Universal service advocates such as Litan are on especially shaky ground when charging that citizens should be "required to give something to their country in exchange for the full range of rights to which citizenship entitles them." This cuts against the grain of U.S. history and traditions. Citizens here are expected to be law-abiding, and they are called to jury duty—and to the military if absolutely necessary. They are encouraged (not forced) to vote and to render voluntary service—which Americans famously do. But to require such service before the rights of citizenship are extended is simply contrary to the purposes for which the country was founded and has endured. The Founders had a keen awareness of the ways that the state could tyrannize the people, and taking the people's liberty away to serve some specious government purpose unattached to national survival is a project that would horrify them.

I also raise this practical question: exactly which citizenship rights will Litan deny those people who decline to perform government-approved national service? What will be done to punish the activist who thinks he can do more to serve humanity through a political party than through prescribed government service? Or the young religious missionary who would rather save souls than guard a pier for a few months? How about—at the other end of the virtue spectrum—the young drug dealer who is only too happy to help guard the pier? Will you keep him out of the service of his choice and compel him to do rehab as his form of "service"?

Outside of mass mobilization for war—or in the special case of Israel, a small nation effectively on constant alert—the only modern nations that have conscripted labor to meet assorted, centrally decreed social purposes have been totalitarian regimes. In those lands, the object, as much as anything, has been to indoctrinate youth in the morality of the state. Litan may not have such goals in mind, but many universal service advocates want to use conscription to straighten out the next generation—to their approved standards. No doubt many—most?—think they can inculcate a sense of voluntary service through compulsory service.

In reality, however, no previous generation of youth has been so encouraged to volunteer for various approved, state-sponsored social causes. In many high schools in the United States, students cannot get a diploma without performing a certain number of hours of approved "community service." Does a child who must perform service to graduate from high school develop a high sense of what it means to help others? Does a student who learns that almost anything counts toward the service requirement—so long as he doesn't get paid—develop a keen sense of civil calling? Or does he hone his skill at gaming the system? And why, if we have this service requirement in high school—and some colleges—do we need yet another one for the year after high school?

Unintended Consequences

Universal service (indeed any national service scheme that achieves demographic heft) is a case study in unintended consequences. One surprise for liberals might be a growing disillusionment with the government and the way it wastes money. Today's youth trust the government and are immensely patriotic, but bureaucratized service requirements could cure that. Another unintended consequence might be instruction in how government make-work is a tax on one's freedom and an irritating distraction from education goals and serious career development. Conservatives of a sardonic nature might come to appreciate the prospect of generations growing to adulthood with firsthand experience of government's impertinence. It would not be necessary thereafter to exhort the veterans of such unnecessary compulsion to resist the claims of government over the rest of their lives.

Universal service likewise would be an invitation to scandal. The military draft was bad enough, dispatching the budding scientist to pick up paper on a base's roadsides and sending the sickly malcontent to deliver meal trays to patients in base hospitals. People with powerful parents got cushy positions, while the poor got the onerous tasks. When labor is both free and abundant, it will be squandered and abused. If that was true in eras when mass armies were raised, what can one expect in a time when only a small fraction of the population is needed to operate our high-tech military?

No Financial Justification

The cost of universal service would be prohibitive. Direct costs would include those for assembling, sorting (and sorting out), allocating, and training several million youth in an unending manpower convoy. Indirect costs include clothing and providing initial medical attention, insurance, the law enforcement associated with such large numbers (no small expense in the army, even with presumably higher discipline), housing, and the periodic "leave" arrangements.

The $20,000 per involuntary volunteer estimated by Litan is too low. The more realistic total figure would be more like $27,000 to $30,000. First, the federal cost for a full-time AmeriCorps member is about $16,000, according to AmeriCorps officials. And that, recall, is for an average 10-month stint, so add another $3,000 or so for a 12-month term of service. (The $10,000 figure cited by Litan appears to average the cost of part-time volunteers with that of full-time volunteers.) Giving the involuntary volunteers the AmeriCorps education benefit of some $4,000 brings the total to about $23,000 of federal contribution for the full-time, one-year participant, which, with local or private match, will easily reach a total cost of some $30,000. Few unskilled young people just out of school make that in private employment!

Because organized compulsion costs more than real volunteering, however, the indirect expenses for governments would be still greater. Chief among these are the hidden financial costs of universal national service to the economy in the form of forgone labor. That problem plagued the old draft and would be more acute now. The United States has suffered a labor shortage for most of the past two decades, with the dearth of educated and trained labor especially serious. Yet universal service advocates want to pluck out of the employment ranks some 4 million people a year and apply a command-and-control approach to their optimal use. How can we even calculate the waste?

Litan says that in 1995 the GAO [General Accounting Office] "positively evaluated" a cost-benefit study of three AmeriCorps programs that found them to produce quantifiable monetary benefits of $1.68 to $2.58 for every dollar invested. But Litan overstates the GAO's "positive evaluation" of the private study's findings. The GAO study merely analyzes the methodology of the private study based on the assumptions that are baked into it. These assumptions (of future benefits and their dollar values) are inherently "problematic," based as they are on "projected data." And neither the GAO nor the private study whose methodology it checked says anything about the applicability of the private study to some universal service program. Inferring GAO endorsement for some putative financial benefits from a national service scheme—let alone a program of compulsory national service—is not good economics.

By contrast, a recent review of the literature and evidence of government spending by William Niskanen, former chairman of the President's Council of Economic Advisors (under Ronald Reagan), concluded that "the marginal cost of government spending and taxes in the United States may be about $2.75 per additional dollar of tax revenue." As the late Nobel economist Frederick Hayek said, "There is only one problem with socialism. It does not work."

The cost of universal service for one year would not be $80 billion, with certain additional economic benefits, as Litan would have it, but roughly $120 billion, with considerable additional losses to the economy as a whole.

No Practical or Political Worth

There is no demand for all these volunteers, as charities themselves have pointed out. Nonprofits can absorb only so many unseasoned, unskilled, short-term "volunteers," particularly when some of the "volunteers" are reluctant, to say the least. So what is the point? Is it political?

Some universal service advocates (not Litan) have cited a January 2002 survey by Lake Snell Perry & Associates, The Tarrance Group, Inc. (The survey was conducted for the Center for Information and Research in Civic Learning & Engagement, the Center for Democracy & Citizenship, and The Partnership for Trust in Government at the Council for Excellence in Government.) The study shows strong support among youth for universal service. But these advocates usually neglect to mention that this support is based on a stated assumption in the survey question that such service would be "an alternative to (compulsory) military service should one be instituted." A truer reflection of youthful opinion is found in the survey's largely unreported question on community service as a requirement for high school graduation. That program is overwhelmingly opposed—by a 35 percent margin among current high school students. Interestingly, the same survey shows that "instituting civics and government course requirements in schools is favored by a 15-point margin by current high school students."

This should tell us something. Putting $120 billion, or even $80 billion, into a universal national service scheme would be a waste. But how about spending some tiny corner of that money on teaching kids about real—that is, voluntary—service? How about paying to teach students about representative democracy and their part in it as voters and volunteers or about the way our economy works and how to prepare for successful participation in it? Or to teach them American history (for many, it would be a new course) in a way that inspired them with the stories of men and women, great and humble, who have rendered notable service in their communities, nation, and world.

The way to get a nation of volunteers is to showcase voluntary service, praise it, reward it, and revere it. The way to sabotage voluntary service is to coerce it, bureaucratize it, nationalize it, cloak it in political correctness, and pay for it to the point where the "volunteer" makes out better than the poor soul of the same age who works for a living. Voluntary service blesses the one who serves as well as those to whom he renders service. Universal service would be civic virtue perverted into a civic vice.

POSTSCRIPT

Should a Program of Universal Service Be Created?

Litan describes the George W. Bush administration's strong support for an expanded voluntary national service program, including the creation of the USA Freedom Corps and a $300 million increase in funding for all national service programs. Litan also outlines his universal service proposal: a requirement that all young people, preferably after high school, spend one year either in military or civilian service. One of his arguments for the adoption of the proposal is that the burden of the war on terrorism should not be placed solely upon volunteers. Litan maintains that America cannot rely only on volunteers because more than the military is in harm's way. That is, if we are all potential victims, then we all have an obligation to serve. Litan advances a second argument: universal service is a means of creating "social glue." This means that universal service will "sensitize more fortunate young men and women, at an impressionable point in their lives, to the concerns and experiences of others from different backgrounds and give them an enduring appreciation of what life is like 'on the other side of the tracks.'"

While not opposed to programs that would promote voluntary community service, Chapman is adamantly opposed to compulsory service, whether civilian or military. He grounds his opposition in military, moral, financial, and political considerations. With respect to the military, Chapman maintains that someone who is forced into military service is unlikely to be a good soldier. Chapman's assessment of the financial dimension leads him to conclude that the cost of service is prohibitive. He estimates that out-of-pocket costs could be as high as $120 billion, and this ignores "the hidden financial costs of universal national service to the economy in the form of forgone labor." Chapman concludes his opposition by asserting that universal service would "sabotage voluntary service," transforming a civic virtue into a civic vice.

The debate on universal and compulsory military service has been around for some time. The older literature includes two articles that appear in *Orbis: A Journal of World Affairs* (Summer 1990): "National Service: Unnecessary and Un-American," by Doug Bandow, and "Rebuttal: Necessary and American," by Charles Moskos. Additionally, see Moskos's *A Call to Civic Service—National Service for Country and Community* (Free Press, 1998) and *National Service: An Action Agenda for the 1990s* (National Service Secretariat, 1998). There are several organizations that organize and promote voluntary community service, including the Corporation for National and Community Service (http://www.national service.org); the Global Service Institute (http://gwbweb.wustl.edu/csd/gsi/); and the National AmeriCorps Association (http://www.lifetimeofservice.org).

ISSUE 11

Is It Time to Abolish the Minimum Wage?

YES: Thomas Rustici, from "A Public Choice View of the Minimum Wage," *The Cato Journal* (Spring/Summer 1985)

NO: Charles Craypo, from "In Defense of Minimum Wages," An Original Essay Written for This Volume (2002)

ISSUE SUMMARY

YES: Orthodox neoclassical economist Thomas Rustici asserts that the effects of the minimum wage are clear: it creates unemployment among the least-skilled workers.

NO: Labor economist Charles Craypo argues that a high minimum wage is good for workers, employers, and consumers alike and that it is therefore good for the economy as a whole.

In the midst of the Great Depression, Congress passed the Fair Labor Standards Act (FLSA) of 1938. In one bold stroke, it established a minimum wage rate of $.25 an hour, placed controls on the use of child labor, designated 44 hours as the normal workweek, and mandated that time and a half be paid to anyone working longer than the normal workweek. Fifty years later the debates concerning child labor, length of the workweek, and overtime pay have long subsided, but the debate over the minimum wage rages on.

The immediate and continued concern over the minimum wage component of the FLSA should surprise few people. Although $.25 an hour is a paltry sum compared to today's wage rates, in 1938 it was a princely reward for work. It must be remembered that jobs were hard to come by and unemployment rates at times reached as high as 25 percent of the workforce. When work was found, any wage seemed acceptable to those who roamed the streets with no safety net to protect their families. Indeed, consider the fact that $.25 an hour was 40.3 percent of the average manufacturing wage rate for 1938.

Little wonder, then, that the business community in the 1930s was up in arms. Business leaders argued that if wages went up, prices would rise. This would choke off the little demand for goods and services that existed in the marketplace, and the demand for workers would be sure to fall. The end result would be a return to the depths of the depression, where there was little or no hope of employment for the very people who were supposed to benefit from the Fair Labor Standards Act.

This dire forecast was demonstrated by simple supply-and-demand analysis. First, as modern-day introductory textbooks in economics invariably show, unemployment occurs when a minimum wage greater than the equilibrium wage is mandated by law. This simplistic analysis, which assumes competitive conditions in both the product and factor markets, is predicated upon the assumptions that as wages are pushed above the equilibrium level, the quantity of labor demanded will fall and the quantity of labor supplied will increase. This wage rigidity prevents the market from clearing. The end result is an excess in the quantity of labor supplied relative to the quantity of labor demanded.

The question that should be addressed in this debate is whether or not a simple supply-and-demand analysis is capable of adequately predicting what happens in real-world labor markets when a minimum wage is introduced or an existing minimum wage is raised. The significance of this is not based on idle curiosity. The minimum wage has been increased numerous times since its introduction in 1938. Most recently, effective September 1, 1997, legislation establishing the current minimum wage of $5.15 was signed into law by President Bill Clinton.

Did this minimum wage increase, and other increases before it, do irreparable harm to those who are least able to defend themselves in the labor market, the marginal worker? That is, if a minimum wage of $5.15 is imposed, what happens to all those marginal workers whose value to the firm is something less than $5.15? Are these workers fired? Do firms simply absorb this cost increase in the form of reduced corporate profits? What happens to productivity?

This is the crux of the following debate between Thomas Rustici and Charles Craypo. Rustici argues that the answer is obvious: there will be an excess in the quantity of labor supplied relative to the quantity demanded. In lay terms, there will be unemployment. Craypo rejects this neoclassical view. He recommends judging the minimum wage on the intent of the original legislation: increased aggregate demand and elimination of predatory labor market practices.

Thomas Rustici

A Public Choice View of
the Minimum Wage

*Why, when the economist gives advice to his society, is he so often cooly ig-
nored? He never ceases to preach free trade . . . and protectionism is growing in the United States. He deplores the perverse effects of minimum wage
laws, and the legal minimum is regularly raised each 3 to 5 years. He
brands usury laws as a medieval superstition, but no state hurries to repeal its laws.*

—George Stigler

Introduction

Much of public policy is allegedly based on the implications of economic theory.
However, economic analysis of government policy is often disregarded for political reasons. The minimum wage law is one such example. Every politician
openly deplores the spectacle of double-digit teenage unemployment pervading
modern society. But, when economists claim that scientific proof, a priori and
empirical, dictates that minimum wage laws cause such a regretful outcome,
their statements generally fall on deaf congressional ears. Economists too often
assume that policymakers are interested in obtaining all the existing economic
knowledge before deciding on a specific policy course. This view of the policy-
formation process, however, is naïve. In framing economic policy politicians will
pay some attention to economists' advice, but such advice always will be rejected
when it conflicts with the political reality of winning votes. . . .

Economic Effects of the Minimum Wage

Economic analysis has demonstrated few things as clearly as the effects of the
minimum wage law. It is well known that the minimum wage creates unemployment among the least skilled workers by raising wage rates above free
market levels. Eight major effects of the minimum wage can be discussed: unemployment effects, employment effects in uncovered sectors of the economy,

From Thomas Rustici, "A Public Choice View of the Minimum Wage," *The Cato Journal,* vol. 5, no. 1
(Spring/Summer 1985). Copyright © 1985 by The Cato Institute. Reprinted by permission.

reduction in nonwage benefits, labor substitution effects, capital substitution effects, racial discrimination in hiring practices, human capital development, and distortion of the market process with respect to comparative advantage. Although the minimum wage has other effects, such as a reduction in hours of employment, these eight effects are the most significant ones for this paper.

Unemployment Effects

The first federal minimum wage laws were established under the provisions of the National Recovery Administration (NRA). The National Industrial Recovery Act, which became law on 16 June 1933, established industrial minimum wages for 515 classes of labor. Over 90 percent of the minimum wages were set at between 30 and 40 cents per hour.[1] Early empirical evidence attests to the unemployment effects of the minimum wage. Using the estimates of C. F. Roos, who was the director of research at the NRA, Benjamin Anderson states: "Roos estimates that, by reason of the minimum wage provisions of the codes, about 500,000 Negro workers were on relief in 1934. Roos adds that a minimum wage definitely causes the displacement of the young, inexperienced worker and the old worker."[2]

On 27 May 1935 the Supreme Court declared the NRA unconstitutional, burying the minimum wage codes with it. The minimum wage law reappeared at a later date, however, with the support of the Supreme Court. In what became the precedent for the constitutionality of future minimum wage legislation, the Court upheld the Washington State minimum wage law on 29 March 1937 in *West Coast Hotel v. Parrish.*[3] This declaration gave the Roosevelt administration and Labor Secretary Frances Perkins the green light to reestablish the federal minimum wage, which was achieved on 25 June 1938 when President Roosevelt signed into law the Fair Labor Standards Act (FLSA).

The FSLA included legislation affecting work-age requirements, the length of the workweek, pay rates for overtime work, as well as the national minimum wage provision. The law established minimum wage rates of 25 cents per hour the first year, 30 cents per hour for the next six years, and 40 cents per hour after seven years. The penalty for noncompliance was severe: violators faced a $10,000 fine, six months imprisonment, or both. In addition, an aggrieved employee could sue his employer for twice the difference between the statutory wage rate and his actual pay.[4]

With the passage of the FLSA, it became inevitable that major dislocations would result in labor markets, primarily those for low-skilled and low-wage workers. Although the act affected occupations covering only one-fifth of the labor force,[5] leaving a large uncovered sector to minimize the disemployment effects, the minimum wage was still extremely counterproductive. The Labor Department admitted that the new minimum wage had a disemployment effect, and one historian sympathetic to the minimum wage was forced to concede that "[t]he Department of Labor estimated that the 25-cents-an-hour minimum wage caused about 30,000 to 50,000 to lose their job. About 90% of these were in southern industries such as bagging, pecan shelling, and tobacco stemming."[6]

These estimates seriously understate the actual magnitude of the damage. Since only 300,000 workers received an increase as a result of the minimum wage,[7] estimates of 30,000–50,000 lost jobs reveal that 10–13 percent of those covered by the law lost their jobs. But it is highly dubious that only 30,000–50,000 low-wage earners lost their jobs in the entire country; that many unemployed could have been found in the state of Texas alone, where labor authorities saw devastation wrought via the minimum wage on the pecan trade. The *New York Times* reported the following on 24 October 1938:

> Information received today by State labor authorities indicated that more than 40,000 employees of the pecan nut shelling plants in Texas would be thrown out of work tomorrow by the closing down of that industry, due to the new Wages and Hours Law. In San Antonio, sixty plants, employing ten thousand men and women, mostly Mexicans, will close. . . . Plant owners assert that they cannot remain in business and pay the minimum wage of 25 cents an hour with a maximum working week of forty-four hours. Many garment factories in Texas will also close.[8]

It can reasonably be deduced that even if the Texas estimates had been wildly inaccurate, the national unemployment effect would still have exceeded the Department of Labor's estimates.

The greatest damage, however, did not come in Texas or in any other southern state, but in Puerto Rico. Since a minimum wage law has its greatest unemployment effect on low-wage earners, and since larger proportions of workers in poor regions such as Puerto Rico tend to be at the lower end of the wage scale, Puerto Rico was disproportionately hard-hit. Subject to the same national 25-cents-per-hour rate as workers on the mainland, Puerto Rican workers suffered much more hardship from the minimum wage law. According to Anderson:

> It was thought by many that, in the first year, the provision would not affect many industries outside the South, though the framers of the law apparently forgot about Puerto Rico, and very grave disturbances came in that island. . . . Immense unemployment resulted there through sheer inability of important industries to pay the 25 cents an hour.[9]

Simon Rottenberg likewise points out the tragic position in which Puerto Rico was placed by the enactment of the minimum wage:

> When the Congress established a minimum wage of 25 cents per hour in 1938, the average hourly wage in the U.S. was 62.7 cents. . . . It resulted in a mandatory increase for only some 300,000 workers out of a labor force of more than 54 million. In Puerto Rico, in contrast . . . the new Federal minimum far exceeded the prevailing average hourly wage of the major portion of Puerto Rican workers. If a continuing serious attempt at enforcement . . . had been made, it would have meant literal economic chaos for the island's economy.[10] . . .

After two years of economic disruption in Puerto Rico, Congress amended the minimum wage provisions.[11] The minimum wage was reduced to 12.5 cents per hour, but it was too late for many industries and for thousands of low-wage earners employed by them, who suddenly found unemployment the price they had to pay for the minimum wage.

In sum, the tragedy of the minimum wage laws during the NRA and the FLSA was not just textbook-theorizing by academic economists, but real-world disaster for the thousands who became the victims of the law. But these destructive effects have not caused the law to be repealed; to the contrary, it has been expanded in coverage and increased in amount.

. . . Evidence for the unemployment effects of the minimum wage continues to mount. Many empirical studies since the early 1950s—from early research by Marshall Colberg and Yale Brozen to more recent work by Jacob Mincer and James Ragan—have validated the predictions of economic theory regarding the unemployment effects of the minimum wage law. In virtually every case it was found that the net employment effects and labor-force participation rates were negatively related to changes in the minimum wage. In the face of 50 years of evidence, the question is no longer *if* the minimum wage law creates unemployment, but *how much* current or future increases in the minimum wage will adversely affect the labor market.

Employment in Uncovered Sectors

The labor market can be divided into two sectors: that covered by the minimum wage law, and that not covered. In a partially covered market, the effects of the minimum wage are somewhat disguised. Increasing it disemploys workers in the covered sector, prompting them to search for work in the uncovered sector if they are trainable and mobile. This then drives down the wage rate in the uncovered sector, making it lower than it otherwise would have been. Since perfect knowledge and flexibility is not observed in real-world labor markets, substantial unemployment can occur during the transition period.

Employees in the covered sector who do not lose their jobs get a wage-rate increase through the higher minimum wage. But this comes only at the expense of (1) the disemployed workers who lose their jobs and suffer unemployment during the transition to employment in the uncovered sector, and (2) everyone in the uncovered sector, as their wage rate falls due to the influx of unemployed workers from the covered sector. While increasing the incomes of some low-wage earners, increasing the minimum wage tends to make the lowest wage earners in the uncovered sector even poorer than they otherwise would have been.

Yale Brozen has found that the uncovered household sector served to absorb the minimum wage-induced disemployed in the past.[12] But the "safety valve" of the uncovered portion of the economy is rapidly vanishing with the continual elimination of various exemptions.[13] Because of this trend we can expect to see the level of structural unemployment increase with escalation of the minimum wage.[14]

Nonwage Benefits

Wage rates are not the only costs associated with the employment of workers by firms. The effective labor cost a firm incurs is usually a package of pecuniary and nonpecuniary benefits. As such, contends Richard McKenzie,

> employers can be expected to respond to a minimum wage law by cutting back or eliminating altogether those fringe benefits and conditions of work, like the company parties, that increase the supply of labor but which do not affect the productivity of labor. By reducing such non-money benefits of employment, the employer reduces his labor costs from what they otherwise would have been and loses nothing in the way of reduced labor productivity."[15]

If one takes the view that employees desire both pecuniary and nonpecuniary income, then anything forcing them to accept another mix of benefits would clearly make them worse off. For example, suppose worker A desires his income in the form of $3.00 per hour in wages, an air-conditioned workplace, carpeted floors, safety precautions, and stereo music. If he is *forced* by the minimum wage law to accept $3.25 per hour and fewer nonpecuniary benefits, he is worse off than at the preminimum wage and the *higher* level of nonpecuniary income. A priori, the enactment of minimum wage laws must place the worker and employer in a less-than-optimal state. Thus it may not be the case that only unemployed workers suffer from the minimum wage; even workers who receive a higher wage and retain employment may be net losers if their nonpecuniary benefits are reduced.

Labor Substitution Effects

The economic world is characterized by a plethora of substitutes. In the labor market low-skill, low-wage earners are substitutes for high-skill, high-wage earners. As Walter Williams points out:

> Suppose a fence can be produced by using either one high skilled worker or by using three low skilled workers. If the wage of high skilled workers is $38 per day, and that of a low skilled worker is $13 per day, the firm employs the high skilled worker because costs would be less and profits higher ($38 versus $39). The high skilled worker would soon recognize that one of the ways to increase his wealth would be to advocate a minimum wage of, say, $20 per day in the fencing industry. . . . After enactment of the minimum wage laws, the high skilled worker can now demand any wage up to $60 per day . . . and retain employment. Prior to the enactment of the minimum wage of $20 per day, a demand of $60 per day would have cost the high skilled worker his job. Thus the effect of the minimum wage is to price the high skilled worker's competition out of the market.[16]

Labor competes against labor, not against management. Since low-skill labor competes with high-skill labor, the minimum wage works against the lower-skill, lower-paid worker in favor of higher-paid workers. Hence, the consequences of the law are exactly opposite its alleged purpose.

Table 1

Value of the Minimum Wage, 1955–1995

Year	Value of the Minimum Wage, Nominal Dollars	Value of the Minimum Wage, 1995 Dollars†	Minimum Wage as a Percent of the Average Private Nonsupervisory Wage
1955	$0.75	$3.94	43.9%
1956	1.00	5.16	55.6
1957	1.00	5.01	52.9
1958	1.00	4.87	51.3
1959	1.00	4.84	49.5
1960	1.00	4.75	47.8
1961	1.15	5.41	53.7
1962	1.15	5.36	51.8
1963	1.25	5.74	54.8
1964	1.25	5.67	53.0
1965	1.25	5.59	50.8
1966	1.25	5.43	48.8
1967	1.40	5.90	52.2
1968	1.60	6.49	56.1
1969	1.60	6.21	52.6
1970	1.60	5.92	49.5
1971	1.60	5.67	46.4
1972	1.60	5.51	43.2
1973	1.60	5.18	40.6
1974	2.00	5.89	47.2
1975	2.10	5.71	46.4
1976	2.30	5.92	47.3
1977	2.30	5.56	43.8
1978	2.65	6.00	46.6
1979	2.90	5.99	47.1
1980	3.10	5.76	46.5
1981	3.35	5.68	46.2
1982	3.35	5.36	43.6
1983	3.35	5.14	41.8
1984	3.35	4.93	40.3
1985	3.35	4.76	39.1
1986	3.35	4.67	38.2
1987	3.35	4.51	37.3
1988	3.35	4.33	36.1
1989	3.35	4.13	34.7
1990	3.80	4.44	37.9
1991	4.25	4.77	41.1
1992	4.25	4.63	40.2
1993	4.25	4.50	39.2
1994	4.25	4.38	n/a
1995	4.25	4.25	n/a

†Adjusted for inflation using the CPI-U-X1.
Source: Center on Budget and Policy Priorities

Capital Substitution Effects

To produce a given quantity of goods, some bundle of inputs is required. The ratio of inputs used to produce the desired output is not fixed by natural law but by the relative prices of inputs, which change continuously with new demand and supply conditions. Based on relative input prices, producers attempt to minimize costs for a given output. Since many inputs are substitutes for one another in the production process, a given output can be achieved by increasing the use of one and diminishing the use of another. The optimal mix will depend on the relative supply and demand for competing substitute inputs.

As a production input, low-skill labor is often in direct competition with highly technical machinery. A Whirlpool dishwasher can be substituted for low-skill manual dishwashers in the dishwashing process, and an automatic elevator can take the place of a nonautomatic elevator and a manual operator. This [is] not to imply that automation "destroys jobs," a common Luddite myth. As Frederic Bastiat explained over a century ago, jobs are obstacles to be overcome.[17] Automation shifts the *kinds* of jobs to be done in society but does not reduce their total number. Low-skill jobs are done away with, but higher-skill jobs are created simultaneously. When the minimum wage raises the cost of employing low-skill workers, it makes the substitute of automated machinery an attractive option.

Racial Discrimination in Hiring Practices

At first glance the connection between the level of racial discrimination in hiring practices and the minimum wage may not seem evident. On closer examination, however, it is apparent that the minimum wage law gives employers strong incentives to exercise their existing racial preferences.[18] The minimum wage burdens minority groups in general and minority teenagers most specifically. Although outright racism has often been blamed as the sole cause of heavy minority teenage unemployment, it is clearly not the only factor. William Keyes informs us that

> In the late 1940's and early 1950's, young blacks had a lower unemployment rate than did whites of the same age group. But after the minimum wage increased significantly, especially in 1961, the black youth unemployment rate has increased to the extent that it is now a multiple of the white youth unemployment rate.[19]

To make the case that racism itself is the cause of the employment and unemployment disparity among blacks and whites, one would have to claim that America was more racially harmonious in the past than it is now. In fact, during the racially hostile times of the early 1900s 71 percent of blacks over nine years of age were employed, as compared with 51 percent for whites.[20] The minimum wage means that employers are not free to decide among low-wage workers on the basis of price differentials; hence, they face fewer disincentives to deciding according to some other (possibly racial) criteria.

To see the racial implications of minimum wage legislation, it is helpful to look at proponents of the law in a country where racial hostility is very strong, South Africa. Since minimum wage laws share characteristics in common with equal pay laws, white racist unions in South Africa continually support both minimum wage and equal-pay-for-equal-work laws for blacks. According to Williams:

> Right-wing white unions in the building trades have complained to the South African government that laws reserving skilled jobs for whites have been broken and should be abandoned in favor of equal pay for equal work laws. . . . The conservative building trades made it clear that they are not motivated by concern for black workers but had come to feel that legal job reservation had been so eroded by government exemptions that it no longer protected the white worker.[21]

The reason white trade unions are restless in South Africa is a $1.52-per-hour wage differential between black and white construction workers.[22] Although the owners of the construction firms are white, they cannot afford to restrict employment to whites when blacks are willing to work for $1.52 per hour less. As minimum wages eliminate the wage differential, the cost to employers of hiring workers with the skin color they prefer is reduced. As the cost of discrimination falls, and with all else remaining the same, the law of demand would dictate that more discrimination in employment practices will occur.

Markets frequently respond where they can, even to the obstacles the minimum wage presents minority groups. In fact, during the NRA blacks would frequently be advanced to the higher rank of "executives" in order to receive exemptions from the minimum wage.[23] The free market demands that firms remain color-blind in the conduct of business: profit, not racial preference, is the primary concern of the profit-maximizing firm. Those firms who fail the profit test get driven out of business by those who put prejudice aside to maximize profits. When markets are restricted by such laws as the minimum wage, the prospects for eliminating racial discrimination in hiring practices and the shocking 40–50 percent rate of black teenage unemployment in our cities are bleak.

Human Capital Development

Minimum wage laws restrict the employment of low-skill workers when the wage rate exceeds the workers' marginal productivity. By doing so, the law prevents workers with the least skills from acquiring the marketable skills necessary for increasing their future productivity, that is, it keeps them from receiving on-the-job training.

It is an observable fact, true across ethnic groups, that income rises with age.[24] As human capital accumulates over time, it makes teenagers more valuable to employers than workers with no labor-market experience. But when teenagers are priced out of the labor market by the minimum wage, they lose their first and most crucial opportunity to accumulate the human capital that would make them more valuable to future employers. This stunting reduces their lifetime potential earnings. As Martin Feldstein has commented:

> [F]or the disadvantaged young worker, with few skills and below average education, producing enough to earn the minimum wage is incompatible with the opportunity for adequate on-the-job learning. For this group, the minimum wage implies high short-run unemployment and the chronic poverty of a life of low wage jobs.[25]

Feldstein also finds a significant irony in the minimum wage: "It is unfortunate and ironic that we encourage and subsidize expenditure on formal education while blocking the opportunity for individuals to 'buy' on-the-job training."[26] This is especially hard on teenagers from the poorest minority groups, such as blacks and hispanics—a truly sad state of affairs, since the law is instituted in the name of the poor.

Distortion of the Market Process

Relative prices provide the transmission mechanism by which information is delivered to participants in the market about the underlying relative scarcities of competing factor inputs. They serve as signals for people to substitute relatively less scarce resources for relatively more scarce resources, in many cases without their even being aware of it.[27]

Table 2

Dates and Amounts of Minimum Wage Changes

Date	Amount	As a Percent of the Average Wage in Manufacturing (Old Minimum/New Minimum)
February 1967	$1.40	44.8%/50.2%
February 1968	$1.60	47.6%/54.4%
May 1974	$2.00	37.8%/47.3%
January 1975	$2.10	42.7%/44.9%
January 1976	$2.30	41.7%/45.6%
January 1978	$2.65	38.5%/44.4%
January 1979	$2.90	40.8%/44.6%
January 1980	$3.20	41.7%/44.5%
January 1981	$3.35	40.1%/43.3%
April 1990	$3.80	31.4%/35.6%
April 1991	$4.25	33.6%/37.6%

Whenever relative price differentials exist for input substitutes in the production process, entrepreneurs will switch from higher-priced inputs to lower-priced inputs. In a dynamically changing economy, this switching occurs continually. But when prices are not allowed to transmit market information accurately, as in the case of prices artificially controlled by government, then distorted information skews the market and guides it to something clearly less than optimal.[28]

Minimum wages, being such a distortion of the price system, lead to the wrong factor input mix between labor and all other inputs. As a result, industry migrates to locations of greater labor supply more slowly, and labor-intensive industries tend to remain fixed in non-optimal areas, areas with greater labor scarcity. Large labor pools of labor-abundant geographical areas are not tapped because the controlled price of labor conveys the wrong information to all the parties involved. Thus, the existence of price differentials, as knowledge to be transmitted through relative prices, is hidden.[29] The slowdown of industrial migration keeps labor-abundant regions poorer than they otherwise would be because economic growth there is stifled. As Simon Rottenberg explains for the case of Puerto Rico:

> The aggregate effect of all these distortions was that Puerto Rico could be expected to produce fewer goods and services than would have otherwise been produced and that the rate at which insular per capita income rose toward mainland United States income standards could be expected to be dampened. In sum, the minimum wage law could be expected to reduce the rate of improvement in the standard of life of the Puerto Rican people and to intensify poverty in the island.[30]

In summary, the evidence is in on the minimum wage. All eight major effects of the minimum wage examined here make the poor, disadvantaged, or young in society worse off—the alleged beneficiaries turn out to be the law's major victims. . . .

Conclusion

George Stigler may have startled some economists in 1946 when he claimed that minimum wage laws create unemployment and make people who had been receiving less than the minimum poorer.[31] Fifty years of experience with the law has proven Stigler correct, leaving very few defenders in the economics profession.[32]

But economists have had little success in criticizing this very destructive law. Simon Rottenberg demonstrated the government's disregard for what most economists have to say about this issue in his investigation of the Minimum Wage Study Commission created by Congress in 1977. He noted the numerous studies presented to the commission that without exception found that the law had a negative impact on employment and intensified the poverty of low-income earners. The commission spent over $17 million to conduct the investigation and on the basis of the evidence should have eliminated the law. What was the outcome? The commission voted to *increase the minimum wage by indexing and expanding coverage.* As dissenting commissioner S. Warne Robinson commented about the investigation:

> The evidence is now in, and the findings of dozens of major economic studies show that the damage done by the minimum wage has been far more severe than even the critics of forty years ago predicted. Indeed, the evidence against the minimum wage is so overwhelming that the only way the Commission's majority was able to recommend it be retained was to ask us not to base any decisions on the facts.[33]

It cannot be that our elected representatives in Congress are just misinformed with respect to the minimum wage law. To the contrary, the *Congressional Record* demonstrates that they fully understand the law's effects and how the utilization of those effects can ensure reelection. Economists would do well to realize that governments have little interest in the truth when its implementation would contradict self-serving government policies. Rather than attempting to bring government the "facts," economists should educate the public. This is the only solution to the malaise created when people uncritically accept such governmental edicts as the minimum wage.

Notes

1. Leverett Lyon et al. *The National Recovery Administration: An Analysis and Appraisal* (New York: Da Capo Press, 1972), pp. 318–19.
2. Benjamin M. Anderson, *Economics and the Public Welfare: A Financial and Economic History of the United States, 1914–1946* (Indianapolis: Liberty Press, 1979), p. 336.
3. Jonathan Grossman, "Fair Labor Standards Act of 1938: Maximum Struggle for a Minimum Wage," *Monthly Labor Review* 101 (June 1978): 23.
4. "Wage and Hours Law," *New York Times,* 24 October 1938, p. 2.
5. Grossman, "Fair Labor Standards Act," p. 29.
6. Ibid., p. 28.
7. Ibid., p. 29.
8. "Report 40,000 Jobs Lost," *New York Times,* 24 October 1938, p. 2.
9. Anderson, *Economics and the Public Welfare,* p. 458.
10. Simon Rottenberg, "Minimum Wages in Puerto Rico," in *Economics of Legal Minimum Wages,* edited by Simon Rottenberg (Washington, D.C.: American Enterprise Institute, 1981), p. 330.
11. Rottenberg, "Minimum Wages in Puerto Rico," p. 333.
12. Yale Brozen, "Minimum Wage Rates and Household Workers," *Journal of Law and Economics* 5 (October 1962): 103–10.
13. Finis Welch, "Minimum Wage Legislation in the United States," *Economic Inquiry* 12 (September 1974): 286.
14. Brozen, "Minimum Wage Rates and Household Workers," pp. 107–08.
15. Richard McKenzie, "The Labor Market Effects of Minimum Wage Laws: A New Perspective," *Journal of Labor Research* 1 (Fall 1980): 258–59.
16. Walter Williams, *The State Against Blacks* (New York: McGraw-Hill, 1982), pp. 44–45.

17. Frederic Bastiat, *Economic Sophisms* (Irvington-on-Hudson, N.Y.: Foundation for Economic Education, 1946), pp. 16–19.

18. Walter Williams, "Government Sanctioned Restraints That Reduce the Economic Opportunities for Minorities," *Policy Review* 22 (Fall 1977): 15.

19. William Keyes,"The Minimum Wage and the Davis Bacon Act: Employment Effects on Minorities and Youth," *Journal of Labor Research* 3 (Fall 1982): 402.

20. Williams, *State Against Blacks,* p. 41.

21. Ibid., p. 43.

22. Ibid., pp. 43–44.

23. Lyon, *National Recovery Administration,* p. 339.

24. U.S. Department of Commerce, Bureau of the Census, *Statistical Abstract of the United States 1982–83,* p. 431.

25. Martin Feldstein, "The Economics of the New Unemployment," *The Public Interest,* no. 33 (Fall 1973): 14–15.

26. Ibid., p. 15.

27. Thomas Sowell, *Knowledge and Decisions* (New York: Basic Books, 1980), p. 79.

28. Ibid.

29. Ibid., pp. 167–68.

30. Rottenberg, "Minimum Wages in Puerto Rico," p. 329.

31. George Stigler, "The Economies of Minimum Wage Legislation," *American Economic Review* 36 (June 1946): 358–65.

32. Although there are a few supporters left such as John K. Galbraith, many "liberal" economists such as Paul Samuelson and James Tobin have recently come out against the minimum wage. See Emerson Schmidt, *Union Power and the Public Interest* (Los Angeles: Nash, 1973).

33. Simon Rottenberg, "National Commissions: Preaching in the Garb of Analysis," *Policy Review* no. 23 (Winter 1983): 139.

Charles Craypo

 **NO**

In Defense of Minimum Wages

This article refutes the dominant view held by orthodox neoclassical economists such as Thomas Rustici. These economists assert that minimum wage laws should be abolished because they misallocate resources and cause production inefficiencies. I reject Rustici's conclusion and instead take the position that in most instances high minimum wages are good for workers, employers and consumers alike and hence are good for the economy as a whole.

Three things are wrong with Rustici's neoclassical view of things. It depends on an idealized world that by assumption favors more rather than less market competition as the solution to economic problems. Second, it ignores the reasons why governments enact minimum wage laws in the first place and instead interprets and judges them on inappropriate grounds. Third, the neoclassical argument against minimum wages is supported by contradictory empirical evidence that casts doubt on its theoretical validity and practical significance.

Critics of the orthodox neoclassical interpretation of minimum wages include both neoclassical and institutional applied labor economists. In fact, most of the contradictory empirical studies in recent years have [been] produced by neoclassical economists whose findings prompt them to question the dominant view. In addition to the research of mainstream economists, research critical of the orthodox position has come from the various institutional schools of thought which emphasize evolutionary change and systemic rather than deductive reasoning from an idealized model.

Most of the debate surrounds the federal minimum wage law contained in the Fair Labor Standards Act (FLSA) of 1938, which represented an essential part of President Roosevelt's agenda to get the nation out of the Great Depression. Labor law reformers had long advocated federal wage and hour laws in response to an historic pattern of low earnings among working families and intense wage competition among employers. The courts, however, struck down early attempts to establish federal standards on grounds the separate states had constitutional primacy in such matters. Individual states were reluctant to pass regulatory laws, however, because they feared industry would avoid locating there. The enormities of the depression nevertheless drove working people to strike employers and protest politically. Soon the Supreme Court changed directions and ruled that the constitution does in fact allow Congress to regulate interstate commerce; Congress responded with numerous regulatory laws including the FLSA.

The inherent bias in neoclassical analysis. When polled, a large majority of American economists support Rustici in his opposition to minimum wage increases. This reflects their prior training in the neoclassical wage model, which generally rejects labor standards legislation on grounds that market outcomes are superior to anything government can achieve through regulation. Employers and others lobbying to abolish or weaken minimum wage laws therefore can count on the support of orthodox economists, despite widespread public approval of these laws. Indeed, in 1993, three-fourths of economists polled said that an increase in the minimum wage would increase unemployment, while a similar poll in 1996 found that 84% of the public favored an increase.

This vastly different view of the world underscores the first problem with Rustici's neoclassical analysis. The competitive market model it uses simply does not depict real labor markets accurately. It imagines all sorts of things that do not exist and ignores a great many other things that do. When this analysis is applied to particular labor market problems, such as declining real wages, it is likely to misdiagnose the ailment and to prescribe inappropriate public policy.

The problem is that in explaining how the interaction between worker skill and output determines wages the neoclassical model uses circular reasoning. It presumes that if we know the wage we also know the worth of the worker because market competition ensures that each worker is paid the value of his or her worth, as measured by the value of what each produces. It further presumes that the worker's productive value is determined by his or her level of skill and education, that is, by their accumulated "human capital." Therefore, if one worker is paid more than another worker, then the first worker must be worth more (that is, must have more skill and education) than the second; because the wage is, by definition, equal to output value, which in turn is determined by skill and education. Consequently, every worker must be worth what he or she is being paid, no more and no less. Workers who think they are not being paid enough must be wrong, because if they possessed more human capital they would be worth more therefore paid more.

This is tautological reasoning. It explains everything and nothing because it uses the thing it is trying to explain as the evidence with which to explain it. It does, however, allow neoclassical economists to reject any attempt to regulate wages on the grounds that the worker currently is being paid what he or she is worth. In the world of the neoclassical economist, forcing employers to pay a higher wage will simply place the individual employer at a competitive disadvantage and at the same time discriminate against workers who did not benefit from the regulated wage increase. As a result, neoclassical investigations of minimum wage effects usually ask a single question. How many workers will become unemployable following an increase in the minimum wage. The question derives from the competitive wage model, not from observed experiences or policy objectives.

With this mind-set, it is understandable that Rustici and other orthodox neoclassical economists see the solution to labor market problems, such as low earnings and unemployment, as more rather than less market determination and the elimination of existing regulations. If labor markets deliver less than ideal results it is because they are not free enough. Public policy must be to remove the imperfections. Unions and minimum wages are logical targets in this regard.

The problem with such deductive reasoning is that employers and employees seldom meet as equals in the labor market, although the model assumes that they do. In blue-collar settings, for example, the employment relationship favors employers, who typically offer jobs on a take-it-or-leave-it basis. Individual workers find there are far more workers than there are good jobs and they take what they can get on the terms that are offered. Employers simply have more options in the hiring process than do workers—except perhaps when unemployment is low and workers scarce in the lowest paying, least desirable occupations and industries, at which point employers turn to immigrant labor to fill job vacancies at the going wage levels. Additionally, employers know far more than hourly workers do about supply and demand conditions in local labor markets and are more mobile in terms of where and when to hire. They also can hold out much longer financially than can workers in the event of differences over wages and working conditions. Finally, and importantly, because they own the plant and equipment upon which the worker's livelihood depends, they can threaten to relocate the workplace or to replace the workers with machines or other workers.

In the absence of institutional protections such as union contracts and minimum wages, workers are in constant danger of having to compete with one another to see which of them will work for less pay and under the worst conditions. If one or a few employers are able to reduce labor standards by taking advantage of labor's inherent bargaining weakness, and in the process they expand markets and increase their profits, then the race is on among all employers to take down labor standards. The labor market degenerates into what institutional labor economists call destructive competition. As two institutional labor economists observed decades ago, "When an employer can hire workers for practically his own price, he can be slack and inefficient in his methods, and yet, by reducing wages, reduce his cost of production to the level of his more able competitor" (Commons and Andrews 1936:48).

The irrelevancy of the neoclassical analysis.   This demonstrates the second thing wrong with Rustici's neoclassical interpretation. It examines and evaluates minimum wage laws only on the basis of what would result in a competitive market model. In doing so, it ignores the reasons why such laws are enacted in the first place and whether or not they solve the problems they were intended to solve. The problem with this approach is that it focuses on only one of the three forms of economic efficiency that are essential for a nation to sustain high-levels of production and consumption: a nation's need to provide high standards of living for its citizens.

Robert Kuttner (1997) argues that neoclassical preoccupation with allocative efficiency prevents an examination of macroefficiency and technical efficiency. Macroefficiency concerns a nation's ability to sustain or enhance total production, employment, and family living standards; whereas technical efficiency refers to the ability to generate new products and production methods through industrial invention and innovation. Allocative efficiency, on the other hand, is limited to looking after the immediate interests of the consumer by minimizing production costs and product prices. If only allocative efficiency is taken into account, the long-term interests of both producers and consumers is ignored as the nation neglects its overall economic growth, job and earnings performance, and progress in research/development.

It must be remembered that neither macro- nor technical efficiency necessarily results in optimal allocation efficiency in the short run, that is, in the lowest possible costs of production and consumer prices. Nor does optimal allocative efficiency necessarily help to maximize either macro- or technical efficiency. The postwar success of certain West European and Asian economies, led by Germany and Japan, testifies to the need to distinguish between alternative forms of economic efficiency and between short- and long-run goals and performance. Japanese industrial strategists made these distinctions for example when they targeted the global auto market in the late 1950s. They gave up short-run cost efficiency in return for long-term product and workforce quality on their way to world supremacy in autos by the 1980s (Halberstam 1986).

Because neoclassical economists largely ignore macro- and technical efficiency in their analysis of competitive labor markets, their competitive model cannot estimate the macroeffects of incremental changes in prices and quantities in particular markets. The 1930s, for example, were characterized by the kind of intense wage and price competition that neoclassical economists associate with allocative efficiency. Consequently, the economy should have been performing at its best. But we still refer to what happened instead as the Great Depression.

Remember that the question deriving from the neoclassical market model is "How many workers are made unemployable because the new wage prices them out of competitive labor markets?" That is not, however, the question that advocates of the FLSA were concerned with in 1938, nor what people are concerned with today in view of the long-term decline in median real wages and the increase in unstable jobs. The problem then and now is not the ability to produce enough goods and services, but rather it is creating jobs at wages high enough to buy back what is produced and in the process sustain high living standards for everyone.

This was the task of the 1938 federal minimum wage. It was designed to do two things: (i) increase employment and purchasing power in order to stimulate the slumping economy; and (ii) drive out of the market employers who competed on the basis of cheap labor instead of through better products and state-of-the-art production methods. The country had been in economic crisis for the better part of a decade. It had become increasingly clear that much of the problem was due to low pay, long workweeks, and growing use of child rather than adult labor. Advocates of minimum wages were not the least dissuaded by neo-classical forecasts that some jobs would be lost and some employers driven out of business. That is precisely what they wanted to do, on grounds that a job that does not pay enough to support a family should not exist and an employer who cannot pay a living wage, even though other employers in that industry can and do pay the mandated living wage, should be driven from the marketplace.

In brief, if a job pays less than enough to sustain workers and their dependents at the customary standard of living, then that job is not paying its way in a productive economy because it is being subsidized by some household, charitable organization, or government transfer payment. The beneficiary of this subsidy is either the employer paying the low wage and making a profit by doing so, or the customer paying a low price for the good or service. Fast-food restaurant fare, for example, is cheap in part because fast-food workers earn poverty level wages. Home owners in wealthy suburbs can get their houses cleaned cheaply because the women who clean them live in low-income areas, need the money, and have few job options. A subsidy is a subsidy, whether the worker is part of a poor household or an affluent household and whether the employer is a large or a small business.

If you work for a fast-food restaurant why should your family subsidize the owners of that restaurant? In a like manner, why should taxpayers subsidize manufacturers that employ fathers and mothers who cannot support their families without receiving food stamps or a tax rebate from the government? Why should the large employer have to compete with a smaller rival that is being subsidized by low-income households and taxpayers?

This subsidization does not have to occur. In Australia, for example, restaurant workers, "bag boys" in grocery stores, bartenders in taverns, and other workers who are generally low paid in the United States are paid in excess of $12 an hour. Nevertheless, McDonalds hamburgers and Pizza Hut pizzas still abound in Australia. In the United States unionized waitresses in Las Vegas also earn $12 an hour, before tips, and Las Vegas is one of the fastest growing economic regions in America. Waitresses in other parts of the country commonly receive about half the level of the minimum wage, before tips, which forces them to show a certain amount of servitude in order to earn enough tips to make the job worthwhile (a subsidy to the employer from the customer) and leaves the worker unsure of her or his earnings from day-to-day and week-to-week. Such market outcomes reflect the low-status, devalued nature of these workers and occupations more than it does their value to both customers and employers.

Contradictory evidence for the neoclassical view.   Rustici's neoclassical approach necessarily ignores the economic and social problems associated with low-wage jobs because it concentrates on workers rather than jobs. Such focus also shifts responsibility for low-wage incomes from jobs to workers by focusing on worker behavior rather than industrial strategies and government policies. Recall that the theory assumes the individual worker's wage is determined by his or her worth on the job; it further presumes that this worth is determined in large part by the amount of human capital the worker possesses in terms of formal education (college degrees) and occupational training (vocational and on-the-job training). Thus the job and its requirements are excluded from the analysis and low-wages are linked to the worker's efforts to acquire skill and education. When neoclassical researchers like Thomas Rustici want to verify their theory they study the earnings and employment experiences of groups of workers having low educational and vocational skills on grounds such workers are most likely to lose jobs as a result of minimum wage raises. Most neoclassical studies do indeed find greater unemployment among such groups following minimum wage increases.

But the findings of empirical studies themselves pose the third problem with Rustici's analysis. The results of far too many empirical studies—those conducted by neoclassical as well as institutional labor economists—have contradicted the neoclassical model for it to remain very convincing. During the Progressive Era prior to World War I, for example, government economists surveyed jobs before and after passage of state minimum wage laws covering women workers (Obenauer and von der Nienburg 1915). This and a later study conducted by Commons and Andrews (1936), found that mandated wages alleviated the degenerative effects of low wages and actually enhanced productivity by increasing worker desire and ability to produce. Only "parasitic" employers were threatened by minimum wages and relatively small numbers of jobs were eliminated.

Some years later, Princeton labor economist Richard Lester surveyed southern manufacturing employers after World War II and found they had not laid-off marginal workers in response to minimum wage increases, but instead had maintained their workforces and tried to offset the higher labor cost by increasing output and sales. This allowed them to take advantage of the economies of scale (lower per-unit costs of production) that accompany higher levels of plant and equipment utilization. Lester went on to note that workers doing the same jobs in different plants received different wages over long periods of time—another finding at odds with neoclassical reasoning—therefore, it was not possible to predict the employment effects of a minimum wage raise. His and other studies thus refuted the neoclassical notion of a single competitive wage. Workers with comparable skills often make quite different wages over long periods of time and those with different skills often earn the same wages. "Such matters are elementary and commonplace to a student of labor, but they seem to be largely overlooked by theorists of the [neoclassical] marginalist faith," he concluded (1947:148).

In the 1990s, another group of neoclassical revisionists using much the same investigative methods as Lester, but with more sophisticated equipment and techniques at their disposal, produced similar findings and came to much the same conclusion. Princeton economists David Card and Alan Krueger demonstrated that modest increases in minimum wage rates have little if any negative impact on the most exposed workers—teenagers. Instead of analyzing what happens to workers following minimum wage increases, they, like Lester before them, asked what happened to the jobs themselves. And like Lester, they discovered that employers did not respond as anticipated. Jobs in fast-food restaurants and other low-wage establishments did not decline, and in fact they even increased slightly in New Jersey when that state increased its minimum wage above the federal level. More surprising perhaps, in adjacent Pennsylvania, where no increase in the state minimum wage had occurred, fast-food employment actually fell slightly! Card and Krueger substantiated these findings in similar studies involving fast-food restaurant jobs in Texas and teenage workers in all industries in California (Card and Krueger 1995: Chapters 2 and 3).

These results, clearly at odds with the neoclassical literature, prompted one somewhat shaken but faithful neoclassical reviewer of Card and Krueger's work to conclude in 1995, just as the debate was getting underway on a proposal to raise the federal minimum wage to $5.15, that "we just don't know how many jobs would be lost if the minimum wage were increased to $5.15." Orthodox certainty was beginning to be eroded by the contradictory findings, but the basic model was not questioned. Many neoclassical economists hold doggedly to the view that jobs *must be* lost if minimum wages are increased. Consider, for example, a standard neoclassical labor economics text now in its sixth edition. The authors dismiss the Card-Krueger findings and insist instead that: "While the impact of the minimum wage on employment, especially that of young workers will undoubtedly continue to receive a great deal of research and public policy discussion, the best evidence remains that the overall impact of the law is to lower employment of unskilled workers while increasing the earnings of those who are able to get jobs" (Filer, Hamermesh, and Rees 1996:175).

In sum, neoclassical economists like Rustici find fault with the minimum wage because they contrast it with a theoretical system that is said to provide optimal results; but it is a system that ultimately is nonfalsifiable because of its tautological nature. They purport to refute the minimum wage on grounds it destroys low-wage jobs despite the fact that this is precisely what it is supposed to do. Finally, by limiting the inquiry to the dictates of a model that is inherently hostile to government regulation, they preclude serious debate on regulation as a policy tool.

Alternative analyses of minimum wage laws.   The shortcomings of traditional neoclassical analysis become apparent when considered in terms of macro- and technical efficiency. Wage-based competition during the 1930s reduced already depressed earnings and worker purchasing power, which in turn decreased product demand and caused additional workers to be unemployed. The effect was to cut output, incomes, and profits. With no recovery in sight, large firms could not be expected to make more cars, radios, and appliances than they could sell, nor could they be expected to design and manufacture new products when consumers could afford neither old nor new models.

Economic recovery did not occur until total war production during 1940–45, when all the neoclassical rules of allocative efficiency were repealed: industry was cartelized, wages and prices were controlled, and productive decision making was centralized. Yet, despite the total violation of market rules, the defense plants were running day and night, workers were acquiring formal and informal education and training, incomes and profits were high. Then, from the late 1940s until the mid-1970s, industrial oligopolies and labor unions replaced government in administering the productive system, again in violation of allocative efficiency. But we look back fondly on those decades as the golden age of increased living standards and job security.

Since then, however, the economy has been deregulated in keeping with neoclassical doctrine and both product and labor markets made more competitive by domestic and global changes in industrial structure and behavior. Labor productivity has been increasing, albeit modestly, and labor resources probably have been allocated more efficiently than in the postwar decades, but real earnings are falling, job security declining, and living standards stagnating (Mishel, et al. 1997).

As a society we have three broad policy responses. One, we can remove a certain portion of the population from the productive system by offering social insurance and welfare benefits to able-bodied individuals including laid-off or displaced males and single mothers. This should raise wages by reducing the supply of workers. Two, we can "reform welfare," so to speak, and force welfare recipients to take jobs work under the terms offered by cutting off their welfare support and giving them no alternative. This should lower wages by putting the new low-wage workers in competition with existing ones. Finally, we can raise minimum wages enough to ensure that the lowest paid workers and households are self-sufficient. This would raise wages directly rather than indirectly, eliminate wage and price subsidies to employers and consumers and raise prices, that is, to the extent that higher labor costs are not offset by productivity gains or profit reductions.

Although liberal economists might consider the first remedy better than none, they, like economists generally, resist policies that allow and presumably encourage able-bodied persons to be consumers but not producers in a market-based economy. Other liberal social scientists, however, are more likely to prefer the welfare alternative on ethical and humanitarian grounds. Wealthy societies like the U.S. should, they argue, be willing to provide sustenance for their disadvantaged individuals and families, regardless of any economic inefficiencies that might result. Moreover, they say, all of society benefits when public assistance makes these families more stable and functioning than otherwise.

Surprisingly perhaps, some conservative economists have supported direct welfare payments. They did so, however, as a second best solution. Milton Friedman, for example, once argued that if the political majority is determined to assist the disadvantaged—as it was in the 1960s—then the least interventionist method is to send them government checks and be done with it, rather than pursue minimum wage or other interventionist labor market policies.

It is the second alternative, abolishing financial support, that conservative economists find most consistent with conventional theory. Others agree mainly for moral and ethical reasons. This has been true since industrial poverty first appeared in 1830s Britain (Persky 1997). Free market advocates urged the abolition of welfare support and wage supplements on grounds their elimination would increase the number of laborers and worker productivity while also lowering taxes and birth rates. As a secondary benefit, they and others claimed, it would enhance family stability and values by making parents responsible for their children and both children and wives dependent on and therefore respectful of and obedient to male wage earners. Conservatives are still moved by such thinking.

The third alternative is preferred by liberal economists and policy makers. It seeks to assure low-wage workers self-sufficiency by supplementing their inadequate earnings through the Earned Income Tax Credit, a tax rebate of up to several thousand dollars a year to the employee based on his or her Social Security payments. Advocates favor this approach because it effectively increases the employee's real wage rate and at the same time offsets the undesirable market outcomes of low wages without distorting wage and employment structures and obstructing allocative efficiency. They also believe that the long-run solution is worker training and education to enhance human capital.

Conservative and liberal economists tend to agree on the latter point, although they differ on whether such efforts should be publicly financed and broadly available or individuals should be primarily responsible for their own human capital enhancement.

In view of the bipartisan support for more education—which can accompany any of the three alternative policy responses—a word of caution is in order. More education is always laudable, but by itself cannot solve the problem of low wages. This is because employers use formal educational credentials, especially college degrees, to screen applicants for good jobs. Therefore, as the overall educational level of the work force rises, the amount of education needed to get a given job also increases. This jeopardizes the effectiveness of education as the justification for high pay. For if a college degree were to be conferred magically upon the entire working population tomorrow, who would bus and wait tables the day after? Most likely, employers would find and apply other screening criteria, perhaps relative college rankings or graduate degrees, in order to determine which college grads became managers and which servers.

Moreover, the supply of educated workers does not automatically create the demand for them. American engineering students, for instance, may wonder exactly what it is they are going to engineer when they read about U.S. companies hiring pools of low-wage but college trained information technologists in developing countries to work on computer software projects using high-speed satellite information links, or when they hear about domestic aerospace companies transferring technology overseas in exchange for sales contracts, or of NASA purchasing rocketry equipment from other industrialized countries in order to get the lowest possible price (Barlett and Steele 1996: 49–52, 93–9).

The third alternative is the best. It goes directly to the problem of low-wage jobs by increasing pre-tax earnings and incomes rather than depend on welfare and other transfer payments, let alone on market forces to do so. It is reasonable to presume that with rare exceptions people want the dignity and independence that comes with gainful employment. Society should expect and enable them to work. Doing so makes them participating stakeholders in the productive system, affords them the purchasing power to be effective consumers and fosters the stability and purpose to be involved citizens. But such outcomes depend on the availability of jobs paying enough to afford a decent living.

In addition, the high wage economy is most consistent over time with the three economic efficiencies. High minimum wages are to be preferred because they contribute to sustained economic growth (macroefficiency) and industrial capitalization and innovation (technical efficiency). It is true that minimum wage are inconsistent with neoclassical allocative efficiency in the short-run; but it is the long-run that we should be concerned. High-paid workers stay with their employers, which encourages the latter to invest in worker human capital, which in turn encourages the employers to adopt state-of-the-art production methods and sophisticated product design and performance. High-paid workers also have the purchasing power to buy the goods and services that they and other high-paid workers produce.

A high wage policy is the best hope for a bright future for the American economy. It ensures a proficient labor force in a stable macroeconomy and encourages steady technological advancement. The larger society is only as prosperous as its individual parts. When labor standards are high the larger society prospers.

References

Barlett, Donald L., and James B. Steele. 1996. *America: Who Stole the Dream?* Kansas City: Andrews & McMeel.

Card, David Edward, and Alan B. Krueger. 1995. *Myth and Measurement: The New Economics of the Minimum Wage.* Princeton, NJ: Princeton University Press.

Commons, John R., and John B. Andrews. 1936. *Principles of Labor Legislation* (fourth edition). New York: Augustus M. Kelley (1967 Reprint).

Filer, Randall K., Daniel S. Hamermesh, and Albert Rees. 1996. *The Economics of Work and Pay*, sixth edition. New York: Harper Collins.

Halberstam, David. 1986. *The Reckoning.* New York: Morrow.

Kuttner, Robert. 1997. *Everything For Sale: The Virtues and Limits of Markets.* New York: Alfred A. Knopf.

Lester, Richard A. 1947. "Marginalism, Minimum Wages, and Labor Markets." *American Economic Review* 37 (March) pp. 135–48.

Mishel, Lawrence, Jared Bernstein, and John Schmitt. 1997. *The State of Working America, 1996–97.* Armonk, NY: M. E. Sharpe.

Obenauer, Marie L., and Bertha von der Nienburg. 1915. *Effect of Minimum Wage Determinations in Oregon.* Bureau of Labor Statistics, Bulletin No. 176. Washington: GPO.

Persky, Joseph. 1997. "Classical Family Values: Ending the Poor Laws as They Knew Them." *Journal of Economic Perspectives* 11 (Winter) pp. 179–89.

POSTSCRIPT

Is It Time to Abolish the Minimum Wage?

The impact of the minimum wage can be expressed in many ways. Two particularly rewarding ways of looking at such legislative initiatives are to examine minimum wages over time in real dollars and as a percentage of manufacturing wages.

A clear pattern should emerge from an examination of this data. The 1965–1970 period saw the highest level of the minimum wage in real terms. In constant 1982–1984 dollars, the minimum wage for these years was approximately $4.00 an hour and reached nearly 50 percent of the prevailing manufacturing wage. For the next 20 years, however, the value of the minimum wage in real terms and as a percentage of the manufacturing wage fell. It is only in recent years that it has begun to recover.

The renewed interest in the minimum wage can be traced in part to the research findings of David Card and Alan Krueger. These economists, as Craypo points out, have shaken the economics profession with their empirical research findings that moderate increases in the minimum wage have few negative effects on employment patterns and in some cases are associated with increases in employment. Their work has been published widely in professional journals: *Industrial and Labor Relations Review* (October 1992 and April 1994) and the *American Economic Review* (September 1994 and May 1995). They have also detailed their findings in a book entitled *Myth and Measurement: The New Economics of the Minimum Wage* (Princeton University Press, 1995).

Two vocal critics of Card and Krueger's research are David Neumark and William Wascher. Their empirical studies are supportive of the traditional neoclassical findings that the minimum wage causes unemployment, particularly among teenagers and young adults. See their work published in *Industrial and Labor Relations Review* (September 1992 and April 1994); NBER Working Paper No. 4617 (1994); *Journal of Business and Economic Statistics* (April 1995); and *American Economic Review Papers and Proceedings* (May 1995). Still often considered the best anti–minimum wage statement, however, is George J. Stigler's 1946 essay "The Economics of Minimum Wage Legislation," *American Economic Review*.

ISSUE 12

Are Declining Caseloads a Sign of Successful Welfare Reform?

YES: Michael J. New, from "Welfare Reform That Works: Explaining the Welfare Caseload Decline, 1996–2000," *Policy Analysis No. 435* (May 7, 2002)

NO: Evelyn Z. Brodkin, from "Requiem for Welfare," *Dissent* (Winter 2003)

ISSUE SUMMARY

YES: Cato Institute researcher Michael J. New presents statistical evidence that welfare reform, and not a growing economy, is the primary cause of the recent decline in welfare caseloads. This means that welfare reform has been a success.

NO: Evelyn Z. Brodkin, an associate professor in the School of Social Service Administration at the University of Chicago Law School, contends that in assessing welfare reform, one must look beyond the decline in welfare caseloads and ask, What has happened to those who no longer receive welfare? Her answer to this question evokes in Brodkin nostalgia for the "bad old days" of unreformed welfare.

Given American society's traditional commitment to a market system and its fundamental belief in self-determination, Americans are uncomfortable enacting social welfare legislation that appears to give someone "something for nothing," even if that individual is clearly in need. Thus, when tracing the roots of the existing U.S. social welfare system back to its origins in the New Deal legislation of President Franklin D. Roosevelt during the Great Depression of the 1930s, one sees that many of the earliest programs linked jobs to public assistance. One exception was Aid to Families with Dependent Children (AFDC), which was established as part of the 1935 Social Security Act. This program provided money to families in which there were children but no breadwinner. In 1935, and for many years thereafter, this program was not particularly controversial. Two reasons explain this acceptance of AFDC: the number of beneficiaries was relatively small, and the popular image of an AFDC family was that of a white woman with young children whose husband had died as a result of an illness or industrial accident.

In the early 1960s, as the U.S. economy prospered, poverty and what to do about it captured the attention of the nation. The Kennedy and Johnson administrations focused their social welfare programs on poor individuals—a minority of the population, especially, but not exclusively, a black minority—left behind as the general economy reached record levels of income and employment. Their policies were designed to address the needs of those who were trapped in "pockets of poverty," a description popularized in the early 1960s in the writings of Michael Harrington (1929–1989), a political theorist and prominent socialist. Between 1964 and 1969 the number of AFDC recipients increased by more than 60 percent, and the costs of the program more than doubled. The number of AFDC families continued to grow throughout the 1970s and the 1980s, and the program became increasingly controversial.

The controversy grew for several reasons: an increase in the number of recipients, an increase in costs, and a change in perceptions. The image of the welfare mother changed; she was increasingly perceived as a woman living in an urban public housing project whose children had been deserted by their father or as an unmarried woman who bore more children only to get more welfare.

In the 1980s social critics began to attack AFDC. They charged AFDC with encouraging welfare dependency and teenage pregnancies, dissolving the traditional family, and eroding the basic American work ethic. Welfare reform became an issue in the 1992 and 1996 presidential campaigns. In both of these campaigns, Bill Clinton promised, if elected, to "end welfare as we know it." Welfare reform became a reality eight months into the start of Clinton's second term with the enactment of the Personal Responsibility and Work Opportunity Reconciliation Act (PRWORA). This act abolished the AFDC entitlement that had guaranteed poor families a standardized set of welfare benefits for 60 years and replaced AFDC with a new block program entitled Temporary Assistance for Needy Families (TANF). The new legislation allowed states far more discretion in determining which families would be supported and how much support each of these families would receive.

The question addressed in this issue is whether or not welfare reform is working. Michael J. New presents evidence that the decline in welfare caseloads can be attributed to welfare reform. Evelyn Z. Brodkin looks beyond the caseload decline and its causes, arguing that to evaluate welfare reform it is necessary to determine what has happened to those who no longer receive government assistance.

Michael J. New

 **YES**

Welfare Reform That Works

Introduction

[In 1996] President [Bill] Clinton signed landmark welfare reform legislation into law. While previous attempts at reform resulted in only cosmetic changes, the Personal Responsibility and Work Opportunity Reconciliation Act of 1996 [PRWORA] has had a meaningful and lasting impact on the federal welfare regime. PRWORA ended the entitlement status of Aid to Families with Dependent Children [AFDC] and replaced it with a time-limited assistance and work requirement program called Temporary Assistance to Needy Families [TANF]. Most important, however, PROWRA gave states more leeway to structure their welfare administrations.

Under PROWRA, states receive federal block grant allocations totaling $16.5 billion a year until September 30, 2002. That allocation allows states to use TANF funding in any manner reasonably calculated to accomplish the purposes of TANF so long as the states maintain historical levels of spending agreed to in "maintenance of effort" plans. To continue receiving their full federal TANF allocations, states must also conform to specific requirements regarding current recipients' work participation rates and length of time on the rolls.[1]

Although PROWRA passed by wide margins in the House and Senate in 1996, it was still politically controversial. Then–senate minority leader Tom Daschle (D-S.D.) opposed the bill, calling the work requirements "extremist." Likewise, House Minority Leader Richard Gephardt (D-Mo.) voted against the bill, citing an Urban Institute study that predicted that welfare reform would force more than 1 million children into poverty. Sen. Daniel Patrick Moynihan (D-N.Y.) was even more strident. He proclaimed that the new law "was the most brutal act of social policy since reconstruction." He predicted: "Those involved will take this disgrace to their graves."[2]

Contrary to those alarming predictions, welfare reform went more smoothly than critics expected. A great deal of evidence has demonstrated that

From Michael J. New, "Welfare Reform That Works: Explaining the Welfare Caseload Decline, 1996–2000," *Policy Analysis No. 435* (May 7, 2002). Copyright © 2002 by The Cato Institute. Reprinted by permission.

welfare reform has been effective at reducing dependence on welfare, reducing poverty, and lowering the rate of out-of-wedlock births:

- By 1999 overall poverty and child poverty had substantially declined. Some 4.2 million fewer people, including 2.3 million children, live in poverty today than did in 1996.[3]
- Hunger among children has been reduced by almost 50 percent since the passage of welfare reform.[4]
- By 2001 welfare caseloads had been reduced by 58 percent since welfare reform was enacted.[5]
- During the past six years, there has been a reduction in the rate of increase in out-of-wedlock childbearing.[6]

Even some opponents of PROWRA have acknowledged the success of welfare reform. Wendell Primus, a deputy assistant secretary in the Department of Health and Human Services, who resigned in protest after President Clinton signed the reform bill, remarked last year, "In many ways welfare reform is working better than I thought it would." He added, "The sky is not falling anymore. Whatever we have been doing during the past five years we ought to keep doing."[7]

However, a number of opponents of welfare reform still stubbornly refuse to acknowledge its progress, crediting instead the booming economy. Donna Shalala, who as secretary of Health and Human Services urged President Clinton to veto the welfare reform bill, said, "What happened on welfare reform was this combination of an economic boom and a political push to get people off the welfare rolls."[8] Others who argue that the economy deserves most of the credit for the decline in caseloads, including Marian Wright Edelman of the Children's Defense Fund, expressed concern about what would happen during the most recent economic slowdown.[9]

Their arguments in favor of an "economics" explanation of welfare caseload changes do not hold up to empirical scrutiny. While the strength of the economy does have an effect on the number of people receiving welfare, other economic expansions did not generate welfare caseload declines of similar magnitude. For instance, the economy expanded by 10.63 percent between 1993 and 1996, but the number of individuals receiving welfare declined by only 8.8 percent. Moreover, the economic expansion that took place during the 1980s failed to reduce the total number of individuals receiving AFDC.[10] Finally, welfare caseloads dramatically increased during the economic boom that took place during the mid to late 1960s largely because benefits became more generous.[11]

Existing Research

What, if not the booming economy, is responsible for the decline in welfare caseloads? A great deal of research has been carried out to analyze this question. In 1999 the Council of Economic Advisers analyzed the decline in welfare caseloads and concluded that the economy was responsible for 10 percent of the decline in registrants between 1996 and 1998. The authors argued that welfare reforms were responsible for approximately one-third of the decline and the remainder was the consequence of other, unnamed factors.[12]

In 1999 the Heritage Foundation released a more detailed study on welfare caseload declines. . . . They found that there were substantial differences among the states in their policies toward welfare recipients who were not performing mandated work activities. In some states, recipients would lose their entire TANF check at the first instance of nonperformance. In other states, however, recipients could be assured of keeping almost their entire benefit check regardless of their conduct.[13]

The Heritage analysts found that the strength of state sanctioning policies had a major impact on the magnitude of state welfare caseload declines. In general, the larger caseload reductions occurred in states with more stringent sanctions, and more modest declines took place in states with weaker sanctioning policies. The Heritage study also found that immediate work requirements also led to declines in the number of individuals receiving welfare. Interestingly, however, the authors found that the strength of the economy, as measured by each state's average unemployment rate, did not have a statistically significant impact on caseload declines.[14]

In the summer of 2001 the Manhattan Institute released a study by June O'Neill and M. Anne Hill titled "Gaining Ground? Measuring the Impact on Welfare and Work." . . . The authors concluded that welfare reform is responsible for more than half of the decline in the welfare population since 1996.[15]

However, O'Neill and Hill neglected to consider other factors that likely played a role in the caseload declines. For instance, they did not consider the effect of the relative strength of state sanctions on the number of welfare recipients. In addition, while the authors held benefit levels constant in their regression analysis, they did not elaborate on their findings. They also did not state whether they considered only benefits available through TANF or included benefits available to welfare recipients from other programs including the Women, Infants, and Children program, food stamps, and Medicare.

A final study that provides useful insights about welfare caseloads is William A. Niskanen's 1996 *Cato Journal* article "Welfare and the Culture of Poverty." Niskanen used 1992 data to examine the specific impact of welfare benefits on a variety of social pathologies. Holding a variety of demographic, cultural, and economic factors constant, he found that increases in AFDC benefits led to statistically significant increases in the numbers of welfare recipients, people in poverty, births to single mothers, abortions, and violent crimes.[16] That article is useful to this analysis because it provides evidence that higher levels of benefits lead to higher welfare caseloads.

Historically, benefit levels have been a politically salient issue. In his 1984 book *Losing Ground,* Charles Murray convincingly argued that increases in welfare benefits, which were legislated during the Great Society period, were largely responsible for the welfare caseload expansion that took place during the mid to late 1960s. According to Murray, before the increase in benefits, a woman facing an unplanned pregnancy had three basic choices. She could give the child up for adoption, get married, or fend for herself. However, when welfare benefits were increased, staying on welfare suddenly became an economically viable option for many unwed mothers.[17] Not surprisingly, welfare caseloads and the number of single-parent families soared.[18] Since the evidence suggests that high welfare benefits led to an increase in welfare caseloads during the 1960s, it seems reasonable that an analysis of benefit levels might help to explain the decline in caseloads during the 1990s.

Overall, previous and current research has identified three major factors that appear to affect fluctuations in welfare caseloads: the strength of sanctions, the performance of the economy, and the level of benefits. In order to determine the impact of each of those factors on welfare caseloads, I use state-level data to examine the effects of each of the foregoing determinants. A comparison of the states should prove fruitful because, during the past five years, states have experienced varying amounts of success in reducing their welfare caseloads. For instance, between August 1996 and August 2000, Wyoming reduced its welfare caseload by 91 percent. Conversely, Rhode Island reduced its caseload by a comparatively modest 22 percent over the same period. In addition, there are variations in the strength of state economies, the level of benefits states offer, and the stringency of state sanctioning policies. Because different state policies have resulted in different outcomes, a proper analysis of these variables across the states should be able to identify the policies that are the most responsible for the substantial declines in welfare caseloads.

Findings

Previous studies have indicated that the strength of state sanctions may be the most reliable predictor of welfare caseload declines at the state level. Even though the Heritage Foundation dealt with this issue extensively in its 1999 study, the topic is worth revisiting for several reasons. First, the Heritage study examined caseload declines up to June 1998,[19] and more data have been released since that time. Second, data from the U.S. Department of Health and Human Services and the U.S. General Accounting Office indicate that some states have changed their sanctioning policies.[20]

Sanctioning Policies

There are three types of state sanctioning policies:

1. Full family sanctioning: Some states sanction the entire TANF check at the first instance of nonperformance of required work or other activities. This is the strongest sanction a state can apply.
2. Graduated sanctioning: States that do not sanction the entire TANF check at the first instance of nonperformance but will sanction the full TANF check after multiple infractions.
3. Partial sanctioning: Some states sanction only the adult portion of the TANF check, even after repeated infractions. This enables recipients to retain the bulk of their TANF benefits even if they fail to perform workfare or other required activities.[21]

[Table 1] lists the sanctioning policies, the years they were in effect, and the monthly TANF benefit for the 50 states and the District of Columbia. Table 2 gives the average decline in caseload under the three types of sanctioning policies, as well as variations of those three types.

The results indicate that states with full family sanctions have, on average, experienced larger caseload declines than states with graduated sanctions.

Table 1

State Sanctioning Policies and TANF Benefits

State	Years With Full Family Sanction	Years With Graduated Sanction	Years With Partial Sanction	Monthly TANF Benefit
Alabama		1996–2000		$164
Alaska			1996–2000	$923
Arizona		1996–2000		$347
Arkansas	1996–1998		1998–2000	$204
California			1996–2000	$565
Colorado		1996–2000		$356
Connecticut		1996–2000		$636
District of Columbia			1996–2000	$379
Delaware		1996–2000		$338
Florida	1996–2000			$303
Georgia		1996–2000		$280
Hawaii	1998–2000		1996–1998	$570
Idaho	1996–2000			$276
Illinois		1996–2000		$377
Indiana			1996–2000	$288
Iowa	1998–2000	1996–1998		$426
Kansas	1996–2000			$429
Kentucky		1996–2000		$262
Louisiana		1996–2000		$190
Maine			1996–2000	$418
Maryland	1996–2000			$388
Massachusetts		1996–2000		$565
Michigan		1996–2000		$459
Minnesota			1996–2000	$532
Mississippi	1996–2000			$120
Missouri			1996–2000	$292
Montana			1996–2000	$450
Nebraska	1996–2000			$364
Nevada		1996–2000		$348
New Hampshire			1996–2000	$550
New Jersey		1996–2000		$424
New Mexico		1996–2000		$389

State	Years With Full Family Sanction	Years With Graduated Sanction	Years With Partial Sanction	Monthly TANF Benefit
New York			1996–2000	$577
North Carolina		1998–2000	1996–1998	$272
North Dakota		1996–2000		$490
Ohio	1996–2000			$362
Oklahoma	1996–2000			$292
Oregon		1996–2000		$460
Pennsylvania		1996–2000		$421
Rhode Island			1996–2000	$554
South Carolina	1996–2000			$201
South Dakota		1996–2000		$430
Tennessee	1996–2000			$185
Texas			1996–2000	$188
Utah		1996–2000		$426
Vermont		1996–1999	2000	$656
Virginia	1996–2000			$354
Washington			1996–2000	$546
West Virginia		1996–2000		$253
Wisconsin	1996–2000			$628
Wyoming	1998–2000	1996–1998		$340

Sources: Data on sanctioning policies are from U.S. Department of Health and Human Services, "State Implementation of Major Changes to Welfare Policies 1992–1998," aspe.hhs.gov/hsp/Waiver-Policies99/W3JOBSsnct.htm; U.S. General Accounting Office, "Welfare Reform: State Sanction Policies and Number of Families Affected," March 2000, pp. 44–47; and State Policy Documentation Project, "Summary of State Sanction Policies," www.spdp.org/tanf/sanctions.htm. Data on TANF benefits are from U.S. House of Representatives, Committee on Ways and Means, *2000 Green Book: Background Material and Data on Programs within the Jurisdiction of the Committee on Ways and Means,* aspe.hhs.gov/2000gb/sec7.txt.

Table 2

Average Welfare Caseload Decline

Type of Sanction	Decline
Full family sanction for 4 years (12 states)	60.85%
Graduated sanction for 4 years (20 states)	52.17%
Partial sanctions for 4 years (13 states)	40.56%
Full family sanctions for 2 years, partial sanctions for 2 years (2 states)	43.62%
Full family sanctions for 2 years, graduated sanctions for 2 years (2 states)	65.75%
Graduated sanctions for 3 years, partial sanctions for 1 year (1 state)	36.32%
Overall average	51.36%

Sources: Data on sanctioning policies are from U.S. Department of Health and Human Services, "State Implementation of Major Changes to Welfare Policies 1992–1998," http://aspe.hhs.gov/hsp/Waiver-Policies99/W3JOBSsnct.htm; U.S. General Accounting Office, "Welfare Reform: State Sanction Policies and Number of Families Affected," March 2000, pp. 44–47; and State Policy Documentation Project, "Summary of State Sanction Policies," www.spdp.org/tanf/sanctions.htm. Data on caseloads are from Administration for Children and Families, www.acf.dhhs.gov/news/stats/caseload.htm.

In addition, states with partial sanctions have had the least success in lowering their caseloads. Surprisingly, some of the states that changed their sanctioning policies actually showed the largest average caseload declines. However, this particular finding should be discounted because of the small size of the sample.

An analysis of variance test was run to determine whether the differences in mean caseload decline between the categories are statistically significant. The results . . . indicate that the differences in mean caseload decline between the categories do in fact achieve conventional standards of statistical significance. All of these findings are consistent with previous research on this topic.

Regression Analysis

Previous analysis has shown that other factors, including benefit levels and the strength of the economy, can also affect fluctuations in welfare caseloads. A multivariate regression analysis was used to determine the combined impact of sanctions, benefits, and the economy on the decline of state welfare caseloads. The regression analysis makes it possible to sort out the effects of each individual variable by holding constant the effects of all other variables.

Interpreting the Results

The regression results indicate that each state's ability to sanction welfare recipients not performing mandated work activities plays the most important role in determining how much welfare caseloads decline. This finding is consistent with the foregoing analysis. For each year that a state has a full family sanction in place, the regression model shows that the decline in its welfare caseload will be more than 5 percentage points greater than the decline in a state with a partial sanction. Similarly, for each year a state has a graduated sanction in place, the regression model shows that its caseload decline is more than 2.7 percentage points greater than that of a state with a partial sanction. Both of these findings are statistically significant.

These results are again broadly consistent with the results of the Heritage Foundation's 1999 study, which examined caseload fluctuations for a year and a half and demonstrated that more stringent sanctions resulted in larger caseload declines. The results of this regression also strengthen Heritage's original finding in two important ways. First, this study shows that the relationship between sanctions and caseload declines is not a short-term phenomenon. Examination of caseload declines for four years demonstrates that the relationship between caseload declines and sanctions is stable over a longer time period. Second, this study is able to take into account the fact that some states changed their sanctioning policies in 1998 and 1999, which adds strength to the analysis.

Figure 1 shows the impact of sanctions. It shows how the various sanctioning policies influence the percentage decline in state welfare caseloads in a hypothetical state with average real income growth (9.18 percent) and average TANF benefits as a percentage of state per capita personal income (16.81 percent). Figure 1 also indicates that the caseload will decline 61.54 percent in four

Figure 1

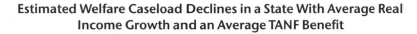

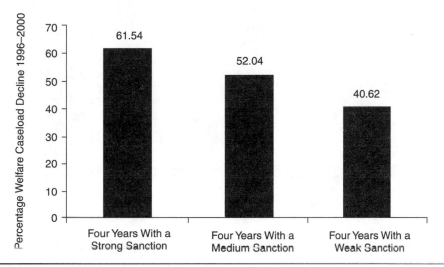

Estimated Welfare Caseload Declines in a State With Average Real Income Growth and an Average TANF Benefit

years under a strong sanction, 52.04 percent under a medium sanction, and 40.62 percent under a weak sanction.

Sanctions are not the only variable that has an impact on welfare caseload declines. The economy also has an effect, though its impact is considerably less. The regression model estimates that, for each percentage point increase in real per capita personal income between 1996 and 2000, welfare caseloads declined by an additional 1.166 percentage points. Those results are generally consistent with the Council of Economic Advisers' study, which found that the economy was responsible for part of the decline in welfare caseloads. Conversely, the results are at odds with the Heritage Foundation's findings that the economy had no statistically significant impact on caseload fluctuations. However, since most states experienced fairly similar rates of economic growth between 1996 and 2000, little of the actual variation in caseload declines can be attributed to the economy. In fact, the real per capita income growth rate for the state at the 25th percentile is only four percentage points less than the real per capita income growth rate for the state at the 75th percentile.

Figure 2 shows the impact of different rates of per capita personal income growth on welfare caseloads. The regression equation was used to show how fluctuations in personal income growth influence the percentage decline in the welfare caseload in a hypothetical state with a medium sanction and average TANF benefits. Caseloads in states with below-average economic growth (25th percentile, 7.00 percent) decline 49.50 percent; in states with average economic growth (50th percentile, 8.63 percent) they decline 51.40 percent; in states with

Figure 2

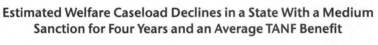

Estimated Welfare Caseload Declines in a State With a Medium Sanction for Four Years and an Average TANF Benefit

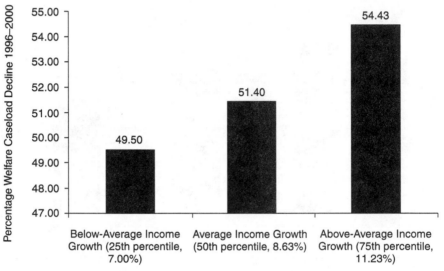

above-average economic growth (75th percentile, 11.23 percent) they decline 54.43 percent.

Figure 2 indicates that the economy had only a marginal impact on welfare caseload declines. The difference in caseload decline between a state with a strong economy and a state with a weak economy was less than five percentage points. Conversely, Figure 1 indicates that differences in sanctioning policy could lead to differences in caseload decline that exceeded 20 percentage points. That indicates that other factors besides the economy are largely responsible for the dramatic decline in welfare caseloads that has taken place over the past five years.

The final factor that the regression model considers is the level of TANF benefits. Although benefits did not have as strong an impact as sanctions, they had an impact nonetheless. The results indicate that states that offered relatively low TANF benefits enjoyed more success in reducing their welfare caseloads. Specifically, if TANF benefits were reduced by 1 percent of state per capita personal income, the regression model estimates that welfare caseloads would decline by .480 percent. That finding approaches conventional standards of statistical significance. This result is consistent with expectations. High cash benefits increase the attractiveness of welfare and create a disincentive to leave the welfare rolls, even with the sanctions and work requirements of TANF. Conversely, low benefits increase the attractiveness of work relative to welfare and give welfare recipients a greater incentive to leave the welfare rolls.

Surprisingly, however, benefit levels have gone largely unexamined in the policy literature on caseload declines. Niskanen demonstrated that benefit levels have an effect on caseloads. Unfortunately, the Heritage Foundation and the Council of Economic Advisers all but ignored TANF benefit levels in their studies. O'Neill and Hill held benefit levels constant in their regression analysis, but they did not report their findings. Even though benefit levels have received little attention from policy analysts in recent years, they merit serious attention in future debates about welfare reform.

Conclusion

Welfare reform was one of the leading public policy stories of the 1990s. Since Congress enacted welfare reform in 1996, the number of people who are receiving welfare has been cut by nearly 60 percent, and both poverty and hunger have declined.[22] That has attracted a great deal of attention, and many scholars have attempted to explain the cause of the large declines in welfare caseloads.

Some states experienced considerably larger caseload declines than others. As a result, many studies analyzing the success of welfare reform have paid close attention to program differentiation among the states. Those studies have presented a number of important insights about the reasons why welfare case loads have declined so sharply in the aftermath of reform. However, shortcomings are evident in many of the studies.

Prior analyses of welfare reform indicate that there are three factors that influence welfare caseload fluctuations: the strength of sanctions, the level of benefits, and the strength of the economy. However, all of the studies cited omit one or more of those factors from their analysis. In addition, since many studies consider caseload declines over a limited period of time since the passage of reform, they are unable to distinguish between policies that cause short-term fluctuations and those that lead to long-term declines.

This study breaks new ground in two ways. First, the use of multivariate regression analysis makes it possible to simultaneously consider the impact of the economy, sanctions, and TANF benefits and to determine which of those factors has had the most impact. Second, although many other studies consider caseload declines for a short period of time after reform, this study tracks declines for four years. Using a longer time frame increases the certainty that the various factors are having a long-term impact on caseloads and are not simply causing a temporary decline.

The most important finding is that the strength of state sanctioning policies had the largest impact on caseload declines between 1996 and 2000. The other variables that are considered, the strength of the economy and TANF benefit levels, achieve statistical significance, but their impact on caseload declines is considerably less than the impact of sanctioning policies. To demonstrate, the regression model estimates that differences in sanctioning policies could result in a 20 percentage point difference in caseload declines. Conversely, holding other factors constant, the model estimates that the difference in caseload decline between a state with a strong economy and a state with a weak economy is only about five percentage points.

Notes

1. Lisa Oliphant, "Four Years of Welfare Reform: A Progress Report," Cato Institute Policy Analysis no. 378, August 22, 2000, p. 2.

2. "Welfare As They Know It," Editorial, *Wall Street Journal,* August 29, 2001, p. A14.

3. U.S. Bureau of the Census, *Poverty in the United States 1999,* Current Population Reports Series P60-210 (Washington: U.S. Government Printing Office, 2000), p. B2.

4. Margaret Andrews et al., "Household Food Security in the United States, 1999," U.S. Department of Agriculture, Economic Research Service, 2000, p. 3.

5. Data on caseloads obtained from Administration for Children and Families, www.acf.dhhs.gov/news/stats/aug-dec.htm.

6. Stephanie Ventura and Christine Bachrach, "Nonmarital Childbearing in the United States 1940–1999," *National Vital Statistics Reports* 48, no. 16 (October 18, 2000): 1–2.

7. Quoted in Blaine Harden, "Two Parent Families Rise after Change in Welfare Laws," *New York Times,* August 12, 2001.

8. "Welfare As They Know It.

9. Ibid.

10. In 1983, 10.9 million individuals were receiving AFDC; by 1989, 12.1 million individuals were receiving AFDC. That is a caseload increase of 11 percent. U.S. Bureau of the Census, *Statistical Abstract of the United States: 1992* (Washington: Government Printing Office, 1992).

11. "Welfare As They Know It."

12. Council of Economic Advisers, "The Effects of Welfare Policy and the Economic Expansion on Welfare Caseloads: An Update," August 3, 1999, executive summary, p. 1.

13. Robert E. Rector and Sarah E. Youssef, *The Determinants of Welfare Caseload Decline* (Washington: Heritage Foundation, 1999), pp. 1–3.

14. Ibid., p. 6.

15. June O'Neill and M. Anne Hill, "Gaining Ground: Measuring the Impact of Welfare Reform on Welfare and Work," Manhattan Institute Civic Report 17, July 17, 2001.

16. William Niskanen, "Welfare and the Culture of Poverty," *Cato Journal* 16, no. 1 (Spring–Summer 1996).

17. Charles Murray, *Losing Ground* (New York: Basic Books, 1984), pp. 154–66.

18. Ibid., pp. 244, 263

19. Rector and Youssef, p. 1.

20. U.S. Department of Health and Human Services, "State Implementation of Major Changes to Welfare Policies 1992–1998," http://aspe.hhs.gov/hsp/Waiver-Policies99/W3JOBSsnct.htm; and U.S. General Accounting Office, "Welfare Reform: State Sanction Policies and Number of Families Affected," March 2000, pp. 44–47.

21. The names of the categories of sanctions are taken from ibid.

22. However, many of the people who have left the welfare rolls are still dependent on various transfer programs; the challenge of transition to self-sufficiency has not yet been met. See Oliphant.

NO

Evelyn Z. Brodkin

Requiem for Welfare

There were few mourners at welfare's funeral. In fact, its demise was widely celebrated when congressional Republicans teamed up with a majority of their Democratic colleagues and then-president Bill Clinton to enact a new welfare law in 1996. The law ended the sixty-one-year old federal commitment to aid poor families and ushered in a commitment to lower welfare rolls and put recipients to work.

To many politicians and the public, anything seemed preferable to the widely discredited program known as Aid to Families with Dependent Children (AFDC). Conservatives were sure that the new welfare would pull up the poor by their bootstraps and redeem them through the virtues of work. Liberals set aside their misgivings, hoping that work would redeem the poor politically and open opportunities to advance economic equality.

More than six years later, the demise of the old welfare remains largely unlamented. But what to make of the changes that have occurred in the name of reform? Often, laws produce more smoke than fire, intimating big change, but producing little. Not this time. In ways both apparent and not fully appreciated, welfare reform has reconfigured both the policy and political landscape. Some of these changes can evoke nostalgia for the bad old days of welfare unreformed.

Reconsidering Welfare's Fate

An immediate consequence of the new law was to defuse welfare as a hot political issue. There's little attention to it these days—apart from some five million parents and children who rely on welfare to alleviate their poverty (and the policy analysts who pore over mountains of data to calculate how it "works"). Legislators have shown no appetite for restarting the welfare wars of prior years. And is it any wonder? The news about welfare has looked good—at least, superficially. Caseloads have plummeted since implementation of the new welfare, dropping 57 percent between 1997 and 2001. Some smaller states essentially cleared their caseloads, with Wyoming and Idaho proudly announcing reductions of 88.9 percent and 85.1 percent, respectively. Even states with large, urban populations have cut caseloads by one-half to three quarters. . . .

Out With the "Old" Welfare

Reforming welfare assumed new urgency in the 1990s, an urgency grounded less in policy realities than in electoral politics. Alarms were sounded about a crisis of cost, although for three decades, spending on AFDC amounted to less than 2 percent of the federal budget. The $16 billion the federal government allocated to AFDC was dwarfed by spending on Social Security and defense, each costing more than $300 billion per year. Public opinion polls, however, indicated a different perception. Forty percent of respondents believed that welfare was one of the most expensive national programs, even larger than Social Security or defense.

Polls also indicated that much of the public believed welfare recipients had it too easy, although few knew what welfare really provided. In fact, AFDC gave only meager support to poor families. In 1996, the median monthly benefit for a family of three was $366. Even when combined with food stamps, welfare lifted few poor families above the federal poverty line. Even the much-touted crisis of dependency ("dependent" being a term loosely applied to anyone receiving welfare) was not reflected in the evidence. The share of families receiving welfare for extended periods declined between 1970 and 1985 and leveled off after that. Families that received welfare for more than six years constituted only a small minority of the welfare caseload at any point in time.

Although the hue and cry over a supposed welfare crisis was greatly overblown, Bill Clinton clearly appreciated welfare's potent political symbolism. As a presidential candidate, he famously pledged to "end welfare as we know it," a turn of phrase useful in demonstrating that he was a "new Democrat" unburdened by the liberalism of his predecessors. His proposals for reform emphasized neoliberal themes of work and individual responsibility, but coupled demands for work with provision of social services intended to improve individual employment prospects. The Clinton administration's plans also assumed the enactment of universal health insurance that would help underwrite the well-being of the working poor. But that did not happen. . . .

Clinton became the first elected Democratic President since Franklin Roosevelt to win a second term. But Clinton was no Roosevelt. In fact, he redeemed his pledge to "end welfare" by presiding over the destruction of a pillar of the New Deal welfare state.

Enter the "New" Welfare

The Personal Responsibility and Work Opportunity Reconciliation Act of 1996 replaced AFDC with a program aptly named Temporary Assistance to Needy Families (TANF). AFDC had provided an open-ended entitlement of federal funds to states based on the amount of benefits they distributed to poor families. TANF ended that entitlement, establishing a five-year block grant fixed at $16.5 billion annually (based on the amount allocated to AFDC in its last year) that states could draw down to subsidize welfare and related expenditures.

Mistrusting the states' willingness to be tough enough on work, Congress incorporated detailed and coercive provisions. First, it set time limits for assistance, restricting federal aid to a lifetime maximum of sixty months. If states wanted to exceed those limits, they would have to pay for most of it themselves. Second, parents were required to work or participate in so-called work activities after a maximum of two years of welfare receipt. Third, TANF established escalating work quotas. States that wanted to collect their full portion of federal dollars would have to show, by 2002, that 50 percent of adults heading single-parent households were working thirty hours per week. Fourth, it meticulously specified those work "activities" that would enable states to meet their quotas, among them paid work, job search, and unpaid workfare (in which recipients "worked off" their welfare benefits at minimum wage or provided child care for other welfare recipients). It limited the use of education and vocational training as countable activities.

Although the "work" side of TANF was clearly pre-eminent, there were some modest provisions on the "opportunity" side, with Congress providing $2.3 billion to help subsidize child care for working mothers and $3 billion in a block grant for welfare-to-work programs.

Beyond these prominent features, the new welfare also packed some hidden punches. It rewarded states for cutting welfare caseloads, largely without regard to how they did it. States that reduced their caseloads (whether those losing welfare found work or not) received credit against officially mandated quotas. If Congress was worried about states' slacking off from its tough work demands, the law indicated no concern that they might go too far in restricting access to benefits or pushing people off the welfare rolls. Only caseload reductions counted.

Under the banner of devolution, the law also gave states new authority to design their own welfare programs. While the welfare debate highlighted the professed virtues of innovation, less obvious was the license it gave states to craft policies even tougher and more restrictive than those allowed by federal law.

Pushing welfare decision making to the state and local level has never been good for the poor. In many states, poor families and their allies have little political influence. Moreover, constitutional balanced-budget requirements make states structurally unsuited to the task of protecting vulnerable residents against economic slumps. When unemployment goes up and state tax revenue goes down, the downward pressure on social spending intensifies.

The secret triumph of devolution lay, not in the opportunities for innovation, but in the opportunity for a quiet unraveling of the safety net.

The Unfolding Story of Welfare Transformed[1]

What has happened since 1996? For one thing, the new welfare changed a national program of income assistance to an array of state programs, each with its own assortment of benefits, services, restrictions, and requirements. There has always been wide variation in the amount of cash aid states provided, and federal waivers allowed states to deviate from some national rules. But devolution spurred far greater policy inconsistency by allowing states, essentially, to make their own rules. Consequently, what you get (or whether you get anything at all) depends on where you live.

In addition, devolution set off a state "race to the bottom," not by reducing benefit levels as some had predicted, but by imposing new restrictions that limited access to benefits. States across the nation have taken advantage of devolution to impose restrictions tougher than those required by federal law.

For example, although federal law required recipients to work within two years, most states require work within one year, some require immediate work, and others demand a month of job search before they even begin to process an application for assistance. No longer required to exempt mothers with children under three years old from work requirements, most states permit an exemption only for mothers with babies under one year old, and some have eliminated exemptions altogether. In nineteen states, lifetime limits for welfare receipt are set below the federal maximum of sixty months. Other states have imposed so-called family caps that preclude benefits for babies born to mothers already receiving welfare. If federal policymakers secretly hoped that states would do part of the dirty work of cutting welfare for them, they must be pleased with these results.

However, the picture from the states is anything but consistent or uniformly punitive. Many help those recipients accepting low-wage jobs by subsidizing the costs of transportation, child care, and medical insurance (although often only for one year). Twenty-two states try to keep low-wage workers afloat by using welfare benefits to supplement their incomes, "stopping the clock" on time limits for working parents. Significantly, the federal clock keeps ticking, and states adopting this strategy must use their own funds to support working families reaching the five-year lifetime limit. With state budgets increasingly squeezed by recession, it is hard to predict how strong the state commitment to preserve these supports will be.

Many state and local agencies have already cut back work preparation and placement programs funded under a $3 billion federal welfare-to-work block grant. Those funds spurred a short-term boom in contracting to private agencies. But the block grant expired leaving little evidence that states were able to build new systems for supporting work over the long term. In fact, no one knows exactly what all of this contracting produced, as state and local agencies kept limited records and conducted few careful evaluations. A close look at contracting in Illinois, for example, revealed the creation of a diffuse array of short-term programs operating under contract requirements that left many agencies unable to build anything of lasting value.

There is another strange twist to the convoluted welfare story: in their zest for services over support, states actually shifted government funds from the pockets of poor families to the pockets of private service providers. They distributed 76 percent of their AFDC funds in cash aid to the poor in 1996, but gave poor families only 41 percent of their TANF funds in 2000. Substantial portions of the TANF budget were consumed by child care costs, although it is difficult to say exactly how all the TANF funds were used. The General Accounting Office suggests that there is a fair amount of "supplantation" of services previously funded from other budget lines but now paid for by TANF.

Beyond the Caseload Count

The picture becomes still more complicated when one attempts to peer behind the head count in order to assess what actually happened in the purge of welfare caseloads. Exactly how did states push those caseloads down? What has happened to poor families that no longer have recourse to welfare? What kind of opportunities does the lower wage labor market really offer? Research has only begun to illuminate these crucial questions, but the evidence is disheartening.

Finding good jobs   There are three ways to lower welfare caseloads. One is by successfully moving recipients into good jobs with stable employment where they can earn enough to maintain their families above poverty (or, at least, above what they could get on welfare). Recipients may find jobs on their own, which many do, or with connections facilitated by welfare agencies and service providers.

Financial supports provided by TANF have allowed some recipients to take jobs where they earn too little to make ends meet on their own. Child-care and transportation subsidies make a difference for those workers. They also benefit from federally funded food stamps that stretch the grocery budget. But food stamp use fell off 40 percent after 1994, although fewer families were receiving welfare and more had joined the ranks of the working poor. Absent external pressures, most states made no effort to assure access to food stamps for those losing welfare. In fact, government studies indicate that administrative hassles and misinformation discouraged low-income families from obtaining benefits.

Taking bad jobs   A second way to lower welfare caseloads is to pressure recipients into taking bad jobs. Not all lower wage jobs are bad, but many of those most readily available to former recipients undermine their best efforts to make it as working parents. These jobs are characterized by unstable schedules, limited access to health insurance or pensions, no sick leave, and job insecurity. Because high turnover is a feature of these jobs, at any given moment, many are apt to be available. Indeed, employers seeking to fill these undesirable "high-velocity" jobs, where there is continuous churning of the workforce, are all too eager to use welfare agencies as a hiring hall.

This may partially explain why more than a fifth of those leaving welfare for work return within a year or two. Proponents of the new welfare conveniently blame individual work behavior or attitudes for job churning, but ignore the role of employers who structure jobs in ways that make job loss inevitable. What's a supermarket clerk to do when her manager makes frequent schedule changes, periodically shortens her hours, or asks her to work in a store across town? What happens is that carefully constructed child care arrangements break down, lost pay days break the family budget, and the hours it takes to commute on public transportation become unmanageable. The family-friendly workplace that more sought-after workers demand couldn't be farther from the hard reality of lower wage jobs.

One of the little appreciated virtues of the old welfare is that it served as a sort of unemployment insurance for these lower wage workers excluded from regular unemployment insurance by their irregular jobs. Welfare cushioned the layoffs, turnover, and contingencies that go with the territory. Under the new welfare, these workers face a hard landing because welfare is more difficult to get and offers little leeway to acquire either the time or skills that might yield a job with a future. Over the longer term, low-wage workers may find their access to welfare blocked by time limits. Although the five-year lifetime limit ostensibly targets sustained reliance on welfare, this limit could come back to bite those who cycle in and out of the lower wage labor force. At this point, no one knows how this will play out.

Creating barriers to access   A third way to reduce welfare caseloads is by reducing access—making benefits harder to acquire and keep. Some states explicitly try to divert applicants by imposing advance job-search requirements, demanding multiple trips to the welfare office in order to complete the application process, or informally advising applicants that it may not be worth the hassle. In some welfare offices, caseworkers routinely encourage applicants to forgo cash aid and apply only for Medicaid and food stamps.

Benefits are also harder to keep, as caseworkers require recipients to attend frequent meetings either to discuss seemingly endless demands for documentation or to press them on issues involving work. Everyday life in an urban welfare office is difficult to describe and, for many, even harder to believe. There are the hours of waiting in rows of plastic chairs, the repeated requests for paperwork, the ritualized weekly job club lectures about how to smile, shake hands, and show a good attitude to employers. As inspiration, caseworkers leading job club sessions often tell stories from their own lives of rising from poverty to become welfare workers (positions likely to be cut back as caseloads decline). When clients tell their own tales of cycling from bad jobs to worse and ask for help getting a good job, caseworkers are apt to admonish them for indulging in a "pity party."

Access to welfare may also be constrained through a profoundly mundane array of administrative barriers that simply make benefits harder to keep. A missed appointment, misplaced documents (often lost by the agency), delayed entry of personal data—these common and otherwise trivial mishaps can result in a loss of benefits for "non-cooperation."

The Public Benefits Hotline, a call-in center that provides both advice and intervention for Chicago residents, received some ten thousand calls in the four years after welfare reform, most of them involving hassles of this sort.[2] In other parts of the country, these types of problems show up in administrative hearing records and court cases, where judges have criticized welfare agencies for making "excessive" demands for verification documents, conducting "sham assessments" leading to inappropriate imposition of work requirements, and sanctioning clients for missing appointments when they should have helped them deal with child care or medical difficulties.

Is There a Bottom Line?

The new welfare has produced neither the immediate cataclysm its opponents threatened nor the economic and social redemption its proponents anticipated. Opponents had warned that welfare reform would plunge one million children into poverty. In the midst of an unprecedented economic boom, that didn't happen. But, even in the best of times, prospects were not auspicious for those leaving welfare.

According to the Urban Institute, about half of those leaving welfare for work between 1997 and 1999 obtained jobs where they earned a median hourly wage of only $7.15. If the jobs offered a steady forty hours of work a week (which lower wage jobs usually don't), that would provide a gross annual income of $14,872. That places a mother with two children a precarious $1,000 above the formal poverty line for the year 2000 and a two-parent family with two children nearly $3,000 *below* that line. But more than one-fifth of those leaving welfare for work didn't make it through the year—either because they lost their jobs, got sick, or just couldn't make ends meet. The only thing surprising about these figures is that the numbers weren't higher. Others left or lost welfare, but did not find work, with one in seven adults losing welfare reporting no alternative means of support. Their specific fate is unknown, but most big cities have been reporting worrisome increases in homelessness and hunger.

If there is any bottom line, it is that caseloads have been purged. But neither the market for lower wage workers nor the policies put into practice in the name of welfare reform have purged poverty from the lives of the poor. Even in the last years of the economic boom, between 1996 and 1998, the Urban Institute found that three hundred thousand more individuals in single-parent families slipped into extreme poverty. Although they qualified for food stamps that might have stretched their resources a bit further, many did not get them. Government figures indicate that families leaving welfare for work often lose access to other benefits, which states do not automatically continue irrespective of eligibility.

More recently, census figures have begun to show the effects of recession coupled with an eroded safety net. The nation's poverty rate rose to 11.7 percent in 2001, up from 11.3 percent the prior year. More troubling still, inequality is growing and poverty is deepening. In 2001, the "poverty gap," the gap between the official poverty line and the income of poor individuals, reached its highest level since measurements were first taken in 1979. In California, often a harbinger of larger social trends, a startling two in three poor children now live in families where at least one adult is employed. Can the families of lower wage workers live without access to welfare and other government supports? Apparently, they can live, but not very well.

Slouching Toward Reauthorization

"We have to remember that the goal of the reform program was not to get people out of poverty, but to achieve financial independence, to get off welfare." This statement by a senior Connecticut welfare official quoted in the *New York*

Times is more candid than most. But it illustrates the kind of political rationale that policymakers use to inoculate themselves against factual evidence of the new welfare's failure to relieve poverty.

With TANF facing reauthorization in the fall of 2002, it was clear that reconsideration of welfare policy would take place on a new playing field. Tough work rules, time limits, and devolution were just the starting point. The Bush administration advanced a reauthorization plan that increased work requirements, cut opportunities for education and training, added new doses of moralism, and extended devolution.

The Republican-controlled House passed a TANF reauthorization bill (later deferred by the Senate) requiring recipients to work forty hours a week and demanding that states enforce these requirements for 70 percent of families receiving welfare by 2007. The bill also created incentives for states to require work within a month of granting welfare benefits and continued to credit states for caseload reductions, regardless of whether families losing welfare had jobs that could sustain them.

Families would face harsh new penalties, simply for running afoul of administrative rules. The House-passed measure required states to impose full family sanctions if caseworkers find a recipient in violation of those rules for sixty days. This makes entire families vulnerable to losing aid if a parent misses a couple of appointments or gets tangled in demands to supply documents verifying eligibility, just the type of problem that crops up routinely in states with complicated rules and outdated record-keeping systems.

One of the least mentioned but most dangerous features of the House bill was a "superwaiver" that would allow the executive branch to release states from social welfare obligations contained in more than a dozen federal poverty programs, including not only TANF, but also food stamps and Medicaid. This stealth provision would allow the Bush administration to override existing legislation by fiat. The nominal justification for the superwaiver is that it would ease the path of state innovation and experimentation. It would also ease the path for state cuts in social programs beyond all previous experience.

A more visibly contentious feature of the House bill was a provision to spend $300 million dollars per year on programs to induce welfare recipients to marry. This provision is one of the favorites of the religious right, along with the administration's funding for faith-based social services. These moral redemption provisions may be more important for what they signify to the Republican Party's conservative base than for what they do, as many states have resisted these types of things in the past. However, on this point, it is irresistible to quote America's favorite president, the fictional President Josiah Bartlet of the television series *West Wing*, who quipped: "When did the government get into the yenta [matchmaker] business?"

Of Poverty, Democracy, and Welfare

The demise of the old welfare marked more than an end to a policy that many believed had outlived its usefulness. It also marked the end of welfare *politics* as we knew it. In the tepid debate over reauthorization in the fall of 2002, the bitter conflicts of earlier years over government's role in addressing poverty were replaced by half-hearted tinkering. Even provisions with the potential to induce hand-to-hand combat—such as those on marriage or the superwaiver—elicited relatively low-intensity challenges.

Is this because the new welfare yielded the benefits that liberals had hoped for, removing a contentious issue from the table and conferring legitimation on the poor, not as recipients, but as workers? Did it satisfy conservatives by clearing caseloads and demanding work? That does not seem to be the case.

If the poor have benefited from a new legitimacy, it is hard to see the rewards. Congress has not rushed to offer extensive new work supports. In fact, the House bill contained $8 to $10 billion less for work supports than the Congressional Budget Office estimated would be needed. In 2002, Congress couldn't even agree to extend unemployment insurance for those outside the welfare system who were felled by recession, corporate collapses, and the high-tech slide. While conservatives celebrated the caseload count, they also savored the opportunity to raise the ante with more onerous work requirements and marriage inducements, and even made a bid to eliminate other social protections through the superwaiver. . . .

Some congressional Democrats did take tentative steps against the tide, suggesting provisions that would fund new welfare-to-work services, provide additional job subsidies, increase the child care allotment, provide alternatives to work for recipients categorized as having work "barriers," and restore benefits to legal immigrants who were cut from welfare in 1996. Maryland Representative Benjamin Cardin was chief sponsor of a bill suggesting that states should be held accountable, not only for caseload reduction, but for poverty reduction. This notion had little traction in the 107th Congress and is likely to have even less in the next. Without the foundation of a politics of poverty to build on, such laudable ideas seem strangely irrelevant, even to the Democrats' agenda.

If welfare is a bellwether of broader political developments, there's little mistaking which way the wind is blowing. It has a decidedly Dickensian chill. The politics of poverty that gave birth to the old welfare has been supplanted by the politics of personal piety that gave birth to the new. This reflects a convergence between a neoliberal agenda of market dominance and a neoconservative agenda of middle-class moralism. In this reconfigured politics, personal responsibility is code for enforcement of the market. The new Calvinism advanced by welfare policy treats inequality as a natural consequence of personal behavior and attitude in an impartial marketplace. It is consistent with a shift in the role of the state from defender of the vulnerable and buffer against the market to one of protector-in-chief of both market and morals. This shift does not favor a small state, but a different state, one capable of enforcing market demands on workers, responding to corporate demands for capital (through public subsidies, bailouts, and tax breaks), and, perhaps more symbolically, regulating morality.

Welfare policy neither created, nor could prevent, these developments. Nor is it a foregone conclusion that government will shirk its social responsibilities. After all, America's growing economic inequality is fundamentally at odds with its commitment to political equality.

In contrast to the United States, the policies of Western European countries suggest that there need not be an absolute conflict between the welfare state and the market. Despite their allegiance to the latter, other nations continue to offer greater social protection to their citizens and worry about the democratic consequences of excluding the disadvantaged from the economy and the polity. U.S. policymakers need to move past stale debates pitting work against welfare and the poor against the nonpoor, if they are to advance policies that promote both social inclusion and economic opportunity.

Welfare, though small in scope, is large in relevance because it is a place where economic, social, and political issues converge. The old welfare acknowledged, in principle, a political commitment to relieve poverty and lessen inequality, even if, in practice, that commitment was limited, benefits were ungenerous, and access uneven. The new welfare dramatically changed the terms of the relationship between disadvantaged citizens and their state. It devolved choices about social protection from the State to the states, and it placed the value of work over the values of family well-being and social equity. As bad as the old welfare may have been, there is reason to lament its demise after all.

Notes

1. The discussion in this section draws, in part, on research conducted for the Project on the Public Economy of Work at the University of Chicago, supported by the Ford Foundation, the National Science Foundation, and the Open Society Institute. The author and Susan Lambert are co-directors.

2. The Hotline is a collaborative effort of the Legal Assistance Foundation of Chicago and community antipoverty advocates.

POSTSCRIPT

Are Declining Caseloads a Sign of Successful Welfare Reform?

New offers a brief description of the 1996 welfare reform, particularly that part of the PRWORA called TANF. He presents data that suggest that welfare reform is working, including a 58 percent decline in welfare caseloads over the 1996–2001 period. He isolates three factors that can explain the decline in caseloads: the strength of sanctions (sanctions refer to the amount of reduction in TANF checks a state imposes for the nonperformance of mandated work activities), the performance of the economy, and the level of benefits. Including these three explanations in his empirical analysis, New finds that all three have contributed to the decline in caseloads but that the state sanctioning policies have had considerably more of an impact than the other two factors. Thus, he concludes that welfare reform is indeed working.

Like New, Brodkin details what she considers to be the main provisions of PRWORA and TANF. She provides data indicating what has happened since 1996, including the nearly 60 percent decline in welfare caseloads over the 1996–2001 period. But she interprets the data differently than New, arguing that a true assessment of welfare reform must address three basic questions: What are the methods used by the states to reduce their caseloads? What is the condition of poor families when they no longer are able to receive welfare? and, What kind of opportunities are provided by the low-wage job market? She finds the answers to these questions disappointing. Brodkin concludes her evaluation by asserting that "the new welfare has placed the value of work over the values of family well being and social equity."

The analyses cited by New are a good place to begin further investigation of the welfare reform issue. Information on the government's definition and measurement of poverty can be found in the U.S. Department of Commerce's publication *Poverty in the United States: 2001,* http://www.census.gov/hhes/www/poverty01.html. Other studies of welfare reform include "Welfare Research Perspectives: Past, Present, and Future, 2002 Edition," by Barbara B. Blum and Jennifer Farnsworth Francis (National Center for Children in Poverty, 2002); "Gaining Ground: Women, Welfare Reform and Work," by June E. O'Neill and M. Anne Hill, *NCPA Policy Report No. 251* (February 2002); "Don't Tamper With Welfare Success," by Chris Schafer, *Society's Welfare/Fraser Forum* (July 2002); and "How Exisiting Welfare Reform Distorts Welfare Reality," which can be found on the Applied Research Center Web site at http://www.arc.org/welfare/welfareresearch.html (January 2001). Finally, there are a number of welfare analyses available on the Urban Institute's Web site, which can be found at http://www.urban.org.

European Union in the United States

This site of the European Union in the United States has everything from history to current status, as well as Web links and a search capability.

http://www.eurunion.org

OECD Online

The Organisation for Economic Co-operation and Development (OECD) resulted from the need to rebuild Europe after World War II, but it expanded to become truly international, with policies designed to expand world trade on a multilateral, nondiscriminatory basis.

http://www.oecd.org

International Monetary Fund (IMF)

The home page of the International Monetary Fund links to information about its purpose and activities, news releases, and its publications, among other things.

http://www.imf.org

International Trade Administration (ITA)

The U.S. Department of Commerce's International Trade Administration is dedicated to helping U.S. businesses compete in the global marketplace. At this site it offers assistance through many Web links under such headings as Trade Statistics, Tariffs and Taxes, Market Research, and Export Documentation.

http://www.ita.doc.gov

Social Science Information Gateway (SOSIG)

The Social Science Information Gateway catalogs 16 subjects and lists more URL addresses from European and developing countries than many U.S. sources do.

http://sosig.esrc.bris.ac.uk

The World Bank Group

At this home page of the World Bank you can click on News, Development Topics, Regions and Countries, Partnerships, and more, as well as use its search feature.

http://www.worldbank.org

PART 3

The World Around Us

*F*or many years America held a position of dominance in international trade. That position has been changed by time, events, and the emergence of other economic powers in the world. Decisions that are made in the international arena will, with increasing frequency, influence our lives. Along with globalization, concern about the environment has grown over the years. Among the questions that have arisen is how to sustain the ecosystem in the face of both population and economic growth.

- Are Protectionist Policies Bad for America?

- Should We Sweat About Sweatshops?

- Are the Costs of Global Warming Too High to Ignore?

- Should Pollution Be Put to the Market Test?

- Has the North American Free Trade Agreement Hurt the American Economy?

ISSUE 13

Are Protectionist Policies Bad for America?

YES: Murray N. Rothbard, from "Protectionism and the Destruction of Prosperity," Ludwig von Mises Institute, http://mises.org/fullarticle.asp?title=Protectionism&month=1 (July 13, 1998)

NO: Patrick J. Buchanan, from "Free Trade Is Not Free," Address to the Chicago Council on Foreign Relations (November 18, 1998)

ISSUE SUMMARY

YES: Free trade economist Murray N. Rothbard objects to the prospect of protectionism, which he sees as an attempt by the few who make up special interest groups "to repress and loot the rest of us" who make up the many.

NO: Social critic and three-time presidential hopeful Patrick J. Buchanan argues that America's "new corporate elite" is willing to sacrifice the country's best interests on "the altar of that golden calf, the global economy."

The economic logic that supports international trade has changed little since David Ricardo provided us with his basic insight that the patterns and the gains of trade depend on relative factor prices. More correctly stated, Ricardo argued nearly 200 years ago that if there were differences in the "opportunity costs" of producing goods and services, trade will occur between countries and that, more important, the countries that engage in trade will all benefit.

Although the large majority of economists accept the logic and the policy conclusions of Ricardo's theory, the debate rages on. The debate between "free traders" and those who plead for protection is timeless. The basic logic of international trade is indistinguishable from the basic logic of purely domestic trade. That is, both domestic and international trade must answer the fundamental economic questions: *what* to produce, *how* to produce it, and *for whom* to produce it. The distinction is that the international trade questions are posed in an international arena. This is an arena filled with producers and consumers who speak different languages, use different currencies, and are often suspicious of the actions and reactions of foreigners.

If markets work the way they are expected to work, free trade simply increases the size or the extent of a purely domestic market and, therefore, increases the advantages of specialization. Market participants should be able to buy and consume a greater variety of inexpensive goods and services after the establishment of free trade than they could before free trade. One might ask, then, why some wish to close U.S. borders and deny Americans the benefits of free trade. The answer to this question is straightforward—these benefits do not come without a cost.

There are two sets of winners and two sets of losers in the game of free trade. The most obvious winners are the consumers of the less expensive imported goods. These consumers are able to buy the low-priced color television sets, automobiles, or steel that is made abroad. Another set of winners is the producers of the exported goods. All the factors in the export industry, as well as those in industries that supply the export industry, experience an increase in market demand. Therefore, their income increases. In the United States, agriculture is one such export industry. As new foreign markets are opened, farmers' incomes increase, as do the incomes of those who supply the farmers with fertilizer, farm equipment, gasoline, and other basic inputs.

On the other side of this coin are the losers. The obvious losers are those who own the factors of production that are employed in the import-competing industries. These factors include the land, labor, and capital that are devoted to the production of such U.S.-made items as color television sets, automobiles, and steel. The less expensive foreign imports displace the demand for these products. The consumers of exported goods are also the losers. For example, as U.S. farmers sell more of their products abroad, less of this output is available domestically. As a result, the domestic prices of these farm products and other export goods and services rise.

The bottom line is that there is nothing really "free" in a market system. Competition—whether it is domestic or foreign—creates winners and losers. Historically, we have sympathized with the losers when they suffer at the hands of foreign competitors. However, we have not let our sympathies seriously curtail free trade.

The "free" that Murray N. Rothbard and Patrick J. Buchanan debate in the following selections goes beyond the notion of winners and losers in a marketplace. Rothbard asserts that protectionism is a restraint of trade, which imposes severe losses on foreign and domestic consumers alike. Buchanan argues that we have to think of "America first, and not only first, but also second and third as well" when considering international trade issues.

Murray N. Rothbard  **YES**

Protectionism and the Destruction of Prosperity

Protectionism, often refuted and seemingly abandoned, has returned, and with a vengeance. The Japanese, who bounced back from grievous losses in World War II to astound the world by producing innovative, high-quality products at low prices, are serving as the convenient butt of protectionist propaganda. Memories of wartime myths prove a heady brew, as protectionists warn about this new "Japanese imperialism," even "worse than Pearl Harbor." This "imperialism" turns out to consist of selling Americans wonderful TV sets, autos, microchips, etc., at prices more than competitive with American firms.

Is this "flood" of Japanese products really a menace, to be combated by the U.S. government? Or is the new Japan a godsend to American consumers?

In taking our stand on this issue, we should recognize that all government action means coercion, so that calling upon the U.S. government to intervene means urging it to use force and violence to restrain peaceful trade. One trusts that the protectionists are not willing to pursue their logic of force to the ultimate in the form of another Hiroshima and Nagasaki [Japanese cities destroyed by the first atomic bombs used in warfare].

Keep Your Eye on the Consumer

As we unravel the tangled web of protectionist argument, we should keep our eye on two essential points: (1) protectionism means force in restraint of trade; and (2) the key is what happens to the consumer. Invariably, we will find that the protectionists are out to cripple, exploit, and impose severe losses not only on foreign consumers but especially on Americans. And since each and every one of us is a consumer, this means that protectionism is out to mulct [swindle] all of us for the benefit of a specially privileged, subsidized few—and an inefficient few at that: people who cannot make it in a free and unhampered market.

Take, for example, the alleged Japanese menace. All trade is mutually beneficial to both parties—in this case Japanese producers and American consumers—otherwise they would not engage in the exchange. In trying to stop

From Murray N. Rothbard, "Protectionism and the Destruction of Prosperity," Ludwig von Mises Institute, http://mises.org/fullarticle.asp?title=Protectionism&month=1 (July 13, 1998). Copyright © 1995 by The Ludwig von Mises Institute. Reprinted by permission.

this trade, protectionists are trying to stop American consumers from enjoying high living standards by buying cheap and high-quality Japanese products. Instead, we are to be forced by government to return to the inefficient, higher-priced products we have already rejected. In short, inefficient producers are trying to deprive all of us of products we desire so that we will have to turn to inefficient firms. American consumers are to be plundered.

How to Look at Tariffs and Quotas

The best way to look at tariffs or import quotas or other protectionist restraints is to forget about political boundaries. Political boundaries of nations may be important for other reasons, but they have no economic meaning whatever. Suppose, for example, that each of the United States were a separate nation. Then we would hear a lot of protectionist bellyaching that we are now fortunately spared. Think of the howls by high-priced New York or Rhode Island textile manufacturers who would then be complaining about the "unfair," "cheap labor" competition from various low-type "foreigners" from Tennessee or North Carolina, or vice versa.

Fortunately, the absurdity of worrying about the balance of payments is made evident by focusing on inter-state trade. For nobody worries about the balance of payments between New York and New Jersey, or, for that matter, between Manhattan and Brooklyn, because there are no customs officials recording such trade and such balances.

If we think about it, it is clear that a call by New York firms for a tariff against North Carolina is a pure ripoff of New York (as well as North Carolina) consumers, a naked grab for coerced special privilege by less efficient business firms. If the 50 states were separate nations, the protectionists would then be able to use the trappings of patriotism, and distrust of foreigners, to camouflage and get away with their looting the consumers of their own region.

Fortunately, inter-state tariffs are unconstitutional. But even with this clear barrier, and even without being able to wrap themselves in the cloak of nationalism, protectionists have been able to impose inter-state tariffs in another guise. Part of the drive for continuing increases in the federal minimum-wage law is to impose a protectionist devise against lower-wage, lower-labor-cost competition from North Carolina and other southern states against their New England and New York competitors.

During the 1966 Congressional battle over a higher federal minimum wage, for example, the late Senator Jacob Javits (R-NY) freely admitted that one of his main reasons for supporting the bill was to cripple the southern competitors of New York textile firms. Since southern wages are generally lower than in the north, the business firms hardest hit by an increased minimum wage (and the workers struck by unemployment) will be located in the south.

Another way in which interstate trade restrictions have been imposed has been in the fashionable name of "safety." Government-organized state milk cartels in New York, for example, have prevented importation of milk from nearby New Jersey under the patently spurious grounds that the trip across the Hudson would render New Jersey milk "unsafe."

If tariffs and restraints on trade are good for a country, then why not indeed for a state or region? The principle is precisely the same. In America's first great depression, the Panic of 1819, Detroit was a tiny frontier town of only a few hundred people. Yet protectionist cries arose—fortunately not fulfilled—to prohibit all "imports" from outside of Detroit, and citizens were exhorted to buy only Detroit. If this nonsense had been put into effect, general starvation and death would have ended all other economic problems for Detroiters.

So why not restrict and even prohibit trade, i.e., "imports," into a city, or a neighborhood, or even on a block, or, to boil it down to its logical conclusion, to one family? Why shouldn't the Jones family issue a decree that from now on, no member of the family can buy any goods or services produced outside the family house? Starvation would quickly wipe out this ludicrous drive for self-sufficiency.

And yet we must realize that this absurdity is inherent in the logic of protectionism. Standard protectionism is just as preposterous, but the rhetoric of nationalism and national boundaries has been able to obscure this vital fact.

The upshot is that protectionism is not only nonsense, but dangerous nonsense, destructive of all economic prosperity. We are not, if we were ever, a world of self-sufficient farmers. The market economy is one vast latticework throughout the world, in which each individual, each region, each country, produces what he or it is best at, most relatively efficient in, and exchanges that product for the goods and services of others. Without the division of labor and the trade based upon that division, the entire world would starve. Coerced restraints on trade—such as protectionism—cripple, hobble, and destroy trade, the source of life and prosperity. Protectionism is simply a plea that consumers, as well as general prosperity, be hurt so as to confer permanent special privilege upon groups of less efficient producers, at the expense of more competent firms and of consumers. But it is a peculiarly destructive kind of bailout, because it permanently shackles trade under the cloak of patriotism.

The Negative Railroad

Protectionism is also peculiarly destructive because it acts as a coerced and artificial increase in the cost of transportation between regions. One of the great features of the Industrial Revolution, one of the ways in which it brought prosperity to the starving masses, was by reducing drastically the cost of transportation. The development of railroads in the early 19th century, for example, meant that for the first time in the history of the human race, goods could be transported cheaply over land. Before that, water—rivers and oceans—was the only economically viable means of transport. By making land transport accessible and cheap, railroads allowed interregional land transportation to break up expensive inefficient local monopolies. The result was an enormous improvement in living standards for all consumers. And what the protectionists want to do is lay an axe to this wondrous principle of progress.

It is no wonder that Frederic Bastiat, the great French laissez-faire economist of the mid-19th century, called a tariff a "negative railroad." Protectionists are just as economically destructive as if they were physically chopping up railroads, or planes, or ships, and forcing us to revert to the costly transport of the past—mountain trails, rafts, or sailing ships.

"Fair" Trade

Let us now turn to some of the leading protectionist arguments. Take, for example, the standard complaint that while the protectionist "welcomes competition," this competition must be "fair." Whenever someone starts talking about "fair competition" or indeed, about "fairness" in general, it is time to keep a sharp eye on your wallet, for it is about to be picked. For the genuinely "fair" is simply the voluntary terms of exchange, mutually agreed upon by buyer and seller. As most of the medieval scholastics were able to figure out, there is no "just" (or "fair") price outside of the market price.

So what could be "unfair" about the free-market price? One common protectionist charge is that it is "unfair" for an American firm to compete with, say, a Taiwanese firm which needs to pay only one-half the wages of the American competitor. The U.S. government is called upon to step in and "equalize" the wage rates by imposing an equivalent tariff upon the Taiwanese. But does this mean that consumers can never patronize low-cost firms because it is "unfair" for them to have lower costs than inefficient competitors? This is the same argument that would be used by a New York firm trying to cripple its North Carolina competitor.

What the protectionists don't bother to explain is why U.S. wage rates are so much higher than Taiwan. They are not imposed by Providence. Wage rates are high in the U.S. because American employers have bid these rates up. Like all other prices on the market, wage rates are determined by supply and demand, and the increased demand by U.S. employers has bid wages up. What determines this demand? The "marginal productivity" of labor.

The demand for any factor of production, including labor, is constituted by the productivity of that factor, the amount of revenue that the worker, or the pound of cement or acre of land, is expected to bring to the brim. The more productive the factory, the greater the demand by employers, and the higher its price or wage rate. American labor is more costly than Taiwanese because it is far more productive. What makes it productive? To some extent, the comparative qualities of labor, skill, and education. But most of the difference is not due to the personal qualities of the laborers themselves, but to the fact that the American laborer, on the whole, is equipped with more and better capital equipment than his Taiwanese counterparts. The more and better the capital investment per worker, the greater the worker's productivity, and therefore the higher the wage rate.

In short, if the American wage rate is twice that of the Taiwanese, it is because the American laborer is more heavily capitalized, is equipped with more and better tools, and is therefore, on the average, twice as productive. In a sense,

I suppose, it is not "fair" for the American worker to make more than the Taiwanese, not because of his personal qualities, but because savers and investors have supplied him with more tools. But a wage rate is determined not just by personal quality but also by relative scarcity, and in the United States the worker is far scarcer compared to capital than he is in Taiwan.

Putting it another way, the fact that American wage rates are on the average twice that of the Taiwanese, does not make the cost of labor in the U.S. twice that of Taiwan. Since U.S. labor is twice as productive, this means that the double wage rate in the U.S. is offset by the double productivity, so that the cost of labor per unit product in the U.S. and Taiwan tends, on the average, to be the same. One of the major protectionist fallacies is to confuse the price of labor (wage rates) with its cost, which also depends on its relative productivity.

Thus, the problem faced by American employers is not really with the "cheap labor" in Taiwan, because "expensive labor" in the U.S. is precisely the result of the bidding for scarce labor by U.S. employers. The problem faced by less efficient U.S. textile or auto firms is not so much cheap labor in Taiwan or Japan, but the fact that other U.S. industries are efficient enough to afford it, because they bid wages that high in the first place.

So, by imposing protective tariffs and quotas to save, bail out, and keep in place less efficient U.S. textile or auto or microchip firms, the protectionists are not only injuring the American consumer. They are also harming efficient U.S. firms and industries, which are prevented from employing resources now locked into incompetent firms, and who could otherwise be able to expand and sell their efficient products at home and abroad.

"Dumping"

Another contradictory line of protectionist assault on the free market asserts that the problem is not so much the low costs enjoyed by foreign firms, as the "unfairness" of selling their products "below costs" to American consumers, and thereby engaging in the pernicious and sinful practice of "dumping." By such dumping they are able to exert unfair advantage over American firms who presumably never engage in such practices and make sure that their prices are always high enough to cover costs. But if selling below costs is such a powerful weapon, why isn't it ever pursued by business firms within a country?

Our first response to this charge is, once again, to keep our eye on consumers in general and on American consumers in particular. Why should it be a matter of complaint when consumers so clearly benefit? Suppose, for example, that Sony is willing to injure American competitors by selling TV sets to Americans for a penny apiece. Shouldn't we rejoice at such an absurd policy of suffering severe losses by subsidizing us, the American consumers? And shouldn't our response be: "Come on, Sony, subsidize us some more!" As far as consumers are concerned, the more "dumping" that takes place, the better.

But what of the poor American TV firms, whose sales will suffer so long as Sony is willing to virtually give their sets away? Well, surely, the sensible policy for RCA, Zenith, etc. would be to hold back production and sales until Sony drives itself into bankruptcy. But suppose that the worst happens, and RCA, Zenith, etc. are themselves driven into bankruptcy by the Sony price war? Well, in that case, we the consumers will still be better off, since the plants of the bankrupt firms, which would still be in existence, would be picked up for a song at auction, and the American buyers at auction would be able to enter the TV business and outcompete Sony because they now enjoy far lower capital costs.

For decades, indeed, opponents of the free market have claimed that many businesses gained their powerful status on the market by what is called "predatory price-cutting," that is, by driving their smaller competitors into bankruptcy by selling their goods below cost, and then reaping the reward of their unfair methods by raising their prices and thereby charging "monopoly prices" to the consumers. The claim is that while consumers may gain in the short run by price wars, "dumping," and selling below costs, they lose in the long run from the alleged monopoly. But, as we have seen, economic theory shows that this would be a mug's [fool's] game, losing money for the "dumping" firms, and never really achieving a monopoly price. And sure enough, historical investigation has not turned up a single case where predatory pricing, when tried, was successful, and there are actually very few cases where it has even been tried.

Another charge claims that Japanese or other foreign firms can afford to engage in dumping because their governments are willing to subsidize their losses. But again, we should still welcome such an absurd policy. If the Japanese government is really willing to waste scarce resources subsidizing American purchases of Sony's, so much the better! Their policy would be just as self-defeating as if the losses were private.

There is yet another problem with the charge of "dumping," even when it is made by economists or other alleged "experts" sitting on impartial tariff commissions and government bureaus. There is no way whatever that outside observers, be they economists, businessmen, or other experts, can decide what some other firm's "costs" may be. "Costs" are not objective entities that can be gauged or measured. Costs are subjective to the businessman himself, and they vary continually, depending on the businessman's time horizon or the stage of production or selling process he happens to be dealing with at any given time.

Suppose, for example, a fruit dealer has purchased a case of pears for $20, amounting to $1 a pound. He hopes and expects to sell those pears for $1.50 a pound. But something has happened to the pear market, and he finds it impossible to sell most of the pears at anything near that price. In fact, he finds that he must sell the pears at whatever price he can get before they become overripe. Suppose he finds that he can only sell his stock of pears at 70 cents a pound. The outside observer might say that the fruit dealer has, perhaps "unfairly," sold his pears "below costs," figuring that the dealer's costs were $1 a pound.

"Infant" Industries

Another protectionist fallacy held that the government should provide a temporary protective tariff to aid, or to bring into being, an "infant industry." Then, when the industry was well-established, the government would and should remove the tariff and toss the now "mature" industry into the competitive swim.

The theory is fallacious, and the policy has proved disastrous in practice. For there is no more need for government to protect a new, young, industry from foreign competition than there is to protect it from domestic competition.

In the last few decades, the "infant" plastics, television, and computer industries made out very well without such protection. Any government subsidizing of a new industry will funnel too many resources into that industry as compared to older firms, and will also inaugurate distortions that may persist and render the firm or industry permanently inefficient and vulnerable to competition. As a result, "infant-industry" tariffs have tended to become permanent, regardless of the "maturity" of the industry. The proponents were carried away by a misleading biological analogy to "infants" who need adult care. But a business firm is not a person, young or old.

Older Industries

Indeed, in recent years, older industries that are notoriously inefficient have been using what might be called a "senile-industry" argument for protectionism. Steel, auto, and other outcompeted industries have been complaining that they "need a breathing space" to retool and become competitive with foreign rivals, and that this breather could be provided by several years of tariffs or import quotas. This argument is just as full of holes as the hoary infant-industry approach, except that it will be even more difficult to figure out when the "senile" industry will have become magically rejuvenated. In fact, the steel industry has been inefficient ever since its inception, and its chronological age seems to make no difference. The first protectionist movement in the U.S. was launched in 1820, headed by the Pennsylvania iron (later iron and steel) industry, artificially force-fed by the War of 1812 and already in grave danger from far more efficient foreign competitors.

The Non-Problem of the Balance of Payments

A final set of arguments, or rather alarms, center on the mysteries of the balance of payments. Protectionists focus on the horrors of imports being greater than exports, implying that if market forces continued unchecked, Americans might wind up buying everything from abroad, while selling foreigners nothing, so that American consumers will have engorged themselves to the permanent ruin of American business firms. But if the exports really fell to somewhere near zero, where in the world would Americans still find the money to purchase foreign products? The balance of payments, as we said earlier, is a pseudo-problem created by the existence of customs statistics.

During the day of the gold standard, a deficit in the national balance of payments was a problem, but only because of the nature of the fractional-reserve banking system. If U.S. banks, spurred on by the Fed or previous forms of central banks, inflated money and credit, the American inflation would lead to higher prices in the U.S., and this would discourage exports and encourage imports. The resulting deficit had to be paid for in some way, and during the gold standard era this meant being paid for in gold, the international money. So as bank credit expanded, gold began to flow out of the country, which put the fractional-reserve banks in even shakier shape. To meet the threat to their solvency posed by the gold outflow, the banks eventually were forced to contract credit, precipitating a recession and reversing the balance of payment deficits, thus bringing gold back into the country.

But now, in the fiat-money era, balance of payments deficits are truly meaningless. For gold is no longer a "balancing item." In effect, there is no deficit in the balance of payments. It is true that in the last few years, imports have been greater than exports by $150 billion or so per year. But no gold flowed out of the country. Neither did dollars "leak" out. The alleged "deficit" was paid for by foreigners investing the equivalent amount of money in American dollars: in real estate, capital goods, U.S. securities, and bank accounts.

In effect, in the last couple of years, foreigners have been investing enough of their own funds in dollars to keep the dollar high, enabling us to purchase cheap imports. Instead of worrying and complaining about this development, we should rejoice that foreign investors are willing to finance our cheap imports. The only problem is that this bonanza is already coming to an end, with the dollar becoming cheaper and exports more expensive.

We conclude that the sheaf of protectionist arguments, many plausible at first glance, are really a tissue of egregious fallacies. They betray a complete ignorance of the most basic economic analysis. Indeed, some of the arguments are almost embarrassing replicas of the most ridiculous claims of 17th-century mercantilism: for example, that it is somehow a calamitous problem that the U.S. has a balance of trade deficit, not overall, but merely with one specific country, e.g., Japan.

Must we even relearn the rebuttals of the more sophisticated mercantilists of the 18th century: namely, that balances with individual countries will cancel each other out, and therefore that we should only concern ourselves with the overall balance? (Let alone realize that the overall balance is no problem either.) But we need not reread the economic literature to realize that the impetus for protectionism comes not from preposterous theories, but from the quest for coerced special privilege and restraint of trade at the expense of efficient competitors and consumers. In the host of special interests using the political process to repress and loot the rest of us, the protectionists are among the most venerable. It is high time that we get them, once and for all, off our backs, and treat them with the righteous indignation they so richly deserve.

 **NO**

Free Trade Is Not Free

This is a prestigious forum; and I appreciate the opportunity to address it. As my subject, I have chosen what I believe is the coming and irrepressible conflict between the claims of a new American nationalism and the commands of the Global Economy.

As you may have heard in my last [presidential] campaign, I am called by many names. "Protectionist" is one of the nicer ones; but it is inexact. I am an economic nationalist. To me, the country comes before the economy; and the economy exists for the people. I believe in free markets, but I do not worship them. In the proper hierarchy of things, it is the market that must be harnessed to work for man—and not the other way around.

As for the Global Economy, like the unicorn, it is a mythical beast that exists only in the imagination. In the real world, there are only national economies—Japan's that has lost its animal spirits, South Korea's that is deep in recession, China's which is headed for trouble, Brazil's which is falling, Indonesia and Russia's which are in collapse.

In these unique national economies, critical decisions are based on what is best for the nation. Only in America do leaders sacrifice the interests of their own country on the altar of that golden calf, the Global Economy.

What is Economic Nationalism? Is it some right-wing or radical idea? By no means. Economic nationalism was the idea and cause that brought [George] Washington, [Alexander] Hamilton and [James] Madison to Philadelphia. These men dreamed of creating here in America the greatest free market on earth, by elimination all internal barriers to trade among the 13 states, and taxing imports to finance the turnpikes and canals of the new nation and end America's dependence on Europe. It was called the American System.

The ideology of free trade is the alien import, an invention of European academics and scribblers, not one of whom ever built a great nation, and all of whom were repudiated by America's greatest statesmen, including all four presidents on Mount Rushmore.

The second bill that Washington signed into law was the Tariff Act of 1789. Madison saved the nation's infant industries from being buried by the dumping of British manufactures, with the first truly protective tariff, the Tariff

Act of 1816. "Give me a tariff and I will give you the greatest nation on earth," said [Abraham] Lincoln. "I thank God I am not a free trader," Theodore Roosevelt wrote to Henry Cabot Lodge.

Under economic nationalism, there was no income tax in the United States, except during the Civil War and Reconstruction. Tariffs produced fifty to ninety percent of federal revenue. And how did America prosper? From 1865 to 1913, U.S. growth averaged 4% a year. We began the era with half Britain's production, but ended with twice Britain's production.

Yet, this era is now disparaged in history books and public schools as the time of the Robber Barons, a Gilded Age best forgotten.

Not only did America rise to greatness through the economic nationalism so did every other first-rank power in history—from Britain in the 18th century, to [Otto von] Bismarck's Germany in the 19th, to post-war Japan. Economic nationalism has been the policy of rising nations, free trade the practice of nations that have commenced their historic decline. Today, this idea may be mocked by the talking heads, but it is going to prevail again in America, for it alone comports with the national interests of the United States. And this is the subject of my remarks.

. . . These are good times in America. . . .

Is this our reward for free trade? My answer is no. Though these are good times in America, our growth today is anemic, compared to what it was in the Protectionist Era, and the Roaring Twenties, when growth rates hit seven percent. Free trade does not explain our prosperity; free trade explains the economic insecurity that is the worm in the apple of our prosperity.

The great free-market economist Milton Friedman is credited with the line, "there is no free lunch." Let me amend to Friedman's Law with Buchanan's Corollary: Free trade is no free lunch.

And it is time its costs were calculated.

Back in 1848, another economist wrote that if free trade were ever adopted, societies would be torn apart. His name was Karl Marx, and he wrote: ". . . the Free Trade system works destructively. It breaks up old nationalities and carries antagonism of proletariat and bourgeoisie to the uttermost point . . . the Free trade system hastens the Social Revolution. In this revolutionary sense alone . . . I am in favor of Free Trade."

Marx was right. Here, then, is the first cost of open-borders free trade. It exacerbates the divisions between capital and labor. It separates societies into contending classes, and deepens the division between rich and poor. Under free trade, economic and social elites, whose jobs and incomes are not adversely impacted by imports or immigration, do well. For them, these have been the best of times. Since 1990, the stock market has tripled in value; corporate profits have doubled since 1992; there has been a population explosion among millionaires. America's richest one percent controlled 21 percent of the national wealth in 1949; in 1997 it was 40 percent. Top CEO salaries were 44 times the average wage of their workers in 1965; by 1996 they were 212 times an average worker's pay.

How has Middle America fared? Between 1972 and 1994, the real wages of working Americans fell 19 percent. In 1970, the price of a new house was twice a young couple's income; it is now four times. In 1960, 18 percent of women with children under six were in the work force; by 1995 it had risen 63 percent. The U.S. has a larger percentage of women in its work force than any industrial nation, yet median family income fell 6 percent in the first six years of the 1990s.

Something is wrong when wage earners work harder and longer just to stay in the same place. Under the free trade regime, economic insecurity has become a preexisting condition of life.

A second cost of global free trade is a loss of independence and national sovereignty. America was once a self-reliant nation; trade amounted to only 10 percent of GNP [gross national product]; imports only 4 percent. Now, trade is equal to 25% of GNP; and the trade surpluses we ran every year from 1900–1970 have turned into trade deficits for all of the last 27 years.

Since 1980 our total merchandise trade deficit adds up to $2 trillion. This year's [1998's] trade deficit is approaching $300 billion. Year in and year out, we consume more than we produce. This cannot last.

Look at what this is doing to an industrial plant that once produced 40 percent of all that the world produced. In 1965, 31 percent of the U.S. labor force had manufacturing equivalent jobs. By 1997, it was down to 15 percent, smallest share in 100 years.

More Americans now work in government than in manufacturing. We Americans no longer make our own cameras, shoes, radios, TV's, toys. A fourth of our steel, a third of our autos, half our machine tools, two-thirds of our textiles are foreign made. We used to be the world's greatest creditor nation; now, we are its greatest debtor.

Friends, this is the read-out of the electrocardiogram of a nation in decline. Writes author-economist Pat Choate, "a peek behind the glitter of record stock prices and high corporate profits reveals a deepening economic dry rot—a nation that is eating its seed corn and squandering its economic leadership position, here and abroad."

And American sovereignty is being eroded. In 1994, for the first time, the U.S. joined a global institution, the World Trade Organization, where America has no veto power and the one-nation, one-vote rule applies. Where are we headed? Look at the nations of Europe that are today surrendering control of their money, their immigration policy, their environmental policy, even defense policy—to a giant socialist superstate called the EU [European Union].

For America to continue down this road of global interdependence is a betrayal of our history and our heritage of liberty. What does it profit a man if he gain the whole world, and suffer the loss of his own country?

A third cost of the Global Economy is America's vulnerability to a financial collapse caused by events beyond our control. Never has this country been so exposed. When Mexico, with an economy no larger than Illinois', threatened a default in 1994, the U.S. cobbled together a $50 billion bailout, lest Mexico's default bring on what Michel Camdessus of the IMF [International Monetary Fund] called "global financial catastrophe."

When tiny Asian dominoes began to fall [in 1997], the IMF had to put together $117 billion in bailouts of Thailand, Indonesia, South Korea, lest the Asian crisis bring down all of Latin America and the rest of the world with it.

In the Global Economy, the world is always just one default away from disaster. What in heaven's name does the vaunted Global Economy give us—besides all that made-in-China junk down at the mall—to justify having the U.S. financial system at permanent risk of collapse—if some incompetent foreign regime decides to walk on its debts?

A fourth cost of this Global Economy is the de-industrialization of America and the de-Americanization of our industries. Many of our Fortune 500 corporations have already shed their American identity.

When Gilbert Williamson, then president of NCR [National Cash Register Company, now known as NCR Corporation], was asked about U.S. workers being unable to compete in a global economy, he dismissed the question with this remark: "I was asked the other day about U.S. competitiveness, and I replied that I don't think about it at all. We at NCR think of ourselves as a globally competitive company that happens to be headquartered in the United States."

Many companies still carry fine old American names, but their work forces are becoming less and less American. In 1985, GE employed 243,000 Americans; ten years later, it was down to 150,000. IBM has lopped off half of its U.S. workers in the past decade. Here is author William Greider:

"By 1995, Big Blue had become a truly global firm—with more employees abroad than at home . . . Intel . . . shrank U.S. employment last year from 22,000 to 17,000. Motorola's . . . work force is now only 56 percent American. . . . Ma Bell once made all its home telephones in the U.S. and now makes none here."

Boeing's Philip Condit says he would be happy if, twenty years from now, no one thought of Boeing as an American company.

Here is Carl A. Gerstacker of Dow Chemical: "I have long dreamed of buying an island owned by no nation and of establishing the World Headquarters of the Dow Company on the truly neutral ground of such an island, beholden to no nation or society." A Union Carbide spokesman agreed: "It is not proper for an international corporation to put the welfare of any country in which it does business above that of any other."

To this new corporate elite, putting America first betrays a lack of loyalty to the company. Some among our political elite share this view. Here is Strobe Talbott, [Bill] Clinton's roommate at Oxford and architect of his Russian policy: "All countries," said Talbott in 1991, "are basically social arrangements . . . No matter how permanent and even sacred they may seem at any one time, in fact they are all artificial and temporary . . . within the next hundred years . . . nationhood as we know it will be obsolete; all states will recognize a single, global authority."

This is the transnational elite, our new Masters of the Universe.

The Cold War has been succeeded by a new struggle. "The real divisions of our time," writes scholar Christisan Kopff, "are not between left and right, but between nations and the globalist delusion." That struggle will shape the politics of the new century; and a familiar question is being asked again across

America: When the commands of the Global Economy conflict with call of patriotism, whose side are you on?

If you would see the consequences of free trade ideology, go to Detroit. In the 1950s this was the forge and furnace of the Arsenal of Democracy, with 2 million of the most productive people on earth. Compare Detroit then to Detroit now. Free trade is not free.

Forty years ago, Japan exported 6000 cars. Today, Japan has as large a share of the U.S. auto and truck market as GM.

How did Japan do it? Yes, they built fine cars; but the Japanese did not leave the outcome of this struggle for dominance in the world's first industry to the vagaries of the market place. The Japanese fixed the game.

Japan virtually sealed off its market to U.S. auto imports, subsidized its auto industry and exports, and paid its workers 15% of U.S. wages in factories that would have had to be shut down in the United States. Tokyo's political and industrial elite did not let [economist] Adam Smith [1723–1790] dictate how they would play the game.

In short, Tokyo in the 1970s and 1980s looked on our auto market the way their grandfathers looked on China in the 1920s and 30s—as an inviting target for conquest. They did not read Richard Cobden on free trade; they read Alexander Hamilton, who would never have allowed Japan to overrun our auto industry, our radio industry, or our television industry.

Remember NAFTA. This treaty was going to open Mexico to U.S. auto exports. Well, in 1996, we shipped 46,000 cars to Mexico; and Mexico sent 550,000 cars back to us. Where did Mexico get its booming auto industry? From Michigan, Ohio, and Missouri.

In the 1950s, "Engine Charlie" Wilson immortalized himself with the remark, "What's good for America is good for General Motors, and vice versa." What Engine Charlie said was true, when he said it. We see that now as we watch GM closing factories here and opening up abroad. GM's four newest plants are going up in Argentina, Poland, China, and Thailand. "GM's days of building new plants in North America may be over," says the *Wall Street Journal.*

GM used to be the largest employer in the United States; today, it is the largest employer in Mexico where it has built 50 plants in 20 years. In Juarez alone, there are 18 plants of Delphi Automotive, a GM subsidiary. Across from Juarez, El Paso is becoming a glorified truck stop, as Texans watch their manufacturing jobs go south.

Volkswagen has closed its U.S. plant in the Mon Valley and moved production of its new Beetle into Mexico, where it will produce 450,000 vehicles this year. Wages at Volkswagen's plant in Puebla average $1.69 an hour, one-third of the U.S. minimum wage.

Let me make a simple point here. If you remove all trade barriers between a Third World economy like Mexico and a First World country like the United States, First World manufacturers will head south, to the advantage of the lower wages, and the Third World workers will head north, to the advantage of the higher wages. Economics 101.

Since the free-trade era began, 4000 new factories have been built in northern Mexico, and 35 million immigrants, most of them poor, have come into the United States—among them five million illegal aliens, mostly from Mexico. Free trade is not free.

But the free traders respond: Who cares who makes what, where? What's important is that consumers get the best buy at the cheapest price. But this is Grasshopper Economics. Americans are not only consumers; we are producers and citizens. We have obligations to one another and to our country; and one of those obligations is not to behave like wastrel children squandering a family estate built up over generations. A family estate is something you can sell off—only once.

What is the wealth of nations? Is it stocks, bonds, derivatives—the pieces of paper traded on Wall Street that can be gone with in the wind? No, the true wealth of a nation lies in its factories, farms, fisheries, and mines, in the genius and capacities of its people. Industrial power is at the heart of economic power, and economic power is at the heart of strategic power. America won two world wars and the Cold War because our industrial power and technology proved beyond the ability of our enemies to match.

Is this steady attrition of America's independence in sovereignty irreversible? My answer is no. For the balance of power in America has begun to shift. In 1997, on the vote to give the president a blank check to negotiate trade treaties without Congressional amendment—so-called Fast Track authority, it went down to defeat. When Newt [Gingrich] brought up "fast track" this year [1998], it was crushed again, by 63 votes.

A majority of Americans no longer believe these trade deals are good for America, and a majority of the House now agrees with them. The force is with us. Neither NAFTA [North American Free Trade Agreement] nor GATT [General Agreement on Tariffs and Trade] would pass today.

The day is not too distant when economic nationalism will triumph. Several events will hasten that day. The first is the tidal wave of imports from Asia about to hit these shores. When all those manufactured goods pour in, taking down industries and killing jobs, there will arise a clamor from industry and labor for protection. If that cry goes unheeded, those who turn a stone face to the American workers will be turned out of power.

In the Democratic Party or the Republican Party or the Reform Party or some new party, economic nationalism will find its vehicle and its voice. Rely upon it.

It is already happening—with the crisis in the steel industry.

Here is a perfect example of the folly of free trade. Since the mid-1980s, fifty billion dollars was invested in modernization; a steel worker today is three times as productive as his father; and the industry has only a third as many workers as twenty-five years ago.

Yet, Russia, Japan, South Korea, Brazil and Indonesia—four of them being bailed out with our tax dollars—are dumping steel into our market, taking down our steel industry to save their own. Why do we allow subsidized foreign steel to be dumped into the U.S. to destroy the greatest private steel industry on earth?

Well, says the free trader: If we can get it cheaper, let our industry go, just as we let our televisions go, our textiles go, radios go, and the shoe industry go. Besides, these countries need to sell steel here to get the dollars to pay back their IMF loans. Thus, the United Steelworkers of America are being sacrificed—to make the world safe for Goldman Sachs.

There is another reason the free trade era is coming to a close. One day soon, Americans will wake up and discover that other nations do not believe in free trade, and do not practice our particular faith. China and Japan each run $60 billion in annual trade surpluses at America's expense, but each cordons off its own market to U.S. goods.

We must start looking out for America first. As Andrew Jackson once declared: "We have been too long subject to the policy of [foreign] merchants. We need to become more Americanized, and instead of feeding the paupers and laborers of Europe . . . feed our own, or in a short time . . . we shall all be rendered paupers ourselves."

America First, and not only first, but second and third as well.

POSTSCRIPT

Are Protectionist Policies Bad for America?

The desirability of free trade is an issue on which a large majority of professional economists agree. Survey after survey confirms this. Although economists are ardent supporters of free trade, they must grapple with the reality that the world that Ricardo modeled in 1807 is starkly different from the world we know in this new millennium.

The concern that Ricardo could ignore is the modern ability of capital and technology to cross national boundaries almost at will. This mobility of capital and technology suggests that a country's comparative advantages can radically change in a relatively short period of time. This is a far cry from Ricardo's world. In his world, comparative advantages were stable and predictable. Consider the example that Ricardo used to illustrate comparative advantage: the trade between England and Portugal in cloth and wine. In the nineteenth century, it was highly unlikely that agrarian Portugal would seriously challenge the manufacturing base of England and equally unlikely that dreary English weather would ever produce a wine to compete with the vineyards of sun-drenched Portugal. This kind of trade stability is rarely found in the modern world. Examples abound of comparative advantages won or lost overnight, as dollars and technology chase one another around the globe. Japan provides an interesting case study. Consider how quickly this country moved from dominance among Pacific Rim countries to fighting for its economic life as Korea, Malaysia, and their other Asian neighbors stole market after market from them.

The bottom line is clear. Comparative advantage does lead to economic efficiency, but, as with any market adjustment, there can be serious dislocations as less efficient producers must make way for more efficient producers. In the modern world this occurs quickly and sometimes quite unexpectedly. This does not mean that there is a shortage of advocates of free trade. Conservative "think tanks" provide ample support for Rothbard's position. For example, see the Reason Foundation, which sponsors *Reason Online* (http://reason.com). On October 25, 1999, it posted an article entitled "Buchanomics Rebuked," which is a frontal attack on Buchanan. To place the free trade argument in its historic context, see John V. C. Nye's essay "The Myth of Free-Trade Britain," The Library of Economics and Liberty, http://www.econlib.org/library/Columns/y2003/Nyefreetrade.html (March 3, 2003).

For more on Buchanan's position, see his book *The Great Betrayal: How American Sovereignty and Social Justice Are Being Sacrificed to the Gods of the Global Economy* (Little, Brown, 1998). Also read John Gray's *False Dawn: The Delusions of Global Capitalism* (New Press, 1999).

ISSUE 14

Should We Sweat About Sweatshops?

YES: Richard Appelbaum and Peter Dreier, from "The Campus Anti-Sweatshop Movement," *The American Prospect* (September–October 1999)

NO: Nicholas D. Kristof and Sheryl WuDunn, from "Two Cheers for Sweatshops," *The New York Times Magazine* (September 24, 2000)

ISSUE SUMMARY

YES: Sociologist Richard Appelbaum and political scientist Peter Dreier chronicle the rise of student activism on American campuses over the issue of sweatshops abroad. Students demand that firms be held responsible for "sweatshop conditions" and warn that if conditions do not improve, American consumers will not "leave their consciences at home when they shop for clothes."

NO: News correspondents Nicholas D. Kristof and Sheryl WuDunn agree that the working conditions in many offshore plant sites "seem brutal from the vantage point of an American sitting in his living room." But they argue that these work opportunities are far superior to the alternatives that are currently available in many parts of the world and that what is needed are more sweatshops, not fewer sweatshops.

$\Tau$he sleeping giant of student activism awoke in the late 1990s. This giant slumbered for nearly three decades. It was last heard from in the late 1960s and the early 1970s, when students on college campuses across the United States caused so much disruption that public awareness of the war in Vietnam slowly but surely came into focus. Prior to the antiwar activism, students were at the forefront of the civil rights movement. As in the case of the antiwar activists, the civil rights activists rebelled. They confronted their parents and grandparents but with less violent, less confrontational means than the antiwar activists.

Many argue that in both of these cases public policy might have eventually changed, but if it did change it would have taken much longer for that change to occur. In essence, these social historians maintain that without the idealism of college-aged students, society has a tendency to become inflexible and rigid. It is slower to change and more likely to assume that what exists today should always exist. The lack of student activism and the resulting return to more traditional values was the pattern throughout the late 1970s, the 1980s, and most of the 1990s. That peaceful atmosphere was shattered in the late 1990s.

It all began rather quietly on a talk show cohosted by Kathie Lee Gifford. In 1996 Charles Kernaghan, who is executive director of the National Labor Committee for Worker and Human Rights, charged that the Walmart apparel that bears Gifford's name was produced in offshore sweatshops that employed child labor. On air she roundly denied that charge. Kernaghan persisted. The media eventually covered the charges and the countercharges, and the more the story was denied, the more the media investigated. Kernaghan's allegations turned out to be true. Because of Gifford's high profile and the extensive coverage that this story received, college students soon learned of the widespread use of sweatshops to produce a wide range of items that they habitually wore.

Students were outraged; they wanted action immediately. Just as many of their uncles, aunts, fathers, and mothers had done 30 years earlier, the students staged sit-ins. University presidents could not duck the issue by simply assigning the problem to a study committee. Student activism had returned to college campuses. If university administrators did not want the situation to erupt into the widespread disruption and possible violence that marked the antiwar period, they had to act.

But how could these colleges and universities respond? More important, *should* they respond? They do not purchase their T-shirts and football jerseys directly from factories in China or Brazil; rather, they license firms who request the use of that university's logo to be sewn onto football jerseys or printed on T-shirts. Should colleges and universities require their licensees to guarantee that neither they nor their subcontractors will produce any items bearing the university's logo under sweatshop conditions? Is this wise? College T-shirts and football jerseys are cheap because they are produced in low-wage countries. If the same items were produced in the United States or another high-wage country, their prices would be substantially higher. Should universities deny their students the chance to buy these items at a low cost? If the answer is yes, what happens to the workers in El Salvador and other poor countries who will lose their jobs if the sweatshops are closed down? Is that what student activists want?

These and other questions are raised in the following selections. Richard Appelbaum and Peter Dreier detail the horrors of working in the sweatshops that allow Americans to pay less for their apparel and the student activism that has brought this issue to the attention of the public. Nicholas D. Kristof and Sheryl WuDunn argue that workers in sweatshops do not want to see them closed because they offer the best jobs many workers in poor countries have ever had.

Richard Appelbaum and Peter Dreier  **YES**

The Campus Anti-Sweatshop Movement

If University of Arizona activist Arne Ekstrom was aware of today's widely reported student apathy, he certainly was not deterred when he helped lead his campus anti-sweatshop sit-in. Nor, for that matter, were any of the other thousands of students across the United States who participated in anti-sweatshop activities during the past academic year, coordinating their activities on the United Students Against Sweatshops (USAS) listserv (a listserv is an online mailing list for the purpose of group discussion) and Web site.

Last year's student anti-sweatshop movement gained momentum as it swept westward, eventually encompassing more than 100 campuses across the country. Sparked by a sit-in at Duke University, students organized teach-ins, led demonstrations, and occupied buildings—first at Georgetown, then northeast to the Ivy League, then west to the Big Ten. After militant actions at Notre Dame, Wisconsin, and Michigan made the *New York Times, Business Week, Time,* National Public Radio, and almost every major daily newspaper, the growing student movement reached California, where schools from tiny Occidental College to the giant ten-campus University of California system agreed to limit the use of their names and logos to sweatshop-free apparel. Now the practical challenge is to devise a regime of monitoring and compliance.

The anti-sweatshop movement is the largest wave of student activism to hit campuses since students rallied to free Nelson Mandela by calling for a halt to university investments in South Africa more than a decade ago. This time around, the movement is electronically connected. Student activists bring their laptops and cell phones with them when they occupy administration buildings, sharing ideas and strategies with fellow activists from Boston to Berkeley. On the USAS listserv, victorious students from Wisconsin counsel neophytes from Arizona and Kentucky, and professors at Berkeley and Harvard explain how to calculate a living wage and guarantee independent monitoring in Honduras.

The target of this renewed activism is the $2.5 billion collegiate licensing industry—led by major companies like Nike, Gear, Champion, and Fruit of the Loom—which pays colleges and universities sizable royalties in exchange for the right to use the campus logo on caps, sweatshirts, jackets, and other items. Students are demanding that the workers who make these goods be paid a living wage, no matter where in the world industry operates. Students are also calling for an end to discrimination against women workers, public disclosure of the names and addresses of all factories involved in production, and independent monitoring in order to verify compliance.

These demands are opposed by the apparel industry, the White House, and most universities. Yet so far students have made significant progress in putting the industry on the defensive. A growing number of colleges and clothing companies have adopted "codes of conduct"—something unthinkable a decade ago—although student activists consider many of these standards inadequate.

In a world economy increasingly dominated by giant retailers and manufacturers who control global networks of independently owned factories, organizing consumers may prove to be a precondition for organizing production workers. And students are a potent group of consumers. If students next year succeed in building on this year's momentum, the collegiate licensing industry will be forced to change the way it does business. These changes, in turn, could affect the organization of the world's most globalized and exploitative industry—apparel manufacturing—along with the growing number of industries that, like apparel, outsource production in order to lower labor costs and blunt worker organizing.

The Global Sweatshop

In the apparel industry, so-called manufacturers—in reality, design and marketing firms—outsource the fabrication of clothing to independent contractors around the world. In this labor-intensive industry where capital requirements are minimal, it is relatively easy to open a clothing factory. This has contributed to a global race to the bottom, in which there is always someplace, somewhere, where clothing can be made still more cheaply. Low wages reflect not low productivity, but low bargaining power. A recent analysis in *Business Week* found that although Mexican apparel workers are 70 percent as productive as U.S. workers, they earn only 11 percent as much as their U.S. counterparts; Indonesian workers, who are 50 percent as productive, earn less than 2 percent as much.

The explosion of imports has proven devastating to once well-paid, unionized U.S. garment workers. The number of American garment workers has declined from peak levels of 1.4 million in the early 1970s to 800,000 today. The one exception to these trends is the expansion of garment employment, largely among immigrant and undocumented workers, in Los Angeles, which has more than 160,000 sweatshop workers. Recent U.S. Department of Labor surveys found that more than nine out of ten such firms violate legal health and safety standards, with more than half troubled by serious violations that could lead to severe injuries or death. Working conditions in New York City, the other major domestic garment center, are similar.

The very word "sweatshop" comes from the apparel industry, where profits were "sweated" out of workers by forcing them to work longer and faster at their sewing machines. Although significant advances have been made in such aspects of production as computer-assisted design, computerized marking, and computerized cutting, the industry still remains low-tech in its core production process, the sewing of garments. The basic unit of production continues to be a worker, usually a woman, sitting or standing at a sewing machine and sewing together pieces of limp cloth.

The structure of the garment industry fosters sweatshop production. During the past decade, retailing in the United States has become increasingly concentrated. Today, the four largest U.S. retailers—Wal-Mart, Kmart, Sears, and Dayton Hudson (owner of Target and Mervyns)—account for nearly two-thirds of U.S. retail sales. Retailers squeeze manufacturers, who in turn squeeze the contractors who actually make their products. Retailers and manufacturers preserve the fiction of being completely separate from contractors because they do not want to be held legally responsible for workplace violations of labor, health, and safety laws. Retailers and manufacturers alike insist that what happens in contractor factories is not their responsibility—even though their production managers and quality control officers are constantly checking up on the sewing shops that make their clothing.

The contracting system also allows retailers and manufacturers to eliminate much uncertainty and risk. When business is slow, the contract is simply not renewed; manufacturers need not worry about paying unemployment benefits or dealing with idle workers who might go on strike or otherwise make trouble. If a particular contractor becomes a problem, there are countless others to be found who will be only too happy to get their business. Workers, however, experience the flip side of the enormous flexibility enjoyed by retailers and manufacturers. They become contingent labor, employed and paid only when their work is needed.

Since profits are taken out at each level of the supply chain, labor costs are reduced to a tiny fraction of the retail price. Consider the economics of a dress that is sewn in Los Angeles and retails for $100. Half goes to the department store and half to the manufacturer, who keeps $12.50 to cover expenses and profit, spends $22.50 on textiles, and pays $15 to the contractor. The contractor keeps $9 to cover expenses and profits. That leaves just $6 of the $100 retail price for the workers who actually make the dress. Even if the cost of direct production labor were to increase by half, the dress would still only cost $103—a small increment that would make a world of difference to the seamstress in Los Angeles, whose $7,000 to $8,000 in annual wages are roughly two-thirds of the poverty level. A garment worker in Mexico would be lucky to earn $1,000 during a year of 48 to 60 hour workweeks; in China, $500.

At the other end of the apparel production chain, the heads of the 60 publicly traded U.S. apparel retailers earn an average $1.5 million a year. The heads of the 35 publicly traded apparel manufacturers average $2 million. In 1997, according to the *Los Angeles Business Journal*, five of the six highest-paid apparel executives in Los Angeles all came from a single firm: Guess?, Inc. They took home nearly $12.6 million—enough to double the yearly wages of 1,700 L.A. apparel workers.

꧁꧂

Organizing workers at the point of production, the century-old strategy that built the power of labor in Europe and North America, is best suited to production processes where most of the work goes on in-house. In industries whose production can easily be shifted almost anywhere on the planet, organizing is extremely difficult. Someday, perhaps, a truly international labor movement will confront global manufacturers. But in the meantime, organized consumers may well be labor's best ally. Consumers, after all, are not as readily moved as factories. And among American consumers, college students represent an especially potent force.

Kathie Lee and Robert Reich

During the early 1990s, American human rights and labor groups protested the proliferation of sweatshops at home and abroad—with major campaigns focusing on Nike and Gap. These efforts largely fizzled. But then two exposés of sweatshop conditions captured public attention. In August 1995, state and federal officials raided a garment factory in El Monte, California—a Los Angeles suburb—where 71 Thai immigrants had been held for several years in virtual slavery in an apartment complex ringed with barbed wire and spiked fences. They worked an average of 84 hours a week for $1.60 an hour, living eight to ten persons in a room. The garments they sewed ended up in major retail chains, including Macy's, Filene's and Robinsons-May, and for brand-name labels like B.U.M., Tomato, and High Sierra. Major daily papers and TV networks picked up on the story, leading to a flood of outraged editorials and columns calling for a clamp-down on domestic sweatshops. Then in April 1996, TV celebrity Kathie Lee Gifford tearfully acknowledged on national television that the Wal-Mart line of clothing that bore her name was made by children in Honduran sweatshops, even though tags on the garments promised that part of the profits would go to help children. Embarrassed by the publicity, Gifford soon became a crusader against sweatshop abuses.

For several years, then–Labor Secretary Robert Reich (now the *Prospect*'s senior editor) had been trying to inject the sweatshop issue onto the nation's agenda. The mounting publicity surrounding the El Monte and Kathie Lee scandals gave Reich new leverage. After all, what the apparel industry primarily sells is image, and the image of some of its major labels was getting a drubbing. He began pressing apparel executives, threatening to issue a report card on firms' behavior unless they agreed to help establish industry-wide standards.

In August 1996, the Clinton administration brought together representatives from the garment industry, labor unions, and consumer and human rights groups to grapple with sweatshops. The members of what they called the White House Apparel Industry Partnership (AIP) included apparel firms (Liz Claiborne, Reebok, L.L. Bean, Nike, Patagonia, Phillips-Van Heusen, Wal-Mart's Kathie Lee Gifford brand, and Nicole Miller), several nonprofit organizations (including the National Consumers League, Interfaith Center on Corporate

Responsibility, International Labor Rights Fund, Lawyers Committee for Human Rights, Robert F. Kennedy Memorial Center for Human Rights, and Business for Social Responsibility), as well as the Union of Needletrades, Industrial and Textile Employees (UNITE), the Retail, Wholesale, and Department Store Union, and the AFL-CIO.

After intense negotiations, the Department of Labor issued an interim AIP report in April 1997 and the White House released the final 40-page report in November 1998, which included a proposed workplace code of conduct and a set of monitoring guidelines. By then, Reich had left the Clinton administration, replaced by Alexis Herman. The two labor representatives on the AIP, as well as the Interfaith Center on Corporate Responsibility, quit the group to protest the feeble recommendations, which had been crafted primarily by the garment industry delegates and which called, essentially, for the industry to police itself. This maneuvering would not have generated much attention except that a new factor—college activism—had been added to the equation.

A "Sweat-Free" Campus

The campus movement began in the fall of 1997 at Duke when a group called Students Against Sweatshops persuaded the university to require manufacturers of items with the Duke label to sign a pledge that they would not use sweatshop labor. Duke has 700 licensees (including Nike and other major labels) that make apparel at hundreds of plants in the U.S. and in more than 10 other countries, generating almost $25 million annually in sales. Following months of negotiations, in March 1998 Duke President Nannerl Keohane and the student activists jointly announced a detailed "code of conduct" that bars Duke licensees from using child labor, requires them to maintain safe workplaces, to pay the minimum wage, to recognize the right of workers to unionize, to disclose the locations of all factories making products with Duke's name, and to allow visits by independent monitors to inspect the factories.

The Duke victory quickly inspired students on other campuses. The level of activity on campuses accelerated, with students finding creative ways to dramatize the issue. At Yale, student activists staged a "knit-in" to draw attention to sweatshop abuses. At Holy Cross and the University of California at Santa Barbara, students sponsored mock fashion shows where they discussed the working conditions under which the garments were manufactured. Duke students published a coloring book explaining how (and where) the campus mascot, the Blue Devil, is stitched onto clothing by workers in sweatshops. Activists at the University of Wisconsin infiltrated a homecoming parade and, dressed like sweatshop workers in Indonesia, carried a giant Reebok shoe. They also held a press conference in front of the chancellor's office and presented him with an oversized check for 16 cents—the hourly wage paid to workers in China making Nike athletic shoes. At Georgetown, Wisconsin, Michigan, Arizona, and Duke, students occupied administration buildings to pressure their institutions to adopt (or, in Duke's case, strengthen) anti-sweatshop codes.

In the summer of 1998, disparate campus groups formed United Students Against Sweatshops (USAS). The USAS has weekly conference calls to discuss their negotiations with Nike, the Department of Labor, and others. It has sponsored training sessions for student leaders and conferences at several campuses where the sweatshop issue is only part of an agenda that also includes helping to build the labor movement, NAFTA, the World Trade Organization, women's rights, and other issues.

Last year, anti-sweatshop activists employed the USAS listserv to exchange ideas on negotiating tactics, discuss media strategies, swap songs to sing during rallies, and debate the technicalities of defining a "living wage" to incorporate in their campus codes of conduct. In May, the USAS listserv heated up after the popular Fox television series *Party of Five* included a scene in which one of the show's characters, Sarah (played by Jennifer Love Hewitt), helps organize a Students Against Sweatshops sit-in on her campus. A few real-life activists worried that the mainstream media was trivializing the movement by skirting the key issues ("the importance of unionized labor, the globalization of the economy, etc.") as well as focusing most of that episode on the characters' love life. University of Michigan student Rachel Paster responded:

> Let's not forget that we ARE a student movement, and students do complain about boyfriends and fashion problems. One of the biggest reasons why USAS and local student groups opposing sweatshops have been as successful as we have been is that opposition to sweatshops ISN'T that radical. Although I'm sure lots of us are all for overthrowing the corporate power structure, the human rights issues involved are what make a lot of people get involved and put their energies into rallies, sit-ins, et cetera. If we were a 'radical' group, university administrations would have brushed us off. . . . The fact that they don't is testament to the fact that we have support, not just from students on the far left, but from students in the middle ground who don't consider themselves radicals. Without those people we would NEVER have gotten as far as we have.

Indeed, the anti-sweatshop movement has been able to mobilize wide support because it strikes several nerves among today's college students, including women's rights (most sweatshop workers are women and some factories have required women to use birth control pills as a condition of employment), immigrant rights, environmental concerns, and human rights. After University of Wisconsin administrators brushed aside anti-sweatshop protestors, claiming they didn't represent student opinion, the activists ran a slate of candidates for student government. Eric Brakken, a sociology major and anti-sweatshop leader, was elected student body president and last year used the organization's substantial resources to promote the activists' agenda. And Duke's student government unanimously passed a resolution supporting the anti-sweatshop group, calling for full public disclosure of the locations of companies that manufacture Duke clothing.

The Labor Connection

At the core of the movement is a strong bond with organized labor. The movement is an important by-product of the labor movement's recent efforts, under President John Sweeney, to repair the rift between students and unions that dates to the Vietnam War. Since 1996, the AFL-CIO's Union Summer has placed almost 2,000 college students in internships with local unions around the country, most of whom work on grassroots organizing campaigns with low-wage workers in hotels, agriculture, food processing, janitorial service, and other industries. The program has its own staff, mostly young organizers only a few years out of college themselves, who actively recruit on campuses, looking for the next generation of union organizers and researchers, particularly minorities, immigrants, and women. Union Summer graduates are among the key leadership of the campus anti-sweatshop movement.

UNITE has one full-time staff person assigned to work on sweatshop issues, which includes helping student groups. A number of small human rights watchdog organizations that operate on shoestring budgets—Global Exchange, Sweatshop Watch, and the National Labor Committee [NLC]—give student activists technical advice. (It was NLC's Charles Kernaghan, an energetic researcher and publicist, who exposed the Kathie Lee Gifford connection to sweatshops in testimony before Congress.) These groups have helped bring sweatshop workers on speaking tours of American campuses, and have organized delegations of student activists to investigate firsthand the conditions in Honduras, Guatemala, El Salvador, Mexico, and elsewhere under which workers produce their college's clothing.

Unions and several liberal foundations have provided modest funding for student anti-sweatshop groups. Until this summer USAS had no staff, nor did any of its local campus affiliates. In contrast, corporate-sponsored conservative foundations have, over the past two decades, funded dozens of conservative student publications, subsidized student organizations and conferences, and recruited conservative students for internships and jobs in right-wing think tanks and publications as well as positions in the Reagan and Bush administrations and Congress, seeking to groom the next generation of conservative activists. The Intercollegiate Studies Institute, the leading right-wing campus umbrella group, has an annual budget over $5 million. In comparison, the Center for Campus Organizing, a Boston-based group that works closely with anti-sweatshop groups and other progressive campus organizations, operates on a budget under $200,000.

This student movement even has some sympathizers among university administrators. "Thank God students are getting passionate about something other than basketball and bonfires," John Burness, a Duke administrator who helped negotiate the end of the 31-hour sit-in, told the *Boston Globe.* "But the tone is definitely different. In the old days, we used to have to scramble to cut off phone lines when they took over the president's office, but we didn't have to worry about that here. They just bring their laptops and they do work."

At every university where students organized a sit-in (Duke, Georgetown, Arizona, Michigan, and Wisconsin) they have wrested agreements to require licensees to disclose the specific location of their factory sites, which is necessary for independent monitoring. Students elsewhere (including Harvard, Illinois, Brown, the University of California, Princeton, Middlebury, and Occidental) won a public disclosure requirement without resorting to civil disobedience. A few institutions have agreed to require manufacturers to pay their employees a "living wage." Wisconsin agreed to organize an academic conference this fall to discuss how to calculate living-wage formulas for countries with widely disparate costs of living, and then to implement its own policy recommendations. [See Richard Rothstein, "The Global Hiring Hall: Why We Need Worldwide Labor Standards," *TAP,* Spring 1994.]

The Industry's New Clothes

Last November, the White House-initiated Apparel Industry Partnership created a monitoring arm, the Fair Labor Association (FLA), and a few months later invited universities to join. Colleges, however, have just one seat on FLA's 14-member board. Under the group's bylaws the garment firms control the board's decisionmaking. The bylaws require a "supermajority" to approve all key questions, thus any three companies can veto a proposal they don't like.

At this writing, FLA member companies agree to ban child and prison labor, to prohibit physical abuse by supervisors, and to allow workers the freedom to organize unions in their foreign factories, though independent enforcement has not yet been specified. FLA wants to assign this monitoring task to corporate accounting firms like PricewaterhouseCoopers and Ernst & Young, to allow companies to select which facilities will be inspected, and to keep factory locations and the monitoring reports secret. Student activists want human rights and labor groups to do the monitoring.

This is only a bare beginning, but it establishes the crucial moral precedent of companies taking responsibility for labor conditions beyond their shores. Seeing this foot in the door, several companies have bowed out because they consider these standards too tough. The FLA expects that by 2001, after its monitoring program has been in place for a year, participating firms will be able to use the FLA logo on their labels and advertising as evidence of their ethical corporate practices. [See Richard Rothstein, "The Starbucks Solution: Can Voluntary Codes Raise Global Living Standards?" *TAP,* July-August 1996.]

The original list of 17 FLA-affiliated universities grew to more than 100 by mid-summer of this year. And yet, some campus groups have dissuaded college administrations (including the Universities of Michigan, Minnesota, Oregon, Toronto, and California, as well as Oberlin, Bucknell, and Earlham Colleges) from joining FLA, while others have persuaded their institutions (including Brown, Wisconsin, North Carolina, and Georgetown) to join only if the FLA adopts stronger standards. While FLA members are supposed to abide by each country's minimum-wage standards, these are typically far below the poverty level. In fact, no company has made a commitment to pay a living wage.

The campus movement has succeeded in raising awareness (both on campus and among the general public) about sweatshops as well as the global economy. It has contributed to industry acceptance of extraterritorial labor standards, something hitherto considered utopian. It has also given thousands of students experience in the nuts and bolts of social activism, many of whom are likely to carry their idealism and organizing experiences with them into jobs with unions, community and environmental groups, and other public interest crusades.

So far, however, the movement has had only minimal impact on the daily lives of sweatshop workers at home and abroad. Nike and Reebok, largely because of student protests, have raised wages and benefits in their Indonesian footwear factories—which employ more than 100,000 workers—to 43 percent above the minimum wage. But this translates to only 20 cents an hour in U.S. dollars, far below a "living wage" to raise a family and even below the 27 cents Nike paid before Indonesia's currency devaluation. Last spring Nike announced its willingness to disclose the location of its overseas plants that produce clothing for universities. This created an important split in industry ranks, since industry leaders have argued that disclosure would undermine each firm's competitive position. But Nike has opened itself up to the charge of having a double standard, since it still refuses to disclose the location of its non-university production sites.

Within a year, when FLA's monitoring system is fully operational, students at several large schools with major licensing contracts—including Duke, Wisconsin, Michigan, North Carolina, and Georgetown—will have lists of factories in the U.S. and overseas that produce university clothing and equipment. This information will be very useful to civic and labor organizations at home and abroad, providing more opportunities to expose working conditions. Student activists at each university will be able to visit these sites—bringing media and public officials with them—to expose working conditions (and, if necessary, challenge the findings of the FLA's own monitors) and support organizing efforts by local unions and women's groups.

If the student activists can help force a small but visible "ethical" niche of the apparel industry to adopt higher standards, it will divide the industry and give unions and consumer groups more leverage to challenge the sweatshop practices of the rest of the industry. The campus anti-sweatshop crusade is part of what might be called a "conscience constituency" among consumers who are willing to incorporate ethical principles into their buying habits, even if it means slightly higher prices. Environmentalists have done the same thing with the "buy green" campaign, as have various "socially responsible" investment firms.

Beyond Consumer Awareness

In a global production system characterized by powerful retailers and invisible contractors, consumer action has an important role to play. But ultimately it must be combined with worker organizing and legislative and regulatory remedies. Unionizing the global apparel industry is an organizer's nightmare. With globalization and the contracting system, any apparel factory with a union risks losing its business.

Domestically, UNITE represents fewer than 300,000 textile and garment industry workers, down from the 800,000 represented by its two predecessor unions in the late 1960s. In the low-income countries where most U.S. apparel is now made, the prospects for unionization are dimmer still. In Mexico, labor unions are controlled by the government. China outlaws independent unions, punishing organizers with prison terms. Building the capacity for unfettered union organizing must necessarily be a long-term strategy for union organizers throughout the world. Here, the student anti-sweatshop movement can help. The independent verification of anti-sweatshop standards that students want can also serve the goal of union organizing.

Public policy could also help. As part of our trade policy, Congress could require public disclosure of manufacturing sites and independent monitoring of firms that sell goods in the American market. It could enact legislation that requires U.S. companies to follow U.S. health and safety standards globally and to bar the import of clothing made in sweatshops or made by workers who are denied the basic right to organize unions. In addition, legislation sponsored by Representative William Clay could make retailers and manufacturers legally liable for the working conditions behind the goods they design and sell, thereby ending the fiction that contractors are completely independent of the manufacturers and retailers that hire them. Last spring the California Assembly passed a state version of this legislation. Student and union activists hope that the Democrat-controlled state senate and Democratic Governor Gray Davis—whose lopsided victory last November was largely attributed to organized labor's get-out-the-vote effort—will support the bill.

⌾

Thanks to the student movement, public opinion may be changing. And last spring, speaking both to the International Labor Organization in Geneva and at the commencement ceremonies at the University of Chicago (an institution founded by John D. Rockefeller and a stronghold of free market economics, but also a center of student anti-sweatshop activism), President Clinton called for an international campaign against child labor, including restrictions on government purchases of goods made by children.

A shift of much apparel production to developing countries may well be inevitable in a global economy. But when companies do move their production abroad, student activists are warning "you can run but you can't hide," demanding that they be held responsible for conditions in contractor factories no matter where they are. Students can't accomplish this on their own, but in a very short period of time they have made many Americans aware that they don't have to leave their consciences at home when they shop for clothes.

Nicholas D. Kristof and
Sheryl WuDunn

 **NO**

Two Cheers for Sweatshops

It was breakfast time, and the food stand in the village in northeastern Thailand was crowded. Maesubin Sisoipha, the middle-aged woman cooking the food, was friendly, her portions large and the price right. For the equivalent of about 5 cents, she offered a huge green mango leaf filled with rice, fish paste and fried beetles. It was a hearty breakfast, if one didn't mind the odd antenna left sticking in one's teeth.

One of the half-dozen men and women sitting on a bench eating was a sinewy, bare-chested laborer in his late 30's named Mongkol Latlakorn. It was a hot, lazy day, and so we started chatting idly about the food and, eventually, our families. Mongkol mentioned that his daughter, Darin, was 15, and his voice softened as he spoke of her. She was beautiful and smart, and her father's hopes rested on her.

"Is she in school?" we asked.

"Oh, no," Mongkol said, his eyes sparkling with amusement. "She's working in a factory in Bangkok. She's making clothing for export to America." He explained that she was paid $2 a day for a nine-hour shift, six days a week.

"It's dangerous work," Mongkol added. "Twice the needles went right through her hands. But the managers bandaged up her hands, and both times she got better again and went back to work."

"How terrible," we murmured sympathetically.

Mongkol looked up, puzzled. "It's good pay," he said. "I hope she can keep that job. There's all this talk about factories closing now, and she said there are rumors that her factory might close. I hope that doesn't happen. I don't know what she would do then."

He was not, of course, indifferent to his daughter's suffering; he simply had a different perspective from ours—not only when it came to food but also when it came to what constituted desirable work.

Nothing captures the difference in mind-set between East and West more than attitudes toward sweatshops. Nike and other American companies have been hammered in the Western press over the last decade for producing shoes, toys and other products in grim little factories with dismal conditions. Protests against sweatshops and the dark forces of globalization that they seem to represent have become common at meetings of the World Bank and the World Trade

Organization and, this month, at a World Economic Forum in Australia, livening up the scene for Olympic athletes arriving for the competition. Yet sweatshops that seem brutal from the vantage point of an American sitting in his living room can appear tantalizing to a Thai laborer getting by on beetles.

Fourteen years ago, we moved to Asia and began reporting there. Like most Westerners, we arrived in the region outraged at sweatshops. In time, though, we came to accept the view supported by most Asians: that the campaign against sweatshops risks harming the very people it is intended to help. For beneath their grime, sweatshops are a clear sign of the industrial revolution that is beginning to reshape Asia.

This is not to praise sweatshops. Some managers are brutal in the way they house workers in firetraps, expose children to dangerous chemicals, deny bathroom breaks, demand sexual favors, force people to work double shifts or dismiss anyone who tries to organize a union. Agitation for improved safety conditions can be helpful, just as it was in 19th-century Europe. But Asian workers would be aghast at the idea of American consumers boycotting certain toys or clothing in protest. The simplest way to help the poorest Asians would be to buy more from sweatshops, not less.

On our first extended trip to China, in 1987, we traveled to the Pearl River delta in the south of the country. There we visited several factories, including one in the boomtown of Dongguan, where about 100 female workers sat at workbenches stitching together bits of leather to make purses for a Hong Kong company. We chatted with several women as their fingers flew over their work and asked about their hours.

"I start at about 6:30, after breakfast, and go until about 7 p.m.," explained one shy teenage girl. "We break for lunch, and I take half an hour off then."

"You do this six days a week?"

"Oh, no. Every day."

"Seven days a week?"

"Yes." She laughed at our surprise. "But then I take a week or two off at Chinese New Year to go back to my village."

The others we talked to all seemed to regard it as a plus that the factory allowed them to work long hours. Indeed, some had sought out this factory precisely because it offered them the chance to earn more.

"It's actually pretty annoying how hard they want to work," said the factory manager, a Hong Kong man. "It means we have to worry about security and have a supervisor around almost constantly."

It sounded pretty dreadful, and it was. We and other journalists wrote about the problems of child labor and oppressive conditions in both China and South Korea. But, looking back, our worries were excessive. Those sweatshops tended to generate the wealth to solve the problems they created. If Americans had reacted to the horror stories in the 1980's by curbing imports of those sweatshop products, then neither southern China nor South Korea would have registered as much progress as they have today.

The truth is, those grim factories in Dongguan and the rest of southern China contributed to a remarkable explosion of wealth. In the years since our first conversations there, we've returned many times to Dongguan and the surrounding towns and seen the transformation. Wages have risen from about $50 a month to $250 a month or more today. Factory conditions have improved as businesses have scrambled to attract and keep the best laborers. A private housing market has emerged, and video arcades and computer schools have opened to cater to workers with rising incomes. A hint of a middle class has appeared—as has China's closest thing to a Western-style independent newspaper, Southern Weekend.

Partly because of these tens of thousands of sweatshops, China's economy has become one of the hottest in the world. Indeed, if China's 30 provinces were counted as individual countries, then the 20 fastest-growing countries in the world between 1978 and 1995 would all have been Chinese. When Britain launched the Industrial Revolution in the late 18th century, it took 58 years for per capita output to double. In China, per capita output has been doubling every 10 years.

In fact, the most vibrant parts of Asia are nearly all in what might be called the Sweatshop Belt, from China and South Korea to Malaysia, Indonesia and even Bangladesh and India. Today these sweatshop countries control about one-quarter of the global economy. As the industrial revolution spreads through China and India, there are good reasons to think that Asia will continue to pick up speed. Some World Bank forecasts show Asia's share of global gross domestic product rising to 55 to 60 percent by about 2025—roughly the West's share at its peak half a century ago. The sweatshops have helped lay the groundwork for a historic economic realignment that is putting Asia back on its feet. Countries are rebounding from the economic crisis of 1997–98 and the sweatshops—seen by Westerners as evidence of moribund economies—actually reflect an industrial revolution that is raising living standards in the East.

Of course, it may sound silly to say that sweatshops offer a route to prosperity, when wages in the poorest countries are sometimes less than $1 a day. Still, for an impoverished Indonesian or Bangladeshi woman with a handful of kids who would otherwise drop out of school and risk dying of mundane diseases like diarrhea, $1 or $2 a day can be a life-transforming wage.

This was made abundantly clear in Cambodia, when we met a 40-year-old woman named Nhem Yen, who told us why she moved to an area with particularly lethal malaria. "We needed to eat," she said. "And here there is wood, so we thought we could cut it and sell it."

But then Nhem Yen's daughter and son-in-law both died of malaria, leaving her with two grandchildren and five children of her own. With just one mosquito net, she had to choose which children would sleep protected and which would sleep exposed.

In Cambodia, a large mosquito net costs $5. If there had been a sweatshop in the area, however harsh or dangerous, Nhem Yen would have leapt at the chance to work in it, to earn enough to buy a net big enough to cover all her children.

For all the misery they can engender, sweatshops at least offer a precarious escape from the poverty that is the developing world's greatest problem. Over the past 50 years, countries like India resisted foreign exploitation, while countries that started at a similar economic level—like Taiwan and South Korea—accepted sweatshops as the price of development. Today there can be no doubt about which approach worked better. Taiwan and South Korea are modern countries with low rates of infant mortality and high levels of education; in contrast, every year 3.1 million Indian children die before the age of 5, mostly from diseases of poverty like diarrhea.

The effect of American pressure on sweatshops is complicated. While it clearly improves conditions at factories that produce branded merchandise for companies like Nike, it also raises labor costs across the board. That encourages less well established companies to mechanize and to reduce the number of employees needed. The upshot is to help people who currently have jobs in Nike plants but to risk jobs for others. The only thing a country like Cambodia has to offer is terribly cheap wages; if companies are scolded for paying those wages, they will shift their manufacturing to marginally richer areas like Malaysia or Mexico.

Sweatshop monitors do have a useful role. They can compel factories to improve safety. They can also call attention to the impact of sweatshops on the environment. The greatest downside of industrialization is not exploitation of workers but toxic air and water. In Asia each year, three million people die from the effects of pollution. The factories springing up throughout the region are far more likely to kill people through the chemicals they expel than through terrible working conditions.

By focusing on these issues, by working closely with organizations and news media in foreign countries, sweatshops can be improved. But refusing to buy sweatshop products risks making Americans feel good while harming those we are trying to help. As a Chinese proverb goes, "First comes the bitterness, then there is sweetness and wealth and honor for 10,000 years."

POSTSCRIPT

Should We Sweat About Sweatshops?

Economists have not remained mute as this debate has raged across college campuses. In a letter circulated across American campuses in September 2000, 90 academics, mostly economists, urged college and university presidents not to yield to student pressure demanding the adoption of strict codes of conduct for the manufacturers of university apparel that is produced in poor countries. There were many distinguished signers, including Nobel Laureate Robert Lucas, several former presidents of the American Economic Association, several former presidents of the Econometric Society, and Paul McCracken, former chairman of the President's Council of Economic Advisers. These market-oriented economists warned against codes of conduct that required offshore plants to pay wages that are above the prevailing wage rates. They asserted that these higher wages might result "in shifts in employment that will worsen the collective welfare of the very workers in poor countries who are supposed to be helped." This group is supported by the Academic Consortium on International Trade (ACIT), an organization of economists and lawyers dedicated to the establishment of free trade on a worldwide basis. Their Web site is at http://www.spp.umich.edu/rsie/acit/.

In "White Hats or Don Quixotes? Human Rights Vigilantes in the Global Economy," NBER Working Paper No. W8102 (January 2001), published by the National Bureau of Economic Research, Kimberly Ann Elliott and Richard Freeman examine the pros and cons of codes of conduct for multinationals working in poor countries. They analyze the incentives for corporations to respond to the demand for more equitable treatment of the workforce in these offshore facilities. They conclude that the pressure applied by student activist groups and others who are concerned about sweatshop conditions may be one of those cases "when 'doing good' actually does good." Elliott and Freeman also suggest that a counterpetition to the Academic Consortium on International Trade is being prepared by Robert Pollin of the University of Massachusetts at Amherst and James K. Galbraith of the University of Texas at Austin. As of April 2001 that petition had not appeared.

There is a wealth of antisweatshop literature to examine, much of which is produced by organized labor. The National Labor Committee, for example, provides a wellspring of data on this topic. They can be found on the Internet at http://www.nlcnet.org. In addition, there is an article on sweatshop abuses in nearly every issue of *Working USA,* a journal sponsored by organized labor. In addition to various organized labor groups, you might also check out the Global Alliance for Workers and Communities. This is an initiative of the International Youth Foundation in partnership with the John D. and Catherine T. MacArthur Foundation. Their Web site is http://www.theglobalalliance.org.

Other pro–worker rights organizations are the Campaign for Labor Rights, the Clean Clothes Campaign, the Collegiate Living Wage Association, the Ethical Trading Initiative, the Global Exchange, the International Labour Organisation, the International Labor Rights Fund, the Investor Responsibility Research Center, Sweatshop Watch, and the UNITE! Stop Sweatshops Campaign.

On the other side you will have no difficulty finding material to support globalization. Start with the National Retail Federation (NRF), which is the largest retail trade organization in the world. It represents 1.4 million U.S. retail establishments, which employ nearly 1 in every 5 American workers—about 20 million workers in all. See the NRF's Web site at http://www.nrf.com. The ACIT also provides an up-to-date list of articles that support globalization, which often entails acceptance of sweatshop use. Some of these articles are Daniel W. Drezner, "Bottom Feeders," *Foreign Policy* (November/December 2000); Michael Barkey, "Globalization, Social Justice and the Plight of the Poor," Acton Commentary, http://www.acton.org/ppolicy/comment/article.php?id=22 (August 2000); Philip Knight, "A Forum for Improving Globalisation," *Financial Times* (August 1, 2000); Thomas Friedman, "Knight Is Right," *The New York Times* (June 20, 2000); "Assessing Globalization," World Bank Briefing Papers (April 2000); "Globalization: Threat or Opportunity?" IMF Issues Brief (April 12, 2000); and "Trade and Poverty: Is There a Connection?" WTO Special Study No. 5 (March 2000).

ISSUE 15

Are the Costs of Global Warming Too High to Ignore?

YES: Lester R. Brown, from *Eco-Economy: Building an Economy for the Earth* (W. W. Norton, 2001)

NO: Lenny Bernstein, from "Climate Change and Ecosystems," A Report of the George C. Marshall Institute (2002)

ISSUE SUMMARY

YES: Lester R. Brown, founder and president of the Earth Policy Institute, describes his vision of an environmentally sustainable economy, which includes food supplies, population growth issues, water availability, climatic changes, and renewable energy.

NO: Lenny Bernstein, head of L. S. Bernstein & Associates, which advises companies and trade associations on political and scientific developments on global environmental issues, acknowledges that ecosystems are sensitive to climate change, but he argues that the change that we have seen repeated again and again over the course of history can lead to benefits for our children and our children's children.

The severe weather that has plagued much of the United States from the late 1980s to the present has offered some memorable events for Americans. National forests have burst into wildfires; electric bills have skyrocketed as air conditioners in homes and businesses have been run at full strength day and night; and local officials have banned car washing and lawn sprinkling to conserve precious water as lakes, streams, and reservoirs have fallen to critically low levels. Citizens and public policymakers alike have increasingly come to believe that the world has entered the long-predicted and much-feared period of global warming, which many associate with the "greenhouse effect."

In the past decade or so, stretching back to the 1992 United Nations Earth Summit in Rio de Janeiro, there have been a series of international agreements or attempted agreements to limit the amount of greenhouse gas emissions. The 1992 summit is worth noting in that regard. That summit produced a landmark treaty that suggested that stabilizing the world environment must be undertaken irrespective of costs. More than 180 countries, including the United States, ratified this treaty. It set the stage for a decade of international negotiations all aimed at rolling back toxic emissions—primarily in the industrialized world—to 1990 levels. In spite of these good intentions, there is little evidence that any measurable success was achieved. This might be attributed to the fact that the U.S. Senate has not ratified the implementing instrument—the 1997 Kyoto Protocol—which failed by a 95–0 vote in July 1997.

The Senate's concerns were that the treaty exempted developing countries and posed serious problems for the U.S. economy at large. Both of these problems can be traced to the fact that the only way to reduce greenhouse gas emissions, which are essentially carbon dioxide gases, would be to stop burning fossil fuels: coal, oil, natural gas, wood, and peat. Eliminating these emissions by taxing them or by imposing regulations comes at a high price. Poor countries cannot afford to do this, and the United States is unwilling to pay the high price. President George W. Bush, for his part, put the final coup de grace to the Kyoto Protocol in March 2001. He rejected the protocol, saying that it was "fatally flawed in fundamental ways." He went on to note that since climate change was a serious concern, he would ask the National Academy of Sciences to review the state of our understanding of global warming and to issue a report. That 2001 report is entitled *Climate Change Science: An Analysis of Some Key Questions* and can be accessed online at http://www.nap.edu/books/0309075742/html/.

This report and the debate over the Kyoto Protocol continue to be controversial. Most acknowledge that social and economic development has impacted the concentration levels of greenhouse gases in our atmosphere, but some people do challenge this widely held belief. Whatever the cause of the accumulated greenhouse gases in our atmosphere, what experts do know is that since the beginning of the Industrial Revolution, concentrations of these gases have increased by 30 percent. More worrisome, perhaps, is the fact that each year the world adds another 6 billion tons of carbon dioxide to the atmosphere.

At the crux of this debate are the consequences of the toxic wastes that we are dumping into the air—air that we depend upon for our very existence. No one seems to know for certain just how the environment will respond to these accumulated greenhouse gases. Many contend that in a very short period of time there will be a sharp rise in surface temperatures. If that turns out to be the case, modern civilization and the ecosystem will be in for dire consequences. Others believe that there might be a more gradual and more modest increase in global warming. This increase might be relatively easy to adjust to and perhaps even lead to benefits for the ecosystem and humankind.

In the following selections, Lester R. Brown argues that economic growth is generally incompatible with the environment but that by basing the economy in an ecological framework, environmentally sustainable economic development can be achieved. Lenny Bernstein maintains that human activities will not have a severe impact on ecosystems and that, in fact, ecosystems that adapt appropriately will benefit from human-induced climate change.

The Economy and the Earth

In 1543, Polish astronomer Nicolaus Copernicus published "On the Revolutions of the Celestial Spheres," in which he challenged the view that the Sun revolved around the earth, arguing instead that the earth revolved around the Sun. With his new model of the solar system, he began a wide-ranging debate among scientists, theologians, and others. His alternative to the earlier Ptolemaic model, which had the earth at the center of the universe, led to a revolution in thinking, to a new worldview.

Today we need a similar shift in our worldview, in how we think about the relationship between the earth and the economy. The issue now is not which celestial sphere revolves around the other but whether the environment is part of the economy or the economy is part of the environment. Economists see the environment as a subset of the economy. Ecologists, on the other hand, see the economy as a subset of the environment.

Like Ptolemy's view of the solar system, the economists' view is confusing efforts to understand our modern world. It has created an economy that is out of sync with the ecosystem on which it depends.

Economic theory and economic indicators do not explain how the economy is disrupting and destroying the earth's natural systems. Economic theory does not explain why Arctic Sea ice is melting. It does not explain why grasslands are turning into desert in northwestern China, why coral reefs are dying in the South Pacific, or why the Newfoundland cod fishery collapsed. Nor does it explain why we are in the early stages of the greatest extinction of plants and animals since the dinosaurs disappeared 65 million years ago. Yet economics is essential to measuring the cost to society of these excesses.

Evidence that the economy is in conflict with the earth's natural systems can be seen in the daily news reports of collapsing fisheries, shrinking forests, eroding soils, deteriorating rangelands, expanding deserts, rising carbon dioxide (CO_2) levels, falling water tables, rising temperatures, more destructive storms, melting glaciers, rising sea level, dying coral reefs, and disappearing species. These trends, which mark an increasingly stressed relationship between the economy and the earth's ecosystem, are taking a growing economic toll. At some point, this could overwhelm the worldwide forces of progress,

From Lester R. Brown, *Eco-Economy: Building an Economy for the Earth* (W. W. Norton, 2001), pp. 3–4, 6–23. Copyright © 2001 by The Earth Policy Institute. Reprinted by permission of W. W. Norton & Company, Inc. Notes omitted.

leading to economic decline. The challenge for our generation is to reverse these trends before environmental deterioration leads to long-term economic decline, as it did for so many earlier civilizations.

These increasingly visible trends indicate that if the operation of the sub-system, the economy, is not compatible with the behavior of the larger system—the earth's ecosystem—both will eventually suffer. The larger the economy becomes relative to the ecosystem, and the more it presses against the earth's natural limits, the more destructive this incompatibility will be.

An environmentally sustainable economy—an eco-economy—requires that the principles of ecology establish the framework for the formulation of economic policy and that economists and ecologists work together to fashion the new economy. Ecologists understand that all economic activity, indeed all life, depends on the earth's ecosystem—the complex of individual species living together, interacting with each other and their physical habitat. These millions of species exist in an intricate balance, woven together by food chains, nutrient cycles, the hydrological cycle, and the climate system. Economists know how to translate goals into policy. Economists and ecologists working together can design and build an eco-economy, one that can sustain progress. . . .

Economists rely on the market to guide their decisionmaking. They respect the market because it can allocate resources with an efficiency that a central planner can never match (as the Soviets learned at great expense). Ecologists view the market with less reverence because they see a market that is not telling the truth. For example, when buying a gallon of gasoline, customers in effect pay to get the oil out of the ground, refine it into gasoline, and deliver it to the local service station. But they do not pay the health care costs of treating respiratory illness from air pollution or the costs of climate disruption.

Ecologists see the record economic growth of recent decades, but they also see an economy that is increasingly in conflict with its support systems, one that is fast depleting the earth's natural capital, moving the global economy onto an environmental path that will inevitably lead to economic decline. They see the need for a wholesale restructuring of the economy so that it meshes with the ecosystem. They know that a stable relationship between the economy and the earth's ecosystem is essential if economic progress is to be sustained.

We have created an economy that cannot sustain economic progress, an economy that cannot take us where we want to go. Just as Copernicus had to formulate a new astronomical worldview after several decades of celestial observations and mathematical calculations, we too must formulate a new economic worldview based on several decades of environmental observations and analyses.

Although the idea that economics must be integrated into ecology may seem radical to many, evidence is mounting that it is the only approach that reflects reality. When observations no longer support theory, it is time to change the theory—what science historian Thomas Kuhn calls a paradigm shift. If the economy is a subset of the earth's ecosystem, as [I contend], the only formulation of economic policy that will succeed is one that respects the principles of ecology.

The good news is that economists are becoming more ecologically aware, recognizing the inherent dependence of the economy on the earth's ecosystem. For example, some 2,500 economists—including eight Nobel laureates—have endorsed the introduction of a carbon tax to stabilize climate. More and more economists are looking for ways to get the market to tell the ecological truth. This spreading awareness is evident in the rapid growth of the International Society of Ecological Economics, which has 1,200 members and chapters in Australia/New Zealand, Brazil, Canada, India, Russia, China, and throughout Europe. Its goal is to integrate the thinking of ecologists and economists into a transdiscipline aimed at building a sustainable world.

Economy Self-Destructing

The economic indicators for the last half-century show remarkable progress. . . . [T]he economy expanded sevenfold between 1950 and 2000. International trade grew even more rapidly. The Dow Jones Index, a widely used indicator of the value of stocks traded on the New York Stock Exchange, climbed from 3,000 in 1990 to 11,000 in 2000. It was difficult not to be bullish about the long-term economic prospect as the new century began.

Difficult, that is, unless you look at the ecological indicators. Here, virtually every global indicator was headed in the wrong direction. The economic policies that have yielded the extraordinary growth in the world economy are the same ones that are destroying its support systems. By an conceivable ecological yardstick, these are failed policies. Mismanagement is destroying forests, rangelands, fisheries, and croplands—the four ecosystems that supply our food and, except for minerals, all our raw materials as well. Although many of us live in a high-tech urbanized society, we are as dependent on the earth's natural systems as our hunter-gatherer forebears were.

To put ecosystems in economic terms, a natural system, such as a fishery, functions like an endowment. The interest income from an endowment will continue in perpetuity as long as the endowment is maintained. If the endowment is drawn down, income declines. If the endowment is eventually depleted, the interest income disappears. And so it is with natural systems. If the sustainable yield of a fishery is exceeded, fish stocks begin to shrink. Eventually stocks are depleted and the fishery collapses. The cash flow from this endowment disappears as well.

As we begin the twenty-first century, our economy is slowly destroying its support systems, consuming its endowment of natural capital. Demands of the expanding economy, *as now structured,* are surpassing the sustainable yield of ecosystems. Easily a third of the world's cropland is losing topsoil at a rate that is undermining its long-term productivity. Fully 50 percent of the world's rangeland is overgrazed and deteriorating into desert. The world's forests have shrunk by about half since the dawn of agriculture and are still shrinking. Two thirds of oceanic fisheries are now being fished at or beyond their capacity; overfishing is now the rule, not the exception. And overpumping of underground water is common in key food-producing regions.

Over large areas of the world, the loss of topsoil from wind and water erosion now exceeds the natural formation of new soil, gradually draining the land of its fertility. In an effort to curb this, the United States is retiring highly erodible cropland that was earlier plowed in overly enthusiastic efforts to expand food production. This process began in 1985 with the Conservation Reserve Program that paid farmers to retire 15 million hectacres, roughly one tenth of U.S. cropland, converting it back to grassland or forest before it became wasteland.

In countries that lack such programs, farmers are being forced to abandon highly erodible land that has lost much of its topsoil. Nigeria is losing over 500 square kilometers of productive land to desert each year. In Kazakhstan, site of the 1950s Soviet Virgin Lands project, half the cropland has been abandoned since 1980 as soil erosion lowered its productivity. This has dropped Kazakhstan's wheat harvest from roughly 13 million tons in 1980 to 8 million tons in 2000—an economic loss of $900 million per year.

The rangelands that supply much of the world's animal protein are also under excessive pressure. As human populations grow, so do livestock numbers. With 180 million people worldwide now trying to make a living raising 3.3 billion cattle, sheep, and goats, grasslands are simply collapsing under the demand. As a result of overstocking, grasslands are now deteriorating in much of Africa, the Middle East, Central Asia, the northern part of the Indian subcontinent, and much of northwestern China. Overgrazing is now the principal cause of desertification, the conversion of productive land into desert. In Africa, the annual loss of livestock production from the cumulative degradation of rangeland is estimated at $7 billion, a sum almost equal to the gross domestic product of Ethiopia.

In China, the combination of overplowing and overgrazing to satisfy rapidly expanding food needs is creating a dust bowl reminiscent of the U.S. Dust Bowl of the 1930s—but much larger. In a desperate effort to maintain grain self-sufficiency, China has plowed large areas of the northwest, much of it land that is highly erodible and should never have been plowed.

As the country's demand for livestock products—meat, leather, and wool—has climbed, so have the numbers of livestock, far exceeding those of the United States, a country with comparable grazing capacity. In addition to the direct damage from overplowing and overgrazing, the northern half of China is literally drying out as aquifers are depleted by overpumping.

These trends are converging to form some of the largest dust storms ever recorded. The huge dust plumes, traveling eastward, affect the cities of northeast China—blotting out the sun and reducing visibility. Eastward-moving winds also carry soil from China's northwest to the Korean Peninsula and Japan, where people regularly complain about the dust clouds that filter out the sunlight and blanket everything with dust. Unless China can reverse the overplowing and overgrazing trends that are creating the dust bowl, these trends could spur massive migration into the already crowded cities of the northeast and undermine the country's economic future.

The world is also running up a water deficit. The overpumping of aquifers, now commonplace on every continent, has led to falling water tables as pumping exceeds aquifer recharge from precipitation. Irrigation problems are as old as irrigation itself, but this is a new threat, one that has evolved over the last half-century with the advent of diesel pumps and powerful electrically driven pumps.

Water tables are falling under large expanses of the three leading food-producing countries—China, India, and the United States. Under the North China Plan, which accounts for 25 percent of China's grain harvest, the water table is falling by roughly 1.5 meters (5 feet) per year. The same thing is happening under much of India, particularly the Punjab, the country's breadbasket. In the United States, water tables are falling under the grain-growing states of the southern Great Plains, shrinking the irrigated area. . . .

Economic demands on forests are also excessive. Trees are being cut or burned faster than they can regenerate or be planted. Overharvesting is common in many regions, including Southeast Asia, West Africa, and the Brazilian Amazon. Worldwide, forests are shrinking by over 9 million hectacres per year, an area equal to Portugal.

In addition to being overharvested, some rainforests are now being destroyed by fire. Healthy rainforests do not burn, but logging and the settlements that occur along logging roads have fragmented and dried out tropical rainforests to the point where they often will burn easily, ignited by a lightning strike or set afire by opportunistic plantation owners, farmers, and ranchers desiring more land.

In the late summer of 1997, during an El Niño–induced drought, tropical rainforests in Borneo and Sumatra burned out of control. This conflagration made the news because the smoke drifting over hundreds of kilometers affected people not only in Indonesia but also in Malaysia, Singapore, Viet Nam, Thailand, and the Philippines. A reported 1,100 airline flights in the region were canceled due to the smoke. Motorists drove with their headlights on during the day, trying to make their way through the thick haze. Millions of people became physically sick.

Deforestation can be costly. Record flooding in the Yangtze River basin during the summer of 1998 drove 120 million people from their homes. Although initially referred to as a "natural disaster," the removal of 85 percent of the original tree cover in the basin had left little vegetative cover to hold the heavy rainfall.

Deforestation also diminishes the recycling of water inland, thus reducing rainfall in the interior of continents. When rain falls on a healthy stand of dense forest, roughly one fourth runs off, returning to the sea, while three fourths evaporates, either directly or through transpiration. When land is cleared for farming or grazing or is clearcut by loggers, this ratio is reversed—three fourths of the water returns to the sea and one fourth evaporates to be carried further inland. As deforestation progresses, nature's mechanism for watering the interior of large continents such as Africa and Asia is weakening.

Evidence of excessive human demands can also be seen in the oceans. As the human demand for animal protein has climbed over the last several decades, it has begun to exceed the sustainable yield of oceanic fisheries. As a result, two thirds of oceanic fisheries are now being fished at their sustainable yield or beyond. Many are collapsing. In 1992, the rich Newfoundland cod fishery that had been supplying fish for several centuries collapsed abruptly, costing 40,000 Canadians their jobs. Despite a subsequent ban on fishing, nearly a decade later the fishery has yet to recover.

Farther to the south, the U.S. Chesapeake Bay has experienced a similar decline. A century ago, this extraordinarily productive estuary produced over 100 million pounds of oysters a year. In 1999, it produced barely 3 million pounds. The Gulf of Thailand fishery has suffered a similarly dramatic decline: depleted by overfishing, the catch has dropped by over 80 percent since 1963, prompting the Thai Fisheries Department to ban fishing in large areas.

The world is also losing its biological diversity as plant and animal species are destroyed faster than new species evolve. This biological impoverishment of the earth is the result of habitat destruction, pollution, climate alteration, and hunting. With each update of its *Red List of Threatened Species,* the World Conservation Union (IUCN) shows us moving farther into a period of mass extinction. In the latest assessment, released in 2000, IUCN reports that one out of eight of the world's 9,946 bird species is in danger of extinction, as is one in four of the 4,763 mammal species and nearly one third of all 25,000 fish species.

Some countries have already suffered extensive losses. Australia, for example, has lost 16 of 140 mammal species over the last two centuries. In the Colorado River system of the southwestern United States, 29 of 50 native species of fish have disappeared partly because their river habitats were drained dry. Species lost cannot be regained. As a popular bumper sticker aptly points out, "Extinction is forever."

The economic benefits of the earth's diverse array of life are countless. They include not only the role of each species in maintaining the particular ecosystem of which it is a part, but economic roles as well, such as providing drugs and germplasm. As diversity diminishes, nature's pharmacy shrinks, depriving future generations of new discoveries.

Even as expanding economic activity has been creating biological deficits, it has been upsetting some of nature's basic balances in other areas: With the huge growth in burning of fossil fuels since 1950, carbon emissions have overwhelmed the capacity of the earth's ecosystem to fix carbon dioxide. The resulting rise in atmospheric CO_2 levels is widely believed by atmospheric scientists to be responsible for the earth's rising temperature. The 14 warmest years since recordkeeping began in 1866 have all occurred since 1980.

One consequence of higher temperatures is more energy driving storm systems. Three powerful winter storms in France in December 1999 destroyed millions of trees, some of which had been standing for centuries. Thousands of buildings were demolished. These storms, the most violent on record in France, wreaked more than $10 billion worth of damage—$170 for each French citizen. Nature was levying a tax of its own on fossil fuel burning.

In October 1998, Hurricane Mitch—one of the most powerful storms ever to come out of the Atlantic—moved through the Caribbean and stalled for several days on the coast of Central America. While there, it acted as a huge pump pulling water from the ocean and dropping it over the land. Parts of Honduras received 2 meters of rainfall within a few days. So powerful was this storm and so vast the amount of water it dropped on Central America that it altered the topography, converting mountains and hills into vast mud flows that simply inundated whole villages, claiming an estimated 10,000 lives. Four fifths of the crops were destroyed. The huge flow of rushing water removed all the top-soil in many areas, ensuring that this land will not be farmed again during our lifetimes.

The overall economic effect of the storm was devastating. The wholesale destruction of roads, bridges, buildings, and other infrastructure set back the development of Honduras and Nicaragua by decades. The estimated $8.5 billion worth of damage in the region approached the gross domestic product of both countries combined. . . .

Perhaps the most disturbing consequence of rising temperature is ice melting. Over the last 35 years, the ice covering the Arctic Sea has thinned by 42 percent. A study by two Norwegian scientists projects that within 50 years there will be no summer ice left in the Arctic Sea. The discovery of open water at the North Pole by an ice breaker cruise ship in mid-August 2000 stunned many in the scientific community.

This particular thawing does not affect sea level because the ice that is melting is already in the ocean. But the Greenland ice sheet is also starting to melt. Greenland is three times the size of Texas and the ice sheet is up to 2 kilometers (1.2 miles) thick in some areas. An article in *Science* notes that if the entire ice sheet were to melt, it would raise sea level by some 7 meters (23 feet), inundating the world's coastal cities and Asia's rice-growing river floodplains. Even a 1-meter rise would cover half of Bangladesh's riceland, dropping food production below the survival level for millions of people.

As the twenty-first century begins, humanity is being squeezed between deserts expanding outward and rising seas encroaching inward. Civilization is being forced to retreat by forces it has created. Even as population continues to grow, the habitable portion of the planet is shrinking.

Aside from climate change, the economic effects of environmental destruction and disruption have been mostly local—collapsing fisheries, abandoned cropland, and shrinking forests. But if local damage keeps accumulating, it will eventually affect global economic trends. In an increasingly integrated global economy, local ecosystem collapse can have global economic consequences.

Lessons From the Past

In *The Collapse of Complex Civilizations,* Joseph Tainter describes the decline of early civilizations and speculates about the causes. Was it because of the degradation of their environment, climate change, civil conflict, foreign invaders? Or, he asks, "is there some mysterious internal dynamic to the rise and fall of civilizations?"

As he ponders the contrast between civilizations that once flourished and the desolation of the sites they occupied, he quotes archeologist Robert McAdams, who described the site of the ancient Sumerian civilization located on the central floodplain of the Euphrates River, an empty, desolate area now outside the frontiers of cultivation. Adams described how the "tangled dunes, long disused canal levees, and the rubble-strewn mounds of former settlement contribute only low, featureless relief. Vegetation is sparse, and in many areas it is almost wholly absent. . . . Yet at one time, here lay the core, the heartland, the oldest urban, literate civilization in the world."

The early Sumerian civilization of the fourth millennium BC was remarkable, advancing far beyond any that had existed before. Its irrigation system, based on sophisticated engineering concepts, created a highly productive agriculture, one that enabled farmers to produce a surplus of food that supported the formation of the first cities. Managing the irrigation system required a complex social organization, one that may have been more sophisticated than any that had gone before. The Sumerians had the first cities and the first written language, the cuneiform script. They were probably as excited about it as we are today about the Internet.

It was an extraordinary civilization, but there was an environmental flaw in the design of the irrigation system, one that would eventually undermine its agricultural economy. Water from behind dams was diverted onto the land, raising crop yields. Some of the water was used by the crops, some evaporated into the atmosphere, and some percolated downward. Over time, this percolation slowly raised the water table until eventually it approached the surface of the land. When it reached a few feet from the surface it began to restrict the growth of deep-rooted crops. Somewhat later, as the water climbed to within inches of the surface, it began to evaporate into the atmosphere. As this happened, the salt in the water was left behind. Over time, the accumulation of salt reduced the productivity of the land. The environmental flaw was that there was no provision for draining the water that percolated downward.

The initial response of the Sumerians to declining wheat yields was to shift to barley, a more salt-tolerant plant. But eventually the yields of barley also declined. The resultant shrinkage of the food supply undermined the economic foundation of this great civilization. . . .

One unanswerable question about these earlier civilizations was whether they knew what was causing their decline. Did the Sumerians understand that rising salt content in the soil was reducing their wheat yields? If they knew, were they simply unable to muster the political support needed to lower water tables, just as we today are struggling unsuccessfully to lower carbon emissions?

Learning From China

The flow of startling information from China helps us understand why our economy cannot take us where we want to go. Not only is China the world's most populous country, with nearly 1.3 billion people, but since 1980 it has been the world's fastest-growing economy—expanding more than fourfold. In effect, China is telescoping history, demonstrating what happens when large numbers of poor people rapidly become more affluent.

As incomes have climbed in China, so has consumption. The Chinese have already caught up with Americans in pork consumption per person and they are now concentrating their energies on increasing beef production. Raising per capita beef consumption in China to that of the average American would take 49 million additional tons of beef. If all this were to come from putting cattle in feedlots, American-style, it would require 343 million tons of grain a year, an amount equal to the entire U.S. grain harvest.

In Japan, as population pressures on the land mounted during a comparable stage of its economic development, the Japanese turned to the sea for their animal protein. Last year, Japan consumed nearly 10 million tons of seafood. If China, with 10 times as many people as Japan, were to try to move down this same path, it would need 100 million tons of seafood—the entire world fish catch.

In 1994, the Chinese government decided that the country would develop an automobile- centered transportation system and that the automobile industry would be one of the engines of future economic growth. Beijing invited major automobile manufacturers, such as Volkswagen, General Motors, and Toyota, to invest in China. But if Beijing's goal of an auto-centered transportation system were to materialize and the Chinese were to have one or two cars in every garage and were to consume oil at the U.S. rate, China would need over 80 million barrels of oil a day—slightly more than the 74 million barrels per day the world now produces. To provide the required roads and parking lots, it would also need to pave some 16 million hectacres of land, and area equal to half the size of the 31 million hectacres of land currently used to produce the country's 132-million-ton annual harvest of rice, its leading food staple.

Similarly, consider paper. As China modernizes, its paper consumption is rising. If annual paper use in China of 35 kilograms per person were to climb to the U.S. level of 342 kilograms, China would need more paper than the world currently produces. There go the world's forests.

We are learning that the western industrial development model is not viable for China, simply because there are not enough resources for it to work. Global land and water resources are not sufficient to satisfy the growing grain needs in China if it continues along the current economic development path. Nor will the existing fossil-fuel-based energy economy supply the needed energy, simply because world oil production is not projected to rise much above current levels in the years ahead. Apart from the availability of oil, if carbon emissions per person in China ever reach the U.S. level, this alone would roughly double global emissions, accelerating the rise in the atmospheric CO_2 level.

China faces a formidable challenge in fashioning a development strategy simply because of the density of its population. Although it has almost exactly the same amount of land as the United States, most of China's 1.3 billion people live in a 1,500-kilometer strip on the eastern and southern coasts. Reaching the equivalent population density in the United States would require squeezing the entire U.S. population into the area east of the Mississippi and then multiplying it by four.

Interestingly, the adoption of the western economic model for China is being challenged from within. A group of prominent scientists, including many in the Chinese Academy of Sciences, wrote a white paper questioning the government's decision to develop an automobile-centered transportation system. They pointed out that China does not have enough land both to feed its people and to provide the roads, highways, and parking lots needed to accommodate the automobile. They also noted the heavy dependence on imported oil that would be required and the potential air pollution and traffic congestion that would result if they followed the U.S. path.

If the fossil-fuel-based, automobile-centered, throwaway economy will not work for China, then it will not work for India with its 1 billion people, or for the other 2 billion people in the developing world. In a world with a shared ecosystem and an increasingly integrated global economy, it will ultimately not work for the industrial economies either.

China is showing that the world cannot remain for long on the current economic path. It is underlining the urgency of restructuring the global economy, of building a new economy—an economy designed for the earth.

The Acceleration of History

. . . Until recently, population growth was so slow that it aroused little concern. But since 1950 we have added more people to world population than during the preceding 4 million years since our early ancestors first stood upright. Economic expansion in earlier times was similarly slow. To illustrate, growth in the world economy during the year 2000 exceeded that during the entire nineteenth century.

Throughout most of human history, the growth of population, the rise in income, and the development of new technologies were so slow as to be imperceptible during an individual life span. For example, the climb in grainland productivity from 1.1 tons per hectare in 1950 to 2.8 tons per hectacre in 2000 exceeds that during the 11,000 years from the beginning of agriculture until 1950.

The population growth of today has no precedent. Throughout most of our existence as a species, our numbers were measured in the thousands. Today, they measure in the billions. Our evolution has prepared us to deal with many threats, but perhaps not with the threat we pose to ourselves with the uncontrolled growth in our own numbers.

The world economy is growing even faster. The sevenfold growth in global output of goods and services since 1950 dwarfs anything in history. In the earlier stages of the Industrial Revolution, economic expansion rarely exceeded 1 or 2 percent a year. Developing countries that are industrializing now are doing so much faster than their predecessors simply because they do not have to invent the technologies needed by a modern industrial society, such as power plants, automobiles, and refrigerators. They can simply draw on the experiences and technology of those that preceded them. . . .

The pace of history is also accelerating as soaring human demands collide with the earth's natural limits. National political leaders are spending more time dealing with the consequences of the collisions described earlier—collapsing fisheries, falling water tables, food shortages, and increasingly destructive storms—along with a steadily swelling international flow of environmental refugees and the many other effects of overshooting natural limits. As change has accelerated, the situation has evolved from one where individuals and societies change only rarely to one where they change continuously. They are changing not only in response to growth itself, but also to the consequences of growth.

The central question is whether the accelerating change that is an integral part of the modern landscape is beginning to exceed the capacity of our social institutions to cope with change. Change is particularly difficult for institutions dealing with international or global issues that require a concerted, cooperative effort by many countries with contrasting cultures if they are to succeed. For example, sustaining the existing oceanic fish catch may be possible only if numerous agreements are reached among countries on the limits to fishing in individual oceanic fisheries. And can governments, working together at the global level, move fast enough to stabilize climate before it disrupts economic progress?

The issue is not whether we know what needs to be done or whether we have the technologies to do it. The issue is whether our social institutions are capable of bringing about the change in the time available. As H.G. Wells wrote in *The Outline of History*, "Human history becomes more and more a race between education and catastrophe."

The Option: Restructure or Decline

Whether we study the environmental undermining of earlier civilizations or look at how adoption of the western industrial model by China would affect the earth's ecosystem, it is evident that the existing industrial economic model cannot sustain economic progress. In our shortsighted efforts to sustain the global economy, as currently structured, we are depleting the earth's natural capital. We spend a lot of time worrying about our economic deficits, but it is the ecological deficits that threaten our long-term economic future. Economic deficits are what we borrow from each other; ecological deficits are what we take from future generations.

Herman Daly, the intellectual pioneer of the fast-growing field of ecological economics, notes that the world "has passed from an era in which manmade capital represented the limiting factor in economic development (an 'empty' world) to an era in which increasingly scarce natural capital has taken its place (a 'full' world)." When our numbers were small relative to the size of the planet, it was humanmade capital that was scarce. Natural capital was abundant. Now that has changed. As the human enterprise continues to expand, the products and services provided by the earth's ecosystem are increasingly scarce, and natural capital is fast becoming the limiting factor while humanmade capital is increasingly abundant.

Transforming our environmentally destructive economy into one that can sustain progress depends on a Copernican shift in our economic mindset, a recognition that the economy is part of the earth's ecosystem and can sustain progress only if it is restructured so that it is compatible with it. The preeminent challenge for our generation is to design an eco-economy, one that respects the principles of ecology. A redesigned economy can be integrated into the ecosystem in a way that will stabilize the relationship between the two, enabling economic progress to continue.

Unfortunately, present-day economics does not provide the conceptual framework needed to build such an economy. It will have to be designed with an understanding of basic ecological concepts such as sustainable yield, carrying capacity, nutrient cycles, the hydrological cycle, and the climate system. Designers must also know that natural systems provide not only goods, but also services—services that are often more valuable than the goods.

We know the kind of restructuring that is needed. In simplest terms, our fossil-fuel-based, automobile-centered, throwaway economy is not a viable model for the world. The alternative is a solar/hydrogen energy economy, an urban transport system that is centered on advanced-design public rail systems and that relies more on the bicycle and less on the automobile, and a comprehensive reuse/recycle economy. And we need to stabilize population as soon as possible.

How do we achieve this economic transformation when all economic decisionmakers—whether political leaders, corporate planners, investment bankers, or individual consumers—are guided by market signals, not the principles of ecological sustainability? How do we integrate ecological awareness into economic decisionmaking? Is it possible for all of us who are making economic decisions to "think like ecologists," to understand the ecological consequences of our decisions? The answer is probably not. It simply may not be possible.

But there may be another approach, a simpler way of achieving our goal. Everyone making economic decisions relies on market signals for guidance. The problem is that the market often fails to tell the ecological truth. It regularly underprices products and services by failing to incorporate the environmental costs of providing them.

Compare, for example, the cost of wind-generated electricity with that from a coal-fired power plant. The cost of the wind-generated electricity reflects the costs of manufacturing the turbine, installing it, maintaining it, and delivering the electricity to consumers. The cost of the coal-fired electricity includes building the power plant, mining the coal, transporting it to the power plant, and distributing the electricity to consumers. What it does not include is the cost of climate disruption caused by carbon emissions from coal burning— whether it be more destructive storms, melting ice caps, rising sea level, or record heat waves. Nor does it include the damage to freshwater lakes and forests from acid rain, or the health care costs of treating respiratory illnesses caused by air pollution. Thus the market price of coal-fired electricity greatly understates its cost to society.

One way to remedy this situation would be to have environmental scientists and economists work together to calculate the cost of climate disruption, acid rain, and air pollution. This figure could then be incorporated as a tax on coal-fired electricity that, when added to the current price, would give the full cost of coal use. This procedure, followed across the board, would mean that all economic decisionmakers—governments and individual consumers—would have the information needed to make more intelligent, ecologically responsible decisions.

We can now see how to restructure the global economy so as to restore stability between the economy and the ecosystem on which it rests. When I helped to pioneer the concept of environmentally sustainable economic development some 27 years ago, at the newly formed Worldwatch Institute, I had a broad sense of what the new economy would look like. Now we can see much more of the detail. We can build an eco-economy with existing technologies. It is economically feasible if we can get the market to tell us the full cost of the products and services that we buy.

The question is not how much will it cost to make this transformation but how much it will cost if we fail to do it. Øystein Dahle, retired Vice President of Esso for Norway and the North Sea, observes, "Socialism collapsed because it did not allow prices to tell the economic truth. Capitalism may collapse because it does not allow prices to tell the ecological truth."

NO

Lenny Bernstein

Climate Change and Ecosystems

Introduction

This report examines the basis for claims that projected human-induced climate change will have a severe impact on ecosystems. Past Marshall Institute Reports, most recently *Climate Science and Policy: Making the Connection,* have questioned the basis for projections that human activities will have a severe impact on the climate of the 21st century. This report does not repeat those arguments, but discusses the possible impact on ecosystems of different levels of climate change, as indicated by temperature rise, independent of time frame or cause.

There are many definitions of ecosystem. This report will use one developed by the Intergovernmental Panel on Climate Change (IPCC):

> A distinct system of interacting living organisms, together with their physical environment. The boundaries of what could be called an ecosystem are somewhat arbitrary, depending on the focus of interest or study. Thus the extent of an ecosystem may range from very small spatial scales to, ultimately, the entire Earth.

The ecosystems we discuss typically cover many thousand square miles, for example, the habitat of a bird species or a river's watershed.

Before considering specific claims of potential ecosystem damage, it is important to recognize that climate has always impacted on ecosystems and that human activities have been impacting on ecosystems for tens of thousands of years.

All of the plants and animals, including humans, that live on Earth are sensitive to climate and will respond to climate change. Climate is a key determinant of what crops can be grown in a particular area. Paleontologists argue that past climate changes were a factor, perhaps the major factor, in the extinction of the dinosaurs and many other species.

Human activities have had impacts on ecosystems since indigenous people, such as the Australian Aborigines, first used fire to clear underbrush to improve their hunting. Both primitive and modern people have caused the extinction of species, e.g. the moa in New Zealand and the passenger pigeon in North America.

The overwhelming majority of the Earth's ecosystems have been affected by human activities. Some of these activities have been planned, e.g., the conversion of forest to farmland. Others activities have been unplanned. For example, as documented in a recent issue of *Audubon*, the removal of wolves and other predators, and bans on hunting, have led to a dramatic increase in the U.S. deer population. This, in turn, has reduced the population of the plants deer like to eat, while increasing in the population of plants deer do not like to eat, thus changing the ecosystem.

Given the pervasive nature of human impacts, ecosystems can be divided into two categories:

- intensively-managed; farmland, managed forests and grasslands, and to a lesser extent, fisheries; and
- lightly-impacted; essentially unmanaged, natural wildlife areas and the oceans.

Concerns about intensely-managed ecosystems focus on the potential impact that climate change will have on the ability of these systems to produce the food and fiber they have traditionally supplied to the global economy. Concerns about lightly-impacted ecosystems focus on the potential for climate change to cause widespread species extinction.

This report examines the question: How sensitive are intensively-managed and lightly-impacted ecosystems to different levels of climate change? In the course of answering this question, it is necessary to consider the relative importance of climate change compared with other human impacts, such as habitat disruption and local or regional pollution, in determining the rate of species extinction.

Three climate changes are discussed in this report: higher atmospheric concentrations of CO_2, warmer temperatures, and increased precipitation. All IPCC projections are for higher CO_2. Based on projection of higher CO_2, climate models project increases in temperature for all parts of the world. They also project increases in average precipitation, but are less consistent in the projections of the regional distribution of precipitation. Most areas of the world are projected to get more precipitation than they now do, a few are projected to get less.

The IPCC Third Assessment Report includes projections of precipitation based on nine climate models using two emissions scenarios: high emissions and low emissions. The results were evaluated for 23 regions of the world, and for two seasons: winter and summer. This resulted in 92 comparisons (23 regions x 2 emissions scenarios x 2 seasons). IPCC reported that in a third (32) of the comparisons, the models gave inconsistent results. In 9 other comparisons they showed no significant change in precipitation. In 40 comparisons, they showed increases in precipitation, and in 11 comparisons they showed decreases. While these comparisons represent the best available modeling results, they hide large differences in the predictions of individual models. As the IPCC reports:

> The magnitude of regional precipitation changes varies considerably amongst models, with the typical range being around 0 to 50% where the direction of change is strongly indicated and around -30 to +30% where it is not.

Given the physical basis for assuming a wetter world, and the preponderance of modeling results, we will assume that most ecosystems will experience wetter conditions in the future.

Intensively-Managed Ecosystems

Society depends on ecosystems for a wide range of goods. Most of the food we eat, the wood we use for construction, and the natural fibers we use for clothing, are products of intensively-managed ecosystems. We also depend on both intensively-managed and lightly-impacted ecosystems for a wide variety of services including water purification and recreational opportunities. Since these ecosystems are sensitive to climate change, it is reasonable to ask whether changes in climate will diminish the ability of ecosystems to continue supplying these goods and services. The debate on the validity of this concern centers on the ability of human society to adapt intensively-managed ecosystems to climate change.

As climate changes, which it has and will in the future, human society will have to adapt to that change; adaptation is a necessity, not an option. But humanity's need to adapt to climate change is not a new phenomena, and both sides of the debate are succinctly captured by Brian Fagan, Professor of Archeology at the University of California, Santa Barbara, in his book, *The Little Ice Age:*

> Humanity has been at the mercy of climate change for its entire existence. Infinitely ingenious, we have lived through eight, perhaps nine, glacial episodes in the past 730,000 years. Our ancestors adapted to the universal but irregular global warming since the end of the Ice Age with dazzling opportunism. They developed strategies for surviving harsh drought cycles, decades of heavy rainfall or unaccustomed cold; adopted agriculture and stock-raising, which revolutionized human life; founded the world's first preindustrial civilization in Egypt, Mesopotamia, and the Americas. The price of sudden climate change, in famine, disease, and suffering, was often high.

Optimists point to the infinite ingenuity and dazzling opportunism Prof. Fagan refers to as evidence that humanity will be able to respond to any future climate change. Pessimists point to the high human costs of past climate changes. Which of these will shape the future?

The majority of studies of the impacts of climate change on intensively-managed ecosystems have the following characteristics:

- they assume today's technology with either no or limited adaptation;
- they use the impacts of severe weather events as predictors of the impacts of climate change; and
- they invariably show high negative impacts.

These studies are misleading. Severe weather events occur in the short-term, offering no opportunity for adaptation. But climate is the long-term average of weather, and climate change, whether natural or human-induced, will take decades to centuries to occur. During that time human society will continue to benefit from advances in knowledge and technology, and hence become more capable of adapting to different climate conditions.

The benefits of adaptation have been clearly demonstrated in the evolution of thinking about the potential impacts of climate change on agriculture. Early studies did not consider adaptation. They assumed no change in the behavior of farmers in response to changing climate. This was known as the "dumb farmer" hypothesis, and was at odds with all of human experience, which indicates that farmers and others whose livelihood is sensitive to climate are very attuned to climate change and adapt to it on a continuous basis.

Later studies considered adaptation by the individual farmer, i.e., planting species that were better matched to climate conditions. For example, wheat farmers have a wide variety of species to choose from, some of which are better adapted than others to the warmer, wetter conditions that are projected by climate models. Choosing these better adapted species would minimize the potential adverse impacts of climate change, and in many cases provide a net benefit. Still more sophisticated studies consider both farmer adaptation and marketplace adaptation. If climate changed sufficiently, wheat farmers might become corn farmers, and corn farmers might grow fruit and vegetables. Using a "smart farmer" assumption led to very different results, often showing that climate change yielded net benefits.

Benefits of Adaptation

The limited number of studies which take growth in adaptive capacity into account often show benefits for climate change. One such study by Adams *et al.* considers the impacts of climate change on U.S. agriculture in 2060, taking into account projected changes in the agricultural market to that time and allowing for the full range of adaptation. The authors considered the effects of changes in temperature, precipitation and atmospheric carbon dioxide (CO_2) content on agricultural yields. Photosynthesis, the process by which atmospheric CO_2 and water vapor are converted into plant matter, is enhanced by higher levels of atmospheric CO_2, though plants respond to increased CO_2 at different rates.

Adams, *et al.* looked at a series of cases in which atmospheric CO_2 concentration was increased from its 1999 level of about 365 ppm to 530 ppm, temperature increased by as much as $5°C$, and precipitation increased by as much as 15%. These climate changes are larger than those typically projected by climate models for 2060. Farmers were allowed to adapt by either optimizing their current crops or by switching crops.

The authors found that for all cases studied, the U.S. benefited from improvements in the agricultural sector, with the benefits being split between consumers, who enjoyed lower food prices because of higher agricultural productivity, and the farmers who benefited from higher income. Not all cases resulted in benefits to both sides, nor were the benefits spread equally across all agricultural areas in the country, but the net effect for the U.S. economy was positive.

The physical basis for these benefits is fairly easy to understand. The benefits of higher CO_2 concentration have already been discussed. Warmer climates mean longer growing seasons and less chance of crop damage from frost. Much of the U.S. agricultural area suffers from periodic droughts, so increased precipitation also provides benefits.

A similar study by [Brent L.] Sohngen and [Robert] Mendelsohn for the U.S. timber industry projects benefits under the same range of climate change conditions. The authors conclude:

> Overall, the timber market is likely to adapt to climate change, thereby ameliorating the potential problem associated with ecological change. This work shows how harvest schedules will adjust from region to region and from moment to moment so as to use timber stocks efficiently during the transition period (to equilibrium climate change). These adjustments occur regardless of the specific climate and ecological scenario. This chapter also shows how timberland owners will adjust their replanting behavior by responding to future ecological and economic conditions. Despite the apparent severity of some ecological effects, market behavior offsets the potential damages through adaptation.

Overall, Mendelsohn and Neumann project that the benefits to managed ecosystems would result in a modest (+0.2%) benefit to the U.S. economy in 2060 for their moderate climate change case (+2.5 °C, +7% precipitation). This result was generalized by the IPCC. In assessing these results, the IPCC concluded that there was medium confidence that small increases in temperature would have a net positive effect on the economies of developed nations.

The IPCC defines "small increases in temperature," as 0–2 °C. This literature also indicates that most, if not all, of the benefit comes from gains in intensively-managed ecosystems.

While the IPCC agrees that moderate climate change would be beneficial to managed ecosystems in the developed world, it raises two concerns: first, that more than 2 °C warming would have adverse effects, even in the developed world, and second, that even small amounts of climate change would have adverse effects in the developing world. Again, much of the basis for these concerns is the projected impact of climate change on intensely-managed ecosystems. The [following] paragraphs examine the validity of these concerns.

The basis for the IPCC's concerns about the inability of intensively-managed ecosystems to adapt to large amounts of climate change appears to lie in the fact that the studies collected by Mendelsohn and Neumann, and other similar exercises, show declining benefits at large amounts of climate change. The extent to which these results are a function of model limitation or represent real limitations in the ability of intensively-managed ecosystems to adapt is unknown. As Mendelsohn and Neumann state:

> . . . it is important to recognize the significant limitations involved in projecting climate, biophysical, and economic conditions over the next century. Although this book seeks to improve the arsenal of methodologies to measure the economic impact of climate change, none of the existing methods are perfect replicas of the experience that society will face if climate gradually warms over the next century.

. . . For the US, which has been subjected to more analysis than any other part of the world, the benefits extend out to double the temperature level considered by the IPCC (5°C vs. 2.5°C). More scientific study and modeling will be needed to determine the extent to which this result can be generalized to other countries and regions. However, there is clearly room for more optimism than exhibited by the IPCC.

Adaptation in the Developing World

The question of whether adaptation can provide benefits for intensively-managed ecosystems in the developing world is more complex. The benefits of higher CO_2 concentration are equally applicable in developed and developing countries. However, most developing countries are in the tropics, and would see no benefit, but potential adverse effects, from rising temperature. The IPCC points out many cases in which extremely high temperatures will inhibit critical stages of plant growth for existing crop species. These studies often do not consider the potential for developing more heat resistant crops or opportunities for adaptation through crop switching. Also, it should be noted that climate models typically project less than global average warming in the tropics.

In many developing countries, the growing season is 365 days of the year and frost does not exist. Thus longer growing season and less potential frost damage are not considerations. Some of these countries also have generous rainfall, so additional rainfall will provide little additional benefit. Others are either arid or desert countries, in which case, additional rainfall is a major benefit. No single description fits all cases.

The IPCC recognizes that there is considerable opportunity for the agriculture and forestry sectors to adapt to climate change, and that there is evidence that they have done so in the past. But it then raises concerns that the poorest and most vulnerable countries will not have the ability to adapt. This conclusion overlooks two factors.

First, there is little reason to believe that developing nations cannot take advantage of improvements in agricultural technology and use them to adapt to any changes in climate. Some of the poorest countries in the world were the ones that benefited most in the 1950s and '60s from adopting the suite of agricultural technologies (improved plant varieties, increased used of fertilizer and irrigation) known as the "Green Revolution," which dramatically raised food production in much of the developing world. Countries with relatively stable governments benefited most. Democratic countries, such as India, were able to take quick advantage of these developments, but even dictatorships, such as Syria, which became self-sufficient in grain in 1991, saw improvements in food production. In today's world, despite a growing population, famine is a problem only in those countries which are at war or have unstable governments. . . .

Second, CO_2 emissions are the result of economic activity, which generates wealth, which in turn results in adaptive capacity. Since projected climate change and the ability to adapt to it are both the result of economic activity, we need to consider the future level of economic activity in developing nations.

The IPCC Special Report on Emissions Scenarios (SRES), published in 2000, provides a wide range of scenarios of the changes in CO_2 emissions and per capita income for both developed and developing nations from 1990 to 2100. As the IPCC is careful to point out, scenarios are not predictions, they are alternate images of how the future might unfold. This report does not address the analytical basis for these scenarios or whether any of them are likely. They are used solely as a basis for assessing the potential growth in the adaptive capacity of developing nations.

The IPCC scenarios all show a faster rate of economic growth in developing nations than in developed nations, resulting in a narrowing of the economic gap between the developed and developing worlds. This higher rate of economic growth also results in developing nations emitting a higher fraction of the world's CO_2 emissions in 2100 than they currently do. The emissions scenarios that lead to the highest level of projected temperature rise to 2100 are the scenarios that have the highest level of economic growth in the developing world.

The SRES does not give country-by-county projections but divides the world into four regions:

1. The countries that were OECD members in 1990,
2. Russia and Eastern Europe,
3. Asia, and
4. Africa and Latin America.

The first two regions are developed nations, the last two, the developing nations.

The SRES authors developed 40 baseline scenarios; none of these scenarios include overt actions to control greenhouse gas emissions. . . .

[Table 1] summarizes the SRES projections for population, total CO_2 emissions, CO_2 emissions per capita, and GDP [gross domestic product] per capita for 1990 and 2100 for the illustrative scenarios with the highest (A1FI) and lowest (B1) global CO_2 emissions.

What the numbers in Table 1 show is a dramatic narrowing of current differences between developed and developing nation per capita CO_2 emissions and GDP during the 21st century. Even in the IPCC's lowest economic growth illustrative scenario, A2 (not shown), developing nation GDP per capita increases more than ten-fold (2.3%/yr.) during the 21st century, and the ratio of developed nation to developing nation GDP per capita decreases to 4.2. It is reasonable to assume that this growth in the wealth of developing nations will be accompanied by a growth in their ability to adapt food production to climate variability and change. At a minimum, the adaptive capacity of developing nations should be roughly equivalent to that of developed nations today. In many cases it should exceed that level.

Pessimists argue that these broad averages hide pockets of poverty that will be resistant to economic growth. The evidence is overwhelming that poverty is caused by government corruption and the lack of rule of law, property rights and individual freedom. These problems dwarf the potential impacts

Table 1

SRES Projections: CO$_2$ Emissions and GDP per Capita

	1990	2100 Highest Emissions	2100 Lowest Emissions
Population, Billions			
Developed Nations	1.3	1.4	1.4
Developing Nations	4.0	5.7	5.7
Total CO$_2$ Emissions (GtC)*			
Developed Nations	4.1	10.0	1.1
Developing Nations	3.1	18.2	3.1
% Developing Nations	43	65	74
CO$_2$ per Capita (Tonnes C)			
Developed Nations	3.2	7.1	0.79
Developing Nations	0.78	3.2	0.54
Ratio	4.1	2.2	1.5
GDP per Capita (1990 US$)			
Developed Nations	13,800	109,500	71,700
Developing Nations	850	69,800	40,000
Ratio	16.1	1.6	1.8

*GtC = billion metric tonnes carbon

of climate change and need to be addressed on an urgent basis, independent of concerns about potential climate change.

Lightly-Impacted Ecosystems

. . . Before discussing the potential impact of climate change on species extinction, we will consider the extent to which humans are and have been responsible for the extinction of other species. The most dramatic and well-known cases involve over-hunting, which led to the extinction of such species as the dodo, moa, and passenger pigeon, and almost led to the extinction of the American buffalo. But, habitat destruction has also been a major cause of species extinction. Conversion of natural habitats to intensive-managed farms and forests has caused the extinction of both plant and animal species.

More recently, the introduction of invasive species, non-native plants or animals that have no natural enemies, has been another factor contributing to the stress on endangered species. Some of these species have been purposely introduced (e.g. kudzu, which was introduced in the southeastern U.S. for erosion control), while the introduction of others was inadvertent (e.g. zebra mussels, which entered the Great Lakes in the ballast water of ships).

While there is no debate that humans have been, and continue to be, responsible for the extinction of some species, there is an active debate as to how serious the problem is. We do not know how many species there are, nor what the background rate of species extinction is, nor how many species are becoming extinct as the result of human activities.

The current best estimate of the number of species on the Earth is between 10 and 80 million, of which only some 1.6 million have been identified. Such a wide range indicates deficiencies in the current estimating methodologies. Systematic studies invariably discover new species, even in intensively studied areas. For example, in 1998, about 12,000 species were known to exist in the Great Smoky Mountains National Park. In that year, the All Taxa (Species) Biodiversity Inventory project was started with the goal of raising the total number of species identified in the park to 100,000. Thus far, 1,480 new species have been identified in the park, 144 of which are new to science.

Background rates of extinction are similarly unknown. Fossil records indicate massive extinctions in the past, the most famous being the extinction of the dinosaurs 65,000,000 years ago. This extinction is now believed to have been caused when a massive asteroid hit the Earth creating a large, sudden change in climate. Fossil records also indicate that most of the species that existed over the Earth's history are now extinct. However, there is no accepted estimate for the number of species that would become extinct as the result of natural evolutionary processes during a "normal" year.

Estimates of the number of species becoming extinct because of human activities vary widely. One widely-quoted number is 40,000 per year, but as has been documented by Bjorn Lomborg in his book *The Skeptical Environmentalist*, this number can be traced to a speculation by Norman Myers, a well known environmentalist. Even critics of Lomborg's approach, such as Thomas Lovejoy, Chief Biodiversity Advisor to the President of the World Bank and a former Director of the World Wildlife Fund—US, agree that Myers provided no basis for his estimate. At the other extreme of the estimates for human-induced species extinction, documentary evidence exists for the extinction of only 1,033 species since 1600. Even those who believe that humans are not causing large-scale species extinction agree that this number is highly likely to be low, since undocumented extinctions as the result of human activities are certain to have occurred. . . .

Climate Change and Species Extinction

The starting point for concerns about the potential impacts of climate change on endangered species is indisputable: all plants and animals living on the Earth are sensitive to climate. All, with the possible exception of humans, have a preferred climate. These preferences are often shown as a plot of the type of ecosystem that will be prevalent as a function of average temperature and rainfall. Any change in climate will put stress on some plant or animal species. However, translating these generalities into threats to specific species is far from easy. The IPCC summarizes the problems involved as follows:

> Modeling changes in biodiversity in response to climate change presents some significant challenges. It requires projections of climate change at high spatial and temporal resolution and often depends on the balance between variables that are poorly handled by climate models (e.g., local pre-

cipitation and evaporative demand). It also requires an understanding of how species interact with each other and how these interactions affect the communities and ecosystems of which they are a part. In addition, the focus of attention in the results is often particular species that may be rare or show unusual biological behavior.

To address these knowledge gaps, the IPCC calls for:

Improvement of regional scale models coupled with transient ecosystem models that deal with multiple pressures with appropriate spatial and temporal resolution and include spatial interactions between ecosystems within landscapes.

The term "landscape" refers to "groups of ecosystems (e.g., forests, rivers, lakes, etc.) that form a visible entity to humans.

Elsewhere the IPCC documents the huge difficulties involved in developing regional climate models. The challenges in developing transient ecosystem models are just as large, and coupling the two would be still another difficult task. Yet, the IPCC is correct in its conclusion that this is what would be needed for a predictive model of the effect of climate change on plant and animal species. Faced with the difficulty of developing predictive models and quantitative assessment tools, any discussion of the impacts of climate change on species is limited to qualitative statements. . . .

Any discussion of the role of climate change in future rates of species extinction must also consider the relative threats posed by climate change vs. habitat disruption and other human activities. Given the high level of uncertainty about both current and future rates of species extinction, we can only speculate about the relative importance of climate change vs. habitat disruption or other human activities.

One study has attempted such speculation and concluded that the dominant factors determining biodiversity decline will be climate change in polar regions and land-use change (habitat disruption) in the tropics. Temperate ecosystems were estimated to experience the least biodiversity change because major land-use changes have already occurred. There are far more plant and animal species, and apparently a far higher number of species becoming extinct, in the tropics than in polar regions. Therefore on a global basis, habitat disruption will continue to be the major impact on animal and plant species.

Not all of the impacts on ecosystems of projected climate change will be negative. As in the case of agriculture, a warmer, wetter, higher CO_2 world will be beneficial for uncultivated plants. Global ecosystem models project higher net biomass production, and observations of a variety of tree species indicate that they are already responding to higher atmospheric concentrations of CO_2 and higher temperatures with increased growth rates. Warmer, wetter conditions, and increased biomass production, also could be expected to benefit some animal species.

Animal and Plant Responses to Climate Change

There is agreement among experts that animals that are capable of moving will attempt to migrate in response to climate change. The movements of commercially important species, such as cod, in response to changes in ocean temperature, have been documented for centuries. More recent studies show that a variety of animal species have moved in response to the warming of the 20th century.

Individual plants cannot migrate, but plant species can and do migrate in response to changes in climate. All plants have seed dispersal mechanisms and therefore are constantly trying to establish seedlings in new areas. Seedlings thrive in a more desirable climate, but fail in a less desirable climate, moving the range of the plant as climate changes. The total change in range can be dramatic. Fossil evidence indicate that since the end of the last Ice Age, the balsam fir migrated from the southeastern U.S. to northern Canada, while the black spruce migrated from the central plains to Alaska.

While it is agreed that plants and animals could migrate in response to climate change, at least four further concerns are raised about the likelihood that this will occur to a sufficient degree to prevent large scale species extinction:

1. human activities, particularly habitat disruption, will block potential migration routes;
2. even if they can migrate, the members of a given ecosystem will migrate at different rates leading to imbalances that will result in species extinctions;
3. plants may not be able to migrate fast enough to keep up with projected rates of climate change; and
4. plants and animals that live in restricted niches, e.g., near mountain tops, will have no place to migrate.

These concerns assume no human intervention to help wild species to adapt to climate change. In light of the growing and successful effort to reintroduce species such as beaver and wolf to their former habitats, to replant native plants, and to remove invasive plant species, this assumption is overly conservative.

Can Species Migrate Given Habitat Disruption and Other Human Activities?

Human activities have fragmented the areas in which many plants and animals can thrive. The remaining habitats are often pictured as "islands," which climate change could make unattractive to the species that live there. Migration to other "islands" could be difficult or impossible because the paths for that migration would be blocked by farms, cities, etc. However, recent studies raise questions about this conceptual model. Many species have been shown to either make use of fairly limited habitats or use multiple habitats to provide the area they need.

A recent *New York Times* article quoted Dr. John Wiens, a professor of ecology at Colorado State University, as follows:

> "We need to shift our thinking away from isolated areas in the midst of inhospitable human development," he said. "They're not oceanic islands." Only if biologists think of fragments in the context of an overall landscape, he went on, can they help manage, conserve and restore these habitats.

The *New York Times* article went on to cite the work of Dr. Diane Debinski, a professor of animal ecology at Iowa State University. She found that even "habitat sensitive" species, which tend to stay in the interior of a particular "island," were present in greater number when those habitats were replicated in an attempt to provide a larger area of suitable habitat for these species. These results show that species are able to make use of all available suitable habitats, even if they are fragmented.

As noted above, habitat disruption is projected to be the largest contributor to human-induced species extinction in the 21st century. The steps that society will need to take to reverse this trend should also make it possible for plant and animal species to migrate in face of whatever climate change may occur in the future. . . .

Can Plants Migrate Fast Enough?

The IPCC summarizes the knowledge about the rate of plant species migration as follows:

> Many studies of past changes have estimated natural rates of migration of trees ranging from 40 to 500 meters per year. . . . Gear and Huntly calculated from several sites in Britain migration rates of Scot's pine of only 40–80 meters per year. However, for other species, such as white spruce, much faster dispersal rates of 1–2 kilometers per year have also been reported. It is not always clear whether observed past rates were maximal rates of migration or whether they were limited by the rate at which the climate changed.

The IPCC concludes that these rates of migration are slower than the 1.5–5.5 kilometers per year that trees would have to migrate to keep up with projected rates of warming. However, this analysis assumes that a tree's habitat is a fixed point. Viable trees have ranges that cover many kilometers. Climate change might reduce that range in the short-term, but climate change alone should not lead to significant rates of extinction. Adaptation, for example, by transplanting tree species, could be beneficial in speeding migration.

Can Species With Already Limited Habitats Survive?

If climate warms, the migration path for plants and animals that live on mountains will be upward. This option is limited, since the plant or animal will soon run out of mountain. Since soil conditions typically become poorer with increasing altitude, other factors may limit migration long before the top of the mountain is reached. For species that have very limited habitats, in the extreme, a single mountain, this could lead to extinction. No doubt some of the past climate-related extinctions occurred for this reason. However, most alpine species have broader habitats than a single mountain and would survive, albeit with a changed habitat.

Summary: Can Plants and Animals Adapt to Climate Change?

The answer to this question has to be yes, since plants and animals have been adapting to climate change for billions of years. However, not all plant and animal species will be successful in adapting. If biologists are correct that natural climate change has been a major factor in past species extinctions, any change in climate, whether natural or human-induced, will increase the risk that some marginal species will become extinct.

Despite the concern about climate change, habitat disruption will continue to be the largest threat posed by human activities to the survival of plant and animal species. Many innovative programs are being undertaken to help plants and animals counter the adverse effects of habitat disruption, and these programs will help make these species more resilient to climate change. However, understanding of ecosystem interactions and the potential impacts of climate change on those interactions is simply inadequate.

Migration is the major response that plants and animals can make to climate change. Many concerns have been raised about the ability of plants and animals to migrate given habitat disruption, scenarios involving high rates of climate change during the 21st century, etc. Societal efforts to counter adverse effects by relocating endangered plant and animal species to more favorable habitats could reduce the impact of these changes. . . .

Conclusions

The destruction of ecosystems and species extinction as a consequence of projected climate change have been reported widely by the media and drive much of the perception of the global warming debate. This study examined available scientific evidence to fairly evaluate the claim that anticipated changes in the Earth's climate will result in unacceptable ecosystem impacts.

There is no question that ecosystems are sensitive to climate change and that any significant change is likely to have detrimental consequences for some ecosystems and some species. However, the scope of these consequences is limited by the ability to adapt to an evolving climate.

With continued adaptation, intensively-managed ecosystems, such [as] farms and commercial forests, can benefit from the levels of climate change projected by the IPCC for the 21st century. Developed countries already have the necessary adaptive capacity, and developing countries will acquire the necessary adaptive capacity as their wealth increases.

Ecosystems, such as wildlife areas, which are currently lightly impacted by human activities, would also benefit from adaptation, but the understanding necessary to plan that adaptation is currently inadequate.

To address these questions in a manner that will provide information and analysis needed to evaluate risks and consequences, decision makers need better tools and better information. These include better models, more robust data collection, and better techniques for estimating species and effects on them.

POSTSCRIPT

Are the Costs of Global Warming Too High to Ignore?

It is reasonable to ask how the scientific community attempts to measure changes in the Earth's surface temperature. Certainly, written records only shed light on a tiny fraction of the Earth's long history, and even in the record books that we do have, written temperature records of more than 100 years ago are not available for large parts of the world.

In place of that written history the scientific community has turned to the physical records left by climatic changes. These appear in the growth rates of trees, sea sediment bore holes, pollen counts, the remains of coral colonies, ice cores, and mountain glacier deposits. They tell us that our world has undergone remarkable changes in the 10,000 years since the end of the last major ice age, which closed the Pleistocene epoch. It is important to examine two major climatic disturbances, which appear in more recent times—the past 1,000 years. Scientists call one of these disturbances the "Little Ice Age," which occurred approximately 1300–1900 A.D. The other anomaly occurred around 1000–1300 A.D. This relatively mild climatic period is called the Medieval Warm Period. It is remarkable in that in some regions radical increases in temperatures occurred. Some suggest that it may help explain the population explosion during the medieval period in Europe. This warm weather may also help explain why this period was marked by the construction of many European cathedrals. See H. H. Lamb, *Climate, History and the Modern World,* 2d ed. (Routledge, 1995).

An apparent conclusion is that global warming is not as clear-cut as some suggest. Simply because we can measure an increase in surface temperatures over a significant period of time may not in and of itself mean that we are experiencing global warming that can be traced to human activity. Rather, this warming may be the natural course of events—events that the world has experienced repeatedly over its long history. For more on that view, read Patrick J. Michaels and Robert Balling, Jr., *Satanic Gases: Clearing the Air About Global Warming* (Cato Institute, 2000). In it, the authors argue that those who warn of global warming have blown the issue all out of proportion and in the process have ignored all the evidence that suggests the contrary.

The other side is not mute on this issue. Indeed, there are many Web sites devoted to the issue of global warming. To read about the Kyoto Protocol, see http://unfccc.int/resource/convkp.html. Alternatively, visit the United Nations Industrial Development Organization's (UNIDO) Web site at http://www.unido.org/doc/3941. For a scholarly, balanced view, turn to Warwick J. McKibbin and Peter Wilcoxen's *Climate Change Policy After Kyoto: A Blueprint for a Realistic Approach* (Brookings Institution Press, 2002.)

ISSUE 16

Should Pollution Be Put to the Market Test?

YES: Alan S. Blinder, from *Hard Heads, Soft Hearts: Tough-Minded Economics for a Just Society* (Addison-Wesley, 1987)

NO: Frank Ackerman and Kevin Gallagher, from "Getting the Prices Wrong: The Limits of Market-Based Environmental Policy," Global Development and Environment Institute Working Paper 00-05 (October 2000)

ISSUE SUMMARY

YES: Alan S. Blinder, a former member of the Board of Governors of the Federal Reserve System, urges policymakers to use the energy of the market to solve America's environmental problems.

NO: Economist Frank Ackerman and environmental policy analyst Kevin Gallagher contend that there is an important distinction between using market forces as a "tool" and using competitive markets as a "blueprint" to solve environmental problems. They argue that environmental goals should be set through the use of "public deliberation" and that at times those goals "may have no inherent relationship to the market."

$\mathbf{M}$arkets sometimes fail. That is, markets sometimes do not automatically yield optimum, economically efficient answers. This is because prices sometimes do not reflect the true social costs and benefits of consumption and production. The culprit here is the presence of externalities. Externalities are spillover effects that impact third parties who had no voice in the determination of an economic decision.

If, for example, my friend and coeditor Frank J. Bonello decided to "cut a few corners" to hold down the costs of his commercially produced banana cream pies, he might well create a *negative externality* for his neighbors. That is, if in the dark of night, Bonello slipped to the back of his property and dumped his banana skins, egg shells, and other waste products into the St. Joe River, which borders his property, part of the cost of producing banana cream pies would be borne by those who live downstream from the Bonello residence. Since the full costs of production are not borne by Bonello, he can set a competitively attractive price and sell many more pies than his competitors, whom we assume must pay to have their waste products carted away.

If Bonello is not forced to internalize the negative externality associated with his production process, the price attached to his pies gives an improper market signal with regard to the true scarcity of resources. In brief, because Bonello's pies are cheaper than his competitors', demanders will flock to his doorstep to demand more and more of his pies, unknowingly causing him to dump more and more negative externalities on his neighbors downstream.

In this case, as in other cases of firms casting off negative externalities, the public sector may have to intervene and mandate that these externalities be internalized. This is not always an easy task, however. Two difficult questions must be answered: (1) Who caused the external effect? Was it only Bonello's banana cream pie production? and (2) Who bore the costs of the negative externality, and what are their losses? These questions require detective work. We must not only identify the source of the pollution, but we must also identify the people who have been negatively affected by its presence and determine their "rights" in this situation. Once this has been achieved, the difficult task of evaluating and measuring the negative effects must be undertaken.

Even if this can be successfully negotiated, one last set of questions remains: What alternative methods can be used to force firms to internalize their externalities, and which of these methods are socially acceptable and economically efficient? This is the subject of the debate that follows.

Alan S. Blinder warns about the limitations inherent in a market solution to the pollution problem; however, he still strongly advocates using the market to rid the world of the harmful effects of pollution. Frank Ackerman and Kevin Gallagher, on the other hand, contend that there are clear limits to the effectiveness of private market solutions. They maintain that, many times, old-fashioned regulations can be even more effective.

Alan S. Blinder

 **YES**

Cleaning Up the Environment: Sometimes Cheaper Is Better

We cannot give anyone the option of polluting for a fee.

—Senator Edmund Muskie
(in Congress, 1971)

In the 1960s, satirist Tom Lehrer wrote a hilarious song warning visitors to American cities not to drink the water or breathe the air. Now, after the passage of more than two decades and the expenditure of hundreds of billions of dollars, such warnings are less appropriate—at least on most days! Although the data base on which their estimates rest is shaky, the Environmental Protection Agency (EPA) estimates that the volume of particulate matter suspended in the air (things like smoke and dust particles) fell by half between 1973 and 1983. During the same decade, the volume of sulfur dioxide emissions declined 27 percent and lead emissions declined a stunning 77 percent. Estimated concentrations of other air pollutants also declined. Though we still have some way to go, there is good reason to believe that our air is cleaner and more healthful than it was in the early 1970s. While the evidence for improved average water quality is less clear (pardon the pun), there have at least been spectacular successes in certain rivers and lakes.

All this progress would seem to be cause for celebration. But economists are frowning—and not because they do not prize cleaner air and water, but rather because our current policies make environmental protection far too costly. America can achieve its present levels of air and water quality at far lower cost, economists insist. The nation is, in effect, shopping for cleaner air and water in a high-priced store when a discount house is just around the corner. Being natural cheapskates, economists find this extravagance disconcerting. Besides, if we shopped in the discount store, we would probably buy a higher-quality environment than we do now. . . .

Is Pollution an Economic Problem?

. . . Nothing in this discussion . . . implies that the appropriate level of environmental quality is a matter for the free market to determine. On the contrary, the market mechanism is ill suited to the task; if left to its own devices, it will certainly produce excessive environmental degradation. Why? Because users of clean air and water, unlike users of oil and steel, are not normally made to pay for the product.

Consider a power plant that uses coal, labor, and other inputs to produce electricity. It buys all these items on markets, paying market prices. But the plant also spews soot, sulfur dioxide, and a variety of other undesirables into the air. In a real sense, it "uses up" clean air—one of those economic goods which people enjoy—without paying a penny. Naturally, such a plant will be sparing in its use of coal and labor, for which it pays, but extravagant in its use of clean air, which is offered for free.

That, in a nutshell, is why the market fails to safeguard the environment. When items of great value, like clean air and water, are offered free of charge it is unsurprising that they are overused, leaving society with a dirtier and less healthful environment than it should have.

The analysis of why the market fails suggests the remedy that economists have advocated for decades: charge polluters for the value of the clean air or water they now take for free. That will succeed where the market fails because an appropriate fee or tax per unit of emissions will, in effect, put the right price tag on clean air and water—just as the market now puts the right price tag on oil and steel. Once our precious air and water resources are priced correctly, polluters will husband them as carefully as they now husband coal, labor, cement, and steel. Pollution will decline. The environment will become cleaner and more healthful. . . .

The Efficiency Argument

It is now time to explain why economists insist that emissions fees can clean up the environment at lower cost than mandatory quantitative controls. The secret is the market's unique ability to accommodate individual differences—in this case, differences among polluters.

Suppose society decides that emissions of sulfur dioxide must decline by 20 percent. One obvious approach is to mandate that every source of sulfur dioxide reduce its emissions by 20 percent. Another option is to levy a fee on discharges that is large enough to reduce emissions by 20 percent. The former is the way our current environmental regulations are often written. The latter is the economist's preferred approach. Both reduce pollution to the same level, but the fee system gets there more cheaply. Why? Because a system of fees assigns most of the job to firms that can reduce emissions easily and cheaply and little to firms that find it onerous and expensive to reduce their emissions.

Let me illustrate how this approach works with a real example. A study in St. Louis found that it cost only $4 for one paper-products factory to cut particulate emissions from its boiler by a ton, but it cost $600 to do the same job at a brewery. If the city fathers instructed both the paper plant and the brewery to cut emissions by the same amount, pollution abatement costs would be low at the paper factory but astronomical at the brewery. Imposing a uniform emissions tax is a more cost-conscious strategy. Suppose a $100/ton tax is announced. The paper company will see an opportunity to save $100 in taxes by spending $4 on cleanup, for a $96 net profit. Similarly, any other firm whose pollution-abatement costs are less than $100 per ton will find it profitable to cut emissions. But firms like the brewery, where pollution-abatement costs exceed $100 per ton, will prefer to continue polluting and paying the tax. Thus the profit motive will automatically assign the task of pollution abatement to the low-cost firms—something no regulators can do.

Mandatory proportional reductions have the seductive appearance of "fairness" and so are frequently adopted. But they provide no incentive to minimize the social costs of environmental clean-up. In fact, when the heavy political hand requires equal percentage reductions by every firm (or perhaps from every smokestack), it pretty much guarantees that the social clean-up will be far more costly than it need be. In the previous example, a one-ton reduction in annual emissions by both the paper factory and the brewery would cost $604 per year. But the same two-ton annual pollution abatement would cost only $8 if the paper factory did the whole job. Only by lucky accident will equiproportionate reductions in discharges be efficient.

Studies that I will cite later . . . suggest that market-oriented approaches to pollution control can reduce abatement costs by 90 percent in some cases. Why, economists ask, is it more virtuous to make pollution reduction hurt more? They have yet to hear a satisfactory answer and suspect there is none. On the contrary, virtue and efficiency are probably in harmony here. If cleaning up our air and water is made cheaper, it is reasonable to suppose that society will buy more clean-up. We can have a purer environment and pay less, too. The hard-headed economist's crass means may be the surest route to the soft-hearted environmentalist's lofty ends.

The Enforcement Argument

Some critics of emissions fees argue that a system of fees would be hard to enforce. In some cases, they are correct. We obviously cannot use effluent charges to reduce concentrations of the unsightly pollutant glop if engineers have yet to devise an effective and dependable devise for measuring how much glop firms are spewing out. If we think glop is harmful, but are unable to monitor it, our only alternative may be to require firms to switch to "cleaner" technologies. Similarly, emissions charges cannot be levied on pollutants that seep unseen—and unmeasured—into groundwater rather than spill out of a pipe.

In many cases, however, those who argue that emissions fees are harder to enforce than direct controls are deceiving themselves. If you cannot measure emissions, you cannot charge a fee, to be sure. But neither can you enforce mandatory standards; you can only delude yourself into thinking you are enforcing them. To a significant extent, that is precisely what the EPA does now. Federal antipollution regulations are poorly policed; the EPA often declares firms in compliance based on nothing more than the firms' self-reporting of their own behavior. When checks are made, noncompliance is frequently uncovered. If emissions can be measured accurately enough to enforce a system of quantitative controls, we need only take more frequent measurements to run a system of pollution fees.

Besides, either permits or taxes are much easier to administer than detailed regulations. Under a system of marketable permits, the government need only conduct periodic auctions. Under a system of emissions taxes, the enforcement mechanism is the relentless and anonymous tax collector who basically reads your meter like a gas or electric company. No fuss, no muss, no bother—and no need for a big bureaucracy. Just a bill. The only way to escape the pollution tax is to exploit the glaring loophole that the government deliberately provides: reduce your emissions.

Contrast this situation with the difficulties of enforcing the cumbersome command-and-control system we now operate. First, complicated statutes must be passed; and polluting industries will use their considerable political muscle in state legislatures and in Congress to fight for weaker laws. Next, the regulatory agencies must write detailed regulations defining precise standards and often prescribing the "best available technology" to use in reducing emissions. Here again industry will do battle, arguing for looser interpretations of the statutes and often turning the regulations to their own advantage. They are helped in this effort by the sheer magnitude of the information-processing task that the law foists upon the EPA and state agencies, a task that quickly outstrips the capacities of their small staffs.

Once detailed regulations are promulgated, the real problems begin. State and federal agencies with limited budgets must enforce these regulations on thousands, if not millions, of sources of pollution. The task is overwhelming. As one critic of the system put it, each polluter argues:

> (1) he is in compliance with the regulation; (2) if not, it is because the regulation is unreasonable as a general rule; (3) if not, then the regulation is unreasonable in this specific case; (4) if not, then it is up to the regulatory agency to tell him how to comply; (5) if forced to take the steps recommended by the agency, he cannot be held responsible for the results; and (6) he needs more time. . . .

Other Reasons to Favor Emissions Fees

Yet other factors argue for market-based approaches to pollution reduction.

One obvious point is that a system of mandatory standards, or one in which a particular technology is prescribed by law, gives a firm that is in compliance with the law no incentive to curtail its emissions any further. If the law says that the firm can emit up to 500 tons of glop per year, it has no reason to spend a penny to reduce its discharges to 499 tons. By contrast, a firm that must pay $100 per ton per year to emit glop can save money by reducing its annual discharges as long as its pollution-abatement costs are less than $100 per ton. The financial incentive to reduce pollution remains.

A second, and possibly very important, virtue of pollution fees is that they create incentives for firms to devise or purchase innovative ways to reduce emissions. Under a system of effluent fees, businesses gain if they can find cheaper ways to control emissions because their savings depend on their pollution abatement, not on how they achieve it. Current regulations, by contrast, often dictate the technology. Firms are expected to obey the regulators, not to search for creative ways to reduce pollution at lower cost.

For this and other reasons, our current system of regulations is unnecessarily adversarial. Businesses feel the government is out to harass them—and they act accordingly. Environmental protection agencies lock horns with industry in the courts. The whole enterprise takes on the atmosphere of a bullfight rather than that of a joint venture. A market-based approach, which made clear that the government wanted to minimize the costs it imposed on business, would naturally create a more cooperative spirit. That cannot be bad.

Finally, the appearance of fairness when regulations take the form of uniform percentage reductions in emissions, as they frequently do, is illusory. Suppose Clean Jeans, Inc. has already spent a considerable sum to reduce the amount of muck it spews into the Stench River. Dirty Jeans, Inc., just downriver, has not spent a cent and emits twice as much. Now a law is passed requiring every firm along the Stench to reduce its emissions by 50 percent. That has the appearance of equity but not the substance. For Dirty Jeans, the regulation may be a minor nuisance. To comply, it need only do what Clean Jeans is already doing voluntarily. But the edict may prove onerous to Clean Jeans, which has already exploited all the cheap ways to cut emissions. In this instance, not only is virtue not its own reward—it actually brings a penalty! Such anomalies cannot arise under a system of marketable pollution permits. Clean Jeans would always have to buy fewer permits than Dirty Jeans. . . .

Objections to "Licenses to Pollute"

Despite the many powerful arguments in favor of effluent taxes or marketable emissions permits, many people have an instinctively negative reaction to the whole idea. Some environmentalists, in particular, rebel at economists' advocacy of market-based approaches to pollution control—which they label "licenses to pollute," a term not meant to sound complimentary. Former Senator Muskie's dictum, quoted at the beginning of this chapter, is an example. The question is: Are the objections to "licenses to pollute" based on coherent arguments that should sway policy, or are they knee-jerk reactions best suited to T-shirts?* My own view is that there is little of the former and much of the latter. Let me explain.

Some of the invective heaped upon the idea of selling the privilege to pollute stems from an ideologically based distrust of markets. Someone who does not think the market a particularly desirable way to organize the production of automobiles, shirts, and soybeans is unlikely to trust the market to protect the environment. As one congressional staff aide put it: "The philosophical assumption that proponents of [emissions] charges make is that there is a free-market

---

*Earlier in his book, Blinder warns his readers about simplistic answers to complex questions. He concludes that "if it fits on a T-shirt, it is almost certainly wrong."—Eds.

system that responds to . . . relative costs. . . . I reject that assumption." This remarkably fatuous statement ignores mountains of evidence accumulated over centuries. Fortunately, it is a minority view in America. Were it the majority view, our economic problems would be too severe to leave much time for worry about pollution.

Some of the criticisms of pollution fees are based on ignorance of the arguments or elementary errors in logic. As mentioned earlier, few opponents of market-based approaches can even explain why economists insist that emissions fees will get the job done more cheaply.

One commonly heard objection is that a rich corporation confronted with a pollution tax will pay the tax rather than reduce its pollution. That belief shows an astonishing lack of respect for avarice. Sure, an obstinate but profitable company *could* pay the fees rather than reduce emissions. But it would do that only if the marginal costs of pollution abatement exceed the fee. Otherwise, its obduracy reduces its profits. Most corporate executives faced with a pollution tax will improve their bottom lines by cutting their emissions, not by flouting the government's intent. To be sure, it is self-interest, not the public interest, that motivates the companies to clean up their acts. But that's exactly the idea behind pollution fees. . . .

One final point should lay the moral issue to rest. Mandatory quantitative standards for emissions are also licenses to pollute—just licenses of a strange sort. They give away, with neither financial charge nor moral condemnation, the right to spew a specified amount of pollution into the air or water. Then they absolutely prohibit any further emissions. Why is such a license morally superior to a uniform tax penalty on all pollution? Why is a business virtuous if it emits 500 tons of glop per year but sinful if it emits 501? Economists make no claim to be arbiters of public morality. But I doubt that these questions have satisfactory answers.

The choice between direct controls and effluent fees, then, is not a moral issue. It is an efficiency issue. About that, economists know a thing or two.

Having made my pitch, I must confess that there are circumstances under which market-based solutions are inappropriate and quantitative standards are better. One obvious instance is the case of a deadly poison. If the socially desirable level of a toxin is zero, there is no point in imposing an emission fee. An outright ban makes more sense.

Another case is a sudden health emergency. When, for example, a summertime air inversion raises air pollution in Los Angeles or New York to hazardous levels, it makes perfect sense for the mayors of those cities to place legal limits on driving, on industrial discharges, or on both. There is simply no time to install a system of pollution permits.

A final obvious case is when no adequate monitoring device exists, as in the case of runoff from soil pollution. Then a system of emissions fees is out of the question. But so also is a system of direct quantitative controls on emissions. The only viable way to control such pollution may be to mandate that cleaner technologies be used.

But each of these is a minor, and well recognized, exception to an overwhelming presumption in the opposite direction. No sane person has ever proposed selling permits to spill arsenic into water supplies. None has suggested that the mayor of New York set the effluent tax on carbon monoxide anew after hearing the weather forecast each morning. And no one has insisted that we must meter what cannot be measured. Each of these objections is a debater's point, not a serious challenge to the basic case for market-oriented approaches to environmental protection. . . .

Rays of Hope: Emissions Trading and Bubbles

There are signs, however, that environmental policy may be changing for the better. The EPA seems to be drifting slowly, and not always surely, away from technology-driven direct controls toward more market-oriented approaches. But not because the agency has been convinced by the logic of economists' arguments. Rather, it was driven into a corner by the inexorable illogic of its own procedures. Necessity proved to be the midwife of common sense.

The story begins in the 1970s, when it became apparent that many regions of the country could not meet the air quality standards prescribed by the Clean Air Act. Under the law, the prospective penalty for violating of the standards was Draconian: no new sources of pollution would be permitted in these regions and existing sources would not be allowed to increase their emissions, implying a virtual halt to local economic growth. The EPA avoided the impending clash between the economy and the environment by creating its "emissions-offsets" program in 1976. Under the new rules, companies were allowed to create new sources of pollution in areas with substandard air quality as long as they reduced their pollution elsewhere by greater amounts. Thus was emissions trading born.

The next important step was invention of the "bubble" concept in 1979. Under this concept, all sources of pollution from a single plant or firm are imagined to be encased in a mythical bubble. The EPA then tells the company that it cares only about total emissions into the bubble. How these emissions are parceled out among the many sources of pollution under the bubble is no concern of the EPA. But it is vital to the firm, which can save money by cutting emissions in the least costly way. A striking example occurred in 1981 when a DuPont plant in New Jersey was ordered to reduce its emissions from 119 sources by 85 percent. Operating under a state bubble program, company engineers proposed instead that emissions from seven large stacks be reduced by 99 percent. The result? Pollution reduction exceeded the state's requirement by 2,300 tons per year and DuPont saved $12 million in capital costs and $3 million per year in operating costs.

Partly because it was hampered by the courts, the bubble concept was little used at first. But bubbles have been growing rapidly since a crucial 1984 judicial decision. By October 1984, about seventy-five bubbles had been approved by the EPA and state authorities and hundreds more were under review or in various stages of development. The EPA estimated the cost savings from all these bubbles to be about $800 million per year. That may seem a small sum compared to the more than $70 billion we now spend on environmental protection. But remember that the whole program was still in the experimental stage, and these bubbles covered only a tiny fraction of the thousands of industrial plants in the United States.

The bubble program was made permanent only when EPA pronounced the experiment a success and issued final guidelines in November 1986. Economists greeted this announcement with joy. Environmentalist David Doniger . . . complained that, "The bubble concept is one of the most destructive impediments to the cleanup of unhealthy air." By now, many more bubbles have been approved or are in the works. Time will tell who was right.

The final step in the logical progression toward the economist's approach would be to make these "licenses to pollute" fully marketable so that firms best able to reduce emissions could sell their excess abatement to firms for which pollution abatement is too expensive. Little trading has taken place to date, though the EPA's November 1986 guidelines may encourage it. But at least one innovative state program is worth mentioning.

The state of Wisconsin found itself unable to achieve EPA-mandated levels of water quality along the polluted Fox and Wisconsin Rivers, even when it employed the prescribed technology. A team of engineers and economists then devised a sophisticated system of transferable discharge permits. Firms were issued an initial allocation of pollution permits (at no charge), based on historical levels of discharges. In total, these permits allow no more pollution than is consistent with EPA standards for water quality. But firms are allowed to trade pollution permits freely in the open market. Thus, in stark contrast to the standard regulatory approach, the Wisconsin system lets the firms along the river—not the regulators—decide how to reduce discharges. Little emissions trading has taken place to date because the entire scheme has been tied up in litigation. But one study estimated that pollution-control costs might eventually fall by as much as 80 percent compared to the alternative of ordering all firms along the river to reduce their discharges by a uniform percentage.

The state of Wisconsin thus came to the conclusion that economists have maintained all along: that applying a little economic horse sense makes it possible to clean up polluted rivers and reduce costs at the same time—a good bargain. That same bargain is available to the nation for the asking. . . .

A Hard-Headed, Soft-Hearted Environmental Policy

Economists who specialize in environmental policy must occasionally harbor self-doubts. They find themselves lined up almost unanimously in favor of market-based approaches to pollution control with seemingly everyone else lined up on the other side. Are economists crazy or is everyone else wrong?

. . . I have argued the seemingly implausible proposition that environmental economists are right and everyone else really is wrong. I have tried to convey a sense of the frustration economists feel when they see obviously superior policies routinely spurned. By replacing our current command-and-control system with either marketable pollution permits or taxes on emissions, our environment can be made cleaner while the burden on industry is reduced. That is about as close to a free lunch as we are likely to encounter. And yet economists' recommendations are overwhelmed by an unholy alliance of ignorance, ideology, and self-interest.

This is a familiar story. The one novel aspect in the sphere of environmental policy is that the usual heavy hitter of this triumvirate—self-interest—is less powerful here than in many other contexts. To be sure, self-interested business lobbies oppose pollution fees. But, as I pointed out, they can be bought off by allowing some pollution free of charge. Doing so may outrage environmental purists, but it is precisely what we do now.

It is the possibility of finessing vested financial interests that holds out the hope that good environmental policy might one day drive out the bad. For we need only overcome ignorance and ideology, not avarice.

Ignorance is normally beaten by knowledge. Few Americans now realize that practical reforms of our environmental policies can reduce the national clean-up bill from more than $70 billion per year to less than $50 billion, and probably to much less. Even fewer understand the reasons why. If the case for market-based policies were better known, more and more people might ask the obvious question: Why is it better to pay more for something we can get for less? Environmental policy may be one area where William Blake's optimistic dictum—"Truth can never be told so as to be understood and not believed"—is germane.

Ideology is less easily rooted out, for it rarely succumbs to rational argument. Some environmentalists support the economist's case. Others understand it well and yet oppose it for what they perceive as moral reasons. I have argued at length that here, as elsewhere, thinking with the heart is less effective than thinking with the head; that the economist's case does not occupy the moral low ground; and that the environment is likely to be cleaner if we offer society clean-up at more reasonable cost. As more environmentalists come to realize that T-shirt slogans are retarding, not hastening, progress toward their goals, their objections may melt away.

The economist's approach to environmental protection is no panacea. It requires an investment in monitoring equipment that society has not yet made. It cannot work in cases where the sources of pollution are not readily identifiable, such as seepage into groundwater. And it will remain an imperfect antidote for environmental hazards until we know a great deal more than we do now about the diffusion of pollutants and the harm they cause.

But perfection is hardly the appropriate standard. As things stand now, our environmental policy may be a bigger mess than our environment. Market-based approaches that join the hard head of the accountant to the soft heart of the environmentalist offer the prospect of genuine improvement: more clean-up for less money. It is an offer society should not refuse.

NO

Frank Ackerman and
Kevin Gallagher

Getting the Prices Wrong

Introduction: The Transformation of the Debate

Public discussion and debate over environmental policy has been transformed, in recent years, to focus on the idea of market-based mechanisms. In the 1970s and 1980s, many newly recognized environmental problems were addressed with laws and regulations that told polluters to stop polluting—a straightforward, common-sense approach that is now frequently stigmatized as "command and control." During the 1990s, a near-consensus emerged in policymaking circles for a sharp turn away from past patterns of regulation toward the theoretically greater efficiency and lower cost of environmental taxes, tradeable emission permits, and other market incentives. Today, to cite just one example, the official U.S. position on climate change negotiations slights the obvious regulatory options such as increased vehicle fuel efficiency standards. Instead it relies above all on the hopes that an unprecedented international emissions trading system can be created, and will prove effective.

There are many voices in the chorus of market enthusiasts. Most economists have always called for reliance on the market; in recent years they have gained a much higher public profile, with widely discussed publications, and major conferences on market-based environmental policy at leading universities. The influential "Project 88" papers and conferences in 1988–91 first brought the economists' theories to the attention of a wide and receptive audience of policymakers (Stavins et al. 1988, 1991). Important activist groups and individuals within the environmental movement have become advocates of market-based policies, while researchers continue to elaborate the economic models and theories on which those policies rest.

For some of the participants in the debate, the environment is almost an afterthought. The most passionate free marketeers seek to roll back all government programs, laws, and regulations that affect business and property. For the true believer, the market is the answer regardless of the question, and even irreversible climate change is just another opportunity for private profit:

> ... free market environmentalism suggests two avenues for dealing with global warming. The first takes changes in the Earth's temperatures as given

From Frank Ackerman and Kevin Gallagher, "Getting the Prices Wrong: The Limits of Market-Based Environmental Policy," Global Development and Environment Institute Working Paper 00-05 (October 2000). Copyright © 2000 by The Global Development and Environment Institute, Tufts University. Reprinted by permission.

and asks whether individuals have the incentive to respond with innovative solutions. The second focuses on the evolution of property rights to the atmosphere. (Anderson and Leal, 1991: 163).

On a more sensibly nuanced view, the market is the answer to some but not all questions. The challenge is to understand what the market can do, and what it cannot. In the current climate, there is little danger of overlooking the market's strengths. To restore a balanced perspective, more attention needs to be focused in the opposite direction, examining the cases in which market incentives are less effective or appropriate.

Uses of the Market: Tool or Blueprint?

Market-based policies have made an undeniable contribution to environmental protection. Innovations such as emissions trading have in some cases lowered the cost of pollution abatement by increasing flexibility, decreasing the burden of bureaucratic regulation, and using the market to pursue environmental goals in an efficient manner. But such success has not been, and will not be, achieved on every issue.

There is a fundamental distinction between using the market as a *tool* to achieve society's goals, and adopting it as a *blueprint* of those goals. These two similar-sounding positions turn out to have very different implications. Is the market, as tool, the most efficient means to reach the environmental objectives that society has chosen? Or is the competitive market itself the blueprint, the ultimate description of society's objectives, with some environmental concerns penciled in?

Under the tool perspective, environmental goals may be set through a process of public deliberation, and may have no inherent relationship to the market. It is then a pragmatic question to determine when market-based policies offer the best tools for achieving those goals, and when traditional regulation or other approaches are preferable. The answer naturally differs from one issue to the next.

If, on the other hand, the market is the blueprint of society's objectives, then there is little scope for pragmatism and pluralism of political strategies. From this perspective, what matters above all is "getting the prices right," i.e. adjusting selected prices as necessary to reflect the true valuation of environmental costs and benefits. Once the prices are right, the market automatically produces the right allocation of resources and the appropriate level of environmental protection; the less additional intervention, the better the market outcomes will be. On this view, public deliberation about environmental objectives is unnecessary or even harmful; society should do no more than endorse the mechanisms that allow the market to work.

The blueprint offered by the market is spelled out in general equilibrium theory. Under a series of idealized assumptions, a competitive economy is guaranteed to have an equilibrium which is Pareto-optimal, and every Pareto-optimal outcome is an equilibrium for some set of initial conditions. These well-known "fundamental theorems of welfare economics" are ultimately the foundation for the common idea that market outcomes are efficient. Yet the relevance of these abstract theorems is doubly limited, both in theory and in practice.

In the abstract, even if the assumptions of general equilibrium theory are accepted, its results remain mathematically problematical. There is no guarantee that the equilibrium of a general equilibrium model is either unique or stable. Intensive theoretical analysis has found no way around this problem, and in fact has found that the dynamic behavior of small (i.e. mathematically manageable) general equilibrium models is not necessarily a guide to the behavior of related, larger (i.e. more realistic) models (Ackerman 2000).

In reality, the assumptions of general equilibrium theory are inconsistent with what we know about people, firms, and technology. The neoclassical behavioral model and its assumptions of well-informed, narrowly defined maximization clash with the results of most social sciences—and with common sense (van den Bergh et al. 2000). Major firms routinely fail to be as small and competitive as the theory requires; oligopoly and monopoly are obvious, persistent facts of life. Path-dependent technologies, involving "learning by doing" and network effects, further undercut the presumption that market outcomes are reliably optimal or efficient (Arthur 1994).

In short, the equilibrium of a market economy is not necessarily an ideal outcome, either in theory or in practice. Our central argument is that *the market is a reasonable policy tool but not a reasonable blueprint for society's goals.* The market as blueprint fails because there are significant public purposes that cannot be achieved by prices and markets alone. There are many instances in which getting the prices right becomes a narrow or meaningless objective; in such cases, society may intentionally and appropriately choose to "get the prices wrong" in order to pursue more important goals.

Five Forms of Failure

There are at least five general reasons why market-based policies fail to address some of the most basic environmental objectives.

1. Large, irreversible damages must be prevented.

The market does not guarantee that producers will always do the right thing; it only ensures that those who do the wrong thing too often will go out of business. In the textbook model of perfect competition, every surviving producer is forced to adopt the most efficient, least-cost technology, because those who do not keep up with the state of the art will be undersold and driven out by those who do. Implicit in this model is a process of trial and error in which unsuccessful producers may do the wrong things (produce things that are needlessly expensive, or that fail to meet consumer desires) for a while before giving up and trying a different line of work.

This is a useful way to make many resource allocation decisions—*if* there is no great social cost or lasting harm caused by a few failed experiments (Koopmans, 1951; Krutilla, 1967). It is hard to imagine a better way to choose which restaurants should serve your community; the economic and environmental impacts of unsuccessful restaurants are minimal. But the same process of trial and error is less attractive as a strategy for disposal of high-level radioactive waste, where it is essential to get it right the first time and every time. When the potential damages are large and irreversible, as with radioactive waste, then society cannot afford the experimental learning process that is implied by market competition. Reliance on market mechanisms in this case would be an abdication of the most basic responsibility for public health and safety.

Many environmental problems are more analogous to the urgent questions of nuclear waste disposal than to the benign issues of consumer preference and restaurant choice. Threats of extinction of endangered species, destruction of irreplaceable wildernesses and other ecosystems, and emission of toxic and carcinogenic pollutants, all involve large, irreversible damages. The market can safely play a role on these issues only in a firmly regulated context, intentionally constrained by high minimum standards that safeguard the interests of nature and humanity.

2. Outcomes far in the future are important.

Discounting, the standard method for comparison of costs and benefits that occur at different times, is indispensable for near-term decisions but nonsensical for the long run. Application of this form of short-run thinking to our environmental future repeatedly leads to the mistaken conclusion that we should do almost nothing on behalf of future generations.

Discounting is essential, and indeed commonplace, for many practical financial decisions. If offered an investment opportunity with a payoff a few years in the future, you can (and should) compare it to the return you would get by putting the same amount of money into a predictable, safe alternative such as a bank account or government bond. Why does this innocuous bit of accounting become nonsensical when applied to society's long-run choices?

The solutions to many environmental issues such as climate change involve sizeable costs now that have their principle benefits far in the future. For an investment with a ten-year lifetime, one individual can weigh her own initial costs against her own ultimate benefits. But there is no one who will personally experience both the cost of investments in carbon reduction made today, and the resulting benefit of mitigation in climate change 100 or 200 years from now. In fact, there is no way of knowing what value our far-future descendants will place on the environment; they could consider it either much more or much less important than we do today. The problem is that by accepting the use of a discount rate we have implicitly imposed a specific pattern of preferences regarding the relative welfare of present and future generations (Howarth and Norgaard, 1993).

Moreover, thanks to the magic of compound interest, benefits far in the future have a very small present value. At 5% annual interest, $1 left in the bank is worth more than $17,000 after 200 years, and more than $2,000,000 after 300 years. So if it costs as much as $1 today to prevent environmental damages worth $17,000 in the year 2200 or $2 million in 2300, economic theory says our descendants would be better off if we left $1 in the bank for them. As strange as it may sound, this argument is seriously advanced as a reason to go slow and minimize current spending on long-run environmental objectives (Hartwick, 1977; Solow 1986). The only reasonable conclusion is that economic theory does not offer a reasonable understanding of our responsibility to future generations (Bromley, 1998).

3. Many environmental values are not commodities that can be priced.

Economic theory usually assumes that environmental damages can be meaningfully measured in monetary terms. From this it is only a short step to calculating the prices that "should" be applied to clean air, clean water, and other values. The vision of the market as blueprint for environmental protection generally assumes such prices have been put in place, so that the market can balance supply and demand in order to achieve the optimal level of pollution reduction. That is, economists assume that environmental values can be treated as commodities like any others.

This approach is problematical on several levels. On a practical level, there are serious conceptual and technical critiques of the standard methods of monetizing environmental damages by economists and lawyers alike (Diamond and Hausman, 1994; Harvard Law Review, 1992). Economists frequently rely on "contingent valuation" surveys that ask people to place a hypothetical dollar value on some aspect of the environment; the question does not always produce a meaningful answer.

A subtler problem is that every unit of a commodity typically sells at the same price: three tons of steel are worth three times as much as one. However, for pollutants with threshold effects or critical levels, three tons of emissions may have vastly more than three times the impact of one ton. In contrast to traditional regulations, market-based policies such as emission trading are more prone to creating "hot spots" where critical levels of pollutants are exceeded.

On the most fundamental level, there are deep ethical, philosophical, and religious objections to assigning dollar values to human or other life (Anderson, 1993; Kelman, 1981). For many people, the protection of endangered species and unique natural habitats, or the prevention of avoidable deaths and injuries, involve a realm of fundamental principles that transcend the market. From this perspective, monetization of human life and health, or of the existence of other species, is either meaningless or degrading. It is important to talk about these principles and their policy implications, but that conversation cannot be reduced to purely monetary terms (Vatn and Bromley 1994).

4. Volatile market prices can cause wasteful misallocation of resources.

When prices change too fast, the investment that made sense yesterday may no longer be profitable today—as many people have learned the hard way in the stock market. This problem can also affect the environment, when volatile markets send mixed signals about the value of environmental policies and initiatives. Sky-high prices for recycled materials in 1995 inspired more than a billion dollars of investment in new recycled paper mills; by 1997 those new mills had closed, most of them bankrupt (Ackerman and Gallagher, 2000). High oil prices in the early 1980s drove the auto industry to retool for small car production, just before prices fell and consumers went back to buying big cars. More recently, as the restructured electricity industry increasingly relies on auction-style pricing to set electric rates, there have been cases where summer peak power has sold for hundreds of times the normal price. This is sure to be a misleading signal about the value of new generating capacity.

Day trading is not an example of the efficiency of the market. In a world with high, industry-specific sunk costs of both physical and human capital, there is a limit to the velocity at which people and businesses can sensibly respond to new price signals. When the market exceeds that speed limit, it leads to wastefully rapid, extreme changes. The government can improve matters by intervening in such markets, enforcing a reasonable speed limit and establishing a sustainable pace of change.

5. If it's not broken, don't fix it.

It is not always the case that market incentives are superior to old-fashioned environmental controls. There are substantial areas—protection of public health, provision of urban infrastructure, and emissions monitoring, among others—where traditional regulatory or public spending approaches remain more effective than market-based policies. The two strategies provide different benefits: the market minimizes consumer choice and creates incentives for cost minimization; the government can supply public goods, minimize transaction costs, and create a transparent standard of fairness. The relative importance of these contrasting strengths will differ from case to case.

Market-based approaches have much higher costs, and hence more limited advantages, in some circumstances than in others. Economists have analyzed the conditions under which market incentives are more or less effective; for example, when pollution approaches thresholds beyond which damages rise rapidly, the rationale for strict emission controls becomes stronger. There is also some evidence that market incentives, like any other policy, are less effective in practice than they were projected to be in theory (Gustafsson, 1998).

Finally, market incentives frequently involve taxes. (The principle alternative, emissions trading, involves high start-up and transaction costs, and is not appropriate in every case.) No one wants any new taxes; most politicians can't bring themselves to utter the word. Traditional regulation, involving rules that lower or prohibit certain emissions, may be more politically feasible—even if, in a theoretical world divorced from politics, market incentives might appear to be more efficient.

Two Cheers for the Market

Despite this catalogue of things the market cannot accomplish, there are things at which it does excel. Guidelines for the appropriate use of market incentives can begin with the negation of the five points listed above. Market-based policies should be used in cases where: there is little risk of irreversible damages; the relevant outcomes are relatively short-term; there are no fundamental ethical or philosophical issues at stake; prices are not excessively volatile; and traditional regulation is expensive or ineffective.

In more positive terms, the great strength of the market is that it decentralizes information processing and decision-making, allowing each firm to analyze and respond to the data that affects its operations. This is one of the key points of the economic critique of traditional regulation: regulators cannot possibly keep up with all the relevant information on complex, changing technologies, let alone the site-specific information about the relative cost of installing new technologies at each location. When there are complex technical choices, especially when the choices depend on site-specific information, it is more efficient to set broad standards and allow firms to choose the most cost-effective means of meeting those standards.

The allowance trading system for sulfur emissions under the 1990 Clean Air Act Amendments comes close to meeting these standards, although it has not been entirely free of problems. Sulfur emissions have been reduced more rapidly, and at lower cost, than anyone thought possible in 1990—though there are other factors that contributed to this happy outcome, such as the increased availability and lowered price of low-sulfur coal in the 1990s (Ackerman and Moomaw, 1997). Moreover, many observers have concluded that the allowances should have been auctioned by the government, rather than given away to the existing producers. Other changes could make the system more environmentally palatable: if the cap on total emissions was steadily declining, rather than constant, the trading system would not create a permanent "right to pollute."

Still, the process of emissions trading is an interesting innovation that has played at least some part in an environmental success story. Our suggested guidelines for the use of market incentives fit well in this case: the damage from acid precipitation appears to be reversible; it occurs promptly following emission; ethical issues about human life or biodiversity are no more prominent here than they are in any environmental issue; relevant prices are not unusually volatile; and traditional regulation, calling for scrubbers at all coal-burning plants, was indeed expensive and inflexible, while trading allowances between U.S. power plants is simple and fairly cheap to administer. There is a complex choice of strategies for sulfur reduction, in which the best choice depends on site-specific information.

Yet in the current climate of celebration of the market, it is important to stress that this is *not* to say that emissions trading is always a good idea. The proposed application of emissions trading to worldwide carbon emissions fails several of our criteria, and raises technical problems of coverage, administration, verification and enforcement. In general, there is far more danger of exaggerating than of overlooking the potential of market-based policies today. The greater need is to re-legitimize other approaches, and to open a broader dialogue about the full range of options for environmental policy.

References

Ackerman, F., 2000. Still dead after all these years: interpreting the failure of general equilibrium theory. GDAE Working Paper No. 00-01, Tufts University.

Ackerman, F., and Gallagher, K., 2000. Mixed signals: Market Incentives, Recycling, and the Price Spike of 1995. GDAE Working Paper, Tufts University.

Ackerman, F. and Moomaw, W., 1997. SO_2 emissions trading: does it work? *Electricity Journal,* August.

Anderson, E., 1993. Cost-benefit analysis, safety, and environmental quality. *Ethics in Economics.* Cambridge: Harvard University Press, 190–216.

Anderson, T., and Leal, L., 1991. *Free Market Environmentalism.* Boulder: Westview Press, 163.

Arthur, B., 1994. *Increasing Returns and Path Dependence in the Economy.* Ann Arbor: Michigan Press.

van den Bergh, Jeroen C. J. M., Ada Ferrer-i-Carbonell and Guiseppe Munda. 2000. Alternative models of individual behaviour and implications for environmental policy. *Ecological Economics* 32, 43–61.

Bromley, D., 1998. Searching for sustainability: the poverty of spontaneous order. *Ecological Economics* 24, 231–240.

Diamond, P., and Hausman, T., 1994. Contingent valuation: is some number better than any number? *Journal of Economic Perspectives,* v8, n4, 45–64.

Gustafsson, B., 1998. Scope and limits of the market mechanism in environmental management. *Ecological Economics* 24, 259–274.

Hartwick, J. M. 1977. Intergenerational equity and the investing of rents from exhaustible resources. *American Economic Review* 66, 972–974.

Harvard Law Review (unsigned editorial). 1992. "Ask a silly question . . .": contingent valuation of natural resource damages. *Harvard Law Review* 105, 1981–2000.

Howarth, R., and Norgaard, R., 1993. Intergenerational transfers and the social discount rate. *Environment and Resource Economics* 3, 337–358.

Kelman, S., 1981. What price incentives? *Economists and the Environment.* Boston: Auburn House.

Koopmans, T. C. 1951. Analysis of production as an efficient combination of activity. *Activity Analysis of Production and Allocation.* New York: John Wiley, 48.

Krutilla, J., 1967. Conservation reconsidered. *American Economic Review* 57, 777–786.

Solow, R. M. 1986. On the intertemporal allocation of natural resources. *Scandinavian Journal of Economics* 88, 141–149.

Stavins, R. N., et al. 1988. Project 88—Harnessing market forces to protect our environment: Initiatives for the new president (Senators Timothy Wirth and John Heinz, Washington D.C.).

Stavins, R. N., et al. 1991. Project 88 Round II—Incentives for action: Designing market-based environmental strategies (Senators Timothy Wirth and John Heinz, Washington D.C.).

Vatn, A., and D. W. Bromley. 1994. Choice without prices without apology, *Journal of Environmental Economics and Management* 26, 129–148.

POSTSCRIPT

Should Pollution Be Put to the Market Test?

For more than 30 years a massive effort has been put forth in the United States to advance environmental protection by using laws and regulation. At first, federal action was directed toward air- and water-pollution control; this was accomplished by issuing regulations and permits. The second set of initiatives focused on cleaning up hazardous waste dumps. This action was first authorized by the Resource Conservation and Recovery Act (RCRA) of 1976, which established a permit system for disposal sites and regulated underground storage tanks. Later initiatives in this area were authorized by the Comprehensive Environmental Response, Compensation, and Liability Act (CERCLA) of 1980. This act, known as Superfund, created a fund to finance the cleanup of hazardous waste sites.

What is significant is that throughout the 1970s and the 1980s, the control, containment, and elimination of pollution and its effects were accomplished largely by traditional government regulation. Economists such as Blinder argued for policies that capture and utilize the strength of the market. By the 1990s their voices had been heard and the population witnessed a marked shift in public policy. Traditional regulation, which demands a uniform response from all who produce pollutants, was replaced with market-based regulation that invites firms to weigh the benefits and costs of their actions. Traditional regulation simply faded into the background.

This concerns Ackerman and Gallagher, who believe that the pendulum has swung too far. They argue that it is time to recognize that it may be best to return to the good old days of a "command and control" type of regulation. They assert that if the public does not take heed, private market interests could kill the goose that lays the golden egg and, in the process, deny society a perpetual stream of golden eggs.

For a review of the initial legislation in the air pollution area, see Richard H. Schulze, "The 20-Year History of the Evolution of Air Pollution Control Legislation in the U.S.A.," *Atmospheric Environment* (March 1993). For a discussion of some of the ethical issues surrounding pollution permits, see Paul Steichmeier, "The Morality of Pollution Permits," *Environmental Ethics* (Summer 1993). To see how important market incentives are to economists, examine the July 2000 appeal to the Supreme Court signed by more than 40 prominent economists, who urged the Court to let the Environmental Protection Agency (EPA) consider the cost and consequences of clean air regulations. This can be found on the Brookings Institution Web site at http://www.brookings.edu/Comm/news/0007EPA.htm.

ISSUE 17

Has the North American Free Trade Agreement Hurt the American Economy?

YES: Robert E. Scott, from "NAFTA's Hidden Costs: Trade Agreement Results in Job Losses, Growing Inequality, and Wage Suppression for the United States," *EPI Briefing Paper* (April 2001)

NO: Daniel T. Griswold, from "NAFTA at 10: An Economic and Foreign Policy Success," *Free Trade Bulletin* (December 2002)

ISSUE SUMMARY

YES: Economic Policy Institute director Robert E. Scott argues that besides the loss of a significant number of jobs, the North American Free Trade Agreement (NAFTA) has generated a number of less visible harmful effects on the American economy. These include increased income inequality and reduced fringe benefits.

NO: Daniel T. Griswold, associate director of the Cato Institute's Center for Trade Policy Studies, contends that NAFTA has helped the American economy by producing better-paying jobs and contributing to increased manufacturing output in the United States between 1993 and 2001.

The North American Free Trade Agreement (NAFTA) was signed into law in the fall of 1993. The passage of NAFTA was no simple matter. Although the basic agreement was negotiated by the Republican George Bush administration during the late 1980s and early 1990s, the Democratic Bill Clinton administration faced the challenge of convincing Congress and the American people that NAFTA would work to the benefit of the United States as well as Mexico and Canada. In meeting this challenge, President Clinton did not hesitate to use a bit of drama to press the case for NAFTA. He arranged for all former, then-living U.S. presidents (Bush, Ronald Reagan, Jimmy Carter, Gerald Ford, and Richard Nixon) to gather together and speak out in support of NAFTA. The public debate probably reached its zenith with a face-to-face confrontation between H. Ross Perot, a successful businessman who ran for president and was perhaps the most visible and outspoken opponent of NAFTA, and then–vice president Al

Gore on the *Larry King Live* television show. The vote on NAFTA in the House of Representatives reflected the sharpness of the debate; it passed by only a slim margin.

In pressing the case for NAFTA, proponents in the United States raised two major arguments. The first argument was economic: NAFTA would produce real economic benefits. These benefits were purported to include increased employment in the United States and increased productivity. Note that these arguments were based on the economic notions of specialization and comparative advantage. The second argument was political: NAFTA would support the political and economic reforms being made in Mexico and promote further progress in these two domains. These reforms had made Mexico a "better" neighbor— that is, Mexico had taken steps to become more like the United States—and NAFTA would support further positive change. Here the links are between greater economic freedom and increased political freedom as well as greater economic stability and increased political stability.

In opposing NAFTA, critics in the United States countered both of these arguments, focusing mostly on U.S.-Mexican relations. They argued that freer trade between the United States and Mexico would mean a loss of jobs in the United States—Perot's reference to a "giant sucking sound" was the transfer of work and jobs from the United States to Mexico. They also argued that NAFTA did not do enough to protect the environment nor to improve working conditions in Mexico. They felt that the notion of passing NAFTA as a reward to the Mexican government was premature; the government had not done enough to improve economic and political conditions in Mexico.

Implementation of NAFTA began in 1994, and so evaluation at the point of its 10-year anniversary seems particularly timely. In assessing the impact of NAFTA, there are any number of different perspectives that can be employed. Should the focus be economic, political, or both? Should the evaluation concentrate on the benefits and costs to the United States, to Mexico, to Canada, or to all three countries? How much of the history that follows NAFTA can be attributed to NAFTA, and how much can be attributed to other factors? When is the appropriate time for an evaluation? In short, evaluation is no easy task.

But evaluation of NAFTA is important not only for its own sake. President George W. Bush supports an expansion of NAFTA to 34 countries in North, Central, and South America. This expansion is called the Free Trade Agreement of the Americas (FTAA). Clearly, whether or not a person is willing to support FTAA depends in part on whether that person believes that NAFTA has helped or hurt the American economy. Robert E. Scott, in the following criticism of NAFTA, explicitly connects NAFTA and FTAA. Because he believes NAFTA has had negative consequences for the U.S. economy, he is less than enthusiastic about FTAA. Although he does not directly address FTAA, Daniel T. Griswold maintains in the second selection that NAFTA has been a success, and he implies that almost all steps taken in the direction of freer trade will be beneficial to the U.S. economy.

Robert E. Scott

YES

NAFTA's Hidden Costs

The North American Free Trade Agreement (NAFTA) eliminated 766,030 actual and potential U.S. jobs between 1994 and 2000 because of the rapid growth in the net U.S. export deficit with Mexico and Canada. The loss of these real and potential jobs[1] is just the most visible tip of NAFTA's impact on the U.S. economy. In fact, NAFTA has also contributed to rising income inequality, suppressed real wages for production workers, weakened collective bargaining powers and ability to organize unions, and reduced fringe benefits. . . .

Growing Trade Deficits and Job Losses

NAFTA supporters have frequently touted the benefits of exports while remaining silent on the impacts of rapid import growth (Scott 2000). But any evaluation of the impact of trade on the domestic economy must include *both* imports and exports. If the United States exports 1,000 cars to Mexico, many American workers are employed in their production. If, however, the U.S. imports 1,000 foreign-made cars rather than building them domestically, then a similar number of Americans who would have otherwise been employed in the auto industry will have to find other work. Ignoring imports and counting only exports is like trying to balance a checkbook by counting only deposits but not withdrawals.

The U.S. has experienced steadily growing global trade deficits for nearly three decades, and these deficits have accelerated rapidly since NAFTA took effect on January 1, 1994. Although gross U.S. exports to its NAFTA partners have increased dramatically—with real growth of 147% to Mexico and 66% to Canada—these increases have been overshadowed by the larger growth in imports, which have gone up by 248% from Mexico and 79% from Canada, as shown in Table 1. As a result, the $16.6 billion U.S. net export deficit with these countries in 1993 increased by 378% to $62.8 billion by 2000 (all figures in inflation-adjusted 1992 dollars). . . .

The growing U.S. trade deficit has been facilitated by substantial currency devaluations in Mexico and Canada, which have made both countries' exports to the United States cheaper while making imports from the United States more expensive in those markets. These devalued currencies have also encouraged

Table 1

U.S. Trade With Canada and Mexico, 1993–2000, Totals for All Commodities (Millions of Constant 1992 Dollars)

	1993	2000	Dollars	Percent	Jobs lost or gained
Canada					
Domestic exports	$90,018	$149,214	$59,196	66%	563,539
Imports for consumption	108,087	193,725	85,638	79	962,376
Net exports	(18,068)	(44,511)	(26,443)	146	(398,837)
Mexico					
Domestic exports	$39,530	$97,509	$57,979	147%	574,326
Imports for consumption	38,074	132,439	94,364	248	941,520
Net exports	1,456	(34,930)	(36,386)	n.a	(367,193)
Mexico and Canada					
Domestic exports	$129,549	$246,723	$117,174	90%	1,137,865
Imports for consumption	146,161	326,164	180,003	123	1,903,896
Net exports	(16,612)	(79,441)	(62,828)	378	(766,030)

(Columns under "Change since 1993": Dollars, Percent, Jobs lost or gained)

investors in Canada and Mexico to build new and expanded production capacity to export even more goods to the U.S. market.

The Mexican peso was highly overvalued in 1994 when NAFTA took effect (Blecker 1997). The peso lost about 31% of its real, inflation-adjusted value between 1994 and 1995, after the Mexican financial crisis. The peso has gained real value (appreciated) recently because inflation in Mexico has remained well above levels in the U.S. As prices in Mexico rose, its exports became less competitive with goods produced in the U.S. and other countries because the peso's market exchange rate was unchanged between 1998 and 2000. High inflation in Mexico also made imports cheaper, relative to goods purchased in the U.S.

By 2000 the peso's real value had risen to roughly the pre-crisis levels of 1994.[2] Thus, the peso was as overvalued in 2000 as it was when NAFTA took effect. As a result, Mexico's trade and current account balances worsened substantially in 1998–2000, as imports from other countries surged, despite the fact that Mexico's trade surplus with the U.S. continued to improve through 2000. Given Mexico's large overall trade deficits, and the rising value of the peso, pressures are building for another peso crisis in the near future.

The Canadian dollar has depreciated over the past few years. The Canada–U.S. Free Trade Agreement—a precursor to NAFTA—took effect in 1989. Initially, the Canadian dollar rose 4.1% in real terms between 1989 and 1991, as Canada's Central Bank tightened interest rates. During this period, Canada maintained short-term interest rates that averaged 2.25 percentage points above those in the U.S. (1989 to 1994), which caused the initial appreciation in its currency. Canada then began to reduce real interest rates in the mid-1990s. Between 1995 and 2000, short-term interest rates in Canada were 0.75 percentage points *below* U.S. rates, a net swing of 3.0 percentage points. The Canadian dollar began to depreciate in the mid-1990s, as interest rates were reduced, relative to the U.S. Overall, between 1989 and 2000, the Canadian dollar *lost* 27% of its real value against the U.S. dollar.[3] . . .

NAFTA Costs Jobs in Every State

All 50 states and the District of Columbia have experienced a net loss of jobs under NAFTA (Table 2). Exports from every state have been offset by faster-rising imports. Net job loss figures range from a low of 395 in Alaska to a high of

Table 2

NAFTA Job Loss by State, 1993–2000

State	Net NAFTA job loss*	State	Net NAFTA job loss*
U.S. total	766,030	Missouri	16,773
		Montana	1,730
Alabama	16,826	Nebraska	4,352
Alaska	809	Nevada	4,374
Arizona	8,493	New Hampshire	2,970
Arkansas	9,615	New Jersey	19,169
California	82,354	New Mexico	2,859
Colorado	8,172	New York	46,210
Connecticut	9,262	North Carolina	31,909
Delaware	1,355	North Dakota	1,288
District of Columbia	1,635	Ohio	37,694
Florida	27,631	Oklahoma	7,009
Georgia	22,918	Oregon	10,986
Hawaii	1,565	Pennsylvania	35,262
Idaho	2,768	Rhode Island	7,021
Illinois	37,422	South Carolina	10,835
Indiana	31,110	South Dakota	2,032
Iowa	8,378	Tennessee	25,419
Kansas	6,582	Texas	41,067
Kentucky	13,128	Utah	5,243
Louisiana	6,613	Vermont	1,611
Maine	3,326	Virginia	16,758
Maryland	8,089	Washington	14,071
Massachusetts	16,998	West Virginia	2,624
Michigan	46,817	Wisconsin	19,362
Minnesota	13,202	Wyoming	864
Mississippi	11,469		

*Excluding effects on wholesale and retail trade and advertising.

Source: EPI analysis of Bureau of Labor Statistics and Census Bureau data.

82,354 in California. Other hard-hit states include Michigan, New York, Texas, Ohio, Illinois, Pennsylvania, North Carolina, Indiana, Florida, Tennessee, and Georgia, each with more than 20,000 jobs lost. These states all have high concentrations of industries (such as motor vehicles, textiles and apparel, computers, and electrical appliances) where a large number of plants have moved to Mexico. . . .

Long-term Stagnation and Growing Inequality

NAFTA has also contributed to growing income inequality and to the declining wages of U.S. production workers, who make up about 70% of the workforce. NAFTA, however, is but one contributor to a larger globalization process that has led to growing structural trade deficits and has shaped the U.S. economy and society over the last few decades.[4] Rapid growth in U.S. trade and foreign investment, as a share of U.S. gross domestic product, has played a large role in the growth of inequality in income distribution in the last 20 years. NAFTA has continued and accelerated international economic integration, and thus contributed to the growing tradeoffs this integration requires.

The growth in U.S. trade and trade deficits has put downward pressure on the wages of "unskilled" (i.e., non-college-educated) workers in the U.S., especially those with no more than a high school degree. This group represents 72.7% of the total U.S. workforce and includes most middle- and low-wage workers. These U.S. workers bear the brunt of the costs and pressures of globalization (Mishel et al. 2001, 157, 172–79).

A large and growing body of research has demonstrated that expanding trade has reduced the price of import-competing products and thus reduced the real wages of workers engaged in producing those goods. Trade, however, is also expected to increase the wages of the workers producing exports, but growing trade deficits have meant that the number of workers hurt by imports has exceeded the number who have benefited through increased exports. Because the United States tends to import goods that make intensive use of less-skilled and less-educated workers in production, it is not surprising to find that the increasing openness of the U.S. economy to trade has reduced the wages of less-skilled workers relative to other workers in the United States.[5]

Globalization has reduced the wages of "unskilled" workers for at least three reasons. First, the steady growth in U.S. trade deficits over the past two decades has eliminated millions of manufacturing jobs and job opportunities in this country. Most displaced workers find jobs in other sectors where wages are much lower, which in turn leads to lower *average* wages for all U.S. workers. Recent surveys have shown that, even when displaced workers are able to find new jobs in the U.S., they face a reduction in wages, with earnings declining by an average of over 13% (Mishel et al. 2001, 24). These displaced workers' new jobs are likely to be in the service industry, the source of 99% of net new jobs created in the United States since 1989, and a sector in which average compensation is only 77% of the manufacturing sector's average (Mishel et al. 2001,

169). This competition also extends to export sectors, where pressures to cut product prices are often intense.

Second, the effects of growing U.S. trade and trade deficits on wages go beyond just those workers exposed directly to foreign competition. As the trade deficit limits jobs in the manufacturing sector, the new supply of workers to the service sector (displaced workers and new labor market entrants not able to find manufacturing jobs) depresses the wages of those already holding service jobs.

Finally, the increased import competition and capital mobility resulting from globalization has increased the "threat effects" in bargaining between employers and workers, further contributing to stagnant and falling wages in the U.S. (Bronfenbrenner 1997a). Employers' credible threats to relocate plants, to outsource portions of their operations, and to purchase intermediate goods and services directly from foreign producers can have a substantial impact on workers' bargaining positions. The use of these kinds of threats is widespread. A *Wall Street Journal* survey in 1992 reported that one-fourth of almost 500 American corporate executives polled admitted that they were "very likely" or "somewhat likely" to use NAFTA as a bargaining chip to hold down wages (Tonelson 2000, 47). A unique study of union organizing drives in 1993–95 found that over 50% of all employers made threats to close all or part of their plants during organizing drives (Bronfenbrenner 1997b). This study also found that strike threats in National Labor Relations Board union-certification elections nearly doubled following the implementation of the NAFTA agreement, and that threat rates were substantially higher in mobile industries in which employers can credibly threaten to shut down or move their operations in response to union activity. . . .

Bronfenbrenner (2000) described the impact of these threats in testimony to the U.S. Trade Deficit Review Commission:

> Under the cover of NAFTA and other trade agreements, employers use the threat of plant closure and capital flight at the bargaining table, in organizing drives, and in wage negotiations with individual workers. What they say to workers, either directly or indirectly, is if you ask for too much or don't give concessions or try to organize, strike, or fight for good jobs with good benefits, we'll close, we'll move across the border just like other plants have done before.[6]

In the context of ongoing U.S. trade deficits and rising levels of trade liberalization, the pervasiveness of employer threats to close or relocate plants may conceivably have a greater impact on real wage growth for production workers than does actual import competition. There are no empirical studies of the effects of such threats on U.S. wages, so such costs simply have been ignored by other studies of NAFTA.

NAFTA, Globalization, and the U.S. Economy

The U.S. economy created 20.7 million jobs between 1992 and 1999. All of those gains are explained by growth in domestic consumption, investment, and government spending. The growth in the overall U.S. trade deficit eliminated

3.2 million jobs in the same period (Scott 2000). Thus, NAFTA and other sources of growing trade deficits were responsible for a change in the composition of employment, shifting workers from manufacturing to other sectors and, frequently, from good jobs to low-quality, low-pay work.

Trade-displaced workers will not be so lucky during the next economic downturn. If unemployment begins to rise in the U.S., then those who lose their jobs due to globalization and growing trade deficits could face longer unemployment spells, and they will find it much more difficult to get new jobs.

When trying to tease apart the various contributing causes behind trends like the disappearance of manufacturing jobs, the rise in income inequality, and the decline in wages in the U.S., NAFTA and growing trade deficits provide only part of the answer. Other major causes include deregulation and privatization, declining rates of unionization, sustained high levels of unemployment, and technological change. While each of these factors has played some role, a large body of economic research has concluded that trade is responsible for at least 15–25% of the growth in wage inequality in the U.S. (U.S. Trade Deficit Review Commission 2000, 110–18). In addition, trade has also had an indirect effect by contributing to many of these other causes. For example, the decline of the manufacturing sector attributable to increased globalization has resulted in a reduction in unionization rates, since unions represent a larger share of the workforce in this sector than in other sectors of the economy.

So, although NAFTA is not solely responsible for all of the labor market problems discussed in this report, it has made a significant contribution to these problems, both directly and indirectly. Without major changes in the current NAFTA agreement, continued integration of North American markets will threaten the prosperity of a growing share of the U.S. workforce while producing no compensatory benefits to non-U.S. workers. Expansion of a NAFTA-style agreement—such as the proposed Free Trade Area of the Americas—will only worsen these problems. If the U.S. economy enters into a downturn or recession under these conditions, prospects for American workers will be further diminished.

Notes

1. Potential jobs, or job opportunities, are positions that would have been created if the trade deficit with Mexico and Canada had remained constant, in real terms (and holding everything else in the economy constant). The total number of jobs and job opportunities is a measure of what employment in trade-related industries would have been if the U.S. NAFTA trade balance remained constant between 1993 and 2000, holding everything else constant.

2. EPI [Economic Policy Institute] calculations and International Monetary Fund (IMF) (2001).

3. IMF (2001) and EPI calculations. This analysis compares overnight money market rates in Canada (annual averages) with the comparable federal funds rate for the U.S.

4. Globalization includes rapid growth in imports, exports, and the share of trade in the world economy, and even more rapid growth in the international flows of foreign investment around the world. The term is also used to refer

to the international convergence of rules, regulations, and even the social structure and role of government in many countries. This process is often viewed as a "race-to-the-bottom" in global environmental standards, wages, and working conditions.

5. See U.S. Trade Deficit Review Commission (2000, 110–18) for more extensive reviews of theoretical models and empirical evidence regarding the impacts of globalization on income inequality in the U.S.

6. Bronfenbrenner (1999).

References

Blecker, Robert A. 1997. *NAFTA and the Peso Collapse—Not Just a Coincidence.* Briefing Paper. Washington, D.C.: Economic Policy Institute.

Bronfenbrenner, Kate. 1997a. "The effects of plant closings and the threat of plant closings on worker rights to organize." *Supplement to Plant Closings and Workers' Rights: A Report to the Council of Ministers by the Secretariat of the Commission for Labor Cooperation.* Lanham, Md.: Bernan Press.

Bronfenbrenner, Kate. 1997b. "We'll close! Plant closings, plant-closing threats, union organizing, and NAFTA." *Multinational Monitor.* Vol. 18, No. 3, pp. 8–13.

Bronfenbrenner, Kate. 1999. "Trade in traditional manufacturing." Testimony before the U.S. Trade Deficit Review Commission. October 29. <http://www.ustdrc.gov/hearings/29oct99/29oct99con.html>

Bronfenbrenner, Kate. 2000. "Uneasy terrain: The impact of capital mobility on workers, wages, and union organizing." Commissioned research paper for the U.S. Trade Deficit Review Commission. <http://www.ustdrc.gov/research/research.html>

Bureau of the Census. 1994. *U.S. Exports of Merchandise on CD-ROM (CDEX, or EX-145)* and *U.S. Imports of Merchandise on CD-ROM (CDIM, or IM-145).* Preliminary data for December 1993 (month and year to date). Washington, D.C.: U.S. Department of Commerce, Bureau of the Census.

Bureau of the Census. 2001. *U.S. Exports of Merchandise on CD-ROM (CDEX, or EX-145)* and *U.S. Imports of Merchandise on CD-ROM (CDIM, or IM-145).* Preliminary data for December 2000 (month and year to date). Washington, D.C.: U.S. Department of Commerce, Bureau of the Census.

Bureau of Labor Statistics. 1997. *ES202 Establishment Census.* Washington, D.C.: U.S. Department of Labor.

Bureau of Labor Statistics, Office of Employment Projections. 2001a. *Employment Outlook: 1994–2005 Macroeconomic Data, Demand Time Series and Input Output Tables.* Washington, D.C.: U.S. Department of Labor. <ftp://ftp.bls.gov/pub/special.requests/ep/ind.employment/>

Bureau of Labor Statistics, Office of Employment Projections. 2001b. Private email communication with Mr. James Franklin about 2000 price deflator estimates.

California State World Trade Commission. 1996. *A Preliminary Assessment of the Agreement's Impact on California.* Sacramento, Calif.: California State World Trade Commission.

International Monetary Fund. 2001. *International Financial Statistics.* Database and browser, March.

Mishel, Lawrence, Jared Bernstein, and John Schmitt. 2001. *State of Working America: 2000–01.* An Economic Policy Institute book. Ithaca, N.Y.: ILR Press, an imprint of Cornell University Press.

Rothstein, Jesse and Robert E. Scott. 1997a. *NAFTA's Casualties: Employment Effects on Men, Women, and Minorities.* Issue Brief. Washington, D.C.: Economic Policy Institute.

Rothstein, Jesse, and Robert E. Scott. 1997b. *NAFTA and the States: Job Destruction Is Widespread.* Issue Brief. Washington, D.C.: Economic Policy Institute.

Scott, Robert E. 1996. *North American Trade After NAFTA: Rising Deficits, Disappearing Jobs.* Briefing Paper. Washington, D.C.: Economic Policy Institute.

Scott, Robert E. 2000. *The Facts About Trade and Job Creation.* Issue Brief. Washington, D.C.: Economic Policy Institute.

Tonelson, Alan. 2000. *Race to the Bottom.* New York, N.Y.: Westview Press.

Trade Deficit Review Commission. 2000. *The U.S. Trade Deficit: Causes, Consequences, and Recommendations for Action.* Washington, D.C.: U.S. Trade Deficit Review Commission.

Daniel T. Griswold

 **NO**

NAFTA at 10: An Economic and Foreign Policy Success

Ten years ago . . . , leaders of the United States, Canada, and Mexico signed the historic North American Free Trade Agreement [NAFTA]. Although NAFTA remains a lightning rod for critics of free trade, by any measure it has been a public policy success. As a trade agreement, it delivered its principal objective of more trade. Since 1993, the value of two-way U.S. trade with Mexico has almost tripled, from $81 billion to $232 billion, growing twice as fast as U.S. trade with the rest of the world.[1] Canada and Mexico are now America's number one and two trading partners, respectively, with Japan a distant third.

Exaggerated Impact

One reason NAFTA remains controversial today is that advocates and opponents alike were guilty a decade ago of exaggerating its impact. Advocates claimed it would create hundreds of thousands of jobs in the U.S. economy due to a dramatic rise in exports; opponents claimed far more jobs would be destroyed by a flood of imports entering the United States and a stampede of U.S. companies moving to Mexico to take advantage of cheap labor. During a presidential debate in 1992, H. Ross Perot famously predicted, "You're going to hear a giant sucking sound of jobs being pulled out of this country."[2]

In reality, NAFTA was never going to have much of an impact on the U.S. economy. America's GDP [gross domestic product] at the time was almost 20 times larger than Mexico's, and U.S. tariffs against Mexican goods already averaged a low 2 percent.

A Foreign-Policy Triumph

For the United States, NAFTA was more about foreign policy than about the domestic economy. Its biggest payoff for the United States has been to institutionalize our southern neighbor's turn away from centralized protectionism and toward decentralized, democratic capitalism.

By that measure, NAFTA has been a spectacular success. In the decade since signing NAFTA, Mexico has continued along the road of economic and political reform. It has successfully decoupled its economy from the old boom-and-bust, high-inflation, debt-ridden model that characterized it and much of Latin America up until the debt crisis of the 1980s. In 2000, Mexico avoided an election-cycle economic crisis for the first time since the 1970s. Today Mexico and Chile are the two most stable and dynamic economies in Latin America—and the two that have reformed most aggressively.

Just as important, the economic competition and decentralization embodied in NAFTA encouraged more political competition in Mexico. It broke the economic grip in which the dominant Institutional Revolutionary Party (PRI) held the country for most of the last century. It is no coincidence that, within seven years of NAFTA's implementation, Vicente Fox became the first opposition-party candidate elected president after 71 years of the PRI's one-party rule.

"Giant Sucking Sound," Where Art Thou?

With a decade of hindsight, it is difficult to find any evidence of a "giant sucking sound" of jobs, investment, and manufacturing capacity heading south.

American jobs   Trade is not about more jobs or fewer jobs but about better jobs, and NAFTA is no exception. Of course, competition from Mexico closed some U.S. factories, but those closures have allowed resources to shift to sectors where American producers enjoy a greater advantage in efficiency. That's the whole idea of trade: we increase production in sectors and industries where we can produce more efficiently and reduce production in sectors where we are less efficient. The result is a shift to better paying jobs. Meanwhile, the overall level of employment is determined by such macroeconomic factors such as monetary policy, labor-market regulations, and the business cycle.

For the record, the U.S. economy created millions of new jobs after passage of NAFTA. Civilian employment in the U.S. economy grew from 120.3 million in 1993 to 135.1 million in 2001, an increase of almost 2 million jobs per year. The unemployment rate fell steadily after the enactment of NAFTA, from an average of 6.9 percent in 1993 to under 4 percent in 2000.[3] The unemployment rate jumped to 6 percent in 2002, but that was because of the recent and relatively mild recession of 2001—a recession brought on not by NAFTA but by rising interest rates and energy prices and a falling stock market.

Foreign investment   Despite predictions, NAFTA did not cause anything like an exodus of manufacturing investment to Mexico. U.S. investment in Mexico did increase after NAFTA, along with trade, but those flows are a trickle compared to what we invest domestically. In the eight years after the implementation of NAFTA, from 1994 through 2001, U.S. manufacturing companies invested an average of $2.2 billion a year in factories in Mexico.[4] That is a mere 1 percent of the $200 billion invested in manufacturing each year in the domestic U.S. economy.[5]

The small outflow of direct manufacturing investment to Mexico has been overwhelmed by the net inflow of such investment from the rest of the world—an average of $16 billion a year since 1994, most of it from Europe and Japan.[6] At the end of 2001, the stock of U.S. direct manufacturing investment in Mexico was $19.7 billion, less than one-tenth the stock of U.S. investment in high-wage, high-standard Europe.[7]

U.S. manufacturing   Nowhere were the predictions about NAFTA more apocalyptic than in regard to manufacturing. H. Ross Perot accused NAFTA of "deindustrializing our country," and Rep. David Bonior, the soon to be ex-congressman and Democratic Whip from Michigan, predicted flatly that NAFTA "will destroy the auto industry."

In the eight years since the implementation of NAFTA, those predictions have become laughable. Between 1993 and 2001, manufacturing output in the United States, as measured by the U.S. Federal Reserve Board, rose by one-third. Output of motor vehicles and parts rose by 30 percent.[8] In fact, in the first eight years of NAFTA, manufacturing output in the United States rose at an annual average rate of 3.7 percent, 50 percent faster than during the eight years before enactment of NAFTA. (See Figure 1.) Of course, this is not an argument that NAFTA was the primary cause of the acceleration in manufacturing output, but it does

Figure 1

Index of U.S. Manufacturing Output
1986–2002 (1992 = 100)

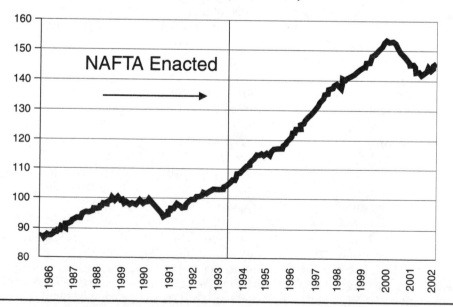

Source: U.S. Federal Reserve Board.

knock the wind out of the myth that NAFTA has somehow caused the "deindustrialization" of America.

Manufacturing employment has fallen in the past few years, but that cannot in any plausible way be blamed on NAFTA. In fact, the number of Americans employed in manufacturing grew by 706,000 in the first four years of NAFTA, from January 1994 to January 1998.[9] The decline in manufacturing jobs since 1998 has not occurred because those jobs have gone to Mexico; it has occurred because of (1) collapsing demand for our exports due to the East Asian financial meltdown in 1997–98, (2) our own domestic slowdown in demand due to the 2001 recession, and (3) the ongoing dramatic improvement in manufacturing productivity—fueled by information technology and increased global competition—that has allowed American factories to produce more and better widgets with fewer workers.

Conclusion

By every reasonable measure, NAFTA has been a public policy success in the decade since it was signed. It has deepened and institutionalized Mexico's drive to modernize and liberalize its economy and political system. It has spurred trade, investment, and integration between the United States and Mexico. And in a more modest way it has enhanced American productivity and prosperity—refuting the critics who were wrong 10 years ago and are just as wrong today.

Notes

1. See Bureau of the Census, "FT900—U.S. International Trade in Goods and Services: 1993," www.census.gov/foreign-trade/Press-Release/ 93_press_ releases/ Final_Revisions_1993; and "U.S. International Trade in Goods and Services— Annual Revision for 2001," www.census. gov/foreign-trade/Press-Release/2001pr/ Final_Revisions_2001.

2. Public Broadcasting System, "Debating Our Destiny: The Third Presidential Debate," *NewsHour*, October 19, 1992, www.pbs.org/newshour/debatingour destiny/92debates/3prez2.html.

3. Joint Economic Committee of Congress (JEC), *Economic Indicators* (Washington: Government Printing Office), October 2002, p. 11.

4. U.S. Department of Commerce, Bureau of Economic Analysis (BEA) "U.S. Direct Investment Abroad," www.bea.doc.gov/bea/di/ di1usdbal.htm.

5. JEC, p. 11.

6. BEA, "Foreign Direct Investment in the U.S.," www.bea.doc.gov/bea/di/ di1fdibal.htm.

7. Maria Borga and Daniel R. Yorgason, "Direct Investment Position for 2001: Country and Industry Detail," *Survey of Current Business* (Bureau of Economic Analysis, July 2002), Table 2.2, p. 33.

8. U.S. Federal Reserve Board, "Industrial Production and Capacity Utilization: Data from January 1986 to Present (Tables 1, 2, and 10), Industrial Production, Seasonally Adjusted," Series B00004, www.federalreserve.gov/releases/g17/ table1_2. htm.

9. In January 1994, 18,155,000 Americans were employed in manufacturing, compared to 18,861,000 in January 1998. See U.S. Bureau of Labor Statistics, "Employment, Hours, and Earnings from the Current Employment Statistics Survey (National), Manufacturing Employment, Seasonally Adjusted," Series EES30000001, data.bls.gov/cgi-bin/surveymost?ee.

POSTSCRIPT

Has the North American Free Trade Agreement Hurt the American Economy?

Scott sees the most visible negative impact of NAFTA to be increased trade deficits and job losses. With respect to the former, he documents a 378 percent increase in the U.S. trade deficit with Canada and Mexico over the 1993–2000 period. As for job loss, he estimates the number to be over 760,000. He states that the job losses have occurred in all 50 states and the District of Columbia. Scott also addresses the less visible but harmful effects of NAFTA. He argues that the loss of jobs in manufacturing has increased job competition in the service sector; thus, there is downward pressure on wages in both sectors. He also refers to "threat effects"—the credible threats of employers to relocate plants, to outsource portions of their operations, and to purchase intermediate goods and services directly from foreign producers. The threat effects have weakened the ability of workers to bargain for higher wages and improved fringe benefits. The job losses, increased job competition, and threat effects combine to increase income inequality. Scott concludes his analysis by arguing that there needs to be major changes in NAFTA. He also cautions that expansion of a NAFTA-style agreement—such as the proposed FTAA—will only worsen the problems he has identified.

Griswold states that NAFTA has delivered on its principal objective of increased trade, with two-way U.S. trade with Mexico tripling from $81 billion in 1993 to $232 billion. Today Canada and Mexico are America's top trading partners. Griswold also asserts that NAFTA has played an important role in the development of more political competition in Mexico. He takes up the criticisms most frequently directed at NAFTA. As to the criticism of job loss, Griswold cites the increase in U.S. employment over the 1993–2001 period, an increase of almost 2 million jobs per year. He attributes the "mild recession of 2001" to rising interest rates, increasing energy prices, and a falling stock market. As to the criticism that NAFTA redirected investment from the United States to Mexico, Griswold argues that investment in Mexico by American manufacturing is almost trivial—"a mere 1 percent of the $200 billion invested in manufacturing each year in the domestic U.S. economy." As to the contention that NAFTA has led to job losses in manufacturing, Griswold offers two counterarguments. First, manufacturing employment actually increased during the first four years of NAFTA. Second, the loss in manufacturing jobs since 1998 is due to other factors, including an increase in manufacturing productivity. Griswold concludes his evaluation by asserting that "by every reasonable measure, NAFTA has been a public policy success in the decade since it was signed."

Both Scott and Griswold provide references that can be used to obtain more data as well as additional analyses of NAFTA. For a more political critique of NAFTA, see *The Selling of "Free Trade": NAFTA, Washington, and the Subversion of American Democracy* by John R. MacArthur (Hill & Wang, 2000). There are also evaluations that were completed earlier in NAFTA's history. Typical of these are two articles published in the October 1997 issue of *The World & I*: "A Successful Agreement," by Joe Cobb, and "A Failed Approach," by Alan Tonelson. Besides controversy on the macro effects of NAFTA, there is significant debate on various elements within the NAFTA agreement. One good example is NAFTA's Chapter 11, the so-called investor-to-state protections. On this issue see William T. Warren, "NAFTA and State Sovereignty: A Pandora's Box of Property Rights," *Spectrum: The Journal of State Government* (Spring 2002) and "Update on NAFTA Chapter 11 Claim re Methanex," GreenYes Archives, http://greenyes.grrn.org/2002/11/msg00069.html (March 2003). For more about FTAA, see "NAFTA Expansion: More About the FTAA," The Sierra Club, http://www.sierraclub.org/trade/ftaa/more.asp and the section entitled "Trade Promotion Authority" in chapter 6 of the 2003 *Economic Report of the President.*

Contributors to This Volume

EDITORS

THOMAS R. SWARTZ was born in Philadelphia, Pennsylvania, in 1937. He received his B.A. from LaSalle University in 1960, his M.A. from Ohio University in 1962, and his Ph.D. from Indiana University in 1965. He is currently a professor of economics at the University of Notre Dame in Indiana and a fellow of the Institute for Educational Initiatives. He and Frank J. Bonello have coauthored or coedited a number of works. In addition to *Taking Sides*, they have coedited *Alternative Directions in Economic Policy* (University of Notre Dame Press, 1978); *The Supply Side: Debating Current Economic Policies* (Dushkin Publishing Group, 1983); and *Urban Finance Under Siege* (M. E. Sharpe, 1993). He has also coedited or coauthored three other books. His most recent book is entitled *Working and Poor in Urban America,* coedited by Kathleen Mass Weigert (University of Notre Dame Press, 1995).

FRANK J. BONELLO was born in Detroit, Michigan, in 1939. He received his B.S. in 1961 and his M.A. in 1963, both from the University of Detroit, and his Ph.D. in 1968 from Michigan State University. He is currently an associate professor of economics at the University of Notre Dame, where he has also served as Arts and Letters College Fellow. He writes in the areas of monetary economics and economic education. *Taking Sides* is his seventh book. In addition to being coeditor on several publications with Thomas R. Swartz, he is the author of *The Formulation of Expected Interest Rates* (Michigan State University Press, 1969) and coauthor, with William I. Davisson, of *Computer-Assisted Instruction in Economic Education: A Case Study* (University of Notre Dame Press, 1976).

STAFF

Jeffrey L. Hahn   Vice President/Publisher
Theodore Knight   Managing Editor
David Brackley   Senior Developmental Editor
Juliana Gribbins   Developmental Editor
Rose Gleich   Permissions Assistant
Brenda S. Filley   Director of Production/Manufacturing
Julie Marsh   Project Editor
Juliana Arbo   Typesetting Supervisor
Richard Tietjen   Publishing Systems Manager
Charles Vitelli   Designer

AUTHORS

FRANK ACKERMAN is a research assistant professor in the Department of Urban and Environmental Policy at Tufts University. He is also the director of the Research and Policy Program at Tuft's Global Development and Environment Institute. He holds a Ph.D. from Harvard University and a B.A. in mathematics and economics from Swarthmore College. He is the author of *Why Do We Recycle? Markets, Values and Public Policy* (Island Press, 1997).

ROBERT ALMEDER is a professor of philosophy at Georgia State University and a member of the editorial board of the *Journal of Business Ethics*. He earned his Ph.D. in philosophy at the University of Pennsylvania, and he is the author of *Harmless Naturalism: The Limits of Science and the Nature of Philosophy* (Open Court, 1998).

RICHARD APPELBAUM is a professor of sociology and global and international studies at the University of California, Santa Barbara. He currently serves as director of the Institute for Social, Behavioral, and Economic Research (ISBER) and as codirector of the ISBER's Center for Global Studies. He is the founding editor of *Competition and Change: The Journal of Global Business and Political Economy,* and he is currently engaged in a multidisciplinary study of the apparel industry in Los Angeles and the Asian Pacific Rim.

ROBERT A. BAADE is the James D. Vail Professor of Economics at Lake Forest College, where he specializes in international trade, international finance, and the economics of sport. He is the author of dozens of articles and essays, and he has been invited to give talks across Europe and North America. He holds an M.A. and a Ph.D from the University of Wisconsin, and he was elected "The Great Teacher" at Lake Forest in 2002.

LENNY BERNSTEIN is head of L. S. Bernstein & Associates, L.L.C., a corporate consulting firm that focuses on the political and scientific developments associated with climate change and other global environmental issues. He holds a Ph.D. in chemical engineering from Purdue University, and he has authored more than 30 articles on the social, economic, and environmental consequences of climatic change.

ALAN S. BLINDER is the Gordon S. Rentschler Memorial Professor of Economics at Princeton University. He is a former vice chairman of the Federal Reserve's Board of Governors and a former member of President Bill Clinton's Council of Economic Advisors. He earned his M.S. in economics from the London School of Economics in 1967 and his Ph.D. from the Massachusetts Institute of Technology in 1971. His many publications include *Central Banking in Theory and Practice* (MIT Press, 1998).

MICHAEL J. BOSKIN is a senior fellow at the Hoover Institution and the Tully M. Friedman Professor of Economics at Stanford University in Stanford, California. He is also an adjunct scholar at the American Enterprise Institute and a research associate at the National Bureau of Economic Research. He is the author or editor of over 100 articles and books, including *Some Thoughts on Improving Economic Statistics* (Hoover Institution Press, 1998).

EVELYN Z. BRODKIN is an associate professor in the School of Social Service Administration, a lecturer in the Law School, and a faculty affiliate of the Northwestern University/University of Chicago Joint Center for Research on Poverty. Codirector of the Project on the Public Economy of Work, she has published widely on issues of welfare policy, social politics, and administrative reform. She earned her M.P.A. from Northeastern University in 1976 and her Ph.D. from the Massachusetts Institute of Technology in 1983.

LESTER R. BROWN is the founder and president of the Earth Policy Institute. He also founded the Worldwatch Institute, for which he served as president for its first 26 years. As president, he launched the annual *State of the World* report, the bimonthly magazine *World Watch,* the annual *Vital Signs,* and the institute's *News Briefs.* He has received many prizes and awards, including the 1987 United Nations' Environment Prize and the 1994 Blue Planet Prize. He earned his M.S. from the University of Maryland in 1959 and his M.P.A. from Harvard University in 1962. His many publications include *Plan B: Rescuing a Planet Under Stress and a Civilization in Trouble* (Earth Policy Institute, 2003).

PATRICK J. BUCHANAN, who sought the 1996 Republican nomination for the presidency, is a political analyst and a frequent television commentator. He is the author of *The Great Betrayal: How American Sovereignty and Social Justice Are Being Sacrificed to the Gods of the Global Economy* (Little, Brown, 1998) and *The Death of the West: How Dying Populations and Immigrant Invasions Imperil Our Country and Civilization* (Thomas Dunne Books, 2000).

CHARLES T. CARLSTROM is an economic adviser in the research department at the Federal Reserve Bank of Cleveland. His principal field of research is macroeconomics, particularly monetary economics and public finance, and he also has an interest in organ markets. His many articles have been published in such journals as *Economic Review, Contemporary Economic Policy,* and *Proceedings.* He holds an M.A. and a Ph.D. in economics from the University of Rochester.

BRUCE CHAPMAN, a specialist in public policy development, has been president of the Discovery Institute since 1990. A former director of the U.S. Census Bureau, he has also served as deputy assistant to President Ronald Reagan and as the U.S. ambassador to the United Nations Organizations in Vienna, Austria. In 1967 he made an early case for an all-volunteer military in *The Wrong Man in Uniform* (Trident).

THOMAS V. CHEMA is a partner in the law firm Arter & Hadden LLP. He has also served as executive director of the Gateway Development Corporation of Greater Cleveland. He earned his J.D. from Harvard Law School in 1971.

CHARLES CRAYPO is an emeritus professor of economics at the University of Notre Dame in Indiana. He is the author of *The Economics of Collective Bargaining: Case Studies in the Private Sector* (BNA Books, 1986) and coeditor, with Bruce Nissen, of *Grand Designs: The Impact of Corporate Strategies on Workers, Unions, and Communities* (Cornell University Press, 1993).

WILLIAM A. DARITY, JR., is the Cary C. Boshamer Professor of Economics at the University of North Carolina. His research focuses on inequality by race, class, and ethnicity; North-South theories of development and trade; the history of economic thought and political economy; the Atlantic slave trade and the Industrial Revolution; and social psychological effects of unemployment exposure. He is coauthor, with Samuel L. Myers, Jr., of *Persistent Disparity: Race and Economic Inequality in the U.S. Since 1945* (Edward Elgar, 1998). He earned his Ph.D. in economics from the Massachusetts Institute of Technology in 1978.

JAMES DEVINE is a professor in the economics department at Loyola Marymount University. His more specialized work centers on macroeconomics, along with labor economics, money and banking, and economic history, and he is a member of the American Economics Association, the Association for Social Economics, and the Union for Radical Political Economics. He earned his Ph.D. in economics from the University of California, Berkeley, in 1981.

PETER DREIER is the Dr. E. P. Clapp Distinguished Professor of Politics and director of the Urban & Environmental Policy Program of the Urban & Environmental Policy Institute at Occidental College in Los Angeles, California. Prior to joining the Occidental faculty in 1993, he served nine years as director of housing at the Boston Redevelopment Authority and as senior policy adviser to Mayor Ray Flynn of Boston, Massachusetts. He has also taught at Tufts University.

JOEL FRIEDMAN is a senior fellow on the national policy staff of the Center on Budget and Policy Priorities. There he divides his time between federal tax and budget issues and the International Budget Project. Prior to joining the center, he worked in the South African Ministry of Finance, where he spent nearly four years as the U.S. Treasury's resident budget adviser. He has also served as director of budget analysis for the Democratic Staff of the House Budget Committee and as a financial economist in the Budget Review Division of the Office of Management and Budget. He holds an M.P.A. from the Woodrow Wilson School of Public and International Affairs.

MILTON FRIEDMAN is a senior research fellow at Stanford University's Hoover Institution on War, Revolution and Peace. He is also the Paul Snowden Russell Distinguished Service Professor Emeritus of Economics at the University of Chicago, and he was a member of the research staff of the National Bureau of Economic Research from 1937 to 1981. He received the 1976 Nobel Prize in economic science for his work in consumption analysis and monetary history and theory and for demonstrating stabilization policy complexity. He and his wife, Rose D. Friedman, who also writes on economic topics, are coauthors of several publications, including *Two Lucky People* (University of Chicago Press, 1998). He holds an M.A. from the University of Chicago and a Ph.D. from Columbia University.

KEVIN GALLAGHER is a research associate on the Sustainable Hemispheric Integration Project at Tufts University's Global Development and Environment Institute. He holds a master's degree in international environmental policy from Tufts University, where he is currently a doctoral candidate.

ALFREDO GOYBURU is a policy analyst in the Center for Data Analysis at the Heritage Foundation. He previously worked as a regional and energy economist for WEFA, a leader in economic information and forecasting, and as an economist for the New York state legislature, where he studied the impact of tax policy. He holds an advanced economics degree from the University of Albany.

ROBERT GREENSTEIN is the founder and executive director of the Center on Budget and Policy Priorities. Prior to founding the center, he was administrator of the Food and Nutrition Service at the U.S. Department of Agriculture, where he directed the agency that operates the federal food assistance programs. Considered an expert on the federal budget and, in particular, the impact of tax and budget proposals on low-income people, he has written numerous reports, analyses, op-ed pieces, and magazine articles on poverty-related issues. In 1994 he was appointed by President Bill Clinton to serve on the Bipartisan Commission on Entitlement and Tax Reform.

DANIEL T. GRISWOLD is associate director of the Center for Trade Policy Studies at the Cato Institute. A specialist in the economic effects of international trade and immigration, his studies have focused on the trade deficit, imports and manufacturing, the World Trade Organization, congressional voting on trade, and Mexican immigration. His articles have appeared in such publications as the *Wall Street Journal* and the *Los Angeles Times*, and he is coeditor, with Solveig Singleton, of *Economic Casualties: How U.S. Foreign Policy Undermines Trade, Growth, and Liberty* (Cato Institute, 1999). He holds a master's degree in the politics of the world economy from the London School of Economics.

WENONAH HAUTER is director of Public Citizen's Critical Mass Energy Project. The Critical Mass Energy Project is Public Citizen's energy policy arm, which works to decrease reliance on nuclear and fossil fuels and to promote safe, affordable, and environmentally sound energy alternatives. Hauter has also served as environmental policy director for Citizen Action and as senior organizer for the Union of Concerned Scientists.

JAMES J. HECKMAN is the Henry Schultz Distinguished Service Professor of Economics and director of social program evaluation in the Harris School of Public Policy at the University of Chicago. A senior research fellow of the American Bar Foundation, he was awarded the Bank of Sweden Prize in Economic Sciences in Memory of Alfred Nobel in 2000. Heckman has written on the impact of civil rights and affirmative action programs in the United States, on the impact of taxes on labor supply and human capital accumulation, and on the impact of skill certification programs. He is coeditor, with Burton Singer, of *Longitudinal Analysis of Labor Market Data* (Cambridge University Press, 1985).

CATHERINE HILL is a task force member and study director at the Institute for Women's Policy Research. She is coauthor, with Heidi Hartman and Lois

Shaw, of *Why Privatizing Social Security Would Hurt Women: A Response to the Cato Institute's Proposal for Individual Accounts* (Institute for Women's Policy Research, 2000).

NICHOLAS D. KRISTOF is a writer for the *New York Times,* where he served for 14 years as an Asia correspondent. He is coauthor, with Sheryl WuDunn, of *Thunder From the East: Portrait of a Rising Asia* (Alfred A. Knopf, 2000). He and WuDunn won the 1990 Pulitzer Prize for international reporting for their coverage of the Tiananmen democracy movement in China and its suppression.

ROBERT E. LITAN, an economist and attorney, is vice president and director of the Economic Studies Program and the Cabot Family Chair in Economics at the Brookings Institution. During President Bill Clinton's first term, he served as deputy assistant attorney general and as associate director of the Office of Management and Budget. He has authored, coauthored, or edited 22 books and over 150 articles on government policies affecting financial institutions, regulatory and legal issues, international trade, and the economy in general, including *Sticking Together: The Israeli Experiment in Pluralism,* coauthored with Yaakov Kop (Brookings Institution Press, 2001). He holds a J.D. from Yale Law School and a Ph.D. in economics from Yale University.

PATRICK L. MASON is an associate professor of economics and director of the African American Studies Program at Florida State University. His areas of interest include labor economics, public policy, and political economy, with a particular interest in racial inequality, educational attainment, income distribution, unemployment, economics of identity, family environment and socioeconomic well-being, and transitions in family structure and public policy. He is also an associate editor for the Southern Economic Association and chair of the Committee on the Status of Minorities in the Economics Profession for the American Economic Association. He is the editor of *African Americans, Labor, and Society: Organizing for a New Agenda* (Wayne State University Press, 2001)

NORBERT J. MICHEL is a policy analyst in the Center for Data Analysis of the Heritage Foundation. His areas of expertise include corporate finance and monetary economics, and he is also part of a team of economists who are constructing a new macroeconomic model, which will give the Heritage Foundation economic forecasting capabilities similar to those of the Congressional Budget Office. Prior to joining the foundation, Michel worked for the global energy company Entergy and as an economic researcher for the National Ports and Waterways Institute. He is currently a Ph.D. candidate in financial economics at the University of New Orleans.

MICHAEL J. NEW was a data analyst and research assistant at the Cato Institute. He received his Ph.D. in political science from Stanford University, and he is currently a post-doctoral fellow at the Harvard-MIT data center. His research interests include limitations on government, tax revolts, welfare reform, and campaign finance reform.

RALPH A. RECTOR is a research fellow in the Center for Data Analysis at the Heritage Foundation, where he directs the center's research and development activities, including the development of new computer software and databases. His areas of expertise include tax policy and microeconomic tax analysis. Before joining Heritage, he worked in the Tax Policy Economics Group at Coopers & Lybrand, L.L.P., where he supervised the construction of micro simulation models used to analyze the impact of tax reform on businesses and individuals. He has also served as a tax analyst and revenue estimator at the state and federal levels. He holds a Ph.D. in economics from George Mason University.

GEORGE REISMAN is a professor of economics in the Graziadio School of Business and Management at Pepperdine University and president of the Jefferson School of Philosophy, Economics and Psychology. His articles have appeared in such journals as *The Quarterly Journal of Austrian Economics* and *The American Journal of Economics and Sociology,* and he is the author of *Capitalism: A Treatise on Economics* (Jameson Books, 1996). He holds a Ph.D. in economics from New York University.

CHRISTY D. ROLLOW is a research associate at the Federal Reserve Bank of Richmond.

MURRAY N. ROTHBARD (1926–1995) was a professor of economics at the University of Nevada, Las Vegas, and vice president for academic affairs at the Ludwig von Mises Institute. Over his 45-year professional career, he wrote 25 books and thousands of articles critiquing socialism, statism, relativism, and scientism. He was instrumental in reviving an interest in the Austrian School of Economics.

THOMAS RUSTICI is an instructor and head of undergraduate development in the economics department at George Mason University in Fairfax, Virginia. His articles have appeared in such publications as *The Cato Journal, The Free Market,* and *Religion and Liberty.* He holds master's degrees in economics and public policy from George Mason University.

NANCY SCHEPER-HUGHES is a professor of anthropology at the University of California, Berkeley, where she directs the graduate training program in "Critical Studies in Medicine, Science, and the Body." She is a member of the International Bellagio Task Force on Transplantation, Bodily Integrity, and the International Traffic in Organs and coeditor, with Phillippe Bourgois, of *Violence in War and Peace: An Anthology* (Blackwell, 2004).

ROBERT E. SCOTT, an international economist, is codirector of the research department at the Economic Policy Institute. His areas of expertise include trade, NAFTA, global finance, and international economic comparisons. He has also worked as an assistant professor in the College of Business and Management at the University of Maryland at College Park, and he has been published in such journals as *The Journal of Policy Analysis and Management* and *The International Review of Applied Economics.* He is also coauthor, with Randy Barber, of *Jobs on the Wing: Trading Away the Future of the U.S. Aero-*

space Industry (Economic Policy Institute, 1995). He earned his Ph.D. in economics from the University of California, Berkeley, in 1989.

TYSON SLOCUM joined Public Citizen's Critical Mass Energy Project in December 2000 and is working on electric utility restructuring and oil and gas policy. He gained organizing and research experience with Citizens for Tax Justice.

MICHAEL TANNER directs research on new, market-based approaches to health, welfare, and other entitlements for the Cato Institute's Project on Social Security Choice. Prior to joining the institute, he served as director of research for the Georgia Public Policy Foundation. His writing has appeared in the *Washington Post,* the *Los Angeles Times,* and the *Wall Street Journal,* and he makes frequent television and radio appearances. He is coauthor, with Peter J. Ferrara, of *Common Cents, Common Dreams: A Layman's Guide to Social Security Privatization* (Cato Institute, 1998).

U.S. DEPARTMENT OF HEALTH AND HUMAN SERVICES is the U.S. government's principal agency for protecting the health of all Americans and providing essential human services, especially for those who are least able to help themselves. Among its activities are medical and social science research, improving maternal and infant health, substance abuse treatment and prevention, and providing services for older Americans.

JACKSON WILLIAMS is the legislative counsel for Public Citizen's Congress Watch, where he concentrates on civil justice issues. Prior to that, he was manager of public affairs for the Defense Research Institute, where he also specialized in civil justice policy issues. He is currently a Ph.D. candidate in public policy analysis at the University of Illinois–Chicago, where he has taught courses in political science and law. His articles on policy topics have appeared in the *Southern Illinois University Law Journal, Policy Sciences,* and *Comparative State Politics.*

SHERYL WuDUNN is a writer for the *New York Times,* where she served for 14 years as an Asia correspondent. She is coauthor, with Nicholas Kristof, of *Thunder From the East: Portrait of a Rising Asia* (Alfred A. Knopf, 2000). She and Kristof received the 1990 Pulitzer Prize for international reporting for their coverage of the Tiananmen democracy movement in China and its suppression.

Index